MOON

USA NATIONAL PARKS HIKING

THE TOP 100 TRAILS

JASON FRYE

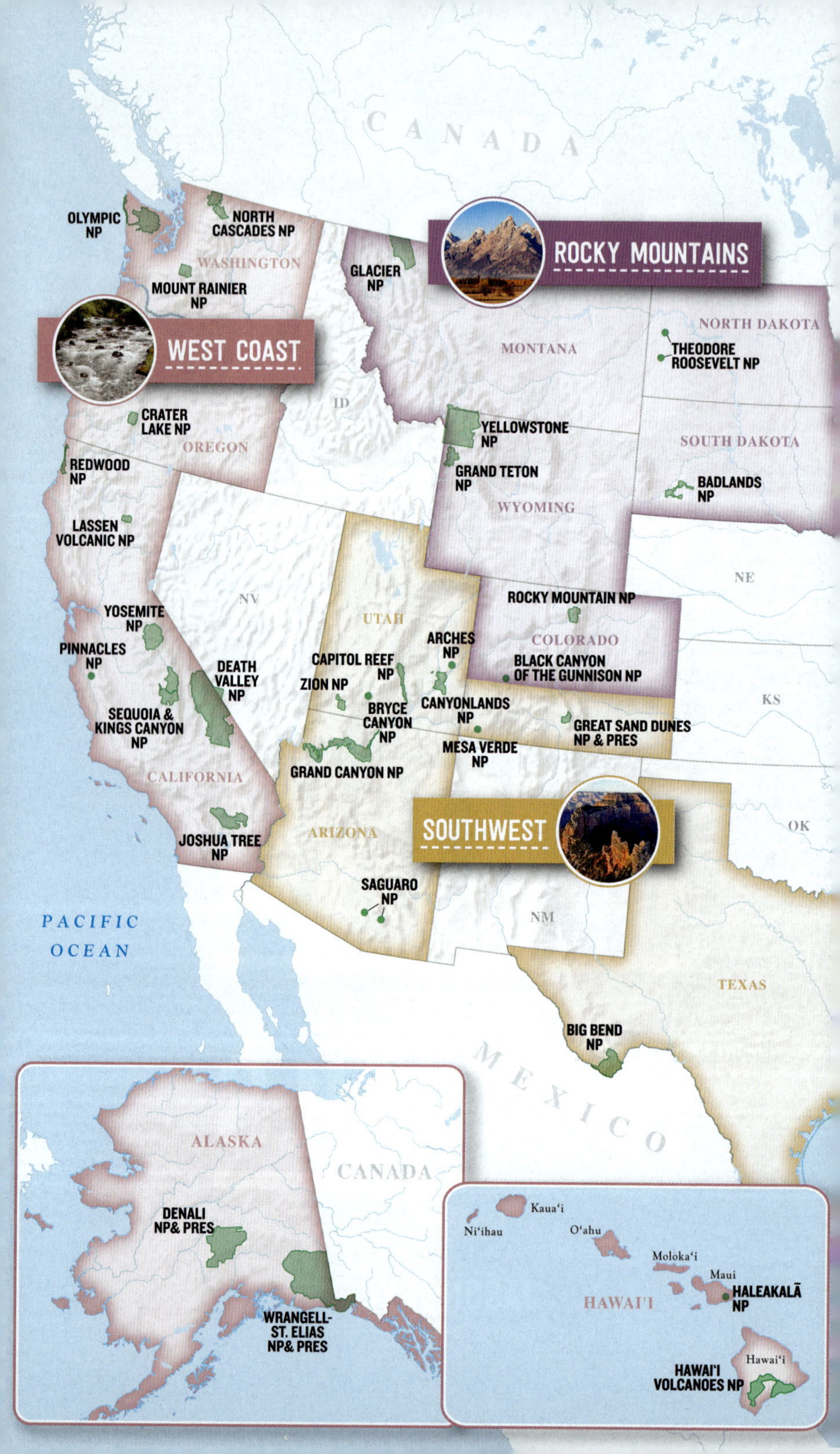

CANADA

ROCKY MOUNTAINS

WEST COAST

SOUTHWEST

OLYMPIC NP

NORTH CASCADES NP

WASHINGTON

MOUNT RAINIER NP

GLACIER NP

MONTANA

NORTH DAKOTA

THEODORE ROOSEVELT NP

ID

CRATER LAKE NP

OREGON

YELLOWSTONE NP

GRAND TETON NP

SOUTH DAKOTA

BADLANDS NP

WYOMING

REDWOOD NP

LASSEN VOLCANIC NP

NV

NE

ROCKY MOUNTAIN NP

UTAH

COLORADO

YOSEMITE NP

PINNACLES NP

ARCHES NP

CAPITOL REEF NP

BLACK CANYON OF THE GUNNISON NP

DEATH VALLEY NP

ZION NP

BRYCE CANYON NP

CANYONLANDS NP

KS

SEQUOIA & KINGS CANYON NP

GREAT SAND DUNES NP & PRES

MESA VERDE NP

GRAND CANYON NP

CALIFORNIA

OK

JOSHUA TREE NP

ARIZONA

SAGUARO NP

NM

PACIFIC OCEAN

TEXAS

BIG BEND NP

MEXICO

ALASKA

CANADA

DENALI NP& PRES

WRANGELL-ST. ELIAS NP& PRES

Kaua'i

Ni'ihau

O'ahu

Moloka'i

Maui

HALEAKALĀ NP

HAWAI'I

Hawai'i

HAWAI'I VOLCANOES NP

USA NATIONAL PARKS HIKING
GREAT LAKES AND NORTHEAST
THE SOUTH
ISLE ROYALE NP
Lake Superior
Lake Huron
Lake Michigan
Lake Ontario
Lake Erie
MAINE
ACADIA NP
VT
NH
MA
CT
RI
NY
NJ
PA
MD
DE
Washington DC
MN
WI
MICHIGAN
IA
INDIANA DUNES NP
CUYAHOGA VALLEY NP
OHIO
INDIANA
IL
WV
SHENANDOAH NP
VIRGINIA
MO
KY
NEW RIVER GORGE NP & PRES
GREAT SMOKY MOUNTAINS NP
NORTH CAROLINA
TENNESSEE
SOUTH CAROLINA
CONGAREE NP
ATLANTIC OCEAN
AR
GA
MS
AL
LA
FL
GULF OF MEXICO
MOON
0 250 mi
0 250 km
© MOON.COM

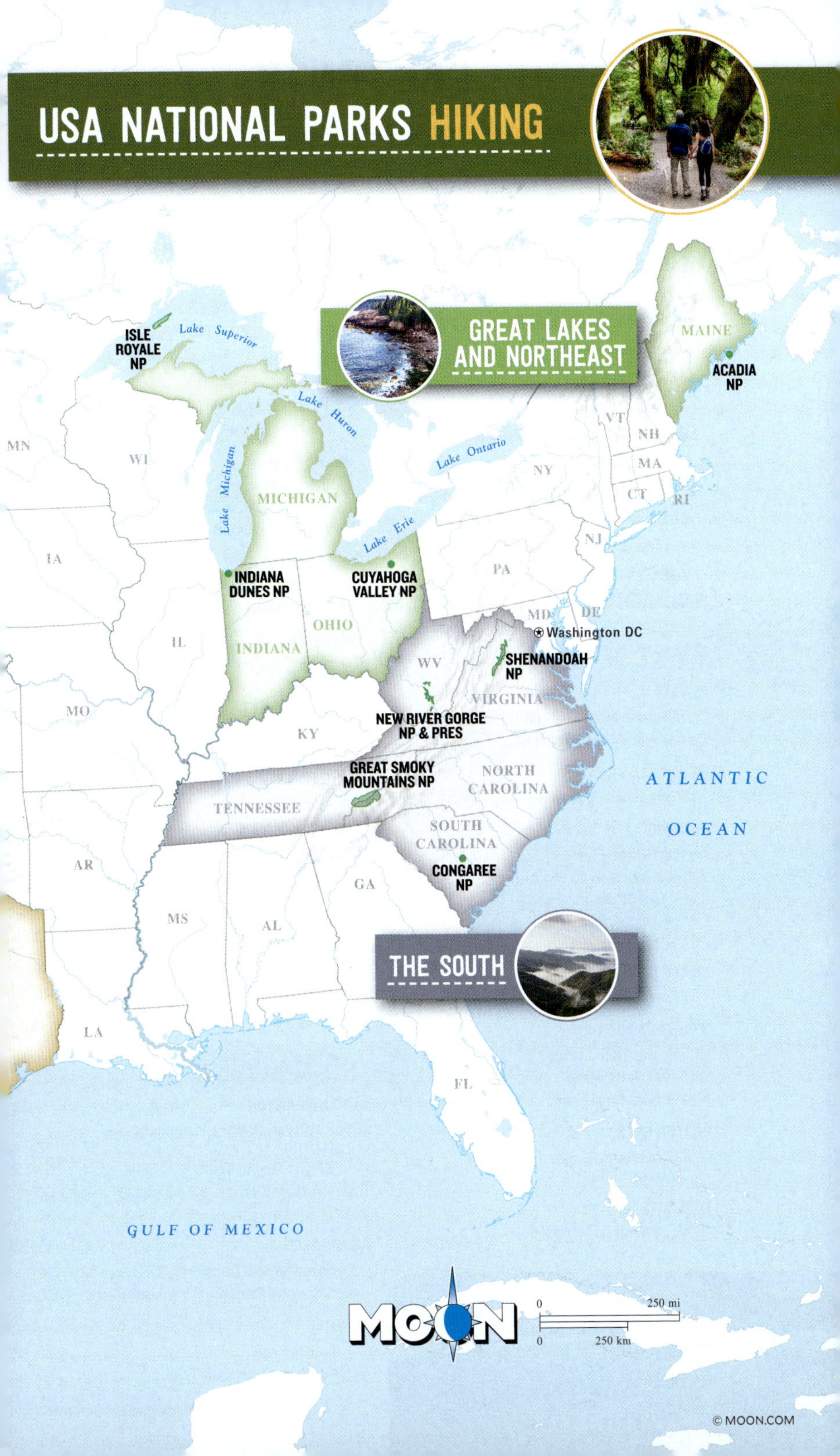

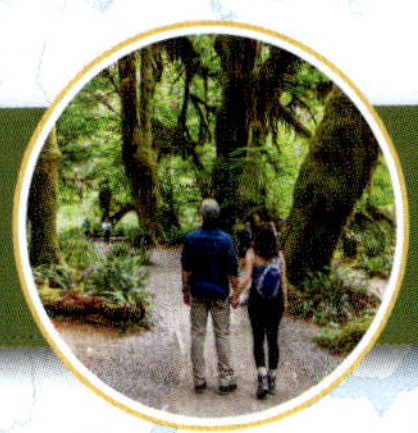

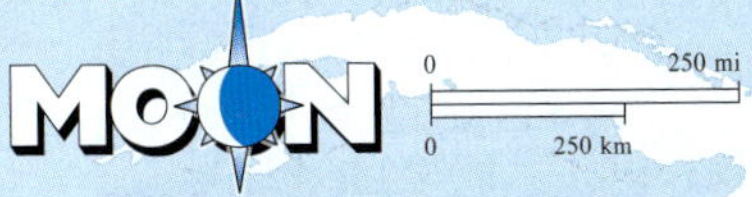

CONTENTS

▌ indicates a top hiking experience

SWIFTCURRENT PASS AND LOOKOUT TRAIL,
GLACIER NATIONAL PARK

HIKING THE NATIONAL PARKS

Within the protected lands of our national parks lie countless trails that lead to breathtaking vistas, alpine lakes, ancient forests, and deserts awash in rare blooms. This book is your gateway to discovering 100 of the most remarkable hikes in these treasured places.

From the skyscraping peaks of the Rocky Mountains to the winding canyons of the Southwest, each hike is a journey into the heart of nature's beauty and resilience. You might come across waterfalls, hot springs, ancient rock art, or hidden caves. Depending on the park, you might see bears, elk, bison, moose, mountain goats, and various types of birds. Whether you're a seasoned trekker or a casual explorer, this guide offers something for everyone, with trails that span all levels of experience, ability, and time.

Every step on these hikes unveils unforgettable views, the crisp scent of nature, and the quiet promise of moments that linger in your heart long after the journey ends. As you lace up your boots and hit the trails, may these pages inspire you to explore, protect, and cherish the wild places that define our national heritage.

Your adventure begins now. The parks are calling—let's go hiking!

TOP 8 EXPERIENCES

1 SWIMMING IN MOUNTAIN LAKES AND STREAMS

Great Smoky Mountains' **Big Creek Trail** (page 492) provides a serene forest setting for leisurely dips, while Crater Lake's **Cleetwood Cove and Wizard Island** hike (pictured; page 94) offers an adventurous plunge amid breathtaking scenery.

2 STANDING AT THE FOOT OF BREATHTAKING WATERFALLS

The waterfall rewards of Olympic's **Quinault Loop** (page 74), Haleakalā's **Pipiwai Trail and Waimoku Falls** (page 182), and Shenandoah's **Cedar Run-Whiteoak Circuit** (pictured; page 456) offer cascading beauty amid diverse landscapes, ranging from lush rain forests to rocky gorges.

3 WANDERING AMONG WILDLIFE IN THEIR NATURAL HABITATS

Spot elusive animals like grizzly bears, mountain goats, elk, and moose, and common (but no less delightful) critters like deer and squirrels (page 34).

4 STARGAZING UNDER MAJESTIC DARK SKIES

Look up on moonless evenings and be rewarded with a celestial show when you do a night hike on the sandy ridges of Great Sand Dunes' **High Dune Trail** (pictured; page 290), join the Astronomy Festival at **The Notch** in Badlands (page 390), or camp at Yosemite's peerless **Cathedral Lakes** (page 112).

3

4

5 CATCHING A SUNRISE OVER SPECTACULAR HOODOOS

Witness the vibrant colors of dawn painting the sky from Bryce Canyon's **Rim Trail** (page 242) for a breathtaking and tranquil experience.

6 CAMPING IN THE BACKCOUNTRY ON A LONG-DISTANCE TRAIL

Adventurers will enjoy a multiday journey along Isle Royale's **Greenstone Ridge Trail** (page 442), featuring solitude, wildlife sightings, and serene views of Lake Superior. Or, for a brag-worthy backpacking trip, take on Grand Canyon's **Rim-to-Rim** (pictured; page 210) hike for endless canyon vistas.

7 WATCHING A SUNSET OVER RUGGED CLIFFS

See a stunning tableau of fiery hues reflecting off red rock and towering cliffs from Arches' **Delicate Arch Trail** (page 260) and New River Gorge's **Endless Wall Trail** (pictured; page 470).

8 CASTING A LINE IN ALPINE LAKES

Hike Glacier's **Trail of the Cedars and Avalanche Lake** (pictured; page 370) and Grand Teton's **Taggart and Bradley Lakes** (page 362) to reel in prized catches while soaking in the beauty of the surrounding mountain landscapes.

7
8

WHERE TO GO

WEST COAST

A cornerstone of the Pacific Northwest, **Olympic** is known for its alpine tundra, dense moss-covered forests, and pristine beaches. In Northern California, **Yosemite** offers dramatic granite cliffs, spectacular waterfalls, and giant sequoia trees. In Southern California, **Joshua Tree** features a surreal desert landscape marked by unique rock formations and the iconic Joshua trees, set against a backdrop of rugged mountains and striking desert skies.

SOUTHWEST

Grand Canyon is famous for its immense, colorful canyon carved by the Colorado River, revealing layered rock formations and dramatic vistas. **Zion,** one of Utah's Mighty Five, has towering sandstone cliffs, narrow slot canyons, and lush river valleys, blending desert and forest scenery. **Great Sand Dunes** boasts the tallest sand dunes in North America, wetlands, and seasonal streams like Medano Creek, which flows through the dunes in spring and summer, creating shimmering water reflections.

ROCKY MOUNTAINS

Rocky Mountain showcases towering snowcapped peaks, expansive meadows, and alpine lakes. **Yellowstone,** the world's first national park,

▲ LONGS PEAK, ROCKY MOUNTAIN NATIONAL PARK

▲ HIKING IN ACADIA NATIONAL PARK

features dramatic geothermal wonders like geysers, hot springs, and bubbling mud pots, alongside vast grasslands and wildlife-rich valleys. **Glacier** offers rugged beauty with towering peaks, shimmering glacial lakes, and vast wilderness.

GREAT LAKES AND NORTHEAST

Acadia, located on Maine's rugged coast, is a stunning blend of rocky shorelines, granite peaks, and lush forests. In the Great Lakes region, **Cuyahoga Valley** is dotted with historic sites, charming covered bridges, sandstone ledges, and cascading waterfalls. Experience five different ecosystems—towering sand dunes, sandy beaches, wetlands, prairies, and forests—on a single hike along the southern shore of Lake Michigan at **Indiana Dunes.**

THE SOUTH

Straddling the border between North Carolina and Tennessee, **Great Smoky Mountains** is the most-visited park in the country. Its trails feature misty mountain vistas and abundant wildlife. **Shenandoah,** located in Virginia's Blue Ridge Mountains, offers a serene escape with its rolling hills, cascading waterfalls, and a portion of the Appalachian Trail. In South Carolina, **Congaree's** boardwalk leads through a towering old-growth floodplain forest.

PASSES AND FEES

ENTRANCE PASSES AND FEES

Most national parks charge an entrance fee (free to $35) that is valid for seven days. To get the most bang for your buck, consider buying the **Interagency Annual Pass** ($80), which is good for all national parks and federal fee areas. Interagency passes are free for fourth graders in the United States, people who are disabled, and military personnel. Seniors have two interagency pass options: Annual ($20), which is valid for one year, and Lifetime ($80).

TIMED ENTRY PASSES

Many national parks have had entrance fees for decades, but a newer idea is the timed entry pass. Timed entry passes help parks manage traffic and deliver a better experience for visitors by limiting access along certain corridors and scenic drives, and in popular sections of a given park. Most parks with a timed entry pass only require it during their peak season. You'll find specific details on timing and fees (most are free, some carry a small—$1-3—charge); the process for making your timed entry reservation; and relevant road, trail, and facility access on each park's website.

FEE-FREE DAYS

Some national parks recognize several fee-free days annually. During fee-free days the entrance fee for the park is waived. Most fee-free days include Martin Luther King Jr. Day (January), the first day of National Park Week (April), the anniversary of the Great American Outdoors Act/National Park Service birthday (August), National Public Lands Day (September), and Veterans Day (November 11).

▲ NORTH RIM CAMPGROUND, GRAND CANYON NATIONAL PARK

PERMITS AND RESERVATIONS

HIKING

Some parks require **permits** (www.recreation.gov) to hike certain trails, such as Angel's Landing in Zion and Half Dome in Yosemite. Permits are often acquired via a **lottery process.**

▲ AUTUMN IN PARADISE, MOUNT RAINIER NATIONAL PARK

Each lottery operates differently; most occur in winter or spring for the upcoming season.

ROADS AND PARKING

Many uber-crowded parks are now requiring reservations (www.recreation.gov; fees vary) to drive certain **roads** or park at **trailheads.** The reservation costs are in addition to entry fees, except for Great Smoky Mountains, which uses a parking pass system in lieu of entry fees. Acadia, Arches, Glacier, Haleakalā, Rocky Mountain, and Yosemite require reservations to access certain roads at certain times. While each park's reservations open at different times, most offer two windows: 60-120 days in advance and 1-7 days in advance. Several other parks are considering reservations for over-crowded areas; check the alerts on the individual park websites or the NPS app when you begin planning your trip.

LODGES AND CAMPGROUNDS

Reservations book up fast for national park lodges and campgrounds. Plan to book as soon as reservation windows open. Book any lodge dinners, tours, or activity reservations concurrently.

To stay overnight at **lodges** inside the parks, make reservations through individual operators for peak seasons (usually summer) 12-13 months in advance. This is especially true for Great Smoky Mountains, Grand Canyon, Yosemite, Yellowstone, Grand Teton, Glacier, Zion, Olympic, and Acadia.

Many **campgrounds** accept reservations (www.recreation.gov) up to six months in advance. Every year, more parks are converting campgrounds from first-come, first-served to the reservation system. When planning your trip, check on the park website to see whether reservations have been added.

SEASONS

HIGH SEASON

Summer is often the best time to visit the national parks. In the East, the foliage is in full green and visitor services are in full swing, while parks across the Rockies and in the mountains of the West are shaking themselves free of high-elevation snows and hitting their peak-season stride from July through the end of **September,** when snowfall dusts mountain peaks and passes and ushers in the end of the season.

Parks across the Southwest shine in **spring** and **fall,** when the deserts and mountains are in bloom and the dangerous triple-digit temperatures of summer are past. But spring and fall can see busy parks as crowds arrive to admire wildflowers and autumn color.

LOW SEASON

Winter is often the low season, when park lodges, campgrounds, and restaurants close for the season, leaving minimal services for visitors. Some national parks enjoy better weather and temperatures in winter thanks to their more moderate climates or tropical locales, while others embrace the snow and cold, offering opportunities for winter recreation—snowshoeing and Nordic skiing, ice climbing, cold weather camping, and more—and singular outdoor experiences.

NATIONAL PARKS APP

The **NPS smartphone app** has information on each national park: road conditions and closures, alerts, weather, ranger programs, maps, trails, activities, and campgrounds. Some parks include driving tours, self-guided walking tours, geyser eruption predictions, and parking lot status. Download the app before you leave home. Select the parks you'll be visiting and download information to use when cell service is not available, which is common in many parks.

▲ JENNY LAKE, GRAND TETON NATIONAL PARK

BEST HIKES BY SEASON

SPRING

- **Abrams Falls Trail, Great Smoky Mountains:** After your waterfall hike, search this pocket of the park for black bear cubs or join a wildflower walk as part of the annual Spring Wildflower Pilgrimage (page 488).
- **Lost Mine Trail, Big Bend:** Mild temperatures and a desert full of blooming cacti and wildflowers delivers beauty with every step (page 294).

SUMMER

- **Cleetwood Cove and Wizard Island, Crater Lake:** Take the plunge into the bracing waters of Crater Lake to celebrate your hike and get a respite from summer's heat (page 94).
- **Grinnell Glacier Trail, Glacier:** Escape to the mountains where summer wildflowers, waterfalls, and glacier-fed lakes offer a balm for everyday life (page 378).

FALL

- **Telescope Peak, Death Valley:** Summit Death Valley's highest point at a time of year when it's easy to explore the valley floor and this sky-scraping peak (page 134).
- **Old Rag Mountain Trail, Shenandoah:** Celebrate autumn with this must-do hike in Virginia, then head south on Skyline Drive and the Blue Ridge Parkway for even more fall color (page 464).

WINTER

- **Delicate Arch Trail, Arches:** A rim of snow makes Delicate Arch and the Utah landscape even more spectacular (page 260).

- **Kīlauea Iki and Crater Rim Trail, Hawai'i Volcanoes:** Try for an endless summer with this Hawai'ian hike that will have you exploring volcanic peaks before you hit the beach (page 186).

ACCESSIBLE TRAILS

Our parks are meant for everyone, but not everyone has the ability to climb or hike their way across the United States. Fortunately a growing list of accessible trails means more of us can experience the outdoors. Depending on your mobility aid and outdoor abilities, you'll find additional trails suited to you in a number of parks. Let this list of accessible trails guide you to your next favorite park, but be sure to check trail conditions and accessibility in your chosen park before you go.

WEST COAST

- **General Sherman Tree and Congress Trail, Sequoia & Kings Canyon:** Boardwalks lead through stands of these improbably tall trees and give every visitor the chance to be wowed (page 116).
- **Quinault Loop, Olympic:** Sections of this hike in Olympic's rain forest and along the shores of Lake Quinault are accessible for nearly all mobility aids thanks to compacted gravel trail segments; beyond the dedicated accessible nature trail, some will find the narrow and often muddy trail difficult (page 74).

SOUTHWEST

- **Pa'rus Trail, Zion:** Get a taste of Utah's rugged landscape at overlook after overlook via a smooth, mostly level concrete path; sunrise and sunset are simply too good to miss (page 226).
- **Rim Trail, Grand Canyon:** This paved trail along the canyon rim gives you phenomenal views of this park's celebrated landscape (page 198).

ROCKY MOUNTAINS

- **Trail of the Cedars, Glacier:** Trail of the Cedars loop's mixed boardwalk-hardscape trail offers an accessible hike with views of glacier-blue water, huge western hemlocks and red cedars, and a lush understory thick with ferns (page 370).
- **Lone Star Geyser Trail, Yellowstone:** This wide, partially paved trail follows an old road and is suitable for wheelchairs and other accessibility aids. Along the way you'll find wildlife, seasonal blooms, and views of the Firehole River, and at the end you'll enjoy geyser views from the boardwalk a safe distance away (page 340).

GREAT LAKES AND NORTHEAST

- **Ocean Path, Acadia:** From Sand Beach to Thunder Hole, this gorgeous seaside trail is fully accessible thanks to a wide concrete and packed-gravel path, boasting dramatic seascapes to one side and stunning mountains on the other (page 408).
- **Brandywine Gorge Loop, Cuyahoga Valley:** Only the upper portion of the boardwalk here is accessible, but it offers a fabulous any-season view of Brandywine Falls (page 420).

THE SOUTH

- **Boardwalk Loop, Congaree:** Explore a blackwater swamp forest full of titanic trees and a surprising array of wildlife on a boardwalk that puts you inches from the creeks and high above the forest floor (page 496).
- **Deep Creek Loop Trail, Great Smoky Mountains:** Leading to Toms Branch and Indian Creek Falls, the first mile (1.6 km) of this trail is broad with a hard-packed surface free of large rocks, roots, or ruts; beyond Indian Creek Falls, the trail grows rocky and steep (page 478).

▼ GENERAL SHERMAN TREE AND CONGRESS TRAIL, SEQUOIA & KINGS CANYON

BEST VIEWS

Glaciers. Deserts. Alpine peaks and the soft curves of the oldest mountain range in North America. Our national parks offer a stunning array of scenery. Whether you're chasing sunsets, photographing morning light on snowcapped mountains, delighting in wildflowers, or seeking a jaw-dropping view to go with your trailside lunch, here are a few hikes that deliver the views of your dreams.

WEST COAST

- **Root Glacier Trail, Wrangell-St. Elias:** Dive into Alaska's culture and incredible scenery with this hike that starts in a historic mining town and ends on a glacier where views of the icefall and towering mountains will leave you in awe (page 56).
- **Panorama Trail, Yosemite:** With waterfalls, gigantic Yosemite Valley views, and a route that lets you experience several of this park's environments, this hike belongs at the top of your Yosemite list (page 106).

SOUTHWEST

- **Bright Angel Trail, Grand Canyon:** You won't tire of the iconic views as you descend into the Grand Canyon. With plenty of places to rest or reverse course, this hike will please novice hikers, kids, and go-the-distance trailmasters (page 202).
- **Fairyland Loop Trail, Bryce Canyon:** Experience the hoodoos, multicolored rock, and storybook landscape of Bryce Canyon on this great-in-any-season hike (page 252).

ROCKY MOUNTAINS

- **Taggart and Bradley Lakes, Grand Teton:** Combining the scenery of alpine peaks and lakes, the chance to fish or go for a chilly swim, and an easy trail perfect for novice hikers, you'll fall in love with the Tetons as soon as you set out (page 362).
- **Highline Trail and Granite Park Chalet, Glacier:** This tough trail pays off with views of valleys and peaks, wildlife encounters, and summer wildflowers that will leave you speechless (page 374).

GREAT LAKES AND NORTHEAST

- **Jordan Pond Path and South Bubble, Acadia:** See mountain reflections in Jordan Pond as you patrol the shoreline on an easy path, then push yourself higher to where a rocky outcrop gives you sweeping views of this patch of Maine (page 400).
- **Ledges Loop Trail, Cuyahoga Valley:** Rise above Ohio's landscape of rolling hills on this cliffside hike for great fall color, cool summer hiking, and an anytime-you-go great day not far from the urban hustle of Cleveland (page 424).

THE SOUTH

- **Old Rag Mountain Trail, Shenandoah:** You'll need a permit for this popular, challenging hike, but if scrambling over, under, and around boulders; clinging to various cliff edges; and enjoying staggering summit views is up your alley, put this hike on your list (page 464).
- **Andrews Bald Trail, Great Smoky Mountains:** Hike to a hilltop bald full of summer blooms, then visit the highest peak in the Smoky Mountains before calling it a day (page 482).

▼ PANORAMA TRAIL, YOSEMITE

POINTS OF PRIDE

Sometimes the pictures and National Parks Passport stamp aren't enough and you need a hike with some serious bragging rights. We've got a few for you whether you're looking for the steepest trail, the highest peak, or the most-remote trailhead.

HARDEST HIKE

- **Rim-to-Rim, Grand Canyon:** On paper this hike is easy—go downhill, cross the river, go uphill—but you need to carry water, camping gear, and food enough for a multiday, marathon-length hike in temperatures that can be sweltering during the day and freezing at night. With planning and training, though, this hike will be one you brag about for decades (page 210).

LONGEST HIKE

- **Wonderland Trail, Mount Rainier:** Plan for at least 10 days of strenuous hiking when you hit the longest trail in this guide. For nearly 100 mi (161 km) you'll circle Mount Rainier on an exhausting, exhilarating hike that requires planning food caches and staying alert for wildlife and weather (page 90).

MOST ELEVATION CHANGE

- **Wonderland Trail, Mount Rainier:** Wonderland's impressive trail profile earned it two spots on our list of superlatives, this time for most elevation change. In your 10 days on the trail, the elevation change comes in at a whopping 24,547 ft (7,482 m), only 3,000 ft (914 m) shy of the summit of Mount Everest (page 90).

STEEPEST HIKE

- **Nuttallburg Trails, New River Gorge:** I grew up hunting and hiking the hills of West Virginia, so finding the steepest hike here was no surprise. Parts of this trail hit a 40.5 percent grade, making for tough going as you climb up or down past evidence of this region's coal mining past (page 474).

HIGHEST MOUNTAIN

- **Longs Peak: Keyhole Route, Rocky Mountain:** Colorado has 53 "14ers"—mountains over 14,000 ft (4,267 m)—and you can summit Longs Peak, a beauty at 14,259 ft (4,346 m), on a high-altitude multiday hike to remember (page 324).

LEAST-VISITED TRAIL

- **Greenstone Ridge Trail, Isle Royale:** Fewer than 25,000 people visit Isle Royale National Park, so when you're on Greenstone Ridge Trail, you're going to have it all to yourself (page 442).

MOST REMOTE TRAIL

- **Savage Alpine Trail, Denali:** Getting to this remote trail takes work. First you have to get to Anchorage, where it's a 4-hour, 240-mi (385-km) drive to the park entrance, where you're still a 2-hour, 15-mi (24-km) drive or shuttle to the trailhead. In short: Plan to visit Denali for a few days and log as many miles on the trail as you can (page 52).

QUIETEST TRAIL

- **Hall of Mosses and Hoh River Trail, Olympic:** In his 2005 book *One Square Inch of Silence,* author Gordon Hempton searched the nation for "the quietest place in the U.S." He found it in the Hoh Rain Forest where the dense rain forest and lack of human-made noise made for a very quiet place. When you visit, find a spot far from the trailhead, take a seat, and get quiet; soon the sounds of nature will overwhelm you and you'll see why Hempton and others fight to reduce noise pollution in our national parks (page 68).

▲ SAVAGE ALPINE TRAIL, DENALI NATIONAL PARK

DRIEST TRAIL

- **Golden Canyon Trail to Red Cathedral, Death Valley:** Death Valley sees less than 2.2 in (5.6 cm) of rain annually, so it makes sense that George Lucas cast the park as Tatooine. Hike Golden Canyon Trail to Red Cathedral and walk in the android footsteps of C-3PO and R2-D2, but avoid this hike in summer at all costs—Death Valley is the driest and the hottest park, clocking a high temperature of 134°F (56.7°C), and summer temperatures easily top 120°F (49°C) (page 124).

WETTEST TRAIL

- **Mist Trail to Vernal Fall, Yosemite:** Mist Trail lives up to its name, and most hikers end up soaked or wrapped in rain gear as they hike to a drier patch of trail (page 98).

CLOSEST TO A MAJOR CITY

- **Blue Hen Falls Trail, Cuyahoga Valley:** This trailhead is 20 mi (32 km) from Cleveland, but Cuyahoga Valley National Park is only 7 mi (11.3 km) from the city, making this park an easy antidote to the rush of urban life (page 416).

STARRIEST SKIES

- **The Notch, Badlands:** Head to Badlands in late July and early August for a spectacular star show and the Badlands Astronomy Festival. The Notch makes for a perfect sunset trail where you'll enjoy expansive celestial views before joining the astronomy festival (page 390).

BEST BACKPACKING HIKES

When you think of long-distance hikes, no doubt you think of the **Triple Crown of Trails** (page 33): Pacific Crest, Continental Divide, and the Appalachian Trails. Those hardcore hikes will test the limits of your endurance, planning, and mettle, and while we'd love to meet each of you on one of these epic treks, the hikes chosen here offer a few nights in the woods and satisfy those who want the trail to just keep going.

WEST COAST

- **Cathedral Lakes, Yosemite:** Explore another of Yosemite's incredible environs when you hike to Cathedral Lakes in Tuolumne Meadows on a route that you can finish in a day, but is best experienced with an overnight or two on the shores of these twin lakes (page 112).
- **Telescope Peak, Death Valley:** Hiking high above Death Valley, you'll enjoy an incredible panoramic scene, but turn this hike into an overnighter for views of the Milky Way and a sunrise you won't forget (page 134).

SOUTHWEST

- **Rim-to-Rim, Grand Canyon:** This marathon-length hike sends you into the depths of the Grand Canyon on a multi-night camping trip full of thigh-burning trail, see-it-to-believe-it scenery, and a sense of "I did that" accomplishment few trails can match (page 210).
- **Chesler Park and The Joint, Canyonlands:** You can tackle this hike in one go, but make the most of it and camp under the stars for wow-worthy celestial views by night and a sunrise that brings ten thousand hues to this wild landscape in the morning (page 276).

ROCKY MOUNTAINS

- **Longs Peak: Keyhole Route, Rocky Mountain:** Take your time on this strenuous hike by adding a night or two in the backcountry, giving you time to acclimate to the altitude, soak up some superb scenery, and put yourself in position for a safe summit push when you make for the top (page 324).

- **Paintbrush Canyon-Cascade Canyon Loop, Grand Teton:** Book your campsite or backcountry reservations to get the most of this hike where alpine lakes, a high-altitude trail, and nightly stargazing make the miles more manageable (page 356).

GREAT LAKES AND NORTHEAST

- **Greenstone Ridge Trail, Isle Royale:** Greenstone Ridge bisects this national park, but you can extend your multi-night backpacking trip by venturing down every spur trail you find, earning yourself a taste of the rocky shores, boggy fens, and dense patches of forest full of wildlife (page 442).

THE SOUTH

- **Big Creek Trail, Great Smoky Mountains:** Big Creek gives you the option for day hikes to waterfalls and swimming holes; overnights to give you more of a taste of the Smoky Mountains; or the chance to connect to the park's vast network of trails, reach notable summits, and even connect with the Appalachian Trail (page 492).

SUSTAINABILITY TIPS

To keep our parks pristine for the next visitors and the next generations, each of us needs to be a little more responsible with our actions. By minding your trash, your pets, and your campfires and campsites, you can take a small action with a large impact.

- **Use a water bottle.** Bring your own refillable water bottle or buy one from a park gift shop. Don't needlessly add disposable plastic to the park refuse collection and recycling infrastructure.
- **Stay on paths.** Staying on designated paths and trails prevents erosion. This is especially crucial in alpine meadows and sensitive wildflower zones. Take photos with your feet on a trail.
- **Carry out your trash.** Bring a small bag or container to corral your trash to pack out rather than letting tidbits drop along a trail or road (while you're at it, collect any litter you see that's safe and sanitary to handle). Think ahead and bring food with little to no packaging.
- **Mind the wildlife.** Keep yourself and the critters safe and healthy by minding your manners when wildlife is present. Don't feed them or leave food scraps around picnic areas or campsites (apple cores and energy bar wrappers are both trash). Maintain a safe distance for observation and photography. And remember, even if the wildlife is friend shaped, don't try to pet it.

For more sustainability tips, check out the principles of **Leave No Trace** (page 524).

ESCAPING THE CROWDS

Our national parks are popular, and rightly so. As visitation increases, however, so do the crowds. Here are some tips to avoid the mayhem.

VISIT IN SHOULDER SEASON

Many parks see their biggest crowds in summer, the traditional and peak travel season across the United States. To dodge the packed parking lots and crowded viewpoints, time your visit for fall or spring instead, or pay a visit to your park in winter when the snowy solitude is a welcome respite. If your park of choice is wildly popular in fall, when the leaves are at their peak, or in spring for wildflowers and adorable baby critters, try to shift your travel a little to see the leaves put on their final hurrah or when wildflowers are beginning to bloom. You might also consider opting for lesser-visited trails or heading to the parks during the week, avoiding the influx of locals and travelers on weekends and holidays. It takes a little more planning, but not much, and the payoff—an exceptional national park visit—is worth the effort.

▲ CAMPING IN JOSHUA TREE NATIONAL PARK

ARRIVE EARLY MORNING OR LATE AFTERNOON

Rush hour at park entrance stations is 10am-4pm. To claim a coveted parking spot at prime sights and trailheads, arrive before 9am (in the busiest and most-visited parks or on weekends, arrive before 7am).

Hike the best-loved trails in early morning or late afternoon, which avoids the crowds common during the busiest part of the day. Aim first for park areas that may require more time or energy to reach. And if your trail is known for sunrise or sunset, get started a little earlier and arrive at that A+ viewpoint with plenty of time to claim your spot.

SPEED THROUGH ENTRANCE STATIONS

You can breeze through entrance stations with an annual park pass. Annual passes and entrance passes for select parks are available online in advance at www.recreation.gov.

Check to see if your park has a timed entry pass, a shuttle system requiring reservations, or if there's a special event planned during your visit. You can often acquire passes, reservations, and tickets online through www.recreation.gov or your specific park.

HAVE AN ALTERNATE PLAN

Be flexible with your itinerary and forgo a hike if it is too crowded. Always have a second trailhead or sight in mind to visit instead. In addition to the 100 hikes in this book, you'll find fantastic national parks travel advice in other Moon titles. Don't hesitate to ask a ranger for advice; they'll know which trails are busy and can direct you to a great alternative.

BEST WITH KIDS

Fill your kids with a love of the outdoors and create new lifelong national parks fans with a visit to some spectacular trails, waterfalls, summits, and streams. From splashing in a mountain stream to earning their Junior Ranger badge, they'll delight you with their joy as they explore the parks by your side. So pack up their little boots and mini hiking poles and hit the trail.

WEST COAST

- **Zumwalt Meadow, Sequoia & Kings Canyon:** Surrounded by gorgeous scenery, bordered by a river perfect for wading, and full of wildflowers and wildlife, Zumwalt Meadows and the short trail here delivers an A+ national parks experience (page 120).
- **Big Tree via Karl Knapp and Cathedral Trees Loop, Redwood:** With kid-high ferns and skyscraping redwoods, this hike will fill your little ones with awe and give them a love for national parks (page 164).

SOUTHWEST

- **Pa'rus Trail, Zion:** Utah's landscape is nothing short of incredible, and the stone spires, eerie canyons, and multicolored rocks practically surround you on Pa'rus Trail, where you'll make memories and snap some holiday card-worthy pics of the kiddos (page 226).
- **Landscape Arch Trail, Arches:** On the way to the largest natural stone arch in the United States, you'll pass smaller arches and odd rock formations guaranteed to land in a "What I Did on My Summer Vacation" essay (page 264).

ROCKY MOUNTAINS

- **Lumpy Ridge and Gem Lake, Rocky Mountain:** With snowcapped mountains in the background, you'll hike past rock formations like Paul Bunyan's Boot, through aspen groves, and to the shore of Gem Lake where you can enjoy lunch on the patch of sandy shore (page 312).
- **Fairy Falls and Grand Prismatic Spring Overlook, Yellowstone:** Before you reach the 197-ft (60-m) waterfall, stop to admire the colorful

Grand Prismatic Spring from a hilltop overlook, then head through a piney forest to your destination (page 334).

GREAT LAKES AND NORTHEAST

- **Ocean Path, Acadia:** From the youngest hikers to the most sullen of teens, everyone will wow at the scenery of the Maine coast. Stop by overlooks for a cute family pic, hit the bouldery beaches to search for critters, or go for a chilly dip at Sand Beach as you make your way along this gentle, paved trail (page 408).
- **Ledges Loop Trail, Cuyahoga Valley:** With great year-round views, cool rocks and cliffs, and the chilly trailside Ice Box Cave, your kids will find plenty to explore (page 424).

THE SOUTH

- **Bearfence Mountain Trail, Shenandoah:** Let the kiddos lead you to their first summit when you top out on Bearfence Mountain and soak up the mountainous scenery. Hit the trail in fall for a stunning color show (page 460).
- **Deep Creek Loop Trail, Great Smoky Mountains:** A broad, easy trail will give little hikers confidence in the woods, but Deep Creek and a trio of trailside waterfalls are the stars of the show. The falls are easy to reach, and Deep Creek is ideal for a summertime swim or, better yet, tubing with the whole family (page 478).

▼ GRAND PRISMATIC SPRING OVERLOOK, YELLOWSTONE NATIONAL PARK

THE TRIPLE CROWN OF HIKING

The Appalachian Trail, Continental Divide Trail, and Pacific Crest Trail make up the iconic Triple Crown of Hiking, and few have thru-hiked or segment-hiked all three. The physical, emotional, and logistical challenges of these hikes is simply monumental, but the challenge still attracts thousands of hikers every year. Following the Appalachian Mountains from Georgia to Maine, the AT clocks in at around 2,190 mi (3,525 km) and passes through Great Smoky Mountains and Shenandoah National Parks. And the CDT follows the Continental Divide along the Rocky Mountains for nearly 3,100 mi (4,988 km). All 2,650 mi (4,265 km) of the PCT follows the Sierra Nevada and Cascades from near Mexico to the Canada border. Complete all three for a whopping 7,940 mi (12,778 km) of trail and the absolute ultimate in hiking bragging rights. Featured trails in our national parks connect to these legendary long hikes, and if you're keen to log a few miles on one or more of them, we've got you covered.

APPALACHIAN TRAIL

- **Bearfence Mountain Trail, Shenandoah:** Part of Bearfence Mountain Trail is shared with the AT, making for easy access to this legendary hike whether you're day hiking, segment hiking, or meeting up with thru-hikers as a trail angel or hiking companion (page 460).
- **Andrews Bald Trail, Great Smoky Mountains:** This trail on the flanks of Kuwohi (formerly known as Clingmans Dome) gives you a couple of ways to connect to the AT, most notably via a spur trail along the trek to the summit of Kuwohi (page 482).
- **Big Creek Trail, Great Smoky Mountains:** In all, 74 mi (119 km) of the AT follows the crest of the Smoky Mountains, but you can connect on Big Creek Trail by following Low Gap Trail 2.5 mi (4 km), past the Walnut Bottom backcountry campsite, to the AT on the ridgeline above (page 492).

▲ DEER FAWN ON THE APPALACHIAN TRAIL, GREAT SMOKY MOUNTAINS NATIONAL PARK

CONTINENTAL DIVIDE TRAIL

- **Highline Trail and Granite Park Chalet, Glacier:** North of Granite Park Chalet, the CDT joins Highline Trail as they both head toward the Canadian border (page 374).
- **Swiftcurrent Pass and Lookout Trail, Glacier:** From the trailhead to Granite Park, this trail is the CDT, so if hiking the CDT is your aim, carry on south from the trailhead or, at Granite Park Chalet, join Highline Trail and the CDT as they head north (page 382).

PACIFIC CREST TRAIL

- **Cathedral Lakes, Yosemite:** At the Cathedral Lakes trailhead you cross the John Muir Trail, a subsection of the PCT; to join the PCT proper, follow Muir Trail east to the junction with the PCT, at which point you can continue east on Muir/PCT or head north on the PCT (page 112).

TOP EXPERIENCE

BEST WILDLIFE WATCHING

Our national parks don't just preserve natural beauty and pieces of cultural heritage—they're also havens for wildlife. Bird watchers, insect and amphibian lovers, and folks hoping to see elk, grizzly bears, black bears, and wolves can find places where the wildlife watching is effortless.

WEST COAST

- **Horseshoe Lake Trail, Denali:** You're almost guaranteed to spot beavers and moose on this hike, though you could also spot red foxes, bald and golden eagles, red squirrels, and the tiny arctic ground squirrel. On rare occasions you'll see a Dall sheep or grizzly bear, but I promise that you'll see millions of mosquitoes (page 48).
- **James Irvine and Miners Ridge Loop, Redwood:** Look for the Roosevelt elk near the trailhead and out on the beach (a rare but exciting sight), and keep your eyes peeled for the rare black bear. You'll also see the bright yellow banana slug, the northern red-legged frog, plenty of birds like woodpeckers and seabirds, and aquatic critters like harbor seals, sea lions, and whales (when they're migrating) once you reach the shore (page 168).

SOUTHWEST

- **Widforss Trail, Grand Canyon:** The Kaibab squirrel (with its tufted ears and bushy white tail) and other small mammals are everywhere along this trail, as are plenty of songbirds and raptors, but you may also spot mule deer, the elusive elk, the ultra-rare mountain lion, and beautiful but seasonal butterflies on this hike (page 206).
- **Garwood Dam and Wildhorse Tank, Saguaro:** Cactus wrens (Arizona's state bird) and roadrunners are common sightings, as are desert tortoises and a number of lizards, plus javelinas, kangaroo rats, and desert cottontails. Keep your eyes open for tarantulas and scorpions as you go along (page 220).

ROCKY MOUNTAINS

- **South Rim Trail to Point Sublime, Yellowstone:** From songbirds to moose to flocks of Canada geese, you'll spot loads of wildlife, and with the chance to see bison, wolves, and grizzly bears, this hike—and nearby Hayden Valley—is a must for wildlife lovers (page 348).
- **Big Plateau and Ekblom Trail Loop, Theodore Roosevelt:** You'll need to take your shoes and socks off to count the critters you spot on this hike: mule deer, coyotes, feral horses, songbirds galore, prairie dogs (and more prairie dogs), and possibly bison and pronghorns (though you stand a better chance of finding these last two on the South Unit Scenic Drive) (page 386).

GREAT LAKES AND NORTHEAST

- **Cowles Bog Trail, Indiana Dunes:** As you venture from biome to biome, you'll find shorebirds and waterfowl, frogs and toads, butterflies and dragonflies, and plenty of songbirds, and you may spot elusive animals like white-tailed deer, coyotes, foxes, or even a beaver (page 430).
- **Greenstone Ridge Trail, Isle Royale:** This hike is a favorite for many reasons, but they all come back to one thing: the solitude of Greenstone Ridge. Thanks to the low visitation numbers, you'll find the wildlife undisturbed, and you stand a good chance of seeing moose, wolves, songbirds and shorebirds, and more (page 442).

THE SOUTH

- **Abrams Falls Trail, Great Smoky Mountains:** Bring a picnic-friendly dinner with you, because after you hike to the falls, you'll want to stick around for evening in Cades Cove when hundreds of white-tailed deer, flocks of wild turkeys, foxes, black bears and their cubs, and other critters come out to forage and feed as the sun sets (page 488).
- **Boardwalk Loop, Congaree:** Chances are good that you'll sight alligators, wild pigs, deer, foxes, turkeys, woodpeckers, and even a snake or two on this trail (page 496).

▼ MOOSE IN DENALI

HIKES AT A GLANCE

#	HIKE NAME	DISTANCE	DURATION	DIFFICULTY	WHY GO	PAGE
			WEST COAST			
	DENALI NATIONAL PARK & PRESERVE					
1	Horseshoe Lake Trail	2.1 mi (3.4 km) round-trip	1.5-2 hr	easy	lakes and rivers	48
2	Savage Alpine Trail	4.1 mi (6.6 km) one-way	3-4 hr	strenuous	mountain views	52
	WRANGELL-ST. ELIAS NATIONAL PARK & PRESERVE					
3	Root Glacier Trail	5.7 mi (9.2 km) round-trip	2.5 hr	easy-moderate	glaciers	56
	OLYMPIC NATIONAL PARK					
4	Hurricane Hill	3.4 mi (5.5 km) round-trip	2-2.5 hr	easy-moderate	mountain views	60
5	Rialto Beach to Hole-in-the-Wall	3.3 mi (5.3 km) round-trip	1.5-2.5 hr	easy	beaches	64
6	Hall of Mosses and Hoh River Trail	6.7 mi (10.8 km) round-trip	3.5-4 hr	easy-moderate	rain forest	68
7	Quinault Loop	4 mi (6.4 km) round-trip	1.5-2 hr	easy	waterfalls	74
	NORTH CASCADES NATIONAL PARK					
8	Agnes Gorge Trail	4.7 mi (7.6 km) round-trip	2-2.5 hr	moderate	mountain views	78
	MOUNT RAINIER NATIONAL PARK					
9	Skyline Trail Loop	5.8 mi (9.3 km) round-trip	3-4 hr	moderate	mountain views	82
10	Silver Falls Loop	2.9 mi (4.7 km) round-trip	2 hr	easy	waterfalls	86
11	Wonderland Trail	93 mi (150 km) round-trip	10-14 days	strenuous	back-packing adventures	90
	CRATER LAKE NATIONAL PARK					
12	Cleetwood Cove and Wizard Island	4.5 mi (7.2 km) round-trip	4 hr	easy-moderate	volcanic craters	94
	YOSEMITE NATIONAL PARK					
13	Mist Trail to Vernal Fall	3 mi (4.8 km) round-trip	1.5-2 hr	moderate	waterfalls	98

#	HIKE NAME	DISTANCE	DURATION	DIFFICULTY	WHY GO	PAGE
14	Half Dome	16 mi (26 km) round-trip	8-10 hr	very strenuous	mountain views	102
15	Panorama Trail	8.5 mi (13.7 km) one-way	4-5 hr	moderate-strenuous	mountain views	106
16	Cathedral Lakes	9.5 mi (15.3 km) round-trip	4-6 hr	strenuous	stargazing	112
	SEQUOIA & KINGS CANYON NATIONAL PARK					
17	General Sherman Tree and Congress Trail	2.9 mi (4.7 km) round-trip	1.5 hr	easy	redwoods	116
18	Zumwalt Meadow	1.6 mi (2.6 km) round-trip	1-2 hr	easy	wildflowers	120
	DEATH VALLEY NATIONAL PARK					
19	Golden Canyon Trail to Red Cathedral	2.9-6 mi (4.7-9.7 km) round-trip	1.5-3 hr	easy	canyons	124
20	Marble Canyon	3.2-5.6 mi (5.1-9 km) round-trip	2-6 hr	moderate	canyons	130
21	Telescope Peak	14 mi (22.5 km) round-trip	7-9 hr	strenuous	mountain views	134
	JOSHUA TREE NATIONAL PARK					
22	Barker Dam	1.3 mi (2.1 km) round-trip	30 min	easy	desert-scapes	138
23	Fortynine Palms Oasis Trail	3 mi (4.8 km) round-trip	2-3 hr	moderate	desert-scapes	142
24	Lost Palms Oasis Trail	7.4 mi (11.9 km) round-trip	4-6 hr	moderate	desert-scapes	148
	LASSEN VOLCANIC NATIONAL PARK					
25	Bumpass Hell Trail	3.2 mi (5.1 km) round-trip	2 hr	easy	geothermal features	152
26	Lassen Peak	4.8 mi (7.7 km) round-trip	4-5 hr	moderate-strenuous	volcanic summits	156
	REDWOOD NATIONAL AND STATE PARKS					
27	Tall Trees Grove	3.6 mi (5.8 km) round-trip	2-3 hr	moderate	redwoods	160
28	Big Tree via Karl Knapp and Cathedral Trees Loop	2.9 mi (4.7 km) round-trip	1-1.5 hr	easy	redwoods	164

(continued)

#	HIKE NAME	DISTANCE	DURATION	DIFFICULTY	WHY GO	PAGE
29	James Irvine and Miners Ridge Loop	11.4 mi (18.3 km) round-trip	6-7 hr	moderate-strenuous	fern-filled canyon	168
	PINNACLES NATIONAL PARK					
30	High Peaks and Balconies Cave Loop	8.4 mi (13.5 km) round-trip	4.5-5 hr	strenuous	caves	172
	HALEAKALĀ NATIONAL PARK					
31	Halemau'u and Haleakalā Overlook Trail	7.3 mi (11.7 km) round-trip	4.5-5 hr	strenuous	volcanic summits	176
32	Pipiwai Trail and Waimoku Falls	3.4 mi (5.5 km) round-trip	2-2.5 hr	moderate	waterfalls	182
	HAWAI'I VOLCANOES NATIONAL PARK					
33	Kīlauea Iki and Crater Rim Trail	3.2 mi (5.1 km) round-trip	2-3 hr	moderate	volcanic craters	186
34	Pu'uloa Petroglyphs Trail	1.2 mi (1.9 km) round-trip	1-1.5 hr	moderate	petroglyphs	190
	SOUTHWEST					
	GRAND CANYON NATIONAL PARK					
35	Rim Trail (Bright Angel Lodge to Mather Point)	6 mi (9.7 km) round-trip	1.5-2.5 hr	easy	canyons	198
36	Bright Angel Trail	3-9 mi (4.8-14.5 km) round-trip	2-8 hr	moderate-strenuous	canyons	202
37	Widforss Trail	10 mi (16.1 km) round-trip	4-6 hr	easy-moderate	canyons	206
38	Rim-to-Rim	24.6 mi (39.6 km) one-way	2-4 days	strenuous	canyons	210
	SAGUARO NATIONAL PARK					
39	Loma Verde Loop	3.7 mi (6 km) round-trip	1-1.5 hr	easy	mountain views	216
40	Garwood Dam and Wildhorse Tank	6.3 mi (10.1 km) round-trip	3 hr	moderate	wildlife watching	220
	ZION NATIONAL PARK					
41	Pa'rus Trail	3 mi (4.8 km) round-trip	2-2.5 hr	easy	year-round scenic views	226
42	Canyon Overlook Trail	1 mi (1.6 km) round-trip	1 hr	easy	canyons	230
43	West Rim Trail to Angels Landing	5.4 mi (8.7 km) round-trip	4 hr	strenuous	mountain views	234

#	HIKE NAME	DISTANCE	DURATION	DIFFICULTY	WHY GO	PAGE
44	The Narrows	5.2-10.2 mi (8.4-16.4 km) round-trip	5-9 hr	strenuous	river hiking	238
	BRYCE CANYON NATIONAL PARK					
45	Rim Trail	11 mi (17.7 km) round-trip	5-7 hr	easy	hoodoos	242
46	Queen's Garden-Navajo Loop	3.2 mi (5.1 km) round-trip	1.5 hr	moderate	hoodoos	246
47	Fairyland Loop Trail	8 mi (12.9 km) round-trip	4-5 hr	strenuous	hoodoos	252
	CAPITOL REEF NATIONAL PARK					
48	Cassidy Arch Trail	3.1 mi (5 km) round-trip	3 hr	moderate-strenuous	arches	256
	ARCHES NATIONAL PARK					
49	Delicate Arch Trail	3 mi (4.8 km) round-trip	2 hr	moderate-strenuous	arches	260
50	Landscape Arch Trail	2.4 mi (3.9 km) round-trip	1 hr	easy	arches	264
	CANYONLANDS NATIONAL PARK					
51	Murphy Point Trail	3.4 mi (5.5 km) round-trip	1 hr	easy	desert-scapes	268
52	Great Gallery Trail	7-10.6 mi (11.3-17.1 km) round-trip	4-6.5 hr	moderate-strenuous	petroglyphs	272
53	Chesler Park and The Joint	10.2 mi (16.4 km) round-trip	5-6 hr	strenuous	canyons	276
	MESA VERDE NATIONAL PARK					
54	Petroglyph Point Trail	2.4 mi (3.9 km) loop	2 hr	moderate-strenuous	petroglyphs	282
55	Soda Canyon Overlook	1.2 mi (1.9 km) round-trip	30-40 min	easy	cliff dwellings	286
	GREAT SAND DUNES NATIONAL PARK & PRESERVE					
56	High Dune Trail	4 mi (6.4 km) round-trip	3 hr	strenuous	sand dunes	290
	BIG BEND NATIONAL PARK					
57	Lost Mine Trail	4.8 mi (7.7 km) round-trip	3 hr	moderate-strenuous	mountain views	294

(continued)

#	HIKE NAME	DISTANCE	DURATION	DIFFICULTY	WHY GO	PAGE
58	Balanced Rock via Grapevine Hills Trail	1.9 mi (3 km) round-trip	1-2 hr	easy-moderate	mountain views	298
59	Santa Elena Canyon	1.6 mi (2.6 km) round-trip	1 hr	easy	canyons	304
ROCKY MOUNTAINS						
ROCKY MOUNTAIN NATIONAL PARK						
60	Lumpy Ridge and Gem Lake	3.8 mi (6.1 km) round-trip	2.5 hr	moderate	aspen groves	312
61	Lake Haiyaha	4.2 mi (6.8 km) round-trip	2-3 hr	moderate	lakes and wildflowers	316
62	Sky Pond via Glacier Gorge Trail	8.6 mi (13.8 km) round-trip	6 hr	strenuous	lakes and waterfalls	320
63	Longs Peak: Keyhole Route	15 mi (24 km) round-trip	10-15 hr	very strenuous	mountain views	324
BLACK CANYON OF THE GUNNISON NATIONAL PARK						
64	North Vista to Exclamation Point	3 mi (4.8 km) round-trip	1.25 hr	easy	canyons	330
YELLOWSTONE NATIONAL PARK						
65	Fairy Falls and Grand Prismatic Spring Overlook	6.8 mi (10.9 km) round-trip	3.5 hr	easy-moderate	geothermal features	334
66	Lone Star Geyser Trail	5.3 mi (8.5 km) round-trip	3-5 hr	easy	geothermal features	340
67	Silver Cord Cascade	2 mi (3.2 km) round-trip	1 hr	easy	waterfalls	344
68	South Rim Trail to Point Sublime	6.6 mi (10.6 km) round-trip	3 hr	easy-strenuous	canyons	348
GRAND TETON NATIONAL PARK						
69	Hidden Falls and Inspiration Point	2 mi (3.2 km) round-trip	2 hr	moderate	waterfalls	352
70	Paintbrush Canyon-Cascade Canyon Loop	19.2 mi (30.9 km) round-trip	13 hr	very strenuous	lakes and waterfalls	356
71	Taggart and Bradley Lakes	3-6 mi (4.8-9.7 km) round-trip	2-4 hr	easy-moderate	lakes	362
72	Teton Crest Trail	31.5-40 mi (50.7-64 km) one-way	3-5 days	very strenuous	back-packing adventures	366

#	HIKE NAME	DISTANCE	DURATION	DIFFICULTY	WHY GO	PAGE
	GLACIER NATIONAL PARK					
73	Trail of the Cedars and Avalanche Lake	0.9-5.9 mi (1.5-9.5 km) loop/ round-trip	0.5-3 hr	easy-moderate	lakes and rain forests	370
74	Highline Trail and Granite Park Chalet	7.4-11.4 mi (11.9-18.3 km) one-way	3.5-6 hr	strenuous	mountain views	374
75	Grinnell Glacier Trail	11 mi (17.7 km) round-trip	6 hr	moderate-strenuous	glaciers	378
76	Swiftcurrent Pass and Lookout Trail	3.6-16.2 mi (5.8-26 km) round-trip	2-8 hr	easy-strenuous	peaks, glaciers, lakes	382
	THEODORE ROOSEVELT NATIONAL PARK					
77	Big Plateau and Ekblom Trail Loop	5.3 mi (8.5 km) round-trip	2-2.5 hr	moderate	wildlife watching	386
	BADLANDS NATIONAL PARK					
78	The Notch	1.5 mi (2.4 km) round-trip	2 hr	moderate-strenuous	canyons	390
	GREAT LAKES AND NORTHEAST					
	ACADIA NATIONAL PARK					
79	Jordan Pond Path and South Bubble	3.5 mi (5.6 km) round-trip	2-4 hr	moderate-strenuous	lakes and mountain views	400
80	Precipice Trail	2 mi (3.2 km) round-trip	1.5-3 hr	very strenuous	thrilling climbs	404
81	Ocean Path	1.6-4.4 mi (2.6-7.1 km)	1.5-2 hr	easy	coastal views	408
82	Gorham Mountain Loop	3.5 mi (5.6 km) round-trip	1.5-2.5 hr	moderate-strenuous	mountain views	412
	CUYAHOGA VALLEY NATIONAL PARK					
83	Blue Hen Falls Trail	2.5 mi (4 km) round-trip	1-2 hr	easy	waterfalls	416
84	Brandywine Gorge Loop	0.8-3.9 mi (1.3-6.3 km) round-trip	35 min-3 hr	moderate	waterfalls	420
85	Ledges Loop Trail	2.3 mi (3.7 km) round-trip	1 hr	easy-moderate	cliffs and ledges	424
	INDIANA DUNES NATIONAL PARK					
86	Cowles Bog Trail	4.3 mi (6.9 km) round-trip	1.5-2 hr	moderate	diverse ecosystems	430

(continued)

#	HIKE NAME	DISTANCE	DURATION	DIFFICULTY	WHY GO	PAGE
87	West Beach Three-Loop Trail	3.6 mi (5.8 km) round-trip	3 hr	moderate	lakes and dunes	434
88	Paul H. Douglas Trail	3.4 mi (5.5 km) round-trip	1-2 hr	moderate	wildflowers and wildlife watching	438
	ISLE ROYALE NATIONAL PARK					
89	Greenstone Ridge Trail	40 mi (64 km) round-trip	2-4 days	moderate-strenuous	back-packing adventures	442
	THE SOUTH					
	SHENANDOAH NATIONAL PARK					
90	Hawksbill Loop Trail	2.7 mi (4.3 km) round-trip	2-3 hr	moderate-strenuous	mountain views	452
91	Cedar Run-Whiteoak Circuit	7.7 mi (12.4 km) round-trip	6-8 hr	strenuous	waterfalls and swimming holes	456
92	Bearfence Mountain Trail	1 mi (1.6 km) round-trip	1-1.5 hr	moderate-strenuous	mountain views	460
93	Old Rag Mountain Trail	5.8-9.3 mi (9.3-15 km) round-trip	7-8 hr	strenuous	mountain views	464
	NEW RIVER GORGE NATIONAL PARK & PRESERVE					
94	Endless Wall Trail	2.2 mi (3.5 km) round-trip	1 hr	easy-moderate	cliffs and ledges	470
95	Nuttallburg Trails	4.6 mi (7.4 km) round-trip	4-5 hr	strenuous	ruins	474
	GREAT SMOKY MOUNTAINS NATIONAL PARK					
96	Deep Creek Loop Trail	1.7-4.4 mi (2.7-7.1 km) round-trip	1-3 hr	easy	waterfalls	478
97	Andrews Bald Trail	3.6 mi (5.8 km) round-trip	3 hr	moderate	wildflowers	482
98	Abrams Falls Trail	5 mi (8 km) round-trip	3 hr	moderate	waterfalls	488
99	Big Creek Trail	10.6 mi (17.1 km) round-trip	5-6 hr	easy	waterfalls and swimming holes	492
	CONGAREE NATIONAL PARK					
100	Boardwalk Loop	2.3 mi (3.7 km) round-trip	1 hr	easy	loblolly pines and bald cypress trees	496

▲ TAGGART LAKE, GRAND TETON NATIONAL PARK

OHANAPECOSH RIVER, MOUNT RAINIER NATIONAL PARK

WEST COAST

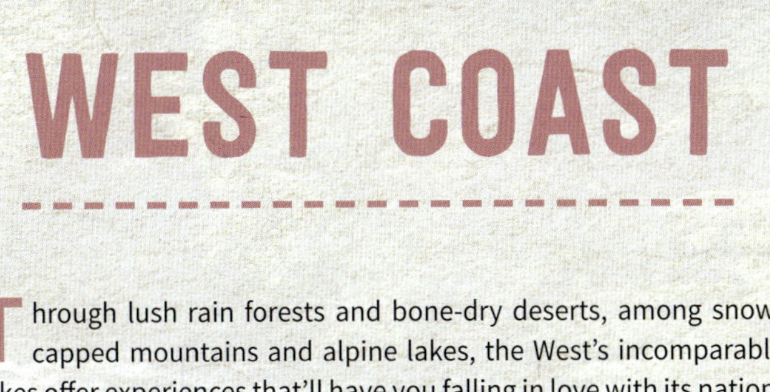

Through lush rain forests and bone-dry deserts, among snow-capped mountains and alpine lakes, the West's incomparable hikes offer experiences that'll have you falling in love with its national parks trails.

In remote Wrangell-St. Elias, Root Glacier delivers the sting of Alaska's winter cold through boots and socks, but you're too distracted by sawtooth mountains to notice. Olympic's Hall of Mosses and Hoh River Trail immerses you in a magical landscape of ancient trees draped in thick green moss, with ferns carpeting the forest floor and a serene, almost otherworldly atmosphere. In Oregon, loop around Witches Cauldron atop Wizard Island, and then dip your feet in the cool water of Crater Lake. Yosemite's Mist Trail delivers on its name and you're soaked as you ascend past waterfalls and emerald pools, yet you dream of tomorrow's Half Dome climb. Witness a stunning sunrise from Hawai'i Volcanoes' crater rim, then descend Kīlauea Iki Trail into the caldera, volcanic dust puffing up with every step.

WEST COAST

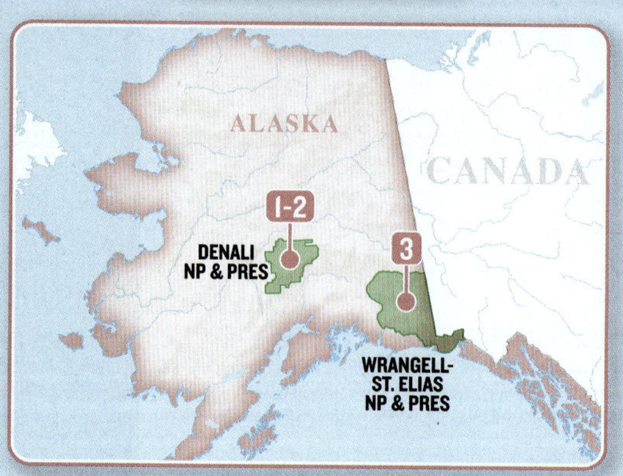

8
NORTH CASCADES N
4-7
OLYMPIC NP
MOUNT RAINIER NP
9-11
WASHINGTON
OREGON
12
CRATER LAKE NP
27-29
REDWOOD NP
LASSEN VOLCANIC NP
25-26
CALIFORNIA
NEVADA
13-16
YOSEMITE NP
PINNACLES NP
30
SEQUOIA & KINGS CANYON NP
17-18
19-21
DEATH VALLEY NP
22-24
JOSHUA TREE NP
PACIFIC OCEAN

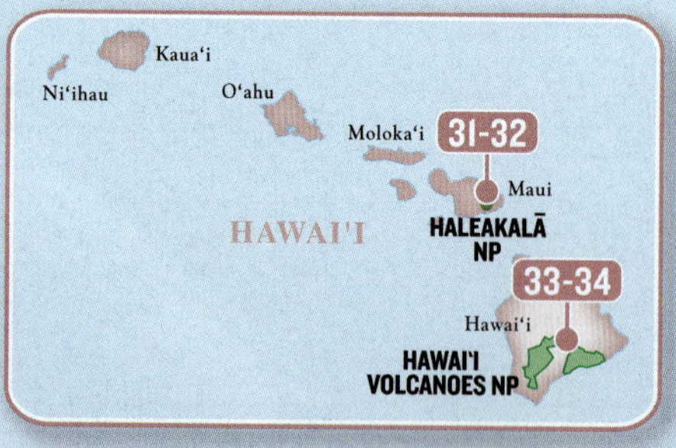

MOON
0 200 mi
0 200 km

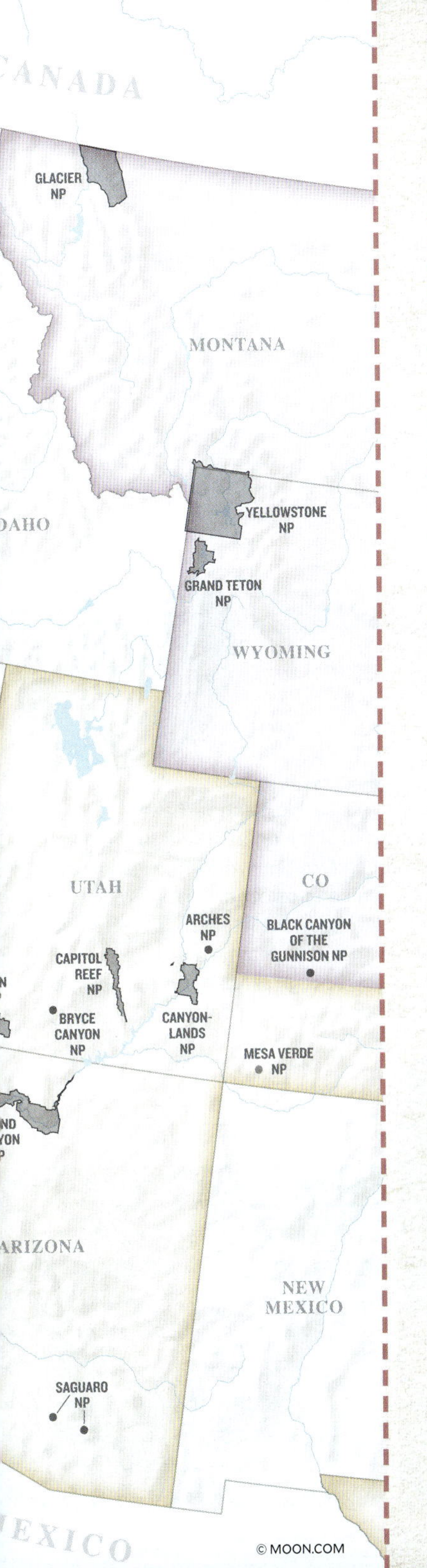
CANADA
GLACIER NP
MONTANA
IDAHO
YELLOWSTONE NP
GRAND TETON NP
WYOMING
UTAH
CO
ARCHES NP
BLACK CANYON OF THE GUNNISON NP
CAPITOL REEF NP
BRYCE CANYON NP
CANYON-LANDS NP
MESA VERDE NP
ARIZONA
NEW MEXICO
SAGUARO NP
MEXICO
© MOON.COM

HORSESHOE LAKE TRAIL

DENALI NATIONAL PARK & PRESERVE, ALASKA

Hike one of Denali National Park's most popular trails and see why the landscape—from towering peaks to rushing rivers to placid lakes—draws so many visitors each year.

- **Distance:** 2.1 mi (3.4 km) round-trip
- **Duration:** 1.5-2 hours
- **Elevation Gain:** 446 ft (136 m)
- **Effort:** Easy
- **When:** May-early Sept.
- **Trailhead:** Horseshoe Lake Trailhead

HIGHLIGHT: Taking a picture along Horseshoe Lake's photogenic west side

This out-and-back lollipop trail takes you along a well-maintained, crushed gravel trail to Horseshoe Lake before paying a visit to the rocky banks of the Nenana River and a beaver dam. You may spot a beaver or two in the water, working on their dam, or out chewing down a tree. You could also spot other wildlife: the wood frog (Denali's only amphibian), which you're more likely to hear than see; small mammals like the pika, the hoary marmot, maybe a red fox or arctic ground squirrel; moose and bears (black and grizzly); maybe a wolf; but certainly birds including golden and bald eagles, gyrfalcons (the largest

BEAVER DAM

BEAVER AT HORSESHOE LAKE

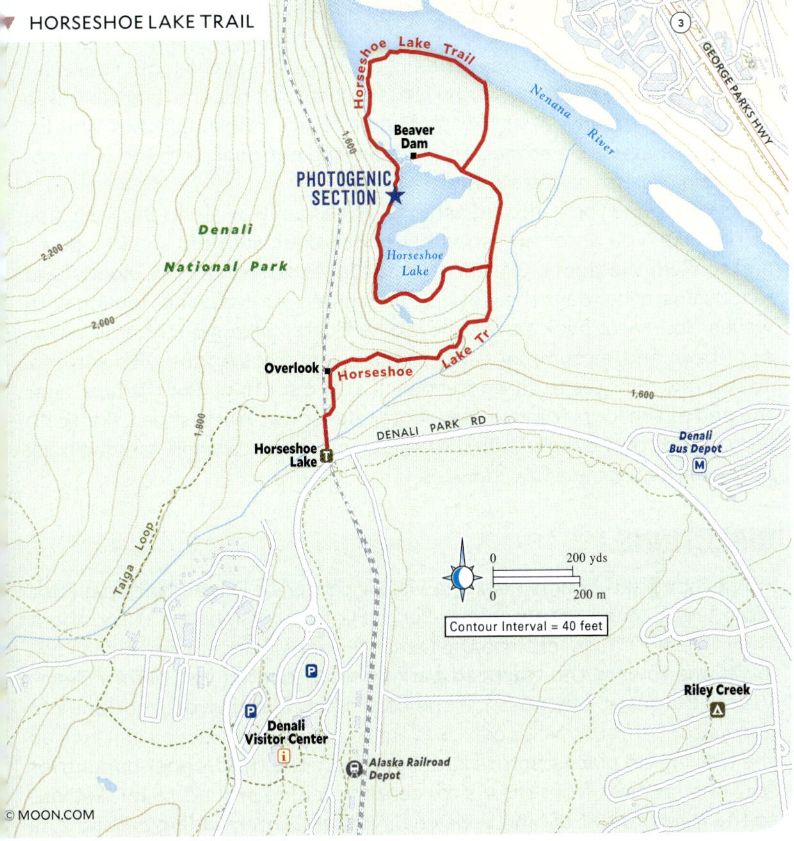

falcon species), songbirds, and possibly even migratory waterfowl like the trumpeter swan. Most likely you'll be in the presence of birds and half a million mosquitoes.

START THE HIKE

The trail begins at the **Horseshoe Lake Trailhead** and immediately climbs to a little ridge with a bench and a great view overlooking the lake and the Nenana River. Steps after the bench, the trail descends 250 ft (76 m) to the lake. Stairs ease the steepest part of the trail, but unless conditions are extremely muddy or icy and snowy, you'll be fine. Near the edge of the lake, you'll find a sign indicating Horseshoe Lake to the left. This is the start of the loop around the lake. Continue straight along the path to circle the lake in a counterclockwise direction.

From the sign, carry on along the undulating trail until you see the sign for the spur trail to the beaver dam. The **beaver dam** is pretty impressive, even more so if you're not familiar with these critters and their constructions. The dam sits at the north end of the lake, and if the beavers have their way, soon they'll form a second lake (maybe technically a pond) here between Horseshoe and the river. Stick around for a while and watch for beavers. If you're lucky, you'll spot them on the shore and going in and out of their dam.

Once you've seen the beaver dam, continue along the loop. Your next stop is the rocky shoreline of the Nenana River. Across the river is an area known as "the Canyon" or "Glitter Gulch" for its twinkling lights. This little community sits a stone's throw from the national park and is one of the main tourism centers in the area.

As you round the bend and begin to make your way along the west side of the lake, you enter an especially **photogenic section,** so slow down and soak up the sights. On still days, the lakes reflect the sky, clouds, and mountains; other days the water is deep green or turgid and rippling with waves. Your view back across the lake will catch hikers on the trail, a sliver of river, and, as summer turns to fall, a few trees bright with autumn. Take a few minutes to sit on the bench at the south end of the lake, near the end of the loop, for your last shoreside look at Horseshoe Lake. From here, return to the main trail, turn right, and ascend the hill, arriving back at the parking lot in a few minutes.

DIRECTIONS

Horseshoe Lake Trail is near the visitor center of Denali National Park. From Healy, head south on the Parks Highway (Highway 3) for about 11 mi (17.7 km). Turn left into the Denali National Park entrance, then follow signs toward the trailhead parking area, located just before Denali Visitor Center at Milepost 1. If the parking area is crowded, continue to the visitor center at Milepost 1.5. From the visitor center, you can pick up the trail in two places: across Park Road from the third/upper parking lot (the one farthest from the visitor center), adding around 1.5 mi (2.4 km) to the hike; or right behind the Denali Visitor Center, adding around 2 mi (3.2 km) to the hike.

BEST NEARBY

Denali Princess Wilderness Lodge

▶ *Mile 238.5 George Parks Hwy., Denali National Park; 907/683-2282; www.princesslodges.com; mid-May–mid-Sept.; rooms from $269*

Unless you're camping inside the park, this is the closest bed you'll find near Denali National Park. Comfortable, stylish, and scenic, it's a lovely spot to call home for a few days. You'll find four restaurants and a pair of cafés at the hotel, serving everything from café drinks, baked goods, and quick-service breakfast and lunch bites to burgers and pizza to breakfast buffets and fine dining takes on salmon, halibut, prime rib, and other hearty dishes. Denali Princess Wilderness Lodge also offers shuttles ($5) to the Denali Visitor Center and Horseshoe Lake Trailhead, laundry facilities, Wi-Fi, a variety of kid-friendly activities, and excursions to and around the park (including whitewater rafting, ATV tours, guided hikes, and more).

NEED TO KNOW

Info: Denali Visitor Center, www.nps.gov/dena

Passes and Reservations: Entry into the park is $15/individual. Passes are available in advance at www.recreation.gov.

Weather Considerations: Temperatures in summer can vary wildly, ranging from 33-77°F (0.5-25°C). Pay attention to your gear, packing your rain kit and warm layers.

Facilities: None at the trailhead. Denali Visitor Center (0.5 mi/0.8 km southwest) has restrooms, flush toilets, and a potable water filling station. You'll also find the rare cellular and Wi-Fi signals here, as well as park and trail maps and park rangers.

▼ HORSESHOE LAKE

2

SAVAGE ALPINE TRAIL

DENALI NATIONAL PARK & PRESERVE, ALASKA

Reach new heights on this alpine hike that offers big views of Denali and the surrounding countryside.

- **Distance:** 4.1 mi (6.6 km) one-way
- **Duration:** 3-4 hours
- **Elevation Gain:** 1,414 ft (431 m)
- **Effort:** Strenuous
- **When:** May-Aug.
- **Trailhead:** Savage Alpine Trailhead

HIGHLIGHT: Enjoying views of the Savage River, Denali, and the countryside

The Savage Alpine Trail connects the Savage River area with Savage River Campground and is a departure from many hikes in this guide: Rather than a round-trip hike, this one is a point-to-point, meaning you'll hike from one trailhead to the other and pick up a shuttle bus ride back to the visitor center when you're done. It's a popular hike in Denali because it offers relatively easy access to alpine environments and pays off with a massive reward at the top of the trail. You'll

▲ SAVAGE RIVER

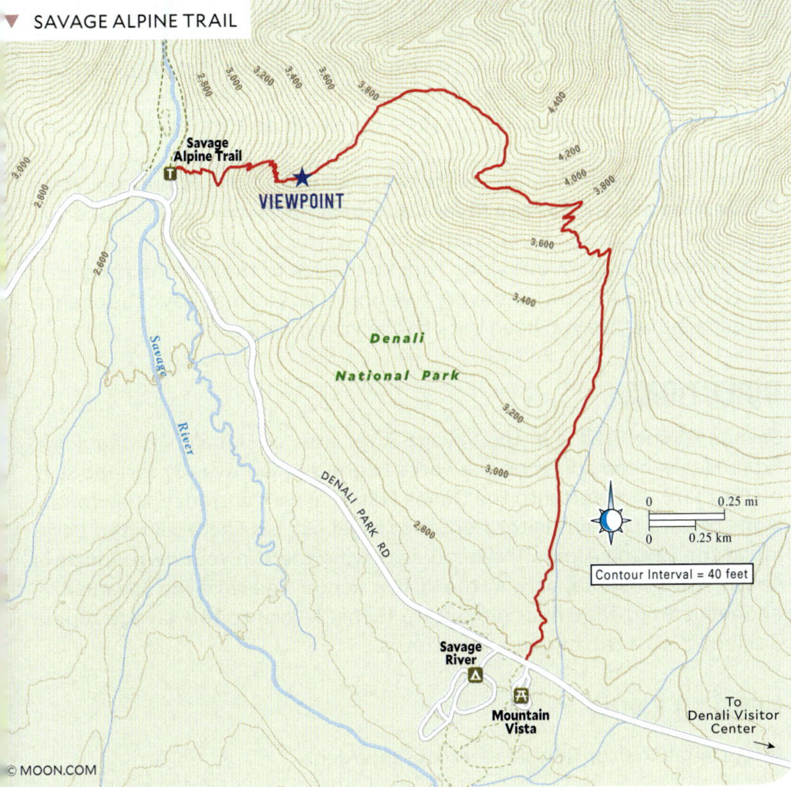

face switchbacks, have countless opportunities to spot wildlife (from Dall sheep to bears to ground squirrels), see some seasonal wildflowers, and get your fill of mountain views, including Denali. If you're camping at Savage River Campground, you can get a pre-dawn start on the trail to catch an absolutely epic sunrise.

START THE HIKE

Take the Savage River Shuttle to the Savage River area where you'll pick up the trail near the toilets on the east side of the Savage River. The trailhead is shared with the Savage River Loop, so as soon as you start the trail, detour uphill to your right and begin to climb. This section is steep but worth it, as you'll soon be rewarded with a look at Denali. Around the 0.2-mi (0.3-km) mark, once you've gained around 200 ft (61 m) of elevation, you'll see the snowy top of Denali off in the distance to the southwest. As you ascend the switchbacks and steep sections here, you'll lose sight of Denali a few times, but each time the mountain reappears, the view gets better and better. Around 0.8 mi (1.3 km), you'll crest a ridge lined with dark rock; you'll have **great views of the Savage River, Denali, and the countryside** from here. When you hit the 1-mi (1.6-km) point, the trail will even out and begin a long, steady, much easier ascent.

The crest of the trail is coming up, and when you're 1.7 mi (2.7 km) into the hike you'll reach the highest point of the trail at 4,157 ft (1,267 m). When you're up this high, keep a look out for wildlife. You may spot Dall sheep; mammals like ground squirrels, pikas, and marmots; and, if you have keen eyes or binoculars, maybe even a bear as it traverses the countryside below.

From here, begin a long, gentle descent toward the **Mountain Vista Picnic Area** and the **Savage River Campground.** At the campground you can catch the Savage River Shuttle back to the Denali Visitor Center, or you can walk 2 mi (3.2 km) along Park Road back to the trailhead and your car or bike. The shuttle runs every two hours, so you may have the chance to rest a bit before you head back to the visitor center.

DIRECTIONS

Savage Alpine Trail is in the Savage River area of Denali National Park. From Healy, head south on the Parks Highway (Highway 3) for about 11 mi (17.7 km). Turn left into the Denali National Park entrance, then follow signs toward Denali Visitor Center at Milepost 1.5. There's limited parking at the Savage Alpine Trailhead, so driving there in your own vehicle is not advised. Instead, park at the visitor center and take the Savage River Shuttle (mid-May-mid-Sept.; free) 15 mi (24 km) to the Savage Alpine Trailhead; it's a trip of nearly two hours.

NEED TO KNOW

Info: Denali Visitor Center, www.nps.gov/dena

Passes and Reservations: Entry into the park is $15/individual. Passes are available in advance at www.recreation.gov.

Weather Considerations: Temperatures in summer can vary wildly, ranging from 33-77°F (0.5-25°C). Pay attention to your gear, packing your rain kit and warm layers.

BEST NEARBY

Savage River Campground

▶ *Mile 14 Denali Park Rd., Denali National Park; 907/683-9532; www.reservedenali.com; mid-May-mid-Sept.; tent/small RV sites from $38.50, large RV sites from $49*

If you're going to camp in Denali National Park & Preserve, do it at the Savage River Campground; it's one of two campgrounds with views of Denali. The campground has seasonal flush toilets and potable water (and year-round vault toilets), and 32 sites for tent and RV campers. Best of all, there are exceptional views from the campground and nearby picnic area, and if you're hiking the Savage River Alpine Loop, you're only steps away from one of the point-to-point trailheads, making it easy to enjoy sunrise—and sunset—from the campground or on the trail. The maximum RV length here is 40 ft (12 m). If you need to pick up camping supplies (food, wood, etc.), do your shopping at one of the camping supply stores, grocery stores, or outdoor outfitters just outside the park.

Facilities: Small parking area and seasonal vault toilets at trailhead. Across the Savage River, a second trailhead and bus turnaround has a few more restrooms. At Savage River Campground, you'll find seasonal flush toilets, year-round vault toilets, and seasonal potable water as well as year-round food storage lockers and seasonal staff.

Other: You'll need plenty of mosquito protection and bear gear like bear spray or maybe even bear bangers (small, firework-like explosives that will scare off most bears).

▼ SAVAGE ALPINE TRAIL

3

ROOT GLACIER TRAIL

WRANGELL-ST. ELIAS NATIONAL PARK & PRESERVE, ALASKA

Get a taste of the Alaskan wilderness and explore Root Glacier and a WWI-era mining town on this hike, where the sights will stun you to silence.

- **Distance:** 5.7 mi (9.2 km) round-trip
- **Duration:** 2.5 hours
- **Elevation Gain:** 840 ft (256 m)
- **Effort:** Easy-moderate
- **When:** June-Sept.
- **Trailhead:** Kennecott Visitor Center

HIGHLIGHT: Looking up at Stairway Icefall from Root Glacier

Our hike begins at the abandoned Kennecott Mill Town, also called the Kennecott Mines National Historic Landmark, where the Kennecott Mining Company operated in the early 1900s, extracting copper from mines near McCarthy and transporting the ore by railroad along the Chitina and Copper Rivers to ships on the coast. You can explore the remains of the mill, check out the little town, and stop by the visitor center before heading north to start the trail, which parallels the toe of the Kennicott Glacier to reach our destination: Root Glacier.

▲ KENNECOTT COPPER MINE BUILDINGS

As a result of climate change and natural cycles, these glaciers are receding, pieces of them disappearing each year. For the moment, both glaciers look like monumental ice rivers flowing down from the summit of Mount Blackburn. Along this trail and at Root Glacier, you'll find wildflowers blooming throughout spring and early summer, and you may spot some wildlife (bears, caribou, hares, moose, mountain goats, and birds like golden and bald eagles).

START THE HIKE

From **Kennecott Visitor Center,** head north along Kennecott Road. For nearly 2 mi (3.2 km), your view will be limited to the trail and the surrounding woods, but look up and you'll see peaks all around, notably Mount Blackburn, Regal Mountain, and Donaho Peak. You may also catch a few fleeting glimpses of the Stairway Icefall, an icefall around 7,000 ft (2,134 m) tall that stands at the head of the valley containing Root Glacier.

At 0.7 mi (1.1 km), turn slightly left onto **Root Glacier Trail.** At 0.8 mi (1.3 km), you'll cross Bonanza Creek via a footbridge, and you'll encounter a second footbridge crossing Jumbo Creek at 1.6 mi (2.6 km). Just after you cross Jumbo Creek, the trail splits; the right fork turns into Erie Mine Trail (this trail does not access the mines) while the left fork leads to Root Glacier. If you're keen on backcountry camping, the **Jumbo Creek Campground** is here by the fork; to camp here, simply tell rangers your itinerary and, if there's space, set up camp and enjoy.

To continue on to **Root Glacier,** take the left fork. The trail will descend and soon you'll be standing on or adjacent to the ice. You can strap on a pair of crampons and explore the glacier, but be aware that the ice is slippery and cold and can be dangerous. Avoid walking on the edge of the glacier as the ice here is "rotten" and may give way underfoot. Be mindful to look for crevasses and holes, avoid ice bridges (who can tell how stable they are?), and keep tabs on your hiking companions.

The best views of the **Stairway Icefall** come when you're out on the glacier, standing on a high point and looking north-northwest up the valley. When you've had your fill of Root Glacier and this scenery, reverse course and head back to Kennecott.

DIRECTIONS

Root Glacier Trail begins at the McCarthy Road and Kennecott Area of Wrangell-St. Elias National Park & Preserve. Getting to the trailhead is a chore; there's no easy way to say it, but when you're visiting a huge, remote park in a huge, remote state, that's how things are going to be. Note that this route is technically passable by 2WD vehicles, but the typical state of the roads—McCarthy Road in particular—leads me to advise you to drive a high-clearance vehicle, preferably a 4WD, in the park. There is nowhere to get fuel inside the park, so bring extra if you're driving.

Start off in Copper Canyon at the Wrangell-St. Elias Headquarters and Visitor Center. Head 50 mi (81 km) southeast via Highway 4/Richardson Highway to the town of Chitina, where you'll find the Chitina Ranger Station. From the ranger station, turn left and drive along McCarthy Road, a 59-mi (95-km) gravel road leading to the town of McCarthy. From McCarthy, you can walk or ride your mountain bike 4.5 mi (7.2 km) along the gravel road to the former mill town of Kennecott. The trail begins at the Kennecott Visitor Center and heads north-northwest.

From McCarthy, you can also take a commercial shuttle to Kennecott; these shuttles are not operated by the National Parks Service but by several private companies, each with their own schedule and pricing. Shuttles run approximately every half hour to an hour; you don't need to make a reservation in advance. If you don't find shuttles waiting at the bridge, there's a list of operators and their contact information on the sign at the Kennicott River Bridge at the end of McCarthy Road. Cell phone service

BEST NEARBY

St. Elias Alpine Guides

▶ *12 Kennicott Millsite, Kennecott; 907/231-6395 or 888/933-5427; www.steliasguides.com*

This corner of Alaska may be remote, but there's a lot to explore if you know where to look. St. Elias Alpine Guides knows where to look. They offer a number of half- and full-day trips on Root Glacier and beyond. Root Glacier hikes start at $115 per person, but you can also ice climb ($170) and explore ice caves under the glacier (from $420). If you want to do a little alpine hiking, guides can take you to Bonanza and Jumbo Mines ($200), but they do even more, from kayaking ($115) to rafting and flightseeing ($395) to huge, multiday, fly-in-and-paddle expeditions (from $1,720). Offerings change season to season, so check to see if they have a trip that fits your Alaska national park goals and budget.

is reliable for most carriers, but there's a courtesy phone at the bridge if you need it.

NEED TO KNOW

Info: Kennecott Visitor Center, www.nps.gov/wrst

Passes and Reservations: No entrance fee or parking pass required.

Weather Considerations: The weather here can be wild and inhospitable, causing some roads to temporarily close or shut down for the season. In summer, heavy rains can swell streams to impassible heights; through fall, winter, and spring you can have deep snows both expectedly and unexpectedly. Visitor centers are open through summer but closed October-April.

Facilities: Pit toilets are available near the Kennecott Visitor Center and the Recreation Hall in the Kennecott Mines National Historic Landmark. Potable water is not available at either location, so ensure you have plenty of water (and a purification system) with you. Primitive toilets are available at the Jumbo Creek Campground.

Other: Crampons are necessary to securely traverse snow and ice. You can bring your own, buy or rent some in Fairbanks or Anchorage, or acquire some from a guide service. You'll also need plenty of mosquito protection and bear gear like bear spray or maybe even bear bangers (small, firework-like explosives that will scare off most bears).

▼ WALKING OUT ON ROOT GLACIER

4

HURRICANE HILL

OLYMPIC NATIONAL PARK, WASHINGTON

Get serious bang for your buck on this easy hike with mile-high views of the Strait of Juan de Fuca, British Columbia, and Cascade and Olympic peaks.

- **Distance:** 3.4 mi (5.5 km) round-trip
- **Duration:** 2-2.5 hours
- **Elevation Gain:** 826 ft (252 m)
- **Effort:** Easy-moderate
- **When:** June-Oct.
- **Trailhead:** Hurricane Hill Trailhead

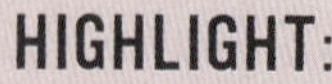

HIGHLIGHT: Taking in the 360-degree panorama atop Hurricane Hill

As you drive to the parking area at the end of Hurricane Hill Road, you'll get a preview of the views to come as the Bailey Range impresses from a distance. Once you park—even before you hit the trail proper—you'll have beautiful short views as wildflowers like the purple bells-of-Scotland and others give springtime and early summer visitors a treat. As you hike the ridgeline to the top of Hurricane Hill, you'll spot more wildflowers and a number of critters: Rabbits, grouse, deer, and marmots are frequently spotted, and, more rarely, you could spot mountain goats or even a bear crossing nearby slopes.

▲ HURRICANE HILL VIEWS

START THE HIKE

From the trailhead, follow the ridgeline to the top of Hurricane Hill. You'll have tremendous views off both sides of the trail. At points like the little rocky knob only 0.3 mi (0.5 km) into the hike, you can hop off-trail and find great vantage points and photo opportunities. A trail junction at 0.4 mi (0.6 km) leads 15 mi (24 km) north

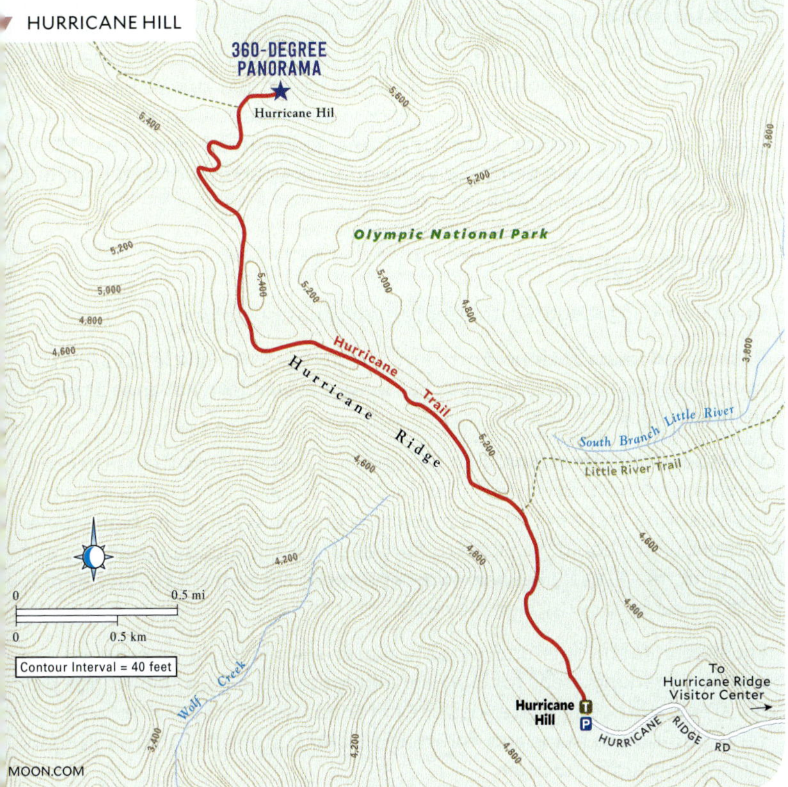

to a trailhead outside the national park and Olympic National Forest; bypass the trail unless you're up for a very long day of hiking. Near this trail junction, your route makes a little dip and begins one of the handful of steep sections you'll encounter. The next is at 1.2 mi (1.9 km), where **switchbacks** will ease the way.

Don't be surprised if you find snow on or near the trail. Just before you reach the switchbacks, you'll often find patches of snow lingering in the deepest, shadiest hollows and folds on the slopes nearby. In winter, folks come to snowshoe and cross-country ski along this route.

After you climb the switchbacks, you'll reach another trail junction, this one branching off to the left. This is the Elwha to Hurricane Hill Trail, one of the many trails in the spiderweb of paths and roads in the national park. Skip it, and in just a few hundred paces you'll be at the summit, standing some 5,760 ft (1,756 m) above the Strait of Juan de Fuca. The **horizon-to-horizon panorama** gives you a look at Port Angeles, Vancouver Island, and the peaks of the Cascades, Olympics, and British Columbia ranges. Snap your pictures—summit selfies, panoramas, epic sunset or sunrise shots—and when you can finally tear yourself away from this view (seriously, it's nothing short of phenomenal), return the way you came to the parking area and your next adventure in Olympic National Park.

DIRECTIONS

Hurricane Hill is in the Hurricane Ridge area of Olympic National Park. From Port Angeles, head south on Race Street and drive about 1.8 mi (2.9 km) to the Olympic National Park visitor center. Bear right just beyond the visitor center onto Hurricane Ridge Road and drive 18 mi (29 km) to Hurricane Ridge. Drive through the parking lot and continue 1.3 mi (2.1 km) to the trailhead.

NEED TO KNOW

Info: Hurricane Ridge Visitor Center, www.nps.gov/olym

Passes and Reservations: Entry into the park is $30/vehicle ($25/motorcycle, $15/pedestrian or cyclist). Passes are available in advance at www.recreation.gov.

Weather Considerations: July-October is generally drier than other seasons, but this region is known for rain, so bring your rain gear just in case. In late spring and early summer, you may find snowfall at the highest elevations, which could translate to flurries or a small accumulation of snow at Hurricane Ridge; likewise, mid-September through October you may find traces of snow at high elevations.

Facilities: Restrooms and potable water are available at primary and overflow parking areas for Hurricane Ridge and the Hurricane Ridge picnic areas. Hurricane Ridge Visitor Center has restrooms and potable water in addition to maps and information, and is staffed with park rangers and volunteers in summer.

Other: The first 0.25 mi (0.4 km) of the trail is paved and easily accessible for those with mobility issues. Note that this trail can get crowded. To avoid crowds, strap on your snowshoes and visit in winter when the views are awesome and the crowds thin. Other times of the year, dodge the crowds by hiking midweek and hitting the trail before 10am (the earlier the better as you'll get that gorgeous morning light) or after 3pm.

BEST NEARBY

Barhop Brewing & Artisan Pizza

▶ *124 W. Railroad Ave., Port Angeles; 360/797-1818; www.barhopbrewing.com; noon-9pm Sun.-Thurs., noon-10pm Fri.-Sat.; $13-26*

Barhop Brewing & Artisan Pizza serves sourdough pizzas (cooked in a stone oven) and house-brewed beers from its spot near the Port Angeles ferry terminal. Beers rotate, but expect big West Coast IPAs, Altbiers, and hefeweizens always on offer. The food menu stays steady (specials notwithstanding), and whether you get a whole pizza or a calzone, you'll get a bite of food that's delicious and, when paired with a tasty beverage, a great reward for a day on the trail.

▲ ALPINE FLOWERS ON HURRICANE RIDGE

5

RIALTO BEACH TO HOLE-IN-THE-WALL

OLYMPIC NATIONAL PARK, WASHINGTON

Take a short, easy walk along the Pacific Ocean to a sea arch that allows you to walk through a bluff at low tide.

- **Distance:** 3.3 mi (5.3 km) round-trip
- **Duration:** 1.5-2.5 hours
- **Elevation Gain:** Negligible
- **Effort:** Easy
- **When:** Year-round, best June-Sept.
- **Trailhead:** Rialto Beach Trailhead

HIGHLIGHT: Exploring the tide pools at Rialto Beach

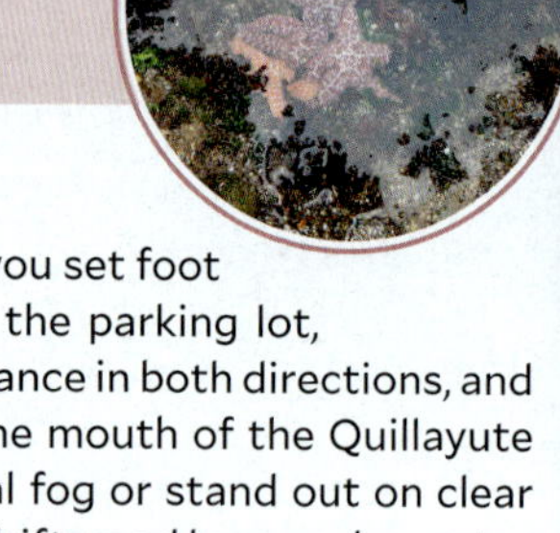

Rialto Beach is captivating, and as soon as you set foot in the sand at the end of the path from the parking lot, you'll see why. The shore stretches to the distance in both directions, and the silhouette or image of James Island at the mouth of the Quillayute River to the south will be shrouded in coastal fog or stand out on clear days. Along the beach, sea stacks, enormous driftwood logs, and, eventually, tide pools offer plenty of opportunities to discover something that wows you. The driftwood can be especially fascinating, as the abrasive

◄ HOLE-IN-THE-WALL

▼ RIALTO BEACH

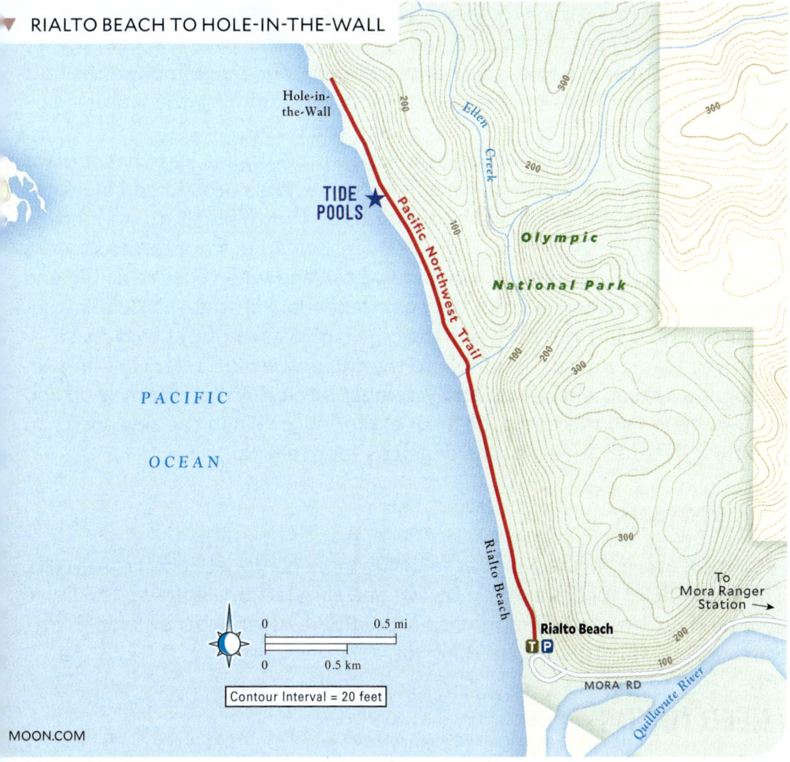

surf and wind have stripped the bark away, revealing interesting patterns beneath.

START THE HIKE

From the parking lot, head north along the beach. There are few landmarks here—it is a beach, after all—but after 0.7 mi (1.1 km) you'll cross **Ellen Creek** where it cuts a channel through the sand. Be careful as you cross because Ellen Creek can grow strong with heavy inland rains, so be mindful of your footing. If the weather's clear, you can look north and see a rocky bump rising from the sea 0.8 mi (1.3 km) beyond the creek; that's Hole-in-the-Wall, and something about the marine fog and mist concealing and revealing the stony outcrop adds to the mystery and sense of adventure here. Sea stacks and rocks appear out of the fog or emerge from high waves. At times it seems you've discovered secret passageways allowing you to proceed farther along the beach.

As you near Hole-in-the-Wall you'll find this shore grows even more rocky, with smaller stones and pebbles scattered around. If you find any flat, smooth rocks, grab a few and try your hand at skipping them across the flat, receding waves. You'll find more **tide pools** here than south of the creek, so spend a few minutes exploring these. They often hold surprising bits of life—sea stars, mollusks clinging to rocks, little fish, and other sea creatures trapped in these temporary pools until the tide rises and they can move back to deeper waters. It's relaxing here thanks to the rhythmic crash and hissing retreat of the surf. You'll see and hear plenty of birds, from bald eagles to a variety of gulls, and if you look to the surf and waves, you'll see guillemots and scoters skimming the water's surface and plucking morsels from the sand and water.

Now you're at **Hole-in-the-Wall.** Hole-in-the-Wall is just that, a giant hole—fine, it's really an arch—in a fin of stone. Walk around and look at it from different angles and light conditions and you'll find it grows more or less striking depending on where you are. Sea arches are formed by the relentless erosive forces of wind and water, and when they're as big and seemingly permanent as this, they gain legendary status—as Hole-in-the-Wall has, growing into a jewel in the crown of Washington's wild coast.

If you want, you can scramble to the top of the bluff over Hole-in-the-Wall. It's a steep, short trail, and you must be cautious on the way up and down. When you've had your fill of exploring, or when the tide starts to come in, head south along the beach to your vehicle.

DIRECTIONS

Rialto Beach is in the Mora area of Olympic National Park. From Forks, drive north 1.5 mi (2.4 km) on US 101 and turn left on Highway 110. Drive 7.8 mi (12.6 km) and turn right on Mora Road. After another 5 mi (8 km), arrive at the Rialto Beach parking lot.

NEED TO KNOW

Info: Mora Ranger Station, www.nps.gov/olym

Passes and Reservations: Entry into the park is $30/vehicle ($25/motorcycle, $15/pedestrian or cyclist). Passes are available in advance at www.recreation.gov.

Weather Considerations: The most important thing to consider is the tide level. Although the trail is accessible at high tide, the beach is a good bit wider at low tide, and the risk of soaking your shoes and pants in a

BEST NEARBY

Quileute Oceanside Resort & RV Park

▶ *330 Ocean Dr., La Push; 360/374-5267; www.quileuteoceanside.com; rooms and cabins from $180, tents from $35, RV sites from $60, pets $30/night*

La Push and the Quileute Nation sit less than 1 mi (1.6 km) from the trailhead on a stretch of coastline that's been the home of the Quileute Tribe for more than a thousand years, and their Quileute Oceanside Resort & RV Park makes a great base camp when exploring the west side of Olympic National Park. There are 33 oceanfront cabins, 10 camper cabins, motel units, a campground, and full-service RV park here (and another Quileute RV park nearby if this one's full). The town of Forks (made internationally famous by the Twilight book and film series), where you'll find groceries, supplies, and restaurants, is 20 minutes east.

high-washing wave is minimal. Waterproof footwear is recommended in any case.

Facilities: Flush toilets and potable water are available at the trailhead.

Other: Rialto Beach is one of the few places in Olympic National Park where you can bring your dog, though they aren't allowed beyond Ellen Creek. If you've brought your pooch (or pooches) along, they can have a pretty good time frolicking on the beach even if they can't get their picture taken at Hole-in-the-Wall.

▼ DRIFTWOOD ON RIALTO BEACH

6

HALL OF MOSSES AND HOH RIVER TRAIL

OLYMPIC NATIONAL PARK, WASHINGTON

Wander beneath blankets of moss hanging from towering trees as you follow family-friendly trails through the Hoh Rain Forest.

- **Distance:** 6.7 mi (10.8 km) round-trip
- **Duration:** 3.5-4 hours
- **Elevation Gain:** 300 ft (91 m)
- **Effort:** Easy-moderate
- **When:** Year-round
- **Trailhead:** Hoh Rain Forest Visitor Center

HIGHLIGHT: Immersing yourself in the Hall of Mosses

This route is a melding of the popular Hall of Mosses loop and a portion of the Hoh River Trail. We're only doing a portion of Hoh River because this trail stretches 17.3 mi (27.8 km) to Glacier Meadows on the flanks of Mount Olympus, the highest peak on the Olympic Peninsula. If you're itching for a longer hike, take a long look at Hoh River Trail. For now, we're keeping it short and focusing on the Mosses-Hoh combo hike.

▲ HOH RAIN FOREST

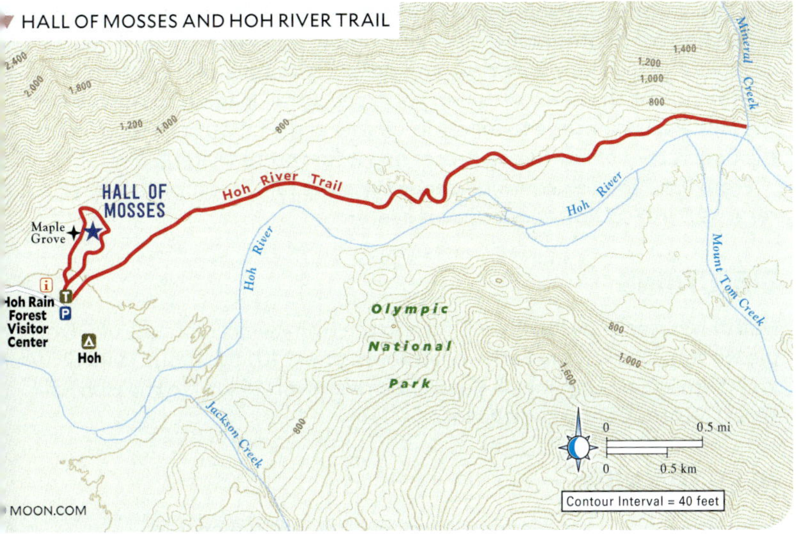

START THE HIKE

You'll start at the **Hoh Rain Forest Visitor Center** and walk only a hundred yards or so until you reach an intersection where signage points you left onto the Hall of Mosses loop. **Hall of Mosses** is only 1.1 mi (1.8 km) long, but it really lives up to its name, immersing you in an incredible landscape of green. Ferns cover the forest floor, trees stretch their bizarre roots out into the path, and moss hangs like sheets from tree branches. To me, living on the southeastern coast of the United States, there are moments when Hall of Mosses is reminiscent of a blend of coastal hikes, where the Spanish moss drips from every tree and damp, fern-rich grottos in Great Smoky Mountains National Park. The side trip to **Maple Grove**—via a 200-ft (61-m) trail—is totally worth it, especially around fall.

While you're here, open all your senses and settle in for a few minutes. Listen closely. It's pretty quiet. The moss, ferns, and foliage absorb quite a bit of sound here, as they do across the national park. In the book *One Square Inch of Silence,* author Gordon Hempton explores the idea of silence (he says it's the absence of human-made sound) and searches for the quietest place in the United States. He finds it here in the Hoh River section of Olympic National Park. It's an interesting idea and project, and the book is a thought-provoking read, especially for folks who love the outdoors.

After you finish the loop, make your way to the first intersection and continue straight to join the **Hoh River Trail.** The trail cuts across the countryside, passing through mossy glades, over fallen trees (it's a wonder how fast they decompose here), and by two campgrounds. Keep your eyes open for wildlife; you can spot a variety of small mammals and birds here, but also elk, black-tailed deer, and even cougars (odds are you're not spotting a cougar, as cats, especially big cats, are very good at keeping it stealthy). Stay on Hoh River Trail for 2.8 mi (4.5 km), to the point where the trail crosses **Mineral Creek.** Mineral Creek cascades down a mossy cliff (no surprise) to your left as it heads to the river, creating a beautiful setting for photography, plein air painting and watercolor (if you can keep your canvas or paper dry), and quiet contemplation. If you look on the far side of the creek crossing you'll see a trail leading to the base of the falls. Resist the urge to follow it—enjoying the falls from afar protects the understory of the forest, preserving it for future visitors.

From here you can continue deeper into the rain forest or turn back to return 2.9 mi (4.7 km) to the visitor center.

DIRECTIONS

Hall of Mosses and Hoh River Trail is in the Hoh Rain Forest area of Olympic National Park. From Forks, head south on US 101 for about 13 mi (20.9 km). Turn left on Upper Hoh Road and drive 18 mi (29 km) to the Hoh Rain Forest Visitor Center parking lot.

NEED TO KNOW

Info: Hoh Rain Forest Visitor Center, www.nps.gov/olym

Passes and Reservations: Entry into the park is $30/vehicle ($25/motorcycle, $15/pedestrian or cyclist). Passes are available in advance at www.recreation.gov.

Weather Considerations: July-Sept. is often drier than other seasons. Be sure to bring your rain gear (rain jacket with hood and rain pants) regardless of the forecast.

Facilities: Flush toilets and potable water are available at Hoh Rain Forest Visitor Center.

Other: On summer afternoons, Olympic National Park uses meter lights to control traffic. Get here early to avoid the crowds.

BEST NEARBY

Creekside Restaurant

▶ *157151 US 101, Forks; 866/662-9928, www.thekalalochlodge.com; hours vary by season; $10-45*

Located inside the Kalaloch Lodge and overlooking the Pacific Ocean and Kalaloch Creek, Creekside Restaurant delivers big on the dinnertime views and serves tasty dishes. Its partnership with local farms and suppliers means this is true local Pacific Northwest cuisine. Salmon, razor clams, Dungeness crab, and other locally caught seafood dominate the menu, but you'll find options to please nearly any palate when you arrive for dinner. The trailhead is a 39-mi (63-km) drive northeast via Upper Hoh Road and US 101.

▲ HALL OF MOSSES AND HOH RIVER TRAIL

▲ HALL OF MOSSES

7

QUINAULT LOOP

OLYMPIC NATIONAL PARK, WASHINGTON

Combine two trails to experience the vast variety of this rain forest—giant trees, a cedar bog, waterfalls, and Lake Quinault.

- **Distance:** 4 mi (6.4 km) round-trip
- **Duration:** 1.5-2 hours
- **Elevation Gain:** 360 ft (110 m)
- **Effort:** Easy
- **When:** June-Sept.
- **Trailhead:** Quinault Rain Forest Trailhead

HIGHLIGHT: Snapping a photo in front of Cascade Falls

The old-growth trees and dense understory of the Olympic temperate rain forest is beautiful and eerie. You'll find a thousand shades of green in the leaves and moss, and when the light slanting through the overstory reaches through tendrils of mist and pockets of fog, the place has a reverent feel; the quiet here, where sound seems to fall flat, absorbed by the vegetation, compounds the feeling. Whether you're new to the trail or spend every weekend in the woods, the discovery of this hike—with creeks, falls, and surprises around many turns of the trail, and those lake views along the last leg—will have you ready to come back to experience this place in another season.

◄ LAKE QUINAULT

▼ LAKE QUINAULT LODGE

START THE HIKE

From the trailhead, start up the trail and take an immediate left on the short 0.5-mi (0.8-km) **Rain Forest Nature Trail Loop,** the first portion of which is accessible. After 0.1 mi (0.2 km), you'll find a trail on the left. Skip it and instead continue to the right along the banks of **Willaby Creek.** At the next mossy kiosk, turn left onto **Quinault Loop Trail** (if you stay to the right, you'll complete the Rain Forest Nature Trail Loop and end your hike after only a few minutes).

The hike climbs a little, undulating with the contours of the land, and as you travel along, you'll be in a quiet part of the forest where the massive 15- to 20-story-tall western hemlocks, Douglas firs, western red cedars, and Sitka spruce seem to absorb sound while also filling the air with a heady, piney aroma. Cross Willaby Creek via a little bridge (ignore the trail just before the bridge; it's closed) and carry on down the trail. Soon you'll enter a bog filled with cedar trees, a place where the footing is often muddy and slippery. A boardwalk provides a cleaner (but not much less slippery) path through the bog. One mi (1.6 km) after crossing Willaby Creek, you'll find a trail on your left heading to Lake Quinault Lodge; if you need to cut this hike short, this is your best option. Otherwise, stay straight and cross a bridge over **Falls Creek.**

In 0.3 mi (0.5 km) you'll come to **Cascade Falls,** a perfect spot to stop for a photo and hang out for a minute or two. You'll reach another fork in

0.2 mi (0.3 km), and here you'll turn left for the lakeshore, crossing Falls Creek thanks to a little bridge. In 0.4 mi (0.6 km) you'll cross **South Shore Road** not far from the **ranger station** and make your way to the shoreline of **Lake Quinault.**

A trail follows the shoreline for nearly 1 mi (1.6 km) to the **Willaby Campground,** passing the ranger station and **Lake Quinault Lodge** along the way. Note that the trail is not always passable. If the lakeside trail is flooded, detour over to South Shore Road and follow it back to Willaby Campground. At the campground, rejoin Quinault Loop Trail where it crosses Willaby Creek via a concrete bridge. The trailhead and parking area is 0.3 mi (0.5 km) beyond the campground.

DIRECTIONS

Quinault Loop is in the Quinault Rain Forest area of Olympic National Park. From Forks, head south on US 101 for 65 mi (105 km). Turn left on Shore Road. Continue 0.4 mi (0.6 km) and turn right into the trailhead parking lot.

NEED TO KNOW

Info: Quinault Rain Forest Ranger Station, www.nps.gov/olym

Passes and Reservations: Entry into the park is $30/vehicle ($25/motorcycle, $15/pedestrian or cyclist). Passes are available in advance at www.recreation.gov.

Weather Considerations: Olympic National Park receives more than 130 inches (3.3 m) of precipitation annually. Your rain gear—waterproof pants, waterproof jacket with hood—is essential and must be in good repair.

Facilities: Flush toilets and potable water are available at the trailhead parking area and Willaby Campground. Information boards provide up-to-date details on trail conditions, weather, wildlife and wildflower spotting, and more.

BEST NEARBY

Lake Quinault Lodge

▶ *345 S. Shore Rd., Quinault; 360/288-2910 or 888/896-3818; www.olympicnationalparks.com; from $305*

Built in 1926, Lake Quinault Lodge is that brilliant blend of grand and rustic that sets national park lodges apart from other accommodations. Huge fireplaces, a great dining room, a pool and game room, and cozy rooms (many with fireplaces) are charming enough to win you over at first sight, but after a night here you'll fall in love with the place. The lodge has a fleet of kayaks and paddleboards to rent and offers guided tours of the national park and nearby forest. The Roosevelt Dining Room serves breakfast ($6-20), lunch ($12-26), and dinner ($20-48) daily.

▲ WILLABY CREEK

8

AGNES GORGE TRAIL

NORTH CASCADES NATIONAL PARK, WASHINGTON

With wildflowers, wildlife, glaciers, and gorges on tap, this hike delivers extensive views and lets you experience the exceptional Cascade Mountains on an easy-to-navigate trail.

- **Distance:** 4.7 mi (7.6 km) round-trip
- **Duration:** 2-2.5 hours
- **Elevation Gain:** 600 ft (183 m)
- **Effort:** Moderate
- **When:** June-late Sept.
- **Trailhead:** Agnes Gorge Trailhead

HIGHLIGHT: Admiring the view of Agnes Mountain and Chickamin Glacier

The Agnes Gorge Trail is located in the remote Stehekin area, accessible only by ferry or private boat, by hiking or horseback riding, or by plane—in other words, you cannot just drive up and start hiking. Yet all your planning and efforts to get to this quiet corner of North Cascades National Park will be rewarded with views of high peaks, deep valleys, wildflowers, wildlife, and a glacier. Come in autumn and the park is awash in color, and in winter, those bold enough (and with the right gear) can enjoy solitude and snowshoeing.

▲ CLAW MARKS FROM BEARS ALONG AGNES GORGE TRAIL

START THE HIKE

Agnes Gorge Trail plunges straight into the forest from Stehekin Valley Road, offering a cool, quiet, leafy respite after the shuttle bus ride to the trailhead. Enjoy the silence and the views of the forest, a mix of trees dominated by ponderosa pines and Douglas firs. After only 0.25 mi (0.4 km) the trail will open up into a hillside meadow where you'll have your first real look into **Agnes Gorge.** For the next mile (1.6 km) you'll traverse this

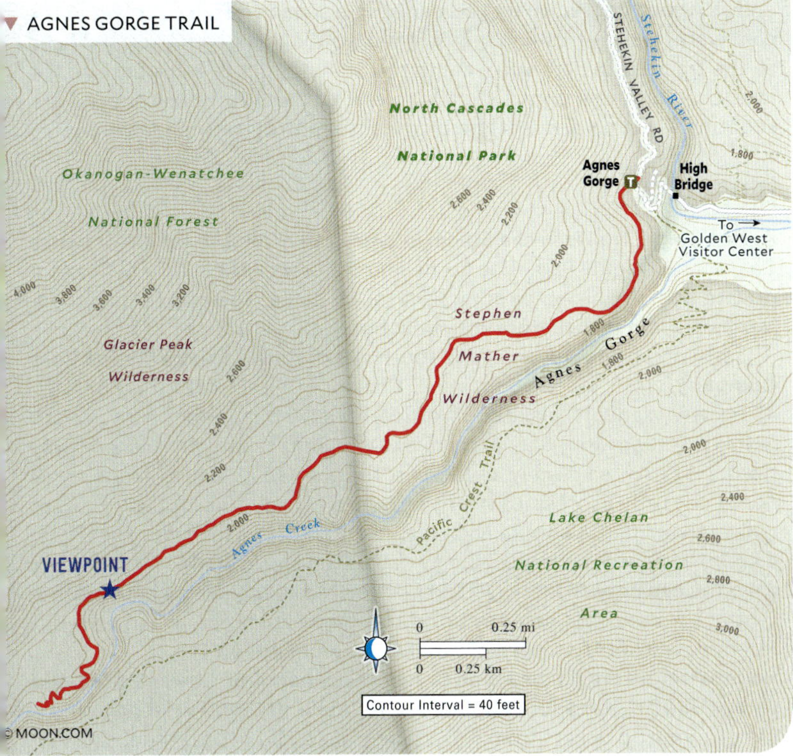

meadow, and if you're here in spring and early summer, you'll be awash in wildflowers. Silvercrown, tiger lilies, chocolate lilies, lupine, wild rose, and paintbrush, among others, bloom here, and they draw a host of butterflies and insects, which draws a crowd of birds for an easy lunch.

An aspen grove stands out in stark contrast to the wildflower blooms and the varied greens of the evergreen forest. Give the aspens a few minutes of your attention and look for claw marks in the bark. If you find any, odds are they were left by bears. It's likely that these claw marks and a few paw prints, maybe a little scat, is all you'll see of bears.

Continue along this undulating trail, and at 1.5 mi (2.4 km) into the hike you'll pass a wooden sign indicating that you've left North Cascade National Park and entered the US Forest Service's **Glacier Peak Wilderness.** If you liked the wildflowers and the views of the Agnes Gorge in that last meadow, you ain't seen nothing yet. Soon after entering the wilderness's domain the view will open up dramatically, revealing **Agnes Mountain** standing 7,861 ft (2,396 m) high, the **Chickamin Glacier** visible over its shoulder. Through here, meadows and patches full of wildflowers and huckleberries line the north slope (above you to the right). Late in the season—toward the end of summer and into September—the huckleberries draw bears hungry for a berry-delicious meal before they head off to hibernate.

Here near the end you'll have views of a cascading waterfall, the rushing creek, and that dramatic mountain background. Follow the trail to its end at **Agnes Creek,** where you can have a snack and dip your feet in the cold water for a refreshing break. When you're done, turn back and head to the trailhead where you'll catch the Stehekin Shuttle Bus back to the lake. Use your time on the shuttle to talk to the driver and other hikers, scouting out trails and waterfalls to visit tomorrow.

DIRECTIONS

Agnes Gorge Trail is in the Stehekin area, a very remote region of North Cascades National Park. The Stehekin area is accessible only by ferry or private boat, by hiking or horseback, or by plane. The pair of passenger ferries serving Stehekin are your best bet.

Departing from Chelan, at the south end of the lake, **Lake Chelan Boat Company** (1418 W. Woodin Ave., Chelan; 509/682-4584 or 888/682-4584; www.ladyofthelake.com; office hours 8:30am-4pm Mon., Wed., and Fri., 9:30am-1pm Sat., 8:30am-9:30pm Sun.; overnight and one-way tickets $25-49, same-day round-trip tickets $75.25 adults) runs three boats, the Lady Express, Lady of the Lake, and Lady Liberty. Lady Express makes the trip in 2.5 hours each way, Lady of the Lake makes the trip in 4 hours each way, and Lady Liberty makes the trip in 70-90 minutes each way. You can book a one-way ticket (if you're hiking, riding a horse, or flying out), a round-trip one-day ticket (for day visitors), or up and back different day tickets for overnight and multi-night stays.

Departing from Fields Point (a few miles north of Chelan), **Stehekin Ferry** (17100 S. Lakeshore Rd., Chelan; 509/669-5045; www.stehekinferry.com; round-trip tickets from $78 adults) runs a pair of passenger catamarans—Stehekin Clipper and Sunny Jo—providing daily service year-round. You're limited to 75 lb (34 kg) of luggage per passenger, with additional weight coming in at $0.25/lb ($0.25/0.5 kg).

BEST NEARBY

North Cascades Lodge at Stehekin

▶ *Stehekin Valley Road, Stehekin; 509/699-2056 or 855/685-4167; www.lodgeatstehekin.com; lodge open mid-May-mid-Oct., kitchen units available year-round; from $250*

This 27-room lakeside lodge and Lake House is one of the only places to stay indoors at Stehekin. You can camp, but if you want to explore Agnes Gorge Trail and the other trails and waterfalls nearby while having access to a hot shower and a restaurant, look no further. Accommodations include cabins with and without kitchens (kitchen units available year-round), and the fully furnished Lake House that sleeps 12. There's a General Store stocked with souvenirs and limited food supplies, and a restaurant (the only full-service restaurant in Stehekin) serving breakfast, grab-and-go and sit-down lunch, and dinner ($10-39). At the General Store you can rent kayaks and paddleboards ($20/hour), and they can help you arrange activities like horseback rides, guided fishing trips, and bicycle rentals; as with most national parks, the folks at the store, lodge, and restaurant can point you to their favorite trails, experiences, and sites nearby.

Ferry schedules vary by line, boat, and time of year, and ticket reservations are advised for each line; refer to individual schedules at time of booking.

Shuttle bus services are provided by **Stehekin Valley Adventures** (509/859-6070; www.stehekinvalleyadventures.com; $10 adults). The shuttle bus departs from Stehekin Landing and stops at Stehekin Pastry Company, Harlequin Bridge, Stehekin Valley Ranch, and High Bridge. Reservations are recommended; book tickets online or by calling or texting.

To reach the town of Chelan from Seattle-Tacoma International Airport, you're looking at a 3-4-hour drive of 184 mi (296 km). Follow I-405 north and east to Bellevue and head east on I-90. At the town of Cle Elum, follow Highway 970, which transitions to US 97. Just outside the town of Peshastin, turn right onto US 2. Take US 2 to the town of Sunnyslope where you'll follow US 97 Alt north along the Columbia River to Chelan. If you're headed to Fields Point, first make your way to Chelan. From Chelan it's a 28-minute, 17.5-mi (28.2-km) drive west along US 97 to South Lakeshore Drive, following South Lakeshore Drive to Fields Point Road and the ferry landing.

NEED TO KNOW

Info: Golden West Visitor Center, www.nps.gov/noca

Passes and Reservations: No entrance fee or parking pass required. Reservations are recommended for the ferry and the shuttle bus.

▲ AGNES CREEK

Weather Considerations: Seasonal snows can force road closures throughout the park. Check the "Current Conditions" page on www.nps.gov/noca for road and trail closures and alerts. The weather's more reliable mid-June-late September, and by then snow is gone from all but the highest trails, but you should still come prepared with your rain gear and warm layers as sudden storms can pop up.

Facilities: Toilets are available at the High Bridge Campground near the trailhead. There's zero cell service in the Stehekin area, but there is a public phone near the ferry landing.

9

SKYLINE TRAIL LOOP

MOUNT RAINIER NATIONAL PARK, WASHINGTON

View the Nisqually Glacier, waterfalls, fields of wildflowers, and a bevy of South Cascade peaks as Rainier towers overhead.

- **Distance:** 5.8 mi (9.3 km) round-trip
- **Duration:** 3-4 hours
- **Elevation Gain:** 1,768 ft (539 m)
- **Effort:** Moderate
- **When:** July-Sept., wildflowers best July-Aug.
- **Trailhead:** Henry M. Jackson Visitor Center

HIGHLIGHT: Taking in dramatic views from Panorama Point

Skyline Trail Loop carries you along the south side of Mount Rainier on a hike so scenic it's dangerously closer to sensory overload territory. Whether you love waterfalls, meadows packed with colorful wildflowers, peering into the deep crevasses of Nisqually Glacier, or looking for marmots, bears, and mountain goats, this hike delivers. Then there are the mountain views—the Tatoosh Range and Mounts Adams, St. Helens, and Hood—all this in the splendid shadow of

▲ SKYLINE TRAIL

Rainier. Ready to be blown away and take about 500 photos, every one of them frame-worthy? Pay attention, as this trail delivers big on the views and the twists and turns.

START THE HIKE

At the **Henry M. Jackson Visitor Center,** grab your trail maps and follow the steps to the top where the paved Skyline Trail leads upward. Take your time and adjust to the altitude—you're about a mile (5,280 ft/1,609 m) high here—on this first stretch of trail. Bypass junctions with other trails to stay straight on Skyline Trail. Soon you'll reach a wide, paved area where the views of the South Cascades draw many, satisfying a good number of hikers and sending them back to their cars.

But the scenery gets better, so leave the pavement behind and press on toward Rainier. In 0.6 mi (1 km) you'll pass Pebble Creek Trail and ascend a steep, rocky slope to **Panorama Point.** The effort to climb this 0.2-mi (0.3-km) slope is worth it, as the views of the Nisqually Glacier, Tatoosh Range, Goat Rocks, and the peaks of Mounts St. Helens, Adams, and Hood will make it hard to leave this spot. Linger for a few minutes, snapping pictures and refueling with a snack and some water before heading off.

Take the trail to the left, **High Skyline Trail.** In 0.4 mi (0.6 km) you'll pass Pebble Creek Trail again, then the loop reaches its apex at 7,100 ft (2,164 m). Again, spend a few moments with this view before carrying on down the trail for another 0.4 mi (0.6 km) to where Golden Gate Trail comes in from the right. If you need a shortcut back to the parking lot, taking this trail will shave about a mile (1.6 km) off the trip, but you'll miss the rest of what Skyline has in store (and you don't want to miss it).

The next 0.7 mi (1.1 km) will see you crossing the **Paradise River,** passing the Paradise Glacier Trail (on the left), and arriving at the **Stevens-Van Trump Historical Monument.** This monument, erected in 1921, marks the site where Hazard Stevens and P. B. Van Trump camped before making the first documented summit of Rainier on August 17, 1870. Sluiskin, their Native American guide, is said to have waited here, certain the men would perish on the trip.

Continue on the trail as it descends into the **Paradise Valley**. For the next 1 mi (1.6 km) you'll pass a number of side trails and countless wildflowers. The wildflowers put on quite the show throughout late spring and early summer, so bring a wildflower guide (or brochure from the visitor center) and see how many you can identify. When you cross the bridge over **Myrtle Falls,** you'll find a path on the left to a viewpoint that has to be one of the best across all the national parks.

After the side trail to that killer viewpoint, you're almost back to the car. The paved trail returns just beyond the bridge, easing that last 0.5 mi (0.8 km) to the parking area. If you want to make a few more wow-worthy photos, come back to the parking area for sunrise, sunset, stormy clouds, or whatever conditions tickle your fancy, and follow the last leg of the trail to the Myrtle Falls viewpoint where you can set up and fill your memory card, sketchbook, or canvas with the sights.

BEST NEARBY

Copper Creek Restaurant

▶ *35707 Hwy. 706 E., Ashford; 360/569-2326; www.coppercreekinn.com; 11am-7pm Mon. and Thurs., 8am-7pm Fri.-Sun.; $10-17*

Pay a visit to the oldest continually operating restaurant in Washington, Copper Creek Restaurant. Not only do you get a dose of history, you'll also get a killer stack of pancakes, a burger you'll crave, and a slice of blackberry pie that's out of this word. Housed in the Copper Creek Inn (for lodging questions, call 360/569-2799, from $160), which opened as a service station in 1925, the business has grown into a collection of inn rooms and cabins large and small, catering to national park and nature lovers with their rustic charm, woodsy settings, and access to the park.

DIRECTIONS

Skyline Trail Loop is in the Paradise area of Mount Rainier National Park. From Highway 7 in Elbe, continue straight on Highway 706 for 13.6 mi (21.9 km) to Mount Rainier National Park's Nisqually Entrance. Continue 17.5 mi (28.2 km) inside the park to the large Paradise parking lot. Restroom facilities are located at the trailhead. The Jackson Visitor Center is open daily in summer, and on weekends and holidays in the winter.

NEED TO KNOW

Info: Henry M. Jackson Visitor Center, www.nps.gov/mora

Passes and Reservations: Entry into the park is $30/vehicle ($25/motorcycle, $15/pedestrian or cyclist), and timed entry passes ($2) are required to access the Paradise Corridor and Sunrise Corridor. Passes are available in advance at www.recreation.gov. For more information, see page 504.

Weather Considerations: This is the Pacific Northwest, a region known for rain, so prepare for rainy conditions any time you visit. As the year turns toward fall and winter, snow becomes more frequent and heavier. Keep in mind that mountains like Rainier create their own weather, so before you head out, check localized weather forecasts specific to your section of the park.

Facilities: Restrooms and water are available at the trailhead.

▼ WILDFLOWERS ALONG SKYLINE TRAIL

10

SILVER FALLS LOOP

MOUNT RAINIER NATIONAL PARK, WASHINGTON

Hike through the forest to a 40-ft (12-m) waterfall fed by glacier runoff and snowmelt.

- **Distance:** 2.9 mi (4.7 km) round-trip
- **Duration:** 2 hours
- **Elevation Gain:** 521 ft (159 m)
- **Effort:** Easy
- **When:** June-Sept.
- **Trailhead:** Ohanapecosh Campground

HIGHLIGHT: Looking at Silver Falls from a different viewpoint

Many folks used to combine the Silver Falls Loop hike with a trip into the Grove of the Patriarchs, but flooding in 2021 wiped out the iconic suspension bridge on the trail to Grove of the Patriarchs, and since construction on a replacement won't begin until 2027, we're going to skip that hike. Instead, let's focus on the 2.9-mi (4.7-km) hike to Silver Falls.

▲ THE TURQUOISE WATER OF OHANAPECOSH RIVER

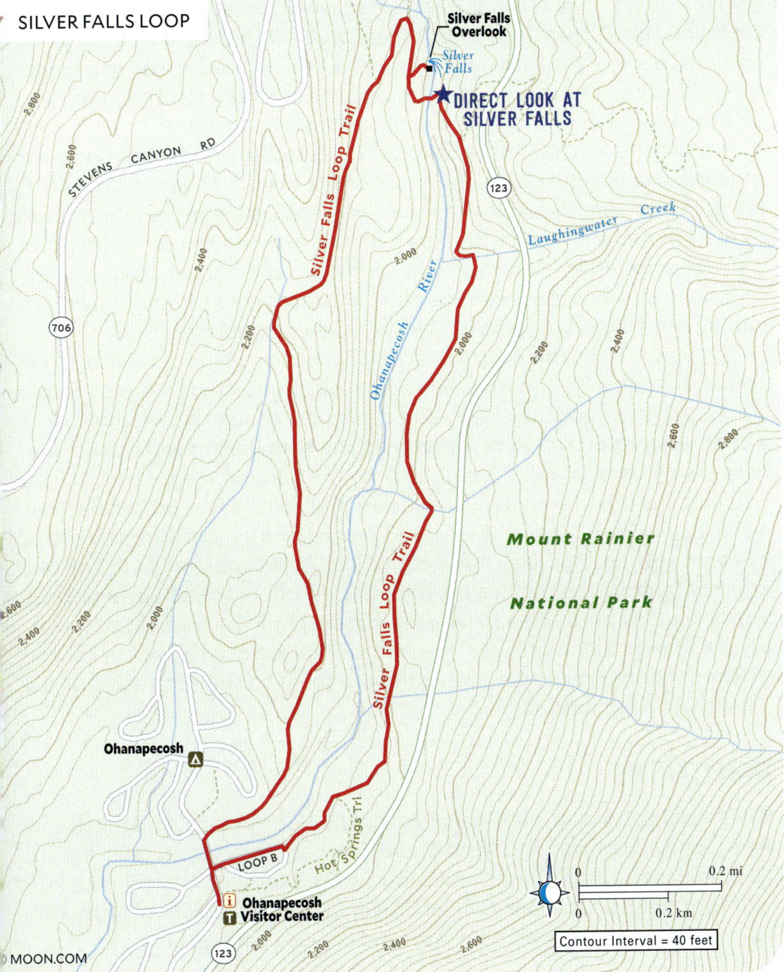

START THE HIKE

Park at the **Ohanapecosh Visitor Center** and walk north along the road, crossing the river into the **Ohanapecosh Campground** and turning right onto Silver Falls Loop Trail. Some describe this trail as "mostly level," but that's not entirely accurate as it does undulate a bit and, in a couple of places, grows quite steep. It's more accurate to say this trail has a slow but steady incline and decline with a few bumps along the way. But you'll hardly notice the handful of steep sections because the forest, the stream of rushing turquoise-tinged waters, and the abundance of trailside mushrooms and mosses will keep you plenty distracted; if you're lucky you'll spot elk or black-tailed deer, fox and American marten, or even a bear.

The first 1.2 mi (1.9 km) leads you up the west side of the **Ohanapecosh River** through a narrow gorge. You'll have glimpses, even a few long looks at the river, but the focus here is on the forest. Don't worry, the river and its odd-colored water will take center stage soon. When you hit that 1.2-mi

(1.9-km) mark, Cowlitz Divide Trail meets Silver Falls Loop Trail on the left. In another 0.1 mi (0.26 km) you'll meet the junction with Eastside Trail, heading north (if Grove of the Patriarchs were open, this trail would lead you there); Silver Falls Loop makes a hairpin turn here, cutting back south, and you'll be able to hear the roar of the falls over the rush of the river.

In another 0.1 mi (0.2 km), a spur trail leads to **Silver Falls Overlook** and a view of the narrow gorge, the chute of the river channel, and the 40-ft (12-m) falls themselves. Notice the water. The Ohanapecosh River is fed by glacier- and snow-melt, and the minerals suspended in the water give it a turquoise look. It's not always turquoise, and it's not turquoise everywhere; at times the river runs clear, at other times (during floods) it's muddy and turgid, but it makes a lovely scene regardless.

The views from the overlook are good, but you'll have a better look down the trail. In yet another 0.1 mi (0.2 km), you'll cross a bridge below the falls (get a good look here) and climb up a couple of switchbacks to **a spot where you can look directly at the thundering waterfall.** From here it's an easy 1.4 mi (2.3 km) back to the parking area. At 1.6 mi (2.6 km) into the hike, Laughingwater Creek Trail joins Silver Falls Loop Trail; at 1.8 mi (2.9 km), 2.2 mi (3.5 km), and 2.4 mi (3.9 km) you'll cross a trio of streams. Hot Springs Trail intersects Silver Falls Loop Trail at 2.6 mi (4.2 km), not far from the trailhead. If you want, detour onto **Hot Springs Trail,** which leads back to the parking area, passing by a few volcanically heated hot springs along the way. The hot springs are maybe best described as warm springs, but when you compare them to the icy waters of the river, they're hot indeed.

DIRECTIONS

Silver Falls Loop is in the Ohanapecosh area of Mount Rainier National Park. Follow Highway 410 from Enumclaw east for 40.7 mi (65.5 km) to Cayuse Pass and turn right on Highway 123. Continue 10.9 mi (17.5 km) and turn right on Stevens Canyon Road. Continue for 12.8 mi (20.6 km), following signs to the visitor center and day-use parking area.

BEST NEARBY

Cliff Droppers

▶ *12968 US Hwy. 12, Packwood; 360/494-2055; 11am-6:45pm Wed.-Fri., 11am-5:45pm Sun.; $9-14*

Big burgers? Fries and tots? Cliff Droppers dishes up a range of burgers, sandwiches, and hot dogs only 25 minutes from the trailhead. You can get a standard cheeseburger, but why when they have the elusive Sasquatch Burger, a double-patty beast of a burger with two kinds of cheese and Canadian bacon? Or an elk or salmon burger? Whatever you get, the meal will be hot, hearty, fast, and delicious.

NEED TO KNOW

Info: Ohanapecosh Visitor Center, www.nps.gov/mora

Passes and Reservations: Entry into the park is $30/vehicle ($25/motorcycle, $15/pedestrian or cyclist). Passes are available in advance at www.recreation.gov. For more information, see page 502.

Weather Considerations: This is a region renowned for precipitation, so be prepared for rain at any time. In early summer you may find patches and pockets of snow at higher elevations; the snowmelt feeds the waterfall and Ohanapecosh River, so after particularly snowy winters, expect to find an especially dramatic waterfall.

Facilities: Water and restrooms are available at the trailhead.

▼ SILVER FALLS

11

WONDERLAND TRAIL

MOUNT RAINIER NATIONAL PARK, WASHINGTON

This multi-night hike circling Mount Rainier delivers everything from star-filled nights to epic sunrise and sunset sessions to daily views of wildflowers, peaks, glacial gorges, and wildlife.

- **Distance:** 93 mi (150 km) round-trip
- **Duration:** 10-14 days
- **Elevation Gain:** 24,547 ft (7,482 m)
- **Effort:** Strenuous
- **When:** July-Sept.
- **Trailhead:** Longmire Wilderness Information Center

HIGHLIGHT: Camping under the stars

National parks were made for epic adventures, and a two-week backpacking trip circling Mount Rainier certainly qualifies as epic. It has everything you want. Valleys, lowland forests, alpine and subalpine environments. Waterfalls and wildlife, season-long patches of snow, and the fleeting beauty of wildflowers. Views for days. Word of warning: The trail is long—we clock it at 85.8 mi (138 km), but park rangers call it 93 mi (150 km), accounting for the difference in "on paper" and "on trail" miles and the number of side-quest trails you explore—and it's a roller-coaster ride. Over the course of the two weeks you'll be on this trail, you'll gain and lose more than 24,000 ft (7,300 m). Come in shape, with proper gear, prepared to put in some hard trail miles to earn a scrapbook full of memories on this phenomenal hike.

◄ BLACK BEAR IN MOUNT RAINIER NATIONAL PARK

▼ SWITCHBACKS ON WONDERLAND TRAIL

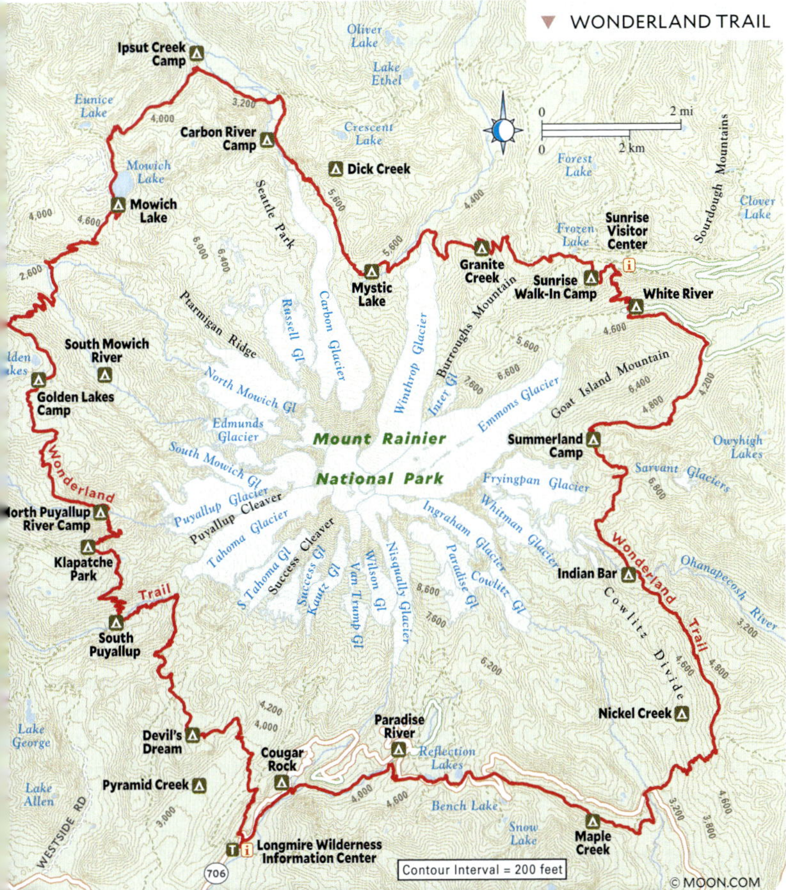

START THE HIKE

The trail begins only a few feet from the **Longmire Wilderness Information Center.** Once you've checked in and activated your wilderness permit, do one final gear check and get on the trail, traveling in a clockwise direction, turning left at the first trail junction.

There are 18 trailside wilderness camps and three non-wilderness camps along Wonderland Trail. Traveling clockwise from Longmire, you'll encounter campsites at Pyramid Creek (no group site), Devil's Dream, South Puyallup River, Klapatche Park (no group site), North Puyallup River, Golden Lakes, South Mowich River, Mowich Lake Campground (non-wilderness campground), Ipsut Creek Campground, Carbon River, Dick Creek (no group site), Mystic Camp, Granite Creek, Sunrise Camp, White River Campground (non-wilderness campground), Summerland, Indian Bar, Nickel Creek, Maple Creek, Paradise River, and Cougar Rock Campgound (non-wilderness campground). Not all campsites can accommodate groups, and parties of 6-12 people will need a group campsite.

Depending on when you get on the trail and your pace, your first night's campsite may be **Devil's Dream,** 5.1 mi (8.2 km) from the trailhead (the NPS calls it 5.8 mi/9.3 km). **South Puyallup** makes a good campsite on night two as you'll wake up fresh and ready to take on a huge challenge first thing in the morning: 1,800 ft (549 m) in elevation gain in only 1.3 mi (2.1 km). Take plenty of breaks, never pass up the chance to check out your surroundings and snap a few pictures, and stay focused on making a steady pace around the mountain and you'll make this trip.

From here the timing of your campsites is up to you. If you and your party are fast, experienced hikers who chew up the trail miles like so much GORP, then you might push for 10-12 mi (16.1-19.3 km) a day and wrap up this hike in little more than a week. If you're taking your time to savor the hike, or if you're new to this type of long backpacking experience, you're going to log fewer miles and use up all or most of the 13 nights/14 days on your permit.

DIRECTIONS

Wonderland Trail begins in the Longmire area of Mount Rainier National Park. Many visitors will be coming into this hike from the Seattle area, if not flying into the Seattle-Tacoma International Airport (SEA). From the airport, it's a two-hour drive of 84.7 mi (136.3 km). Take I-5 south through Tacoma and take exit 127, turning east on Highway 512. Take the next exit onto Steele Street, follow Steele to the Cross-Base Highway, and turn right onto Highway 7. Follow Highway 7 to the town of Elbe, where you'll continue east by staying straight on Highway 706, which leads into the park through the Nisqually Entrance. Turn right into the Longmire Wilderness Information Center as directed by signage.

NEED TO KNOW

Info: Longmire Wilderness Information Center, www.nps.gov/mora

Passes and Reservations: Entry into the park is $30/vehicle ($25/motorcycle, $15/pedestrian or cyclist), and timed entry passes ($2) are required

BEST NEARBY

National Park Inn

▶ *47009 Paradise Rd. E., Ashford; 855/755-2275; https://mtrainierguestservices.com; open year-round; from $189*

I always book a decent to really nice hotel for a couple of nights after a long hike like this, and I advise you to do the same. Nothing's easier that staying in style right by the trailhead and your parking space, and if you snag one of the 25 rooms at National Park Inn, you can take a long, hot shower and finally eat a meal that wasn't cooked over your backpacking stove. Accommodations here are on the decent end of things, with rooms that share a bathroom with the floor as well as rooms that have an en suite bath.

▲ VIEW FROM KLAPATCHE PARK

to access the Paradise Corridor and Sunrise Corridor. You'll also need a wilderness permit ($26) for this hike (keep it with you at all times), a climbing permit ($68) if you're headed above 10,000 ft (3,048 m) or to climb on one of the glaciers, and you'll need reservations at your campsites. Passes, permits, and reservations are available in advance at www.recreation.gov. For more information, see page 508.

Weather Considerations: The weather around Longmire and Mount Rainier is generally quite pleasant during the popular hiking season, with high temperatures in the 66-75°F (19-24°C) range; lows range 43-47°F (6-8°C), so bring an insulated sleeping bag and warm outer layers. Though summer is the sunniest season, wet and cold weather can pop up at any time, making foul-weather gear a must in any backpack. You'll find snow at the 5,000-8,000-ft (1,524-2,438-m) range into mid-July.

Facilities: Restrooms and potable water are available at the Longmire trailhead, with additional facilities in the Longmire Museum and National Park Inn. You can find a few supplies (plus souvenirs and winter gear rental) at the Longmire General Store. Every camp along the trail has cleared tent sites, a pit toilet, and a nearby water source. Some pit toilets are fully enclosed with a door, while others are out in the open.

Other: You'll need to have plenty of food and stove fuel for this hike, and while you can acquire basic supplies at the General Store in Longmire and the Day Lodge at Sunrise (provided they are open), you'll pay dearly for them here in the park. Grocery stores, big box centers, and outdoor outfitters near the park will be able to supply all or most of what you need, but to ensure you have the gear you want and need, your best bet is to gather up your food and fuel caches and mail them to the national park. Find detailed information on caching food and fuel at www.nps.gov/mora.

In addition to your usual camping kit, rain gear, warm layers, and food supply, bring a way to charge electronics like your phone or camera, headlamp, and other devices. You're not required to carry a bear-proof canister, but it's a good idea to have one. For additional planning questions, contact rangers at Mount Rainier National Park.

12

CLEETWOOD COVE AND WIZARD ISLAND

CRATER LAKE NATIONAL PARK, OREGON

Hike the Cleetwood Cove Trail to Crater Lake's shoreline and take a boat to Wizard Island to scale the mini volcano.

- **Distance:** 4.5 mi (7.2 km) round-trip
- **Duration:** 4 hours
- **Elevation Gain:** 1,370 ft (418 m)
- **Effort:** Easy-moderate
- **When:** June-Oct.
- **Trailhead:** Cleetwood Cove parking area

HIGHLIGHT: Hiking around Witches Cauldron

One glance at the conical shape of Wizard Island leads you to a pair of conclusions: why it was named (it looks like a cartoon wizard's hat) and that it looks like a mini volcano (pretty close—some 7,700 years ago a huge volcanic eruption destroyed the mountain and formed Crater Lake; over the centuries, other eruptions formed Wizard Island). This hike is all about seeing and experiencing these Crater Lake icons, from the stunning lakeshore to the short ferry ride to the top of that wizard hat-shaped island.

▲ WIZARD ISLAND IN CRATER LAKE

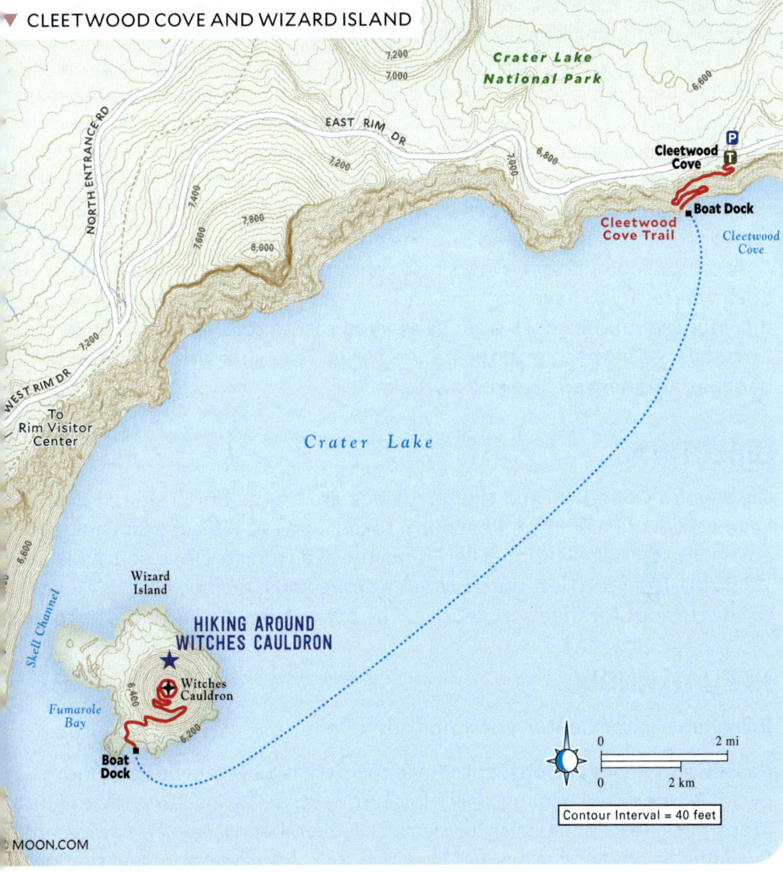

START THE HIKE

Check in at the **Cleetwood Cove parking area,** then cross Rim Drive to the Cleetwood Cove Trailhead where you'll descend the 1.1-mi (1.8-km) trail to the shores of **Crater Lake.** The trail is wide, and as you follow the nine switchbacks to the shore, you'll pass through a forest of lodgepole pine, Shasta red fir, and mountain hemlock; through their branches you'll get fleeting views of the lake, but as you near the shore, the view opens. At the end of the trail you'll find the **dock,** a ticket booth (if you haven't secured tickets for your shuttle boat or tour, this is your last chance), and the shoreline; check in at the ticket booth so they know to save your seat. Tours depart at 9am daily in season, and shuttles depart at 9am and 11:30am daily in season.

Upon arriving at the **Wizard Island dock,** you'll find a restroom and the trailhead. The boats stop here for three hours, so hit the trail first. When you start hiking to the summit, you'll meet a trail junction at 0.1 mi (0.2 km); to the left is Fumarole Bay Trail, while our trail ascends to the right. Follow the signs to the summit and you'll begin a steady ascent through a forest that starts as western hemlock and soon gives way to whitebark pine and a trailside bed of ankle-high pinemat manzanita. You'll likely see a few ground squirrels and hear the band-winged grasshopper, which sounds very much like a lawn sprinkler.

After 1.2 mi (1.9 km) on the trail, you'll reach the summit and a junction. The junction is for a 0.3-mi (0.5-km) loop trail circling the crater atop Wizard Island. The crater—called the **Witches Cauldron**—has wow-worthy scenery every step of the way, with great views of Crater Lake, Mount Scott, Watchman Peak, and other landmarks all around. In midsummer you'll find purple penstemon growing near the summit. Unofficial (or social) trails descend into the pumice-filled crater.

After you complete the loop, head back downhill to the Wizard Island dock where, if you have the time and a towel, you can take a swim or just dip your feet in the cool water. When you return to Cleetwood Cove, it's time for that big ascent to the parking area. Take your time—the trailside benches are there to give you a break.

DIRECTIONS

Cleetwood Cove Trail and the ferry dock are on the north side of Crater Lake National Park. From Roseburg, take Highway 138 east 86.9 mi (140 km) to Crater Lake National Park's northern entrance. Drive south 8.4 mi (13.5 km), then turn left onto East Rim Drive and continue 4.5 mi (7.2 km) to the turnout for Cleetwood Cove. The parking area is north of the road.

NEED TO KNOW

Info: Rim Visitor Center, www.nps.gov/crla

Passes and Reservations: Entry into the park is $30/vehicle ($25/motorcycle, $15/pedestrian or cyclist) May 22-October 31 and $20/vehicle ($15/motorcycle, $15/pedestrian or cyclist) November 1-May 21. Passes are available in advance at www.recreation.gov. A ticket for a shuttle boat ($28) or boat tour ($55) is required to access Wizard Island, available online (www.explorecraterlake.com) or in person. You must check in at the booth at the Cleetwood Cove parking area as well as at a second booth

BEST NEARBY

Rim Drive

Rim Drive encircles Crater Lake along a 33-mi (53-km) loop packed with exceptional views, parking areas, five picnic spots, and several trailheads. Budget for at least two hours to drive the full loop, but be prepared for your trip to be longer as you linger at overlooks, explore a short trail, or get behind some slower-moving traffic. There are 30 overlooks, several waterfalls, and millions of photo opportunities and moments to be awed by nature along the way, so take your time as you make your way around the lake. Note that Rim Drive is closed to automobiles every winter, when it becomes a route for skiing and snowshoeing. Seasonal closure occurs around October or November with the area's first big snowstorm; the road reopens between May and July, depending on weather conditions.

at the base of the trail for shuttles and boat tours. For more information, see page 516.

Weather Considerations: Though Crater Lake National Park is open 24 hours year-round, it does experience seasonal closures due to snow, most frequently November-mid-April. Check the "Current Conditions" page on www.nps.gov/crla.

Be sure to bring plenty of water for this hike and apply sunscreen; time on the boat alone will offer plenty of exposure, and the summit of Wizard Island is also exposed.

Facilities: Restrooms available at the Cleetwood Cove parking area, the Cleetwood Cove ticket booth, and the Wizard Island dock. There are no water stations, so bring plenty of water.

Other: At the time of writing, Cleetwood Cove Trail was set to close for construction. Check for updates before visiting.

▼ VIEW OF CRATER LAKE AND WIZARD ISLAND

13

MIST TRAIL TO VERNAL FALL

YOSEMITE NATIONAL PARK, CALIFORNIA

This world-class hike goes to one of the most photographed waterfalls in the world.

- **Distance:** 3 mi (4.8 km) round-trip
- **Duration:** 1.5-2 hours
- **Elevation Gain:** 1,050 ft (320 m)
- **Effort:** Moderate
- **When:** Year-round, best late Apr.-early May
- **Trailhead:** Happy Isles

HIGHLIGHT: Climbing the granite stairway to Vernal Fall overlook and Emerald Pool

If there's one hike you should take in Yosemite Valley, this is it. In all likelihood the trail to Vernal Fall will be busy, even crowded, as folks make a veritable pilgrimage to one of the most photographed waterfalls in the world. If you hit the trail early you can avoid much of the crowd.

▲ VERNAL FALL FROM MIST TRAIL

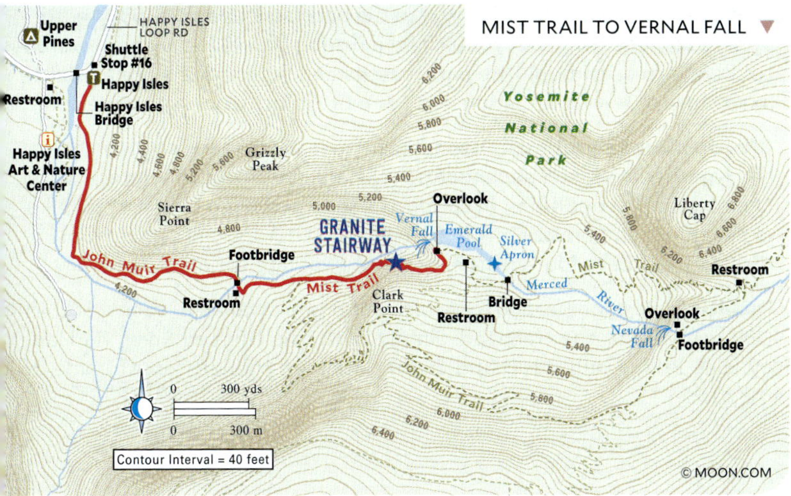

START THE HIKE

Take the free Yosemite Valley Shuttle to the trailhead at **Happy Isles.** You'll set off on the **John Muir Trail,** ascending gently to a **footbridge** where you can see the fall at 0.8 mi (1.3 km). Many folks stop at the footbridge, satisfied with the view, but continue on the **granite staircase** to the top of the falls—the views get more and more stunning as you climb. At 1.1 mi (1.8 km), you'll meet the junction of Muir (branching off to the right) and Mist Trails (straight ahead). Stay on **Mist Trail** until you reach the top of **Vernal Fall** (317 ft/97 m tall) in another 0.5 mi (0.8 km).

When you reach the overlook atop the fall and the lake-like **Emerald Pool,** explore a bit. It's lovely and a good spot to have lunch or linger over a snack and some water. Bring a raincoat or poncho if you don't want to get wet; if you're here in spring when snowmelt has the fall throwing mist all over, you'll get soaked. Once content, you can turn back, descending the stairs (with caution—they can get slippery when the fall is really flowing) and trail back to the parking area, or you can press on, climbing Mist Trail to more waterfalls and wow-worthy views.

DIRECTIONS

Mist Trail and Vernal Fall are in the Yosemite Valley area of Yosemite National Park. From El Portal, take Highway 140 east for 3 mi (4.8 km) to the Arch Rock entrance station. Drive 11.6 mi (18.7 km) east to the day-use parking lot at Curry Village. Board the free Yosemite Valley shuttle bus to Happy Isles, stop number 16. In winter when the shuttle does not run, you must hike from Curry Village, adding 2 mi (3.2 km) to your round-trip.

NEED TO KNOW

Info: Yosemite Valley Welcome Center or Happy Isles Art and Nature Center, www.nps.gov/yose

Passes and Reservations: Entry into the park is $35/vehicle ($30/motorcycle, $20/pedestrian or cyclist), and a reservation ($2) may be required to drive into or through the park. Passes and reservations are available in advance at www.recreation.gov. For more information, see page 504.

Weather Considerations: Yosemite is a year-round park, so planning for the weather is season dependent. Trails may be closed in winter; call to check weather conditions. In spring, the recommended time for this hike, expect high temperatures from 63-71°F (17-21°C) and chilly lows from 38-45°F (3-7°C); have foul-weather gear ready as late spring can see rain.

Facilities: Restrooms and potable water are available about 500 ft (152 m) west of the trailhead. Simply cross the Merced River via Happy Isles Bridge and you'll find the facilities on the left (south) side of the road.

BEST NEARBY

Nevada Fall via Mist Trail

You can bag two more waterfalls and get even more stunning views of Yosemite by extending this hike. From Vernal Fall, continue along Mist Trail as it skirts the edge of Emerald Pool and offers a look at Silver Apron Falls. The trail continues to climb, entering a long set of switchbacks before meeting up with John Muir Trail. Turn right (south) on Muir, paralleling the Merced River. A spur trail at the south end of the little lake here gives you a great look at Nevada Fall. John Muir Trail continues south and west, descending the sweeping ridgelines and providing unbelievable views nearly every step of the way. You'll rejoin the original trail at the point where the John Muir and Mist Trails meet. Turn left on Muir to return to the trailhead. If you combine Vernal and Nevada Fall, this hike comes in at 6.4 mi (10.3 km) with 2,208 ft (673 m) of elevation gain.

▲ VERNAL FALL FROM MIST TRAIL

14

HALF DOME

YOSEMITE NATIONAL PARK, CALIFORNIA

This challenging, bucket-list trek ascends steep granite slopes, culminating in a final, thrilling climb aided by cables to reach breathtaking panoramic views from the summit.

- **Distance:** 16 mi (26 km) round-trip
- **Duration:** 8-10 hours
- **Elevation Gain:** 5,000 ft (1,524 m)
- **Effort:** Very strenuous
- **When:** Apr.-late Sept.
- **Trailhead:** Happy Isles

HIGHLIGHT: Rewarding yourself with summit views atop Half Dome

Half Dome is one of those instantly recognizable landscapes that fills your heart with wonder, and, for many people, is a must-do-once-in-your-life hike. Just be sure you know what you're in for prior to lacing up your boots and heading out on this epic trek. You're looking at 16 mi (26 km) of round-trip hiking, an elevation gain of about 5,000 ft (1,524 m), and so many trail companions you won't believe the number of hikers. Oh, and there are the cables. That's right, steel cables anchored to the granite, plus an assortment of steps carved into the stone and iron hand- and footholds attached to the rock here and there. It's not a hike for the faint of heart, but for the reasonably fit, it's one you can do in one (exhausting) day.

▲ HALF DOME CABLES

However, we can't stress this enough: Half Dome is a potentially dangerous hike. Due to the elevation and exposure, there's the potential for lightning strikes at and near the summit. The slick rock face of Half Dome can grow slippery with any precipitation, making for a deadly situation.

Unfortunately, accidents happen; since 2004 there have been 10 falling deaths on Half Dome, including two tragic accidents in the summer of 2024 (the last reporting period before going to press), so be extra cautious on this hike—and remember, there's nothing wrong with getting to the bottom of the cables and deciding that part of the hike isn't for you.

START THE HIKE

The first part of this hike follows the route to **Vernal Fall** (page 98). When you reach the junction of Mist Trail and John Muir Trail at 1.1 mi (1.8 km), turn right and ascend **John Muir Trail** via a set of switchbacks. You'll stay on this trail for 2.7 mi (4.3 km), passing several fantastic viewpoints and **Nevada Fall.** Around 5 mi (8 km) into the hike you'll find yourself in the **Lower Yosemite Valley** near the **campground** and **ranger station.**

Continue on John Muir Trail for 1.3 mi (2.1 km) to a fork in the trail where Muir heads right and **Half Dome Trail** heads left. Follow Half Dome. Another 1.5 mi (2.4 km) of trail will carry you out of the tree line to the rocky base of **Sub Dome,** Half Dome's smaller sibling, and a brutal set of switchbacks.

At 8 mi (12.9 km) from the trailhead (only 1.8 mi/2.9 km from where you joined Half Dome Trail) is the **steel cables section.** Steel yourself and do a moment of soul-searching before you begin the cable ascent, as turning around when you're halfway up and scared isn't a great option (you'll cause quite the logjam among your fellow hikers). If you decide to climb, you'll want to slip on some sturdy gloves to protect your hands from the cable. The cables require almost equal parts arm and leg strength as you haul yourself up 440 ft (134 m) of near-vertical granite.

When you reach the top, the views are so incredible that you forget all about your exertion. There's plenty of room for everyone on top of **Half Dome;** its vast, mostly flat surface covers about 13 acres (5 ha).

Your return trip of 8 mi (12.9 km) begins with a descent of the steel cables section. Be extremely cautious on the descent, ensuring you have good footing and handholds every step of the way. Once you clear the steel cables, follow the descending trail through the switchbacks and into the tree line at Sub Dome. When you reach the junction with John Muir Trail, turn right and in 1.3 mi (2.1 km) you'll be back at the Lower Yosemite Valley near the campground and ranger station. Some hikers break the trail into smaller segments by overnighting at the campground on the way to Half Dome or on the return trip, and if this sounds like you, you've reached home for the night. Otherwise, it's 5 mi (8 km) back to the trailhead. Follow John Muir Trail as it parallels the Merced River to the junction with Mist Trail. If you want a look from the top of Nevada Fall, you'll find the fall and a viewpoint 0.2 mi (0.3 km) down the John Muir Trail, which you can take all the way back to the trailhead (2.7 mi/4.4 km); otherwise descend Mist Trail, braving the switchbacks, the mist, and the crowds until you're back at the trailhead.

DIRECTIONS

Half Dome is in the Yosemite Valley area of Yosemite National Park. From El Portal, take Highway 140 east for 3 mi (4.8 km) to the Arch Rock entrance station. Drive 11.6 mi (18.7 km) east to the day-use parking lot at Curry Village. Board the free Yosemite Valley shuttle bus to Happy Isles, stop number 16. Buses arrive every 12-22 minutes 7am-10pm, so time your hike accordingly if you're not overnighting at the campground.

BEST NEARBY

Little Yosemite Valley

▶ *5 mi (8 km) from the trailhead along John Muir Trail*

To make the trip to Half Dome easier, some camp at Little Yosemite Valley (wilderness permit required; permits available 24 weeks in advance via lottery at www.recreation.gov; $10/processing, $5/successful permit). This saves the final ascent for the next day, lets you get an early start on the trail, and could even give you one more night in the backcountry if you wanted to hang around after Half Dome. Figure on two hours to hike from Little Yosemite Valley campsites to the summit. There's a composting toilet at the campground, but no potable water.

▲ HALF DOME SUMMIT VIEWS

NEED TO KNOW

Info: Yosemite Valley Welcome Center or Happy Isles Art and Nature Center, www.nps.gov/yose

Passes and Reservations: Entry into the park is $35/vehicle ($30/motorcycle, $20/pedestrian or cyclist), and a reservation ($2) may be required to drive into or through the park. A separate permit is required to hike Half Dome. Passes, reservations, and permits are available in advance at www.recreation.gov. For more information, see page 506.

Weather Considerations: Plan on an early morning start to beat the heat and the possibility of afternoon clouds and/or thundershowers (5am is a common start time).

Facilities: Restrooms and potable water are available about 500 ft (152 m) west of the trailhead. Simply cross the Merced River via Happy Isles Bridge and you'll find the facilities on the left (south) side of the road.

Other: Plan on not seeing your car again for about 10-12 hours, during which time you must have everything you need in your day pack. Bring plenty of water and food, and consider carrying along a pair of gloves to keep your hands from slipping or chafing on the cables. If you're feeling a little squeamish at the thought of falling on the cable section, check your local outdoor store for a via ferrata setup that includes a harness, a Y-shaped energy-absorbing lanyard, and carabiners, and clip yourself into the cables as you climb.

15

PANORAMA TRAIL

YOSEMITE NATIONAL PARK, CALIFORNIA

Panorama Trail descends from a high point overlooking the valley to the valley floor, passing waterfalls, viewpoints, sheer cliffs, and ridgeline walks along the way.

- **Distance:** 8.5 mi (13.7 km) one-way
- **Duration:** 4-5 hours
- **Elevation Gain:** 3,900 ft (1,189 m)
- **Effort:** Moderate-strenuous
- **When:** June-Oct.
- **Trailhead:** Glacier Point

HIGHLIGHT: Taking in views of Yosemite Valley from Panorama Point

Panorama Trail is a point-to-point hike that follows a dazzling route from Glacier Point to Nevada Fall, then down impressive granite stairs past Vernal Fall to Happy Isles. Nearly every step of the way you'll find perfect postcard views of the Yosemite Valley.

START THE HIKE

Begin the trail at **Glacier Point,** elevation 7,214 ft (2,199 m), where you'll have unreal views of Yosemite: Half Dome, Basket Dome, North Dome,

◄ PANORAMA TRAIL

▼ ILLILOUETTE FALL

Contour Interval = 100 feet
0
500 yds
0
500 m
PANORAMA POINT
Panorama Trail
Panorama Cliff
Illilouette Creek
Illilouette Fall
Illilouette Gorge
Buena Vista Trail
Washburn Point
GLACIER POINT RD
Glacier Point
Glacier Point
Four Mile Trail
Yosemite National Park
Yosemite Valley
To Yosemite Valley Welcome Center
Upper Pines
Shuttle Stop #16
Happy Isles
John Muir Trail
Merced River
Vernal Fall Footbridge
Granite Stairway
Mist Trail
Vernal Fall
Emerald Pool
Clark Point
John Muir Trail
Nevada Fall
Mist Trail
Liberty Cap
John Muir Trail
Mount Broderick
Grizzly Peak
© MOON.COM

Liberty Cap, and Vernal and Nevada Falls in the distance. The sights from the trailhead are fantastic, and only get better as you hike. Descend via **Panorama Trail,** where a few switchbacks will carry you to a trail that hugs the contours of the mountain on a steep but steady incline. In 2.7 mi (4.3 km) you'll reach **Illilouette Fall** and begin to ascend. At 3.2 mi (5.1 km), take the spur trail to **Panorama Point** for a secluded spot to rest a bit or to just goggle at the view.

Back on the trail, the ascent lasts for another 1.3 mi (2.1 km) before you descend, meeting up with **John Muir Trail** and passing by **Nevada Fall.** A spur trail at 5.7 mi (9.2 km) leads to a viewpoint of the fall and offers big views down the valley. Continue along Muir until you reach **Mist Trail** on your left 5.9 mi (9.5 km) into the hike.

As you descend Mist Trail you're in for a treat. The valley opens up at your feet, the view growing wider and more spectacular with each step. Soon you'll see **Emerald Pool,** where the Merced River gathers before dropping down Vernal Fall. Continue for 1.4 mi (2.3 km), cross the river, and follow along the edge of Emerald Pool to the top of **Vernal Fall.** Take some time to rest and absorb the view, then make your way down the **granite staircase** on the busy trail to **Happy Isles.**

DIRECTIONS

Panorama Trail is in the Yosemite Valley area of Yosemite National Park. From El Portal, take Highway 140 east for 3 mi (4.8 km) to the Arch Rock entrance station. Drive 12.1 mi (19.5 km) to Yosemite Valley Lodge, where most hikers park their car and join a one-way **Glacier Point Tour** (888/413-8869; www.travelyosemite.com; $28.50), which leads through the valley to Glacier Point near the trailhead for Panorama Trail. Once you complete Panorama Trail and reach Happy Isles, you can take the free Yosemite Valley Shuttle to stop number 7, Yosemite Valley Lodge, and your vehicle.

NEED TO KNOW

Info: Yosemite Valley Welcome Center, www.nps.gov/yose

BEST NEARBY

Taft Point and the Fissures

This easy trail (2.3 mi/3.7 km rt; 1-1.5 hours; 354 ft/108 m of elevation gain) descends (yes, descends) to the 7,500-ft (2,286-m) summit of Taft Point where the views of the Yosemite Valley, including El Capitan and Yosemite Falls, among other iconic landmarks, are so good you'll have a hard time taking a bad photo. The views are great the whole way, but as you near Taft Point you'll see the Fissures. These narrow fractures in the granite are called "joints" and are crazy deep. Be careful here, as the drop-offs are up to 2,000 ft (610 m) of clear air between here and the ground.

Passes and Reservations: Entry into the park is $35/vehicle ($30/motorcycle, $20/pedestrian or cyclist), and a reservation ($2) may be required to drive into or through the park (separate from your bus tour reservation). Passes and reservations are available in advance at www.recreation.gov. For more information, see page 504.

Weather Considerations: Yosemite's weather is generally pleasant, but in summer there's always the chance of a sudden thunderstorm, and in fall you may encounter early snow squalls and the potential for rain; for those reasons, carry foul-weather gear and some sort of insulating layer you can throw on.

Facilities: Restrooms and potable water are available at the Glacier Point parking area adjacent to the trailhead.

▼ HIKERS ON PANORAMA TRAIL

▲ PANORAMA TRAIL

TOP EXPERIENCE

16

CATHEDRAL LAKES

YOSEMITE NATIONAL PARK, CALIFORNIA

Camp lakeside for an evening of fishing, nights full of stargazing, and plenty of time to explore Cathedral Lakes and this part of Tuolumne Meadows.

- **Distance:** 9.5 mi (15.3 km) round-trip
- **Duration:** Overnight, or 4-6 hours as a day hike
- **Elevation Gain:** 1,600 ft (488 m)
- **Effort:** Strenuous
- **When:** June-Sept.
- **Trailhead:** Cathedral Lakes

HIGHLIGHT: Seeing the stars' reflection in Lower or Upper Cathedral Lake

Tuolumne Meadows, a huge subalpine meadow, is a popular destination for Yosemite visitors, though many pass through (with a stop at the visitor center) on a scenic drive along Tioga Road. Rather than breeze through, we're going on an overnight hike. Cathedral Peak stands south-southwest from the visitor center, and

▲ CATHEDRAL PEAK

a pair of lakes—Upper and Lower Cathedral Lake—sit at the foot of the mountain. Some make a hike to either Upper or Lower Cathedral Lake, sometimes both, as a day hike, but for the full Yosemite experience, you should plan to camp here for one or two nights. You'll need to carry in your provisions, use a bear-proof canister for food, and practice those Leave no Trace principles, but that's all a breeze when you get to explore Tuolumne by day and sit in awe of the stars by night.

START THE HIKE

From Cathedral Lakes Trailhead, head south on **John Muir Trail.** You'll reach a trail junction with Budd Lake Trail in 0.3 mi (0.5 km); stay on Muir heading southwest.

A good bit of this hike will be in and among the lodgepole pines, but the view opens up to show the spectacular landscape and the distinctive shape of **Cathedral Peak.** At 3.1 mi (5 km) from the trailhead, the trail forks; following the right trail for 0.5 mi (0.8 km) will lead you to **Lower Cathedral Lake,** while the left trail leads 0.8 mi (1.3 km) to **Upper Cathedral Lake.** Lower Lake is the larger of the two, and there are more campsites on the shoreline here than at Upper Lake; Upper offers better fishing but fewer campsites.

Many hikers come out to Lower Cathedral Lake, head to the west end for a photo of Cathedral Peak reflected in the water below, then head back. A few hikers will make the trek to Upper Cathedral Lake after visiting Lower. If you're doing this as a day hike, be sure to bring a hearty lunch to eat lakeside. But don't day-hike this; plan to camp here because nothing beats camping lakeside.

If you can only camp for one night, camp at Lower Cathedral Lake (campsites on the west side have great views if you can find one), but if you're here for two or more nights, plan to pack up and find a site on the shores of Upper Cathedral Lake. Camping means plenty of **stargazing**—it's amazing at this elevation and with the lakes reflecting the stars above—and the chance to explore off trail. It also means fishing (you'll need a valid California fishing license, available at www.ca.wildlifelicense.com, and you'll need to abide by Yosemite's regulations, available at www.nps.gov/yose).

When you've had your fill of this place (honestly, who can say they've had their fill of this gorgeous spot?), it's time to pack up your gear and head back to the trailhead.

DIRECTIONS

Cathedral Lakes are in the Tuolumne Meadows area of Yosemite National Park. From Groveland, take Highway 120 east 24 mi (39 km) to the Big Oak Flat entrance station. Drive southeast 7.7 mi (12.4 km) to Crane Flat, and then turn left to stay on Highway 120. Drive 37.4 mi (60.2 km) to the Cathedral Lakes Trailhead on the right, by Tuolumne Meadows. Park your car in the pullouts on either side of the road; there is no formal parking lot.

BEST NEARBY

Parsons Memorial Lodge

▶ *1 mi (1.6 km) north of the Tuolumne Meadows Visitor Center along Old Tioga Road Trail*

There are a lot of important historic sites in Yosemite, perhaps none more important than Parsons Memorial Lodge. You'll get plenty of information on Tuolumne Meadows' human and natural histories at the lodge and nearby Soda Springs, and it's plenty interesting, but this is the place where John Muir and Robert Underwood Johnson conceived of establishing the Yosemite Valley and surrounding lands into Yosemite National Park. Put yourself in their shoes and imagine the incredible effort it took to arrive at this virtually unspoiled meadow (even with good roads and fast cars it takes a bit of work to get here today). Now open yourself to the beauty, the solitude, the sights and sounds and smells of this place. Let yourself be inspired and moved by this landscape. Were Muir and Johnson right in saying this place was national park-worthy? I think so, and I think you do too.

NEED TO KNOW

Info: Tuolumne Meadows Visitor Center, www.nps.gov/yose

Passes and Reservations: Entry into the park is $35/vehicle ($30/motorcycle, $20/pedestrian or cyclist), and a reservation ($2) may be required to drive into or through the park. You will need to secure your wilderness permit far in advance in order to camp overnight. Passes, reservations, and permits are available in advance at www.recreation.gov. For more information, see page 508.

Weather Considerations: The weather at Tuolumne Meadows is different from the rest of the valley due to the elevation and geography of this place. You shouldn't encounter much rain June-September, and temperatures will be lower than what you'd find on the valley floor. Expect pleasant daytime temperatures from 65-72°F (18-22°C) and chilly nighttime lows from 32-39°F (0-4°C). Pack a warm sleeping bag and some insulating layers.

Facilities: Restrooms are available near the trailhead but no potable water. Outhouses are available at the campsites.

▼ CATHEDRAL LAKES

17

GENERAL SHERMAN TREE AND CONGRESS TRAIL

SEQUOIA & KINGS CANYON NATIONAL PARK, CALIFORNIA

See Giant Forest's gargantuan giant sequoia trees that have been growing since before King Arthur's knights gathered at the Round Table.

- **Distance:** 2.9 mi (4.7 km) round-trip
- **Duration:** 1.5 hours
- **Elevation Gain:** Less than 500 ft (152 m)
- **Effort:** Easy
- **When:** May-late Sept.
- **Trailhead:** General Sherman Tree

HIGHLIGHT: Looking up (and up and up) at General Sherman and other giant sequoia trees

Boardwalks lead to some of the largest trees on earth, making for an easy trail through groves of giant sequoias that will leave you in awe. The first portion of this trail is accessible, so visitors of nearly all ability levels can get a look at General Sherman, a true colossal.

◄ CONGRESS TRAIL

▼ LOOKING UP FROM CONGRESS TRAIL

GENERAL SHERMAN TREE AND CONGRESS TRAIL

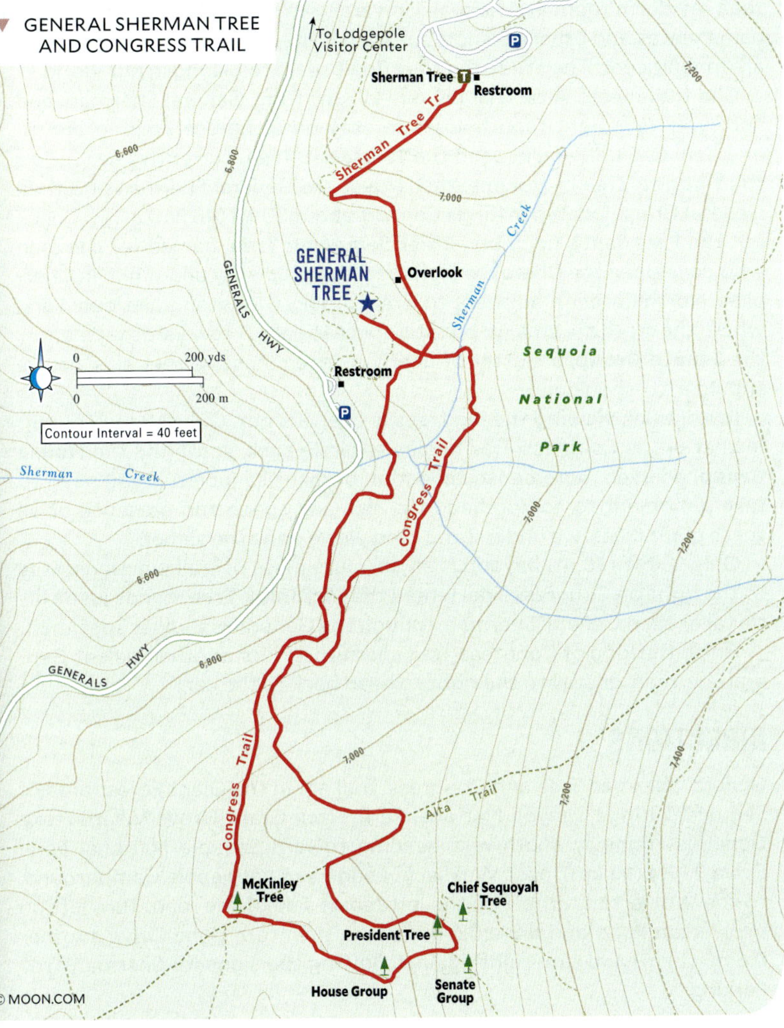

START THE HIKE

Proceed up the wide, paved trail to begin the trek into these giant trees.

At 0.3 mi (0.5 km), an overlook gives you a full view of the staggering **General Sherman.** General Sherman is a giant sequoia standing 275 ft (84 m) high with a circumference at the ground of 102.6 ft (31.3 m); the first large branches don't appear until 130 ft (40 m) up the trunk. Looking at trees like this makes one wonder what our forests looked like 500 years ago.

Only 100 yards (91 m) past the overlook, you'll reach another signboard and junction. Turn left and you'll be on **Congress Trail,** or turn right and you'll be at General Sherman in a few steps. Turn right and visit the General to admire the tree and attempt a selfie that shows this sequoia's monumental scale. Backtrack to Congress Trail and almost immediately you'll find sequoias bigger than most living rooms (truthfully, many are bigger than my dorm room at Marshall University). You'll note that some have name plates and others do not, but even if they're unnamed, these trees are magnificent. They're so big they don't seem to belong in our world.

The trail meets Alta Trail 0.9 mi (1.5 km) from General Sherman, and here you veer right (southwest) to stay on Congress Trail. In another 0.3 mi (0.5 km) you'll reach the **President Tree,** currently the world's third-largest tree by volume; the largest are General Sherman and then General Grant, located in Kings Canyon, about 30 mi (48 km) away. Check out the President's neighbor, **Chief Sequoyah Tree,** named for the man who developed the Cherokee alphabet (there's plenty about him in Cherokee, North Carolina, adjacent to Great Smoky Mountains National Park, where the trees are smaller but still spectacular). A few yards farther on, the **Senate Group,** a cluster of nearly a dozen massive sequoias, grows shoulder-to-shoulder.

If you think viewing the big trees is over, it's not. Only 0.2 mi (0.3 km) farther on, as Congress Trail begins to circle back, you'll find the **House Group,** an even more dense collection of giant sequoias. If you need to take a moment to comprehend the size and space and presence of all these giant trees, we understand (and we've done the same).

Only 100 ft (30 m) beyond is an absolute mess of trail junctions. Stay to the right on Congress Trail where the **McKinley Tree** stands just a little taller than General Sherman, though the General is a wider specimen.

Finish the loop of Congress Trail and turn left for another look at General Sherman, or stay to the right to head back to the car.

DIRECTIONS

General Sherman Tree and Congress Trail are in the Giant Forest area of Sequoia & Kings Canyon National Park. From Grant Grove Village, take Generals Highway southwest heading toward Sequoia National Park. Drive 27 mi (43 km), past Wuksachi Lodge and Lodgepole Campground, to the Wolverton turnoff on the left (east) side of the road. Turn left on Wolverton Road and drive 0.6 mi (1 km), then turn right. Drive another 0.6 mi (1 km) and turn right again, following the signs for Sherman Tree Parking.

BEST NEARBY

Giant Forest Museum

▶ *47050 Generals Highway, Three Rivers, 16 mi (26 km) north of Ash Mountain Entrance; 559/565-3341; www.nps.gov/seki; 9am-6pm daily with seasonal variances; free*

You'll get a lot out of visiting the grove of giant sequoias here, but at Giant Forest Museum, you'll really learn about these amazing trees and the environments that foster such astounding growth. Housed in the historic Giant Forest market building (listed on the National Register of Historic Places), the museum and visitor center has a number of displays, ranger-led talks and hikes, and other programs to help you build a deeper relationship with these trees and this park. Visit the museum before your hike if you can.

NEED TO KNOW

Info: Lodgepole Visitor Center, www.nps.gov/seki

Passes and Reservations: Entry into the park is $35/vehicle ($30/motorcycle, $20/pedestrian or cyclist). Passes are available in advance at www.recreation.gov.

Weather Considerations: Seasonal road closures—due largely to snow and/or avalanche danger—can shut down the route near Lodgepole Visitor Center, which remains unplowed from the Friday after January 1 to the third Friday in March. See www.nps.gov/seki for current road and trail closure information.

Facilities: Restrooms (with accessible facilities) and potable water are available at the trailhead.

▼ GIANT FOREST MUSEUM

18

ZUMWALT MEADOW

SEQUOIA & KINGS CANYON NATIONAL PARK, CALIFORNIA

This is a scenic, easy loop trail that offers stunning views of towering granite cliffs, lush meadows, and the winding Kings River.

- **Distance:** 1.6 mi (2.6 km) round-trip
- **Duration:** 1-2 hours
- **Elevation Gain:** 150 ft (46 m)
- **Effort:** Easy
- **When:** May-late Sept.
- **Trailhead:** Zumwalt Meadow Trailhead

HIGHLIGHT: Watching wildlife frolicking in the meadow around sunrise or sunset

Rather than climb high into the Sierras, this hike keeps you in the foothills surrounded by forests, meadows, and rivers. Zumwalt Meadow is the epitome of this foothills landscape, with high granite cliffs and snowy peaks above, the South Fork Kings River flowing nearby, and a grass-filled meadow.

▲ SOUTH FORK KINGS RIVER

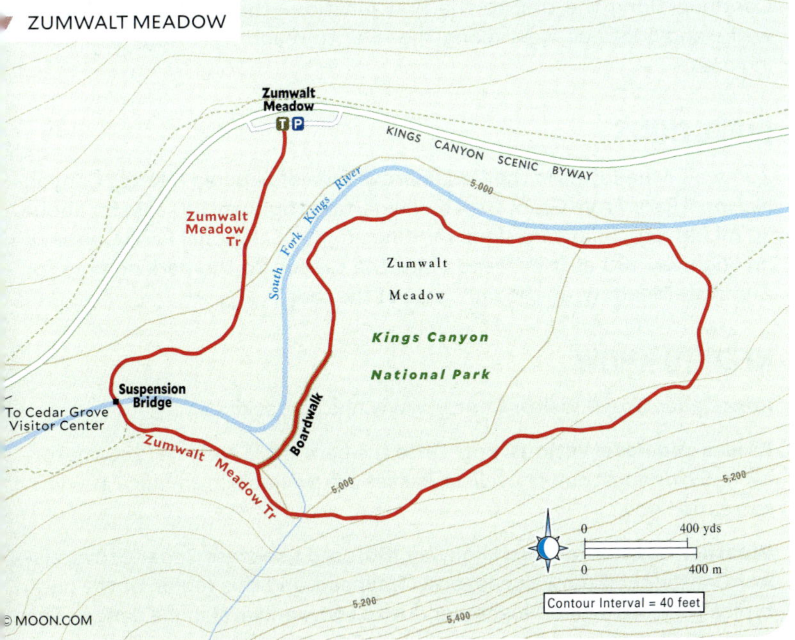

START THE HIKE

From the trailhead a dirt path leads southwest along the **South Fork Kings River** to where a bridge crosses. Look upstream and you'll see North Dome standing tall at 8,715 ft (2,656 m), looking down the valley. It makes an impressive sight, especially in evening light. Once you cross the bridge, the trail can be soggy or even wet depending on the river's level, but you only have a short muddy/wet section to deal with before you reach the **boardwalk.**

At the boardwalk, turn left and go clockwise around the loop. Along this stretch the boardwalk parallels the river, and you'll find ferns, reeds, and brushy horsetail. Cottonwoods, willows, and vine maples grow in abundance, but pine trees are starting to grow here as well.

After 0.3 mi (0.5 km), the boardwalk ends and the trail continues through the forest at the edge of the marsh. This is a **hotspot for wildlife watching:** mule deer and black bears, maybe a bobcat or other small mammal, and plenty of birds. If you want to increase your chance of seeing bears and deer, note that they tend to frequent the meadow in the hours around sunrise and sunset, sticking close to the tree line as they browse for food.

When you leave the river behind, the trail forks. Use the obviously well-traveled path to the right to begin looping back. Round a bend and face southeast and the view changes, with granite as your primary focus. The trail is a little rocky with stone steps easing the way, but with a few big rocks to contend with for good measure. There are many fantastic views to take in here, and they vary depending on the light conditions; again, if you're here around sunset, the glow on the peaks is magnificent.

Continue along the trail to the first junction—the start of the boardwalk—and continue west along the river to reach the bridge and parking area.

DIRECTIONS

Zumwalt Meadow is in the Cedar Grove area of Sequoia & Kings Canyon National Park. From Grant Grove Village, take Highway 180 east for about 30 mi (48 km), following signs for Kings Canyon National Park. Continue on Highway 180 as it descends into the canyon to the parking area for Zumwalt Meadow, on the right side of the road.

NEED TO KNOW

Info: Cedar Grove Visitor Center, www.nps.gov/seki

Passes and Reservations: Entry into the park is $35/vehicle ($30/motorcycle, $20/pedestrian or cyclist). Passes are available in advance at www.recreation.gov.

Weather Considerations: Highway 180, used to access Cedar Grove Visitor Center, the Zumwalt Meadow Trailhead, and this region of the park, typically closes in mid-November due to snow and avalanche danger. The road usually reopens around the fourth Friday in April.

Facilities: Restrooms are available at the trailhead. Water stations are available in the nearby campsites, but for snacks and bottled drinks you'll need to visit the Cedar Grove Lodge's gift shop and market 4.8 mi (7.7 km) south.

BEST NEARBY

Moraine Campground

▶ *Mile 33.1 Highway 180, Kings Canyon National Park; 559/565-3341; www.recreation.gov or www.nps.gov/seki; open late May-Aug.; $32*

There are four campgrounds near Zumwalt Meadow—Sheep Creek, Sentinel, Canyon View, and Moraine—the biggest of which is Moraine with 121 sites (the smallest is Sheep Creek, a group-only campsite with 12 sites for medium-to-large groups of up to 40). Try to book a site at the Moraine Campground, reserving the others as your backup options. Flush toilets and potable water are available in the campsite; showers, food, and supplies can be found in Cedar Grove Village nearby.

▲ ZUMWALT MEADOW BOARDWALK

19

GOLDEN CANYON TRAIL TO RED CATHEDRAL

DEATH VALLEY NATIONAL PARK, CALIFORNIA

Experience the otherworldly landscape of Death Valley on this easy hike that will transport you to Tatooine.

- **Distance:** 2.9-6 mi (4.7-9.7 km) round-trip
- **Duration:** 1.5-3 hours
- **Elevation Gain:** 577 ft (176 m)
- **Effort:** Easy
- **When:** Nov.-Mar.
- **Trailhead:** Golden Canyon parking area

HIGHLIGHT: Scrambling over small ledges to reach Red Cathedral

As you hike through Golden Canyon to Red Cathedral, you might find this landscape otherworldly, and if you do, you're in good company. NASA and its partners have tested Mars rovers in Death Valley, and Golden Canyon (among other locations in the park) appeared in *Star Wars: Episode IV* and *V* as the desert planet Tatooine.

START THE HIKE

Begin the hike in the **Golden Canyon parking area** and follow the path to the left as it leads up a gentle incline into the canyon. Depending on the quality of light, the walls here can range from pale yellow to lemony to

▲ GOLDEN CANYON

GOLDEN CANYON TRAIL TO RED CATHEDRAL

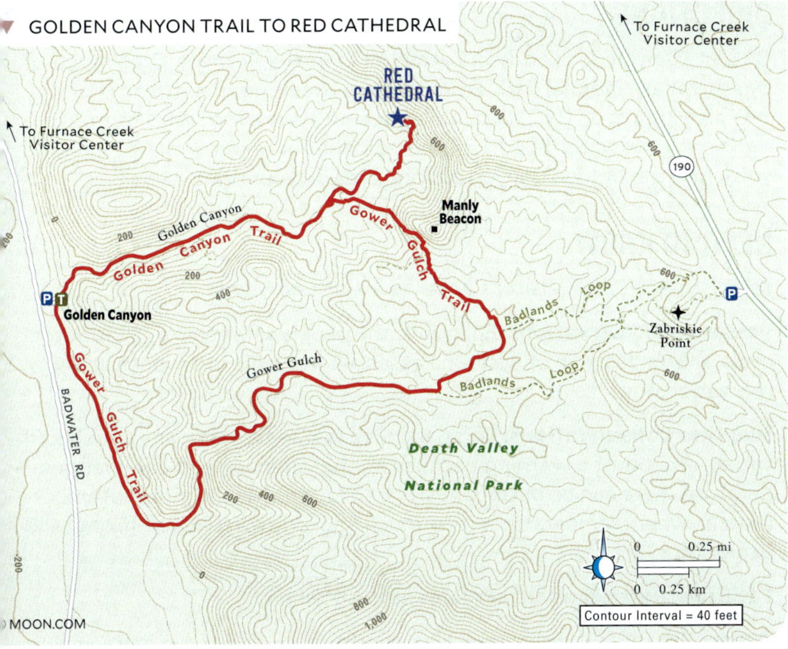

truly golden. At 0.5 mi (0.8 km), you'll reach sea level—that's right, from the trailhead to here, you've been hiking "underwater," or at least below sea level. A spur trail to the right leads to a little overlook. Continue along Golden Canyon as it grows steeper, never issuing much of a challenge, but climbing steadily. As you hike, notice the overhangs and little caves beside the trail. In *Star Wars,* R2-D2 took this path and the Jawas ambushed the astromech droid from one of these caves.

At 1 mi (1.6 km) you'll meet the junction with Gower Gulch Trail and catch a glimpse of the shark fin-like Manly Beacon rising above the canyons; remember this trail, as you can extend the hike by following this route after you check out Red Cathedral. If you noticed the chunky cliff of red rock ahead, you've seen Red Cathedral from a distance, and you'll continue to catch great glimpses of it as the last 0.5 mi (0.8 km) of trail leads you there. At the foot of **Red Cathedral,** you'll find spur trails leading to vantage points to the right and left. Explore as you will, just be mindful of the path (you'll see faint outlines of trail in the yellow dust and dirt) and of your footing as you climb over small ledges to get the best views. You'll need to use a little imagination to envision the cathedral part of Red Cathedral, but the way the rocks have fractured and split, it does resemble columns, pilasters, and carvings from a medieval cathedral. When you've had your fill of the view, turn back and head to the parking area.

If you want to extend the hike, take a left on **Gower Gulch Trail,** which passes beneath **Manly Beacon** and offers several vantage points with views of Manly Beacon and the surrounding landscape. Gower Gulch leads 3.1 mi (5 km) back to the Golden Canyon parking area.

DIRECTIONS

Golden Canyon Trail to Red Cathedral is in the Furnace Creek area of Death Valley National Park. From Furnace Creek, head south on Highway 190, also known as the Death Valley Scenic Byway, for 1 mi (1.6 km). Turn right onto Badwater Road; continue driving for about 2 mi (3.2 km) and you'll find the Golden Canyon parking area on your right.

NEED TO KNOW

Info: Furnace Creek Visitor Center, www.nps.gov/deva

Passes and Reservations: Entry into the park is $30/vehicle ($25/motorcycle, $15/pedestrian or cyclist). Passes are available in advance at www.recreation.gov.

Weather Considerations: This park has a fearsome name, and you should take it as a bit of a warning because spring, summer, and early fall temperatures here can be outrageously hot. Plan to visit the park November-March, when temperatures are much more favorable for hiking and exploring.

Facilities: Restrooms are available at the trailhead.

Other: Bring plenty of water or a sports drink and some salty snacks (you'll need to replenish your electrolytes), pack a sun shirt and wide-brimmed hat, and remember your sunscreen. Hiking poles are a great idea in Death Valley as they offer more stability as you traverse loose sand and gravel on trails. If you're going on longer hikes, it's a good idea to pick up a pair of gaiters to keep stones, sand, and scree out of your boots. Cell service is essentially nonexistent in Death Valley, so load up your maps, playlists, and podcasts before you go, and bring your analog gazetteer, road maps, and trail maps (and this guidebook) with you.

BEST NEARBY

The Inn at Death Valley

▶ *Highway 190, Death Valley; 800/236-7916 or 760/786-2345; www.oasisatdeathvalley.com; from $329*

The Inn at Death Valley is something of a surprise, a bit of Hollywood Golden Age glam in the heat and dry of Death Valley. Built in 1927, The Inn at Death Valley—a AAA Four-Diamond Award winner for going on 40 years—is full of charm, has a spring-fed swimming pool surrounded by palm trees, and offers accommodations from rooms and suites to a pool bungalow and a handful of casitas. It's a pricey stay, but this puts you in the heart of the national park (and offers some much-needed air-conditioning) for easy exploration.

▲ HIKERS IN GOLDEN CANYON

▲ RED CATHEDRAL ABOVE GOLDEN CANYON

20

MARBLE CANYON

DEATH VALLEY NATIONAL PARK, CALIFORNIA

This remote, scenic canyon features narrow, winding pathways through polished, multicolored marble walls and striking desert landscapes.

- **Distance:** 3.2-5.6 mi (5.1-9 km) round-trip
- **Duration:** 2-6 hours
- **Elevation Gain:** 445 ft (136 m)
- **Effort:** Moderate
- **When:** Nov.-Mar.
- **Trailhead:** Mouth of Marble Canyon, 13.4 mi (21.6 km) along Cottonwood Canyon Road

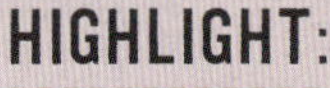

HIGHLIGHT: Exploring the colorful canyon walls of the Second Narrows

A rough, scenic drive into the Cottonwood Mountains pays off in the sculpted narrows and hidden petroglyphs of Marble Canyon. The petroglyphs are plentiful but faint, inspiring full attention to your surroundings. The real highlights are the canyon narrows, twisting in colorful corridors that shoot up to frame small pieces of the sky.

START THE HIKE

The trail is immediately rewarding as it enters the sheer and colorful **narrows;** look for limestone beds with black chert nodules. This first

◀ MARBLE CANYON

▼ PETROGLYPHS IN MARBLE CANYON

section of the trail ends at a **chockstone** wedged between the canyon walls. Some people turn around here, but the **second narrows**—the most spectacular on this hike—lie just beyond this easily passable barrier. Bypass the chockstone with a trail on the right to head into the second narrows. They are deep, twisting, polished, and impressive. The sculpted high walls keep the passage cool and dim even in the heat of the day. The **third narrows** start in another 2.4 mi (3.9 km), after a walk through the mid-canyon. They're less impressive than the first two, but they have walls of polished black-and-white marble.

If you drove to the canyon mouth, a hike through the second narrows is easy and will take an hour or two; it's a simple day hike. Add another 3-4 hours of hiking if you parked before the wash (it is 4.8 mi/7.7 km to the canyon mouth).

DIRECTIONS

Marble Canyon is in the Stovepipe Wells area of Death Valley National Park. The drive to the canyon is half the fun, or half the battle, depending on your vehicle. From Stovepipe Wells Village, head north on Highway 190 for about 10 mi (16.1 km). Look for the Stovepipe Wells Landing Strip and turn right on Cottonwood Canyon Road, an unpaved dirt road. The road starts off with a bang, spitting through sand. Eventually the ground becomes more solid, but the road is washboard with some gravel near the end of this stretch.

At the 8.6-mi (13.8-km) mark, the road enters the Cottonwood Canyon wash and becomes much rougher. A 4WD vehicle is recommended past this point. If you continue driving, there are many places to turn around if needed. At 10.8 mi (17.4 km), the road splits off toward Cottonwood Canyon; stay right to continue to Marble Canyon. The road is marked with a very faint sign that is easy to miss. At 13.4 mi (21.6 km), the road ends at the canyon mouth.

NEED TO KNOW

Info: Furnace Creek Visitor Center, www.nps.gov/deva

Passes and Reservations: Entry into the park is $30/vehicle ($25/motorcycle, $15/pedestrian or cyclist). Passes are available in advance at www.recreation.gov.

Weather Considerations: This park has a fearsome name, and you should take it as a bit of a warning because spring, summer, and early fall temperatures here can be outrageously hot. Plan to visit the park November-March, when temperatures are much more favorable for hiking and exploring.

Facilities: None at the trailhead. The nearest restrooms are at Stovepipe Wells Village 13.1 mi (21.1 km) east.

Other: Bring plenty of water or a sports drink and some salty snacks (you'll need to replenish your electrolytes), pack a sun shirt and wide-brimmed hat, and remember your sunscreen. Hiking poles are a great idea in Death Valley as they offer more stability as you traverse loose sand and gravel on trails. If you're going on longer hikes, it's a good idea to pick up a pair of gaiters to keep stones, sand, and scree out of your boots. Cell service is essentially nonexistent in Death Valley, so load up your maps, playlists, and podcasts before you go, and bring your analog gazetteer, road maps, and trail maps (and this guidebook) with you.

BEST NEARBY

Mesquite Flat Sand Dunes

▶ *2 mi (3.2 km) east of Stovepipe Wells; year-round; free*

The Mesquite Flat Sand Dunes are iconic to Death Valley and are the most popular sight in the park. In order to form, dunes require wind, sand, and a place for the sand to collect. These three things exist in spades in this austere section of the park, just east of the village of Stovepipe Wells. The sculpted dunes are visible from Stovepipe Wells and beyond, rising out of the desert floor to catch the light of the sky in smooth, unbroken crests and lines. Such is the power of the dunes that they seem to draw people from miles around, and you'll find that lots of other people are here to enjoy these vast expanses. The simplicity of the dunes provides a rich experience where you can hike, run in the sand, admire the ripples of the wind, or look for tiny animal tracks. From Stovepipe Wells, drive 2 mi (3.2 km) east on Highway 190 and look for a signed parking area. From here it's less than 0.5 mi (0.8 km) to the base of the dunes.

▲ HIKING IN MARBLE CANYON

21

TELESCOPE PEAK

DEATH VALLEY NATIONAL PARK, CALIFORNIA

Summit the park's highest peak and catch a glimpse of the lowest point in the hemisphere (Badwater Basin) and highest mountain in the Lower 48 (Mount Whitney) on this overnight adventure.

- **Distance:** 14 mi (22.5 km) round-trip
- **Duration:** 7-9 hours
- **Elevation Gain:** 2,929 ft (893 m)
- **Effort:** Strenuous
- **When:** Late spring, May-June
- **Trailhead:** Mahogany Flat Campground

HIGHLIGHT: Summiting Death Valley's highest peak for breathtaking views of Badwater Basin

You can't miss Telescope Peak (11,049 ft/3,368 m), the highest mountain in Death Valley. Any time you have a westward view, this snowcapped peak is there, rising above the rest of the range and looking down on Badwater Basin, the lowest point in North America. To get to the summit you're in for a 14-mi (22.5-km) round-trip hike that's worth every step, switchback, and night you spend under the stars. And you should plan to camp here: at least one night at the trailhead or nearby (to acclimate to the altitude and take advantage of the incredible stargazing), and at least one night at Arcane Meadows only 2 mi (3.2 km) into the hike. Nearly every step of the way, this hike gives you monumental views of Death Valley to the east, the Panamint Valley (and Mount Whitney) to the west, and, at times, both valleys at once.

▲ STARGAZING IN DEATH VALLEY

START THE HIKE

The trail is straightforward: Leave **Mahogany Flat Campground** and 7 mi (11.3 km) later you're at the summit of Telescope Peak. But the hike is more than that. You begin in a forest of pinyon pine, juniper, and mahogany, then the hike opens into a subalpine

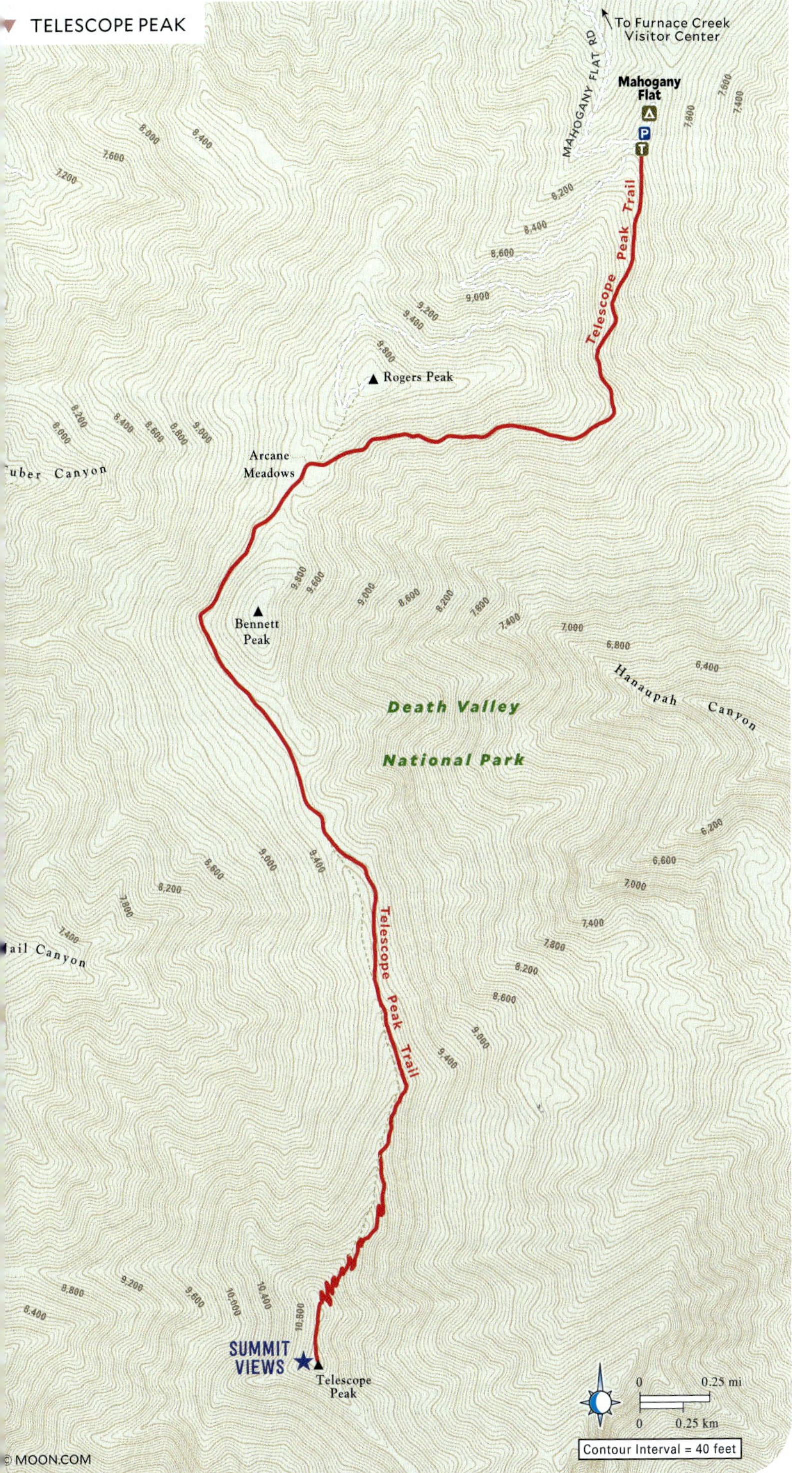
To Furnace Creek
Visitor Center
MAHOGANY FLAT RD
Mahogany
Flat
Telescope Peak Trail
Rogers Peak
Arcane
Meadows
Tuber Canyon
Bennett
Peak
Death Valley
National Park
Hanaupah Canyon
Tail Canyon
Telescope Peak Trail
SUMMIT
VIEWS
Telescope
Peak
0
0.25 mi
0
0.25 km
Contour Interval = 40 feet

environment, swings around **Rogers Peak** (named for John Rogers, partner of William Lewis Manly, who together led a party of gold rush 49ers bound for San Francisco into the valley in 1848; their experiences here lent the place its name: Death Valley) and slowly gains elevation until you reach **Arcane Meadows,** a windswept flat where many hikers camp for the night. From here, it's a straight (well, with a few switchbacks) shot to the summit, and you'll see Telescope Peak growing larger and closer with every step.

At Arcane Meadows, on the ridgeline section of trail, and from the summit of Rogers Peak (accessed via a 0.3-mi/0.5-km spur trail) you'll have sweeping views of **Tuber** and **Jail Canyons** to the west and the three forks of **Hanaupah Canyon** to the east.

Around 4 mi (6.4 km) in, the hike begins to climb more steeply; the last mile (1.6 km) of the hike is all switchbacks. The landscape up here is windswept, rocky, and barren. A few bristlecone pines (they're improbably old) stand on the mountainside above the tree line, and other plants are scrubby, ground-hugging growers. The view from the **summit** is breathtaking. Death Valley—from the salt flats at Badwater to the distant Sierra Nevada—puts on a great show from this vantage point. If you're like me—coming to Death Valley from sea level or a similarly low elevation—you might find the lack of oxygen at this altitude taxing and breathtaking in its own right. Just go slow, stay hydrated and full of electrolytes, and monitor how you feel. Relax and soak up the view from the summit when you arrive.

When you're ready to leave, just turn around and head back the way you came.

DIRECTIONS

Telescope Peak is the highest point within Death Valley National Park. From Stovepipe Wells Village, head west on Highway 190 for about 9 mi (14.5 km), then turn left onto Emigrant Canyon Road. Follow Emigrant Canyon Road 20 mi (32 km) to Charcoal Kilns/Wood Canyon Road, which

BEST NEARBY

Death Valley Dark Sky Festival

▶ *Various locations throughout the park; early Mar.*

When you're in a national park this big, this isolated, and with a peak named "Telescope," stargazing is a must. Go outside at night (and hide the light pollution from distant Las Vegas behind any obstacle) and you'll have a jaw-dropping view of the stars, Milky Way, orbiting satellites, and meteors any day of the year. But in early March, NASA's Goddard Space Flight Center, Jet Propulsion Laboratory, Ames Research Center SETI (Search for Extra-Terrestrial Intelligence), California Institute of Technology, park rangers, and the Death Valley Natural History Association combine their knowledge and expertise to deliver a weekend packed with talks, stargazing, astrophotography meetups, nighttime walks, and more at locations across the park.

▲ TRAIL TO TELESCOPE PEAK

terminates at the Mahogany Flat Campground, where the Telescope Peak trail begins.

A high-clearance or 4WD vehicle is recommended on the final 1.5 mi (2.4 km) of the road. Note that in the event of extreme flooding, Charcoal Kilns Road or other roads and highways leading to the trailhead may be closed for short or long stretches. As of this writing, the route to Wildrose Campground (8.8 mi/14.2 km from the trailhead) was open, but the last 8.8 mi (14.2 km) to Mahogany Flat and this trailhead was closed pending road repairs. Be sure to check www.nps.gov/deva for road and trail closures before you make the trek from the valley floor to this near-alpine trailhead.

NEED TO KNOW

Info: Furnace Creek Visitor Center, www.nps.gov/deva

Passes and Reservations: Entry into the park is $30/vehicle ($25/motorcycle, $15/pedestrian or cyclist). Passes are available in advance at www.recreation.gov.

Weather Considerations: This park has a fearsome name, and you should take it as a bit of a warning because spring, summer, and early fall temperatures here can be outrageously hot. Because you'll be hiking and camping at elevation—staying at Mahogany Flat Campground for the hike to Telescope Peak—the best season is late spring, May-June. However, if you're not heading to high elevation, plan to visit the park November-March, when temperatures are much more favorable for hiking and exploring.

Facilities: Seasonal vault toilets are available at the trailhead and Mahogany Flat Campground, but no potable water. There are no facilities at Arcane Meadows.

Other: Bring plenty of water or a sports drink and some salty snacks (you'll need to replenish your electrolytes), pack a sun shirt and wide-brimmed hat, and remember your sunscreen. Hiking poles are a great idea in Death Valley as they offer more stability as you traverse loose sand and gravel on trails. If you're going on longer hikes, it's a good idea to pick up a pair of gaiters to keep stones, sand, and scree out of your boots. Cell service is essentially nonexistent in Death Valley, so load up your maps, playlists, and podcasts before you go, and bring your analog gazetteer, road maps, and trail maps (and this guidebook) with you.

22

BARKER DAM

JOSHUA TREE NATIONAL PARK, CALIFORNIA

This hike weaves through sandy washes, over boulders, and to a dam and even some petroglyphs.

- **Distance:** 1.3 mi (2.1 km) round-trip
- **Duration:** 30 minutes
- **Elevation Gain:** Negligible
- **Effort:** Easy
- **When:** Oct.-May
- **Trailhead:** Barker Dam Loop Trailhead

HIGHLIGHT: Watching for wildlife at Barker Dam

A fantastic introduction to the landscape and the human history of Joshua Tree National Park, Barker Dam, on the southern edge of the Wonderland of Rocks, has it all: desert landscapes, the namesake Joshua trees, cacti (many in bloom during spring months), a man-made dam and pond, critters from birds to (maybe) bighorn sheep, petroglyphs, and plenty of boulder-able rocks. This 30-minute jaunt into the desert will get you excited for more hikes and more exploration in this beautiful, sandy park.

◀ PETROGLYPHS

▼ GREATER YELLOWLEGS AT BARKER DAM

START THE HIKE

From the **parking area,** take the trail to the left, marked **Barker Dam Loop,** and head into the desert. There are several short spur trails that lead to nearby rock formations and boulders where you're likely to see rock climbers and the chalky paths they and others have taken up, over, and around the rocks. Feel free to detour and check out the rocks, but return to the main trail when you're done. At 0.2 mi (0.3 km) there's a four-way intersection. Proceed straight. To the right is the return from a climber-friendly rock to the right, left is the return path, and straight ahead is your destination.

Very soon after the junction you'll reach the hike's **high point.** It's not very high, but it does require some scrambling. If you're new to rock scrambling, be careful of your footing, take a look at your handholds before you grab them (you don't want to grab a snake), and take your time. You'll find the pond and **Barker Dam** at the 0.4-mi (0.6-km) mark. Native Americans, such as members from the Chemehuevi, Serrano, and Cahuilla Indians, had trails in the desert that connected watering holes, springs, and natural "tanks" like the one here, where ranchers eventually dammed the natural pond to ensure water for their cattle. Water levels in the pond vary from full or overflowing (when there's been a recent rain) to bone dry, but the water, even if there's very little, draws plenty of desert critters. Take a look in the soft sand near the water's edge and you could see tracks from lizards, kangaroo rats, pocket gophers, antelope ground squirrels, and birds. If you're very lucky, very quiet, and very observant, you may even see bighorn sheep drinking at the water's edge. Explore the pond, look for wildlife, take a few shots of the rocks and sky reflecting in the still water, and then move on (it's dark enough here to take some interesting night or astrophotography shots, so if that's your thing, plan accordingly).

In 0.3 mi (0.5 km) from the dam, you'll reach a point with two trail junctions. These trails both lead to Barker Dam Trail and a distant parking lot. Since we're on Barker Dam Loop, skip right past them and proceed around the loop. At 0.9 mi (1.5 km) the trail makes a hairpin turn and meets Barker Dam Trail again. Go a few paces down Barker Dam Trail and you'll find some **petroglyphs.** Check them out, taking only pictures, and return to the trail, which leads to the parking area. You'll reach that four-way junction and proceed right to get to the trailhead. If you go straight here, no big deal; the path will approach a big rock and curve around to meet Barker Dam Loop near the parking area.

DIRECTIONS

Barker Dam is in the central area of Joshua Tree National Park. From Twentynine Palms, head south on Utah Trail, then turn right onto Highway 62 (Twentynine Palms Highway) and continue west for about 4 mi (6.4 km). Turn left onto Park Boulevard, and after approximately 3 mi (4.8 km), turn left into the Barker Dam parking area.

NEED TO KNOW

Info: Joshua Tree Visitor Center, www.nps.gov/jotr

BEST NEARBY

Wall Street Mill

At the Barker Dam Loop Trailhead there's a second trail to the right, on the northeastern side of the parking area. This leads to Wall Street Mill (1.8 mi/2.9 km rt; 30 minutes), a historic site where gold from local mining operations was processed. There's only a little elevation gain (75 ft/23 m), a bit of rock scrambling, and plenty of Joshua trees and interesting rock formations all along this hike. You'll likely see rock climbers on the trail or nearby clinging to rocks. But the draw here isn't the namesake Joshua tree or the climbers, but the more recent human history. Soon into the hike you'll pass a windmill and water pump, an abandoned car now rust-eaten, and the ruins of a house here at the Wonderland Ranch. At the end of the trail there's a trailside tombstone/handmade historical marker and the remains of the mill site. Explore—but safely and responsibly—and take your pictures, then reverse course and head back to the parking area.

Passes and Reservations: Entry into the park is $30/vehicle ($25/motorcycle, $15/pedestrian or cyclist). Passes are available in advance at www.recreation.gov.

Weather Considerations: The best times of year to visit are fall through spring. In fall and spring, you have blooming cacti and the rare desert wildflower, and in winter you have migratory birds visiting the park, especially Barker Dam. Summers get hot, regularly exceeding 100°F (37.7°C) and "cooling" to around 75°F (23.8°C). Rain is unpredictable and infrequent. If you're going to hike in summer, get an early start (before 9am) and bring additional water as well as salty snacks and sun protection.

Facilities: Restrooms are available at the trailhead but no potable water; be sure to bring at least 1 quart or liter per person per hour on the trail.

▼ BARKER DAM

23

FORTYNINE PALMS OASIS TRAIL

JOSHUA TREE NATIONAL PARK, CALIFORNIA

Hike through dry washes, rolling desert terrain, and ridgelines heavy with barrel cactus to reach this pristine fan palm oasis tucked away in a rocky canyon.

- **Distance:** 3 mi (4.8 km) round-trip
- **Duration:** 2-3 hours
- **Elevation Gain:** 636 ft (194 m)
- **Effort:** Moderate
- **When:** Nov.-Apr.
- **Trailhead:** Parking area at the end of Canyon Road

HIGHLIGHT: Enjoying the shaded retreat of Fortynine Palms Oasis, with natural pools and vibrant flora

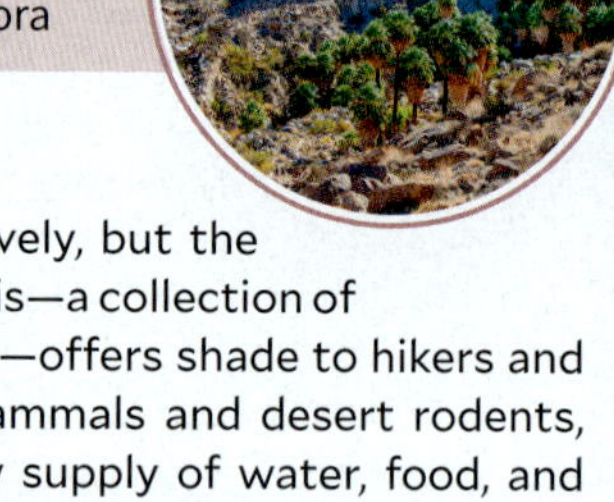

The trail into Fortynine Palms Oasis is lovely, but the destination is positively striking. The oasis—a collection of native fan palms growing in a rocky canyon—offers shade to hikers and wildlife, and gives wildlife—birds, small mammals and desert rodents, even coyotes and bighorn sheep—a steady supply of water, food, and shelter. The hike isn't too difficult, but warmer weather makes it more challenging, so avoid this trail in summer months.

▲ BARREL CACTUS AND WILDFLOWERS ALONG FORTYNINE PALMS OASIS TRAIL

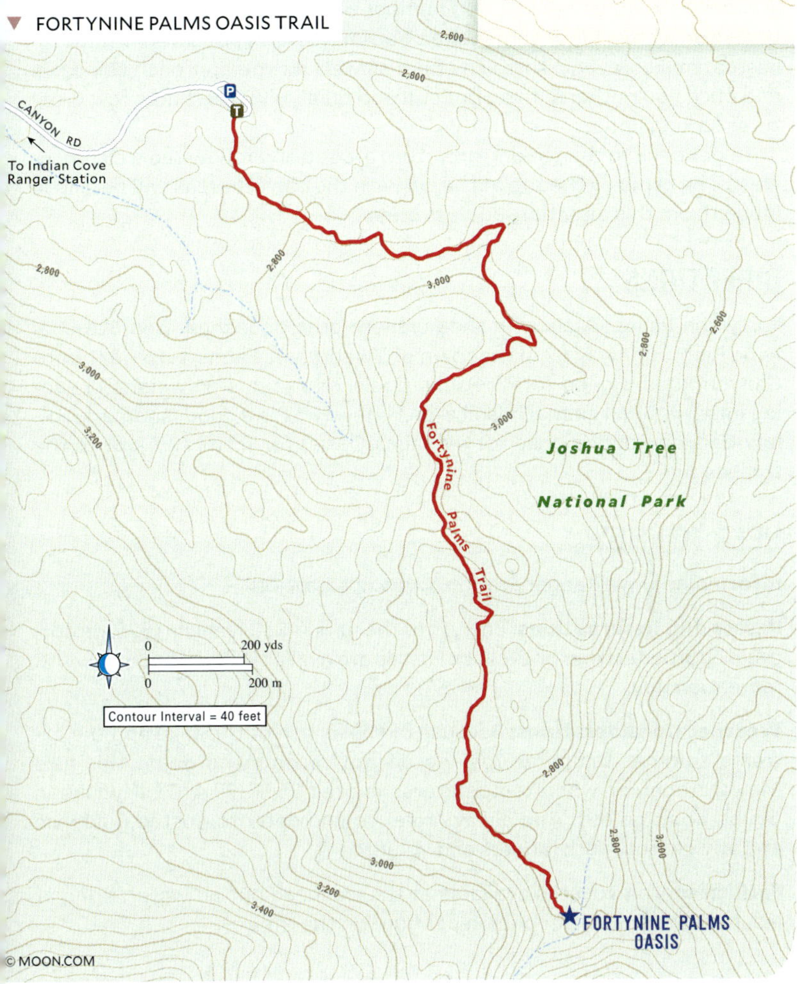

START THE HIKE

The trail climbs immediately from the **parking area,** winding its way through washes to the flanks of the hills and to a ridgeline thick with barrel cactus (they bloom in spring and are quite the sight then), and from here it's a steady descent into the oasis. From the ridge you'll notice the oasis—it sort of stands out in this landscape—building the excitement of getting there.

Joshua Tree has five fan palm oases, and there are only 158 fan palm oases in all of North America, making this destination something of a rarity. Clearly this is a special place, and when you're standing there looking up at the palm trees, you'll be wowed. Historically, the Cahuilla Indians visited the oasis with great frequency. Today hikers and wildlife are the primary visitors. Bighorn sheep like the waters from the cool spring and the relative buffet of vegetation nearby. Coyotes, small mammals and desert rodents, and a good number of migratory and resident birds come for water, food, and shelter. You may even spot a few reptiles—lizards, snakes, even a tortoise—here as well. As you approach **the oasis** and once you're there, if you get still and quiet, you may find a few creatures lurking about.

To get back to the parking area, turn around and follow the trail northwest. The climb to the top of the hill with the barrel cactus will be a little longer from this direction, but less steep.

DIRECTIONS

Fortynine Palms Oasis is in the northern area of Joshua Tree National Park. From Highway 62 in the town of Twentynine Palms, turn right onto Canyon Road, signed for 49 Palms Oasis. (Note: It is only signed heading east.) A small animal hospital on Highway 62 is a good landmark. Follow Canyon Road (signed for 49 Palms Oasis) for 1.7 mi (2.7 km) to the trailhead.

NEED TO KNOW

Info: Indian Cove Ranger Station, www.nps.gov/jotr

Passes and Reservations: Entry into the park is $30/vehicle ($25/motorcycle, $15/pedestrian or cyclist). Passes are available in advance at www.recreation.gov.

Weather Considerations: Because of the length of this hike and the extreme summer temperatures, we do not recommend doing this hike May-October, or when temperatures exceed 85°F (29.4°C). If you're in doubt, don't go out. And always refer to and defer to posted guidance and advice from park rangers and volunteers.

Facilities: A pit toilet is available at the trailhead but no water; bring at least 1 quart or liter per person per hour on the trail.

BEST NEARBY

Crossroads Cafe

▶ *61715 Twentynine Palms Hwy. (Hwy. 62), Joshua Tree; 760/366-5414; www.crossroadscafejtree.com; 7am-9pm daily; $10-17*

Serving breakfast until 1:30pm every day and offering a great mix of burgers, tacos, sandwiches, and salads, Crossroads Cafe is a great Southern California spin on the diner. It looks just right—weathered wood, rusted steel, and desert imagery everywhere—whether you're there for a pre-hike pancake stack, a post-hike taco, or a cup of coffee and a slice of apple pie.

▲ FAN PALMS AT FORTYNINE PALMS OASIS

▲ NIGHT SKY IN JOSHUA TREE NATIONAL PARK

24

LOST PALMS OASIS TRAIL

JOSHUA TREE NATIONAL PARK, CALIFORNIA

This trail undulates through striking desert scenery before dropping down to a secluded canyon and the largest collection of fan palms in the park.

- **Distance:** 7.4 mi (11.9 km) round-trip
- **Duration:** 4-6 hours
- **Elevation Gain:** 1,047 ft (319 m)
- **Effort:** Moderate
- **When:** Nov.-Apr.
- **Trailhead:** Cottonwood Spring/ Palm Oasis parking area

HIGHLIGHT:

Taking in the most stunning collection of California fan palms at Lost Palms Oasis

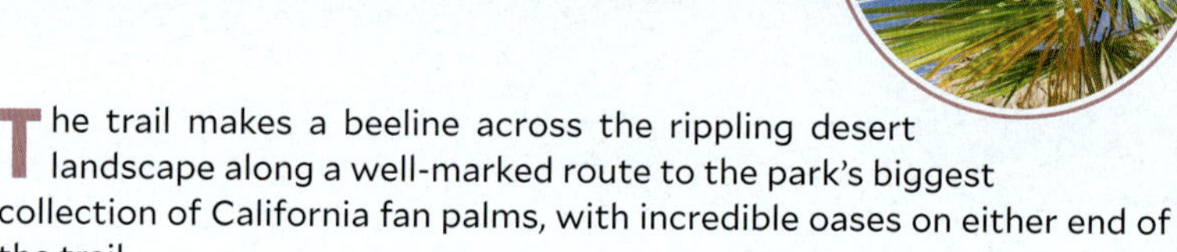
The trail makes a beeline across the rippling desert landscape along a well-marked route to the park's biggest collection of California fan palms, with incredible oases on either end of the trail.

▲ LOST PALMS OASIS

START THE HIKE

Begin at the **Cottonwood Spring/Palm Oasis parking area** where you'll join the trail at the southeastern corner of the lot. This parking area can get crowded, so for the best chance at grabbing a spot—and the best chances to see and hear wildlife—arrive pre-dawn for an early hike in cooler temperatures.

In the parking area, check out **Cottonwood Spring Oasis** for a preview of Lost Palms. Insects, birds, and an interesting array of desert plants make good use of the water, and there's even more at Lost Palms. Once you take a look at this oasis, hit the trail. As you hike, the trail will have some ups and downs, but nothing steep or strenuous (the most difficult things about this hike are the distance and, at certain times, hot temperatures). The trail passes through a series of washes and ridges that contain intriguing desert gardens where barrel cacti, ocotillos, and desert willows grow. In spring you'll find a few blooms here—the rare desert wildflower, but more commonly cactus blossoms. Look for animal tracks on the trail as you hike in.

As you hike, the trail will creep along the foothills of the **Eagle Mountains** before finally depositing you on an overlook with views of a steep canyon and **Lost Palms Oasis,** secreted away in a fold on the rugged canyon hillside. When you see where it is, you'll note how apt the name Lost Palms Oasis is. Try to keep the noise down as you approach and you may see larger mammals like coyotes or bighorn sheep in and among the trees or on nearby game trails and slopes.

You have a short scramble—100-150 yd (91-137 m) or so—over a steep trail to the canyon floor, littered with boulders and palms. Make your way to Lost Palms Oasis for a welcome dose of shade and the chance to spy on some birds and other creatures. When you're done, reverse course and follow the trail back to Cottonwood Spring Oasis.

DIRECTIONS

Lost Palms Oasis is in the Cottonwood Spring area of Joshua Tree National Park. From Indio, take I-10 east for 23.7 mi (38 km). Take exit 168 and turn left on Cottonwood Spring Road; continue on this road until it dead-ends at the Cottonwood Spring/Palm Oasis parking area.

NEED TO KNOW

Info: Cottonwood Visitor Center, www.nps.gov/jotr

Passes and Reservations: Entry into the park is $30/vehicle ($25/motorcycle, $15/pedestrian or cyclist). Passes are available in advance at www.recreation.gov.

Weather Considerations: Because of the length of this hike and the extreme summer temperatures, we do not recommend doing this hike May-October, or when temperatures exceed 85°F (29.4°C). If you're in doubt, don't go out. And always refer to and defer to posted guidance and advice from park rangers and volunteers.

Facilities: A pit toilet is available at the trailhead but no water; bring at least 1 quart or liter per person per hour on the trail.

BEST NEARBY

Cottonwood Campground

▶ *Pinto Basin Road, Cottonwood Springs; 760/367-3001; www.recreation.gov or www.nps.gov/jotr; Sept.-June, closed for high temperatures June-Sept.; $25*

Cottonwood Campground has 62 sites with 3 designated for groups. There are potable water and flush toilets available, but no showers or camp store. In addition to putting you close to this and several other trailheads, staying in the national park has a real advantage: the chance to make stargazing and sunrise/sunset viewing simple. Visit during a meteor shower, an eclipse, or another celestial event and you'll find the park full of folks there for the star show.

▲ FAN PALMS IN LOST PALMS OASIS

25

BUMPASS HELL TRAIL

LASSEN VOLCANIC NATIONAL PARK, CALIFORNIA

Hike to an active geothermal wonderland of superheated fumaroles, thumping mud pots, billowing steam, and boiling acidic pools.

- **Distance:** 3.2 mi (5.1 km) round-trip
- **Duration:** 2 hours
- **Elevation Gain:** 518 ft (158 m)
- **Effort:** Easy
- **When:** June-Oct.
- **Trailhead:** Bumpass Hell Trailhead

HIGHLIGHT: Looping around the bubbling landscape of Bumpass Hell

This primordial landscape is at the heart of the park's most active hydrothermal area. It's a place of unexpected colors in the water and soil, steaming and boiling water, thumping mud pots, and steam vents. Stick to the trail and boardwalks and enjoy the wild color palette and multi-sensory experience of Bumpass Hell.

▲ FUMAROLES AND YELLOW SULFUR CRYSTALS AT BUMPASS HELL

START THE HIKE

The trail begins at the large sign adjacent to the **parking area entrance.** For the first mile (1.6 km), you're in a thick hemlock forest where there are more hemlocks per square acre than you'll find almost anywhere. At 0.5 mi (0.8 km) an **overlook** on the right opens to reveal an impressive set of volcanoes, and signage gives you the story and names the peaks. You'll see Mount Conard, Diamond Peak, Brokeoff Mountain, Mount Diller, and Pilot Pinnacle, all part of the ancient Mount Tehama, a volcano that dwarfed Lassen Peak at 4 mi (6.4 km) across and 11,000 ft (3,353 m) high. Lassen Peak was formed from Mount Tehama's lava flows.

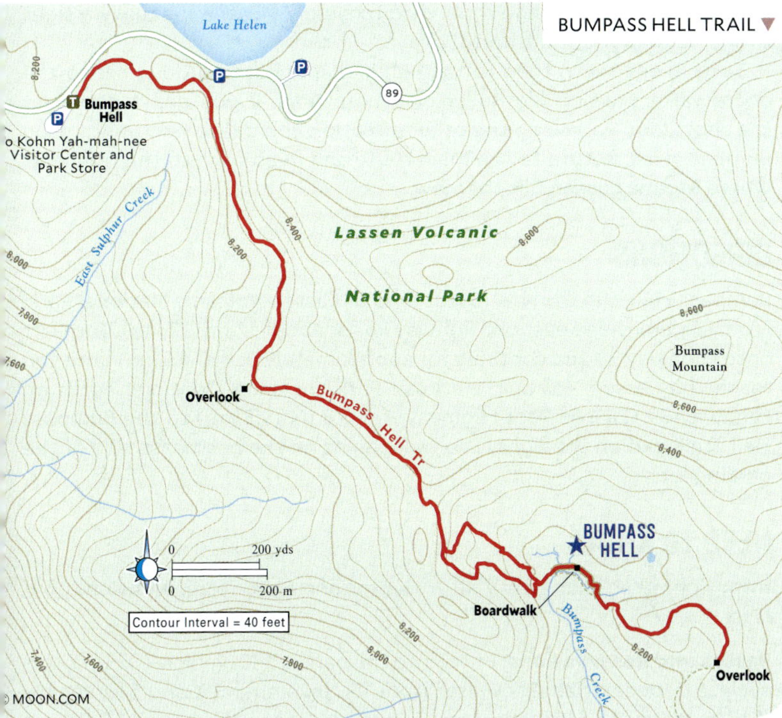

The trail makes its way uphill on a gentle incline, and at 1 mi (1.6 km) in, you're at the highest point and directly above your destination: **Bumpass Hell.** Here the trail descends 200 ft (61 m) along a white, chalky trail (it reminds me of chalk dust, but I'm a former teacher, so no surprise there). This soft, powdery dust is what remains of volcanic rock after steam and sulfuric acid have broken it down. In addition to the chalky trail, you'll find the distinct aroma of hydrogen sulfide—sulfur—making quite the impression.

In just a moment you'll reach a junction where a short loop leads you around geothermal features. Go either direction and explore as you will. It's a mind-bending, otherworldly landscape of steaming turquoise pools, a milky gray creek winding through the valley, and clay minerals leaving a palette of yellow, orange, and red staining the otherwise barren rock.

A network of boardwalks lets you get closer than otherwise possible to the boiling, bubbling landscape, and as this place is bubbling, boiling, steaming, and acid-filled, mind the warning signs that direct you to stay on the path. This 16-acre (6.5-ha) basin has 75 major fumaroles, acid-sulfate hot springs (great for looking at, but not so great for a dip, so obey those signs), and mud pots that thump and thunder as they boil. One of the coolest features is the Big Boiler, Lassen's largest super-heated fumarole where high-velocity steam has hit temperatures of 322°F (161°C).

At the far end of the boardwalk, ascend to a high overlook on the basin's southeast side for a panoramic view of the colorful basin. Depending on the light conditions during your visit, the pyrite pools could range from a dull to brilliant turquoise, and the orange and yellow hues of sulfur and other elements range from vivid to simply vibrant. It's really a sight to see, so take your time here.

Take in the view, then retrace your steps, heading downhill to the boardwalks, passing Big Boiler one more time. If you didn't complete the short loop earlier, go the other direction and gain a new vantage on Bumpass Hell. Return to the main route and head back to the trailhead, where **Mount Lassen** fills the view.

DIRECTIONS

Bumpass Hell is in the southwest area of Lassen Volcanic National Park. From Mineral, head east on Highway 36 for about 17 mi (27 km). Turn left onto Highway 89 and continue for approximately 9 mi (14.5 km) until you reach the Lassen Volcanic National Park entrance. Continue north on Highway 89 (Lassen Park Highway) for 5.8 mi (9.3 km) to the Bumpass Hell Trailhead on the right. The trail begins on the northeast side of the parking lot.

NEED TO KNOW

Info: Kohm Yah-mah-nee Visitor Center and Park Store, www.nps.gov/lavo

Passes and Reservations: Entry into the park is $30/vehicle ($25/motorcycle, $15/pedestrian or cyclist) April 15-November 30, and $10/vehicle ($10/motorcycle, $10/pedestrian or cyclist) December 1-April 14. Passes are available in advance at www.recreation.gov.

Weather Considerations: Lassen Volcanic National Park sees significant snowfall November-May, which can close roads and impact the availability of camping and park services. The park is busiest June-October, when the weather is best and the full suite of park facilities are open. Most of the park is open April-June and October-November, but facilities at higher elevations may be unavailable.

Facilities: Vault toilets are available at the trailhead but no potable water.

BEST NEARBY

Lake Helen

▶ *0.4 mi (0.6 km) east of Bumpass Hell parking area on Lassen Peak Hwy./Hwy. 89*

Two minutes east of Bumpass Hell, Lake Helen sits at the base of Lassen Peak, making for a gorgeous view and offering some fantastic photo opportunities. This deep, intensely blue lake has one of the best views in the park (and it's easy to reach), with reflections of Mount Lassen making it all the more lovely. There's a picnic area (with toilets but no drinking water) on the southeastern corner near the parking area (so pack a cooler and enjoy a bite al fresco), and during summer you can swim in the cool (ok, cold) water along the southern shore.

▲ BUMPASS HELL

26

LASSEN PEAK

LASSEN VOLCANIC NATIONAL PARK, CALIFORNIA

A remarkably well-graded trail leads to the 10,457-ft (3,187-m) summit of Lassen Peak, the world's largest plug dome volcano.

- **Distance:** 4.8 mi (7.7 km) round-trip
- **Duration:** 4-5 hours
- **Elevation Gain:** 1,867 ft (569 m)
- **Effort:** Moderate-strenuous
- **When:** June-Sept.
- **Trailhead:** Lassen Peak Trailhead

HIGHLIGHT: Enjoying the view from Lassen's crater

The centerpiece of Lassen Volcanic National Park is Lassen Peak (10,457 ft/3,187 m), an active volcano and the largest plug dome volcano in the world (a plug dome volcano is one whose primary vent has been blocked by a plug of viscous magma). First protected as a forest preserve, then as a national monument, the decision to name this place a national park came in 1916, after a series of eruptions (starting in 1914 and lasting through 1921) released loads of lava, ash, and gas, destroying several homes and structures and endangering the local populace. In that way, this national park serves to preserve the area for its ongoing natural history and as a safeguard for locals. This hike leads to the summit of Lassen Peak, which, while still active, is safe to visit.

◄ LASSEN PEAK AND PAINTED DUNES

▼ TRAIL TO LASSEN PEAK

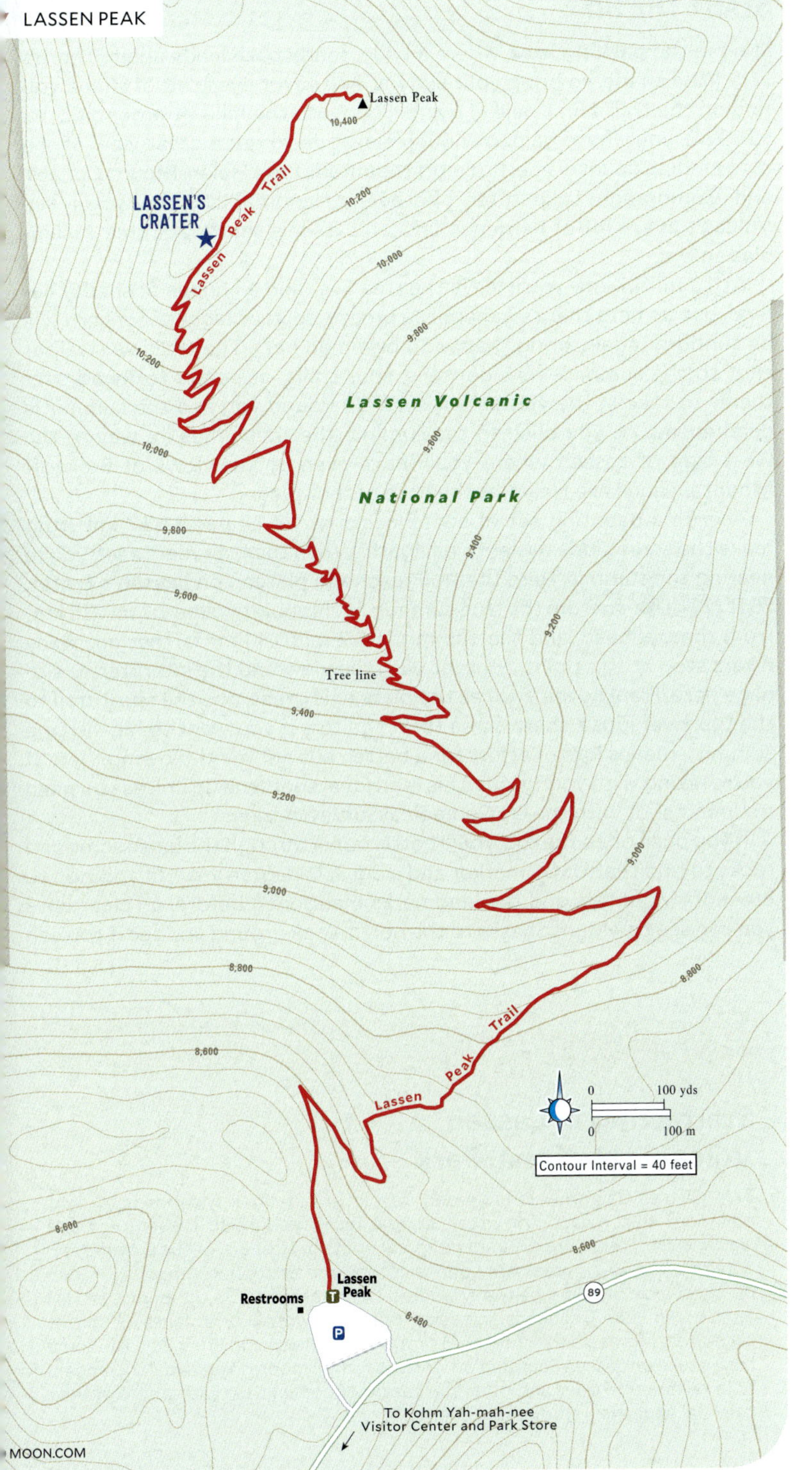

Lassen Peak
10,400
LASSEN'S CRATER
Lassen Peak Trail
10,200
10,000
9,800
Lassen Volcanic National Park
9,600
9,400
9,200
Tree line
9,000
8,800
8,600
Lassen Peak Trail
0
100 yds
100 m
Contour Interval = 40 feet
Lassen Peak
Restrooms
89
8,480
To Kohm Yah-mah-nee Visitor Center and Park Store

START THE HIKE

Start in the **parking area** where a wide, sandy path leads uphill. There's very little shade, so bring your sun hat and savor every bit of shade you find on the trail's first mile (1.6 km). Soon into the hike, at around 0.5 mi (0.8 km), you'll have gained enough elevation to get a great view of the surrounding countryside: Brokeoff Mountain, Lake Helen, Mount Conard, and Cumbraugh Lake offer photogenic landmarks. Soon you'll see Vulcan's Eye, a bit of hardened lava on Lassen's south face that resembles an eye.

At 1.2 mi (1.9 km) you'll leave the tree line (and all hopes of shade) behind, but up here there's generally a breeze, so your biggest concern will be sunburn (again, bring that wide-brimmed hat). The trail is a straight shot to the summit—no side trails, spur trails, or points to "head over there" to take in the view; the view's all around you and the summit is dead ahead. As you push to the summit, the trail winds its way to the west side of Lassen where you'll have even better views of Brokeoff Mountain and Lake Helen, at the base of the volcano.

There's a daunting set of switchbacks at 1.3-1.7 mi (2.1-2.7 km) that make the scree slope easier to navigate. When the trail veers east, you're nearing the summit. Here the trail reaches a plateau on **Lassen's crater,** 75 ft (23 m) or so from the true summit; at this point you're 2.2 mi (3.5 km) from the trailhead, and the summit is 0.2 mi (0.3 km) farther on. Many hikers stop at this point, content with the view and the interpretive signage here. Frankly, the view at the plateau is great, and the short trail to the top, over loose, sharp scree (bring gaiters if you want to hit the true summit), means lots of effort for a better, but not mind-blowing, view. If you're hiking with young kids, this is an ideal spot to stop unless you need a summit shot with the US Geological Survey marker.

If you push on to the top, you'll battle uphill through the loose scree and rocks to find that USGS marker and a big 360-degree view. In addition to Brokeoff Mountain and the landmarks mentioned before, on clear days you can see to Mount Shasta to the north. Look around and see if you can

BEST NEARBY

Stargazing in Lassen Volcanic National Park

This part of California is huge and devoid of big cities with loads of light pollution; this makes for great stargazing. Throughout Lassen Volcanic National Park there are a number of great spots to post up for the evening and admire the stars or break out your telescope and astrophotography kit for an up-close look at some heavenly bodies. Near Lassen Peak, the Bumpass Hell and Lassen Peak Trailheads and spots not far downtrail offer fantastic places for stargazing, as do the shorelines around Lake Helen and Emerald Lake. Some hikers take on Lassen Peak and other trails for full moon hikes, and park rangers hold talks, lead walks, and offer stargazing opportunities (with a side of their celestial expertise) throughout the year.

▲ STARS OVER LASSEN PEAK

note the changes in the landscape indicating the areas most impacted by Lassen's early 20th-century eruptions. If you've spotted the furrowed lines marking the course of mud, snow, and water pouring downhill, you found it. An interesting note about Lassen Peak is that it's California's snowiest, with an average snowfall of 660 in (1,676 cm)—that's 55 ft (16.8 m) of snow annually.

DIRECTIONS

Lassen Peak is in the southwest area of Lassen Volcanic National Park. From Mineral, head east on Highway 36 for about 17 mi (27 km). Turn left onto Highway 89 and continue for approximately 9 mi (14.5 km) until you reach the Lassen Volcanic National Park entrance. Continue north on Highway 89 (Lassen Park Highway) for 6.9 mi (11.1 km) to the Lassen Peak Trailhead, on the left. The trail begins by the large signboard.

NEED TO KNOW

Info: Kohm Yah-mah-nee Visitor Center and Park Store, www.nps.gov/lavo

Passes and Reservations: Entry into the park is $30/vehicle ($25/motorcycle, $15/pedestrian or cyclist) April 15-November 30, and $10/vehicle ($10/motorcycle, $10/pedestrian or cyclist) December 1-April 14. Passes are available in advance at www.recreation.gov.

Weather Considerations: During winter and into spring, when the snowpack is developing and finally receding, there's significant risk of avalanche, so we don't advise a winter summit attempt. In years with heavy snowfall, you may encounter snow on the trail well into summer, so ask park rangers about trail conditions before you set off on your hike.

Facilities: Vault toilets are available at the trailhead but no potable water.

Other: The ascent to Lassen Peak's volcanic summit is deservedly popular. Make sure you're adequately prepared: Start early in the morning to beat the oppressive alpine sun, wear strong sun protection (there's almost no shade along the trail), and carry plenty of water and a few snacks. If you want to beat the crowds, consider hitting the trail at 5am to catch sunrise from the top of this remarkable volcano.

27

TALL TREES GROVE

REDWOOD NATIONAL AND STATE PARKS, CALIFORNIA

In 1963, this redwood grove boasted the world's tallest tree. Taller redwoods have been discovered since, but this grove's awe factor hasn't waned.

- **Distance:** 3.6 mi (5.8 km) round-trip
- **Duration:** 2-3 hours
- **Elevation Gain:** 1,600 ft (488 m)
- **Effort:** Moderate
- **When:** Mar.-Oct.
- **Trailhead:** Tall Trees Grove Trailhead

HIGHLIGHT: Standing among the giants in Tall Trees Grove

Grab an interpretive brochure at the Tall Trees Grove Trailhead and get ready to attack this trail. Or maybe the trail attacks you. In the first 1.5 mi (2.4 km), you'll descend nearly 800 ft (244 m) to the alluvial floodplain of Redwood Creek. If you're doing the trail math you know there's a 1.5-mi (2.4-km) ascent of nearly 800 ft (244 m) waiting for you on the return trip, and that there's not much level terrain on this hike. Don't worry, it's worth every step. The plants are spectacular here, and giant; from the giant coast redwoods to smaller specimens, they tower overhead, as do the Douglas firs, massive rhododendrons, and sword ferns more than 4 ft (1.2 m) tall.

START THE HIKE

From the trailhead, descend and admire the woods. There's no full-grown coast redwoods here, but the other trees are tall and beautiful. When the trail levels out, you're on the alluvial floodplain. Here the trail splits, creating the loop at the end of this lollipop hike (you just hiked the "stick" of the lollipop; now it's time for the sweet part); go left, near the river, and circle **Tall Trees Grove** clockwise.

Check out the creek if you can tear your gaze from the giant trees, or better yet, explore the half-dozen or so spur trails leading to **Redwood Creek.** The grove lives up to its name. These aren't your average trees or even your average very tall trees; these are gargantuan. Dozens of trees exceed 350 ft (107 m), stretching skyward from a sea of ferns and sorrel. Even if you've seen other tall redwoods and giant sequoias, these are breathtaking trees.

TALL TREES GROVE

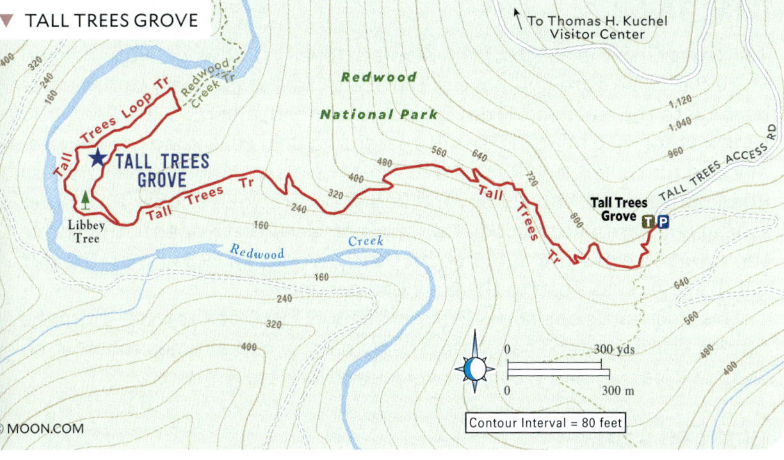

Tall Trees Grove is home to the **Libbey Tree** (found near the start of the loop portion of the hike), once regarded as the world's tallest tree. The 367-ft-tall (112-m) tree graced the cover of National Geographic in July 1964. In 1989, Libbey suffered a loss: A storm removed the top few feet and the tree shrank in size—it's now "only" 362 ft (110 m) or so tall—and dropped from the top spot to number 13 on the list of tallest trees.

At the far eastern end, you enter a grove of maples, very different from the redwoods. Linger here, among the redwoods or on the banks of Redwood Creek as long as you like, then make your way back to the lollipop "stick" and ascend to the parking area.

▲ ROAD TO TALL TREES GROVE

DIRECTIONS

Tall Trees Grove is south of the Klamath River in Redwood National and State Parks. Be sure you have a Tall Trees Trailhead reservation before heading to the trailhead. From Eureka, head north along US 101/Redwood Highway for 42.6 mi (68.6 km). Turn right on Bald Hills Road (not recommended for trailers and RVs). Drive 7 mi (11.3 km) to the Tall Trees Access Road on the right, shortly beyond Redwood Creek Overlook. Turn right, stop at the gate, use the code from your reservation to open it, then drive through and close the gate behind you. Drive 5.8 mi (9.3 km) on the dirt Tall Trees Access Road to the trailhead parking lot.

This trailhead is one hour—including 6 mi (9.7 km) of dirt road—from the nearest visitor center. The road in is curvy, narrow, and, at times, rough, so no RVs, vehicles over 21 ft (6.4 m), or vehicles towing trailers here.

NEED TO KNOW

Info: Thomas H. Kuchel Visitor Center, www.nps.gov/redw

Passes and Reservations: No entrance fee; however, the Park Service limits the number of folks allowed on this trail each day (65 reservations available daily), so you do need to make a Tall Trees reservation if you want to visit. For more information, see page 506.

Weather Considerations: Prepare for rain and cooler temperatures March-May and October-November. Any time of year expect to experience the marine layer fog that hugs the coast of Northern California; at times it can be quite thick, making the view eerie and dampening your clothes.

Facilities: No restrooms or water at the trailhead, but you'll find a vault toilet at the Redwood Creek Overlook (5.4 mi/8.7 km from the trailhead) on Bald Hills Road just before you reach the gate at Tall Trees Access Road.

Other: No dogs are allowed on trails in the contiguous parks system, though dogs (on leash) are permitted in campgrounds and on the beach.

BEST NEARBY

Sue-meg State Park

▶ *4150 Patricks Point Dr., Trinidad; 707/677-3570; www.parks.ca.gov; sunrise-sunset daily*

Sue-meg State Park is a scenic coastal park located in Humboldt County, known for its stunning views of the Pacific Ocean, rugged cliffs, and lush coastal forests. The park features a variety of recreational opportunities, including hiking trails, picnic areas, and access to the beach, making it a perfect spot for wildlife viewing, photography, and enjoying the natural beauty of Northern California's coastline. The area is culturally significant, with a reconstructed Yurok village, offering visitors a glimpse into the rich heritage of the region.

▲ TALL TREES GROVE

28

BIG TREE VIA KARL KNAPP AND CATHEDRAL TREES LOOP

REDWOOD NATIONAL AND STATE PARKS, CALIFORNIA

Wander among impressive groves of coast redwoods, the tallest trees in the world, on this fern-filled trail.

- **Distance:** 2.9 mi (4.7 km) round-trip
- **Duration:** 1-1.5 hours
- **Elevation Gain:** 213 ft (65 m)
- **Effort:** Easy
- **When:** Year-round
- **Trailhead:** Prairie Creek Visitor Center

HIGHLIGHT: Marveling at the humongous Big Tree and redwood groves

It's no wonder George Lucas cast the woods in and around Redwood State and National Park in the role of the Forest Moon of Endor in the Star Wars film franchise. Towering trees, ferns tiny and tall, mist and moss, light filtering through so many layers of leaves it takes on an ethereal quality by the time it reaches the ground—all can make this place feel like another planet. Fortunately, the sound of birdsong and the wonder of nature right here on planet Earth will snap you back to reality and let you enjoy the awesome experience of being surrounded by these majestic trees.

▲ REDWOOD NATIONAL AND STATE PARKS

START THE HIKE

This hike is simple: From the **Prairie Creek Visitor Center,** head north along **Karl Knapp Trail** for 1.1 mi (1.8 km) and turn right at the junction where the path begins to turn east and south. At about 1.3 mi (2.1 km) into the hike you'll arrive at **Big Tree,** the appropriately named big tree—a humongous redwood with a

▼ BIG TREE VIA KARL KNAPP AND CATHEDRAL TREES LOOP

21-ft (6.4-m) diameter—via Foothill and Circle Trails, then continue south along **Cathedral Trees Trail** for 1.4 mi (2.3 km) until you reach the Prairie Creek Visitor Center.

But the hike is more than that. From the trailhead you'll cross a long footbridge over Prairie Creek and enter one of the best redwood groves in the park. Honestly, if all you want is a few minutes immersed in the redwoods, neck craned as you gaze up in an attempt to see the crowns of these trees, you can wrap up your hike in about 10 minutes, but don't; there's more to discover. Karl Knapp Trail is lined with redwoods, and the lush understory—young redwoods, ferns, redwood sorrel—hides another secret: mushrooms and even smaller plants growing beneath. As you hike you'll cross Prairie Creek several times. When you do, check out the water; in autumn coho salmon spawn here, and throughout the year you'll see other creatures in and near the water.

You'll cross the **Newton B. Drury Scenic Parkway** when Karl Knapp Trail hooks back to the south, your indication the Big Tree is nearby. After you head south from Big Tree on Cathedral Trees Trail, the trail gets steeper, climbs to its highest point, and makes a mostly gentle (there is one really steep part) return. The trail is root-filled along this section, which makes you feel like you're in the deep, deep woods, miles from your car, but in reality you're 30 minutes away. When you cross Cal Barrel Road at the 1.8-mi (2.9-km) mark, you'll enter a final grove of huge redwoods before arriving back at the parking area.

DIRECTIONS

Big Tree via Karl Knapp and Cathedral Trees Loop is in Prairie Creek Redwoods State Park, one of the three state parks that make up the "State" part of Redwood National and State Parks. From Eureka, head north along US 101/Redwood Highway for 47.5 mi (76.4 km), then turn left onto the Newton B. Drury Scenic Byway. In 0.2 mi (0.3 km), the Prairie Creek Visitor Center and trailhead are on the left.

NEED TO KNOW

Info: Prairie Creek Visitor Center, www.nps.gov/redw

Passes and Reservations: No entrance fee for Redwood National Park, but there is an $8 day-use fee payable at developed campgrounds and parking areas for Prairie Creek Redwoods State Park. For more information, see page 502.

Weather Considerations: The ocean influence creates a fairly consistent climate on this part of the California coast. November-March see the most rainfall. Bring rain gear to combat the showers and put a layer between you and the heavy coastal fog.

Facilities: At the trailhead you'll find potable water, restrooms with flush toilets, a picnic area, and a gift shop complete with maps, park rangers or volunteer staff, and souvenirs.

Other: No dogs are allowed on trails in the contiguous parks system, though dogs (on leash) are permitted in campgrounds and on the beach.

BEST NEARBY

Trillium Falls Trail

Some rangers call this their favorite short hike in the combined parks, and with a waterfall only 0.5 mi (0.8 km) from the trailhead, plenty of wildflowers (including the trail's namesake trillium) and ferns, and groves of maples and old-growth redwoods, you'll find this moderately difficult trail (2.6 mi/4.2 km rt; 1-1.5 hours; 419 ft/128 m of elevation gain) a delight when paired with the Knapp-Cathedral Loop. Look for Roosevelt elk grazing near the parking area on Davison Road; make the short, steep hike to Trillium Falls (and turn back if you're pressed for time), and continue through the loop to explore more redwoods, pockets of wildflowers, and grassy meadows where you might spy an elk or other wildlife browsing for a meal.

▲ TRILLIUM FALLS

29

JAMES IRVINE AND MINERS RIDGE LOOP

REDWOOD NATIONAL AND STATE PARKS, CALIFORNIA

Wander among venerable redwoods and riffling creeks on this daylong trek to Fern Canyon, where a wealth of waving ferns cling to 50-ft-high (15-m) walls.

- **Distance:** 11.4 mi (18.3 km) round-trip
- **Duration:** 6-7 hours
- **Elevation change:** 1,483 ft (452 m)
- **Effort:** Moderate-strenuous
- **When:** May-Sept.
- **Trailhead:** Prairie Creek Visitor Center

HIGHLIGHT: Getting lost in Fern Canyon

For the first mile of this trail the forest is a mossy collection of maples slowly giving way to the redwood forest. Moss is everywhere (frankly, this hike is a moss- and fern-lover's dream)—covering rocks, growing on trees, dangling from branches—and redwood sorrel runs rampant. Importantly, the trees keep getting bigger. If you're here in fall, winter, or spring, look for mushrooms and the huge banana slugs on the forest floor. Though this hike is already long, clocking in at around six hours for fast hikers, you can turn it into a true daylong adventure, as the trails here cut through redwood

◀ JAMES IRVINE AND MINERS RIDGE LOOP

▼ GOLD BLUFFS BEACH

groves, onto the beach, through a fern-draped gully, and back into this primeval-looking forest.

START THE HIKE

The trail begins at the **Prairie Creek Visitor Center** where you'll start off on the **Karl Knapp Trail.** At 0.1 mi (0.2 km), Knapp splits off to the right and you join the **Nature Trail** on the left for 0.1 mi (0.2 km). Cross **Godwood Creek** on a small bridge and turn right onto James Irvine Trail. In 0.6 mi (1 km), take the switchbacks to the point where Irvine branches off to the right and your trail, **Miners Ridge Trail,** follows the left fork.

Press on along Miners Ridge, even though the forest grows thick and dim (to me, something like Fangorn Forest from *The Lord of the Rings),* listening for the call of the varied thrush, a common bird in this part of the park. The trail will narrow, climb a little, then open up to an area where there are giant (no surprise) huckleberry trees, at times thick as hedgerows, beside the trail. You'll note that the intermittent road noise from US 101 falls away here, giving you more of a sense of solitude and wildness. Carry on west along the trail, passing Clintonia Trail (on your right), and soon the forest will grow close and dim again and you'll hear the pounding surf in the background. You'll be shocked to abruptly leave the thick forest and enter an area that was logged; here the second-growth timber is growing nicely, but it's still a surprise when you've been surrounded by old-growth forest. On the other side of this area, you enter a spruce forest, descend through the evergreens, and emerge at a gravel road. Turn left to the **campground** and cut through it to **Gold Bluffs Beach.**

Walk north on Gold Bluffs Beach (which was mined for gold from around 1850 to 1920 or so) for a little more than 1 mi (1.6 km), hopefully seeing some elk on the shore, and turn inland at the **Fern Canyon parking lot.** You'll know it by the wall of shrubbery separating it from the beach. There are restrooms at the parking area, and the trail proceeds north here. Follow the trail into **Fern Canyon** (ignoring the stairs leading to the return route on James Irvine Trail).

Fern Canyon is a highlight of any national park hike. The sheer walls are covered in ferns—and I mean covered. It's like a fern wallpaper store in here. The walls are narrow, the creek running in all but the driest of seasons, and it's spectacular. Go slow through here, get observant, and enjoy the sound, the quality of the air, and the look of this special place. At the end of Fern Canyon Trail, ascend via a switchback to James Irvine Trail and begin to hike east.

At around 7 mi (11.2 km) into the hike, you'll pass Friendship Ridge Trail (on the left) and cross a creek in a narrow canyon. Take a look at the seasonal, very delicate 25-ft (8-m) waterfall, then continue down the trail. The trail is easy for a good stretch here, passing the junction with Clintonia Trail and descending along a gully. At 9.6 mi (15.4 km) in, you'll climb again, using the switchbacks to ascend the steep bluff where the James Irvine and Miners Ridge Trails meet. From this junction stay straight and enjoy the last 0.8 mi (1.3 km) of forest and trail leading to the parking lot and your car.

DIRECTIONS

James Irvine and Miners Ridge Loop is in Prairie Creek Redwoods State Park, one of the three state parks that make up the "State" part of Redwood National and State Parks. From Eureka, head north along US 101/ Redwood Highway for 47.5 mi (76.4 km), then turn left onto the Newton B. Drury Scenic Byway. In 0.2 mi (0.3 km), you'll reach the Prairie Creek

BEST NEARBY

EdeBee's Snack Shack

▶ *120777 US 101, Orick; 530/716-0202; 11am-4pm Sun.-Thurs., 11am-6:30pm Fri.-Sat.; $7-21*

EdeBee's is only 10 minutes from the trailhead, so whether you grab lunch before your hike or plan to get a bite after you wrap the trail, your meal is only minutes from the hike. Elk burgers are the way to go, though I get it if you feel a little weird ordering elk after admiring these magnificent animals today. If you want to skip the delicious elk burgers, you can opt for a beef burger, fish-and-chips, or a simple grilled cheese, and a basket of fries, tots, or onion rings.

Visitor Center. Several trails, including James Irvine Trail, begin at the large signboard on the lot's north side.

NEED TO KNOW

Info: Prairie Creek Visitor Center, www.nps.gov/redw

Passes and Reservations: No entrance fee for Redwood National Park, but there is an $8 day-use fee payable at developed campgrounds and parking areas for Prairie Creek Redwoods State Park. Hikers heading to Fern Canyon via this route (the James Irvine Trail) do not need a permit; other routes may require an advance permit. For more information, see page 506.

Weather Considerations: Don't expect to keep your feet dry in Fern Canyon; the trail is simply the streambed, so you'll hop logs and rocks and splash your way along. At least one shoe will go in the water. Unless you're visiting in the driest, warmest months of summer, it's smart to pack along water sandals for the canyon walk, or at least an extra pair of dry socks to change into.

Facilities: At this trailhead you'll find potable water, restrooms with flush toilets, a picnic area, and a gift shop complete with maps, park rangers or volunteer staff, and souvenirs.

Other: No dogs are allowed on trails in the contiguous parks system, though dogs (on leash) are permitted in campgrounds and on the beach.

▼ FERN CANYON

30

HIGH PEAKS AND BALCONIES CAVE LOOP

PINNACLES NATIONAL PARK, CALIFORNIA

Condors soar above as you hike, climb, and duck through the heart of the park's rock spires.

- **Distance:** 8.4 mi (13.5 km) round-trip
- **Duration:** 4.5-5 hours
- **Elevation Gain:** 1,864 ft (568 m)
- **Effort:** Strenuous
- **When:** Mar.-May and Sept.-Nov.
- **Trailhead:** Chaparral parking area

HIGHLIGHT: Exploring the pitch-black Balconies Cave with a headlamp or flashlight

This 8.4-mi (13.5-km) hike combines two of the most popular trails in Pinnacles National Park, leading you through a cave, along exposed cliff edges, and in and around the pinnacles. There are two trailheads for this route, the Chaparral parking area (west side of the park) and Old Pinnacles Trailhead (east side); we'll approach this trail from Chapparal and make the loop counterclockwise, starting on Juniper Canyon Trail.

Before you set off on this hike, know there are many areas of extreme exposure that could be unsafe for children or folks who have issues with heights.

▲ CALIFORNIA CONDOR AT PINNACLES NATIONAL PARK

START THE HIKE

From the **Chaparral parking area,** go due south on **Juniper Canyon Trail,** which you'll follow for 1.8 mi (2.9 km), ignoring Tunnel Trail—branching off to the left—at 1.2 mi (1.9 km). Only a few dozen steps into the trail, you'll begin to climb, gently at first, then more and more steeply. Throughout spring, a bevy of trailside wildflowers offer colorful distractions from the gorgeous scenery. Pinnacles National Park is named for the curious stone

▼ HIGH PEAKS AND BALCONIES CAVE LOOP

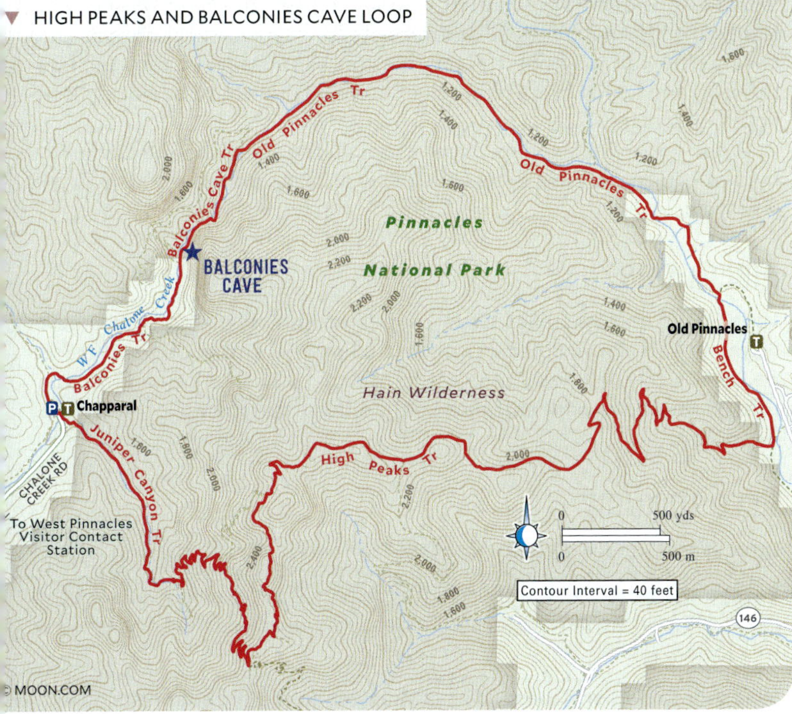

columns rising from the landscape thanks to a 23-million-year-old volcano; you'll see the first pinnacles 0.4 mi (0.6 km) into the hike. Enjoy the pinnacles, the flowers, and the views as you continue to climb.

At the 1.8-mi (2.9-km) mark, turn left on **High Peaks Trail** and keep climbing; you'll soon reach the highest elevations of the hike. Along this stretch the rock formations are a little strange, and you'll have exceptional views of the Salinas Valley and San Andreas Rift Zone. You'll also have the chance to spot a few birds: eagles, falcons, vultures, and possibly the endangered California condor with its massive 9-ft (2.7-m) wingspan. Spur trails to the right lead to peaks and viewpoints if you're inclined to explore further.

At the 2.4-mi mark (3.9 km) the trail gets interesting. It's not a via ferrata, but it does involve some extreme exposure as well as rungs and handholds bolted into the mountain, stone steps, and narrow ledges; watch your footing and take your time here. In 0.6 mi (1 km) you'll reach the junction with Condor Gulch Trail and leave all the climbing and high elevation behind you. Wildflowers abound here in spring, but year-round you'll find great panoramic views. When the trail levels out you'll turn left along **Bench Trail,** joining **Old Pinnacles Trail** in 0.5 mi (0.8 km); there's a parking area across the creek and a primitive restroom.

Old Pinnacles Trail follows and crosses Chalone Creek and the West Fork of Chalone Creek for 1.3 mi (2.1 km), climbing slightly through the chaparral as you go along. As you near **Balconies Cave**—formed by a rockfall—you'll encounter a couple of short, steep sections, then enter the cave proper. Bring a flashlight, but be aware that trail conditions, wildlife considerations, claustrophobia, and/or your own desires may lead you on the Balconies Cliffs Trail instead, a bypass that contains zero caving. The warning aside, the cave is a cool experience (literally and figuratively) and worth every pitch-black step (again, bring a powerful flashlight or headlamp).

When you exit Balconies Cave—or rejoin the trail from the Cliffs Trail bypass—you're an easy, creekside 0.8 mi (1.3 km) from the trailhead and your vehicle.

DIRECTIONS

High Peaks and Balconies Cave Loop is on the west side of Pinnacles National Park. From Soledad, which is 85 mi (137 km) south of San Jose on US 101, take Highway 146 east for about 12 mi (19.3 km) and 25 minutes, through the park entrance to the Chaparral parking lot, which has 43 spots.

NEED TO KNOW

Info: West Pinnacles Visitor Contact Station, www.nps.gov/pinn

Passes and Reservations: Entry into the park is $30/vehicle ($25/motorcycle, $15/pedestrian or cyclist). Passes are available in advance at www.recreation.gov.

Weather Considerations: This park can get hot during summer, and with several long, exposed sections of trail, you'll want sunscreen, a wide-brimmed hat, and a sun shirt or something similar. Bring plenty of water for every member of your party, at minimum 1 quart or liter per person for every two hours on the trail, but double that when temperatures are high.

Facilities: Restrooms (with accessible facilities), potable water, and a water bottle filling station are available at the trailhead.

Other: You'll need a flashlight for this hike—the cave is an actual cave (not just an overhang) and you'll need a bright light in there (trust me, your phone's flashlight just doesn't cut it).

BEST NEARBY

Cocuyo's Mexican Restaurant

▶ *185 Kidder St., Soledad; 831/237-5004; 11am-8pm Mon.-Tues. and Thurs.-Sat., 9am-7pm Sun.; $3-36*

About 25 minutes from the Chaparral parking area and trailhead is Cocuyo's Mexican Restaurant. Their chips and salsa, street tacos, and agua fresca de Jamaica will hit the spot after a day on the trails, but don't be afraid to explore the menu and specials as it's near impossible to put in the wrong order here.

▲ HIKER ON HIGH PEAKS TRAIL

31

HALEMAU'U AND HALEAKALĀ OVERLOOK TRAIL

HALEAKALĀ NATIONAL PARK, HAWAI'I

Explore breathtaking views of the volcano rim and crater floor on this hike through rugged terrains and dramatic elevation changes.

- **Distance:** 7.3 mi (11.7 km) round-trip
- **Duration:** 4.5-5 hours
- **Elevation Gain:** 2,349 ft (716 m)
- **Effort:** Strenuous
- **When:** Year-round
- **Trailhead:** Halemau'u Trailhead

HIGHLIGHT: Watching the sunrise from Haleakalā summit

Haleakalā National Park's Summit District takes you above the clouds on the slopes of a dormant volcano for a wild and unusual view: dawn breaking over a sea of clouds, and when they clear, the crater revealed beneath dazzles with the colors and textures of the soil and scree. Even though it'll be an early start, I recommend **sunrise from the trailhead** or from one of five overlooks beside (or adjacent to via a very short walk) Crater Road. Arriving via Crater Road you'll reach the Halemau'u Trailhead first, but soon encounter Leleiwi Overlook, Crater View at Kalahaku, the Pā Ka'oao and Keonehe'ehe'e Overlooks at the Haleakalā Visitor Center, and the overlook at the 10,006-ft (3,050-m) summit of Pu'u'ula'ula. Each of these overlooks will put you a

◄ SILVERSWORD ON THE CRATER FLOOR

▼ SILVERSWORD IN BLOOM

▼ HALEMAU'U AND HALEAKALĀ OVERLOOK TRAIL

few miles from the trailhead, but not too far (the farthest, Pu'u'ula'ula, is a 6.6-mi/10.6-km, 15-minute drive from the trailhead), making sunrise from any of these incredible vantage points a must when you've already made the trek to Hawai'i.

START THE HIKE

After enjoying the sunrise (preferably with a hearty packed breakfast), you're ready to begin hiking. This is a hike with altitude: The trailhead sits at 7,900 ft (2,408 m), so if you're like me—from sea level or nearby—you'll feel the effects of this elevation. After a few hundred yards of level trail, you begin your descent, gentle at first, but growing steeper as you near the **Rainbow Bridge,** a natural bridge 1.1 mi (1.8 km) into the hike. Rainbow Bridge stands on a narrow fin of ridgeline and has tremendous views. To the left is the **Ko'olau Gap** and to the right, the trail to the crater floor. You'll be able to see both sides at once, revealing a stark difference in the landscape from lush green forests to the Martian-like environs of the crater floor. Some hikers satisfy themselves with the view from here, but to truly appreciate the magnitude of this hike, continue to descend into the crater.

As you pass Rainbow Bridge, the trail enters a winding series of switchbacks. In many national parks, hikers cut the trail to eliminate a few switchbacks, but no one is tempted here as the drop-offs are steep and can be a cause of concern. At 2.6 mi (4.2 km) you'll begin to traverse the relatively flat crater floor, another highlight of the hike. On the **crater floor,** notice the coloration of the landscape around you, which varies from black to deep brown to sandy and intense red, all caused by the mineral content underfoot; the variation in color and the sparseness of the landscape gives it an alien feel. Cross the crater floor as you climb (mostly gently) toward the **Hōlua Cabin,** a wilderness camp area. Here you'll find a pit toilet and the turnaround point for the hike. To get back to the trailhead, you've gotta climb. All those switchbacks and steep sections will present a different challenge as you climb, so take your time and stay hydrated.

DIRECTIONS

Halemau'u and Haleakalā Overlook Trail is in the Summit District of Haleakalā National Park. The Summit District is quite a drive from the larger towns on Maui—you're looking at 2.5 hours from Kahului and 3 hours from Wailea. From Kahului and the airport, take Highway 37 to Highway 377 (the Haleakalā Highway), turning onto Highway 378 in the town of Kula where the Haleakalā Highway leads to the trailhead and summit. Your GPS will tell you this is a drive of 1 hour or so, but that doesn't account for the steepness of the road, the curves, or the times you'll slow down to goggle at the view. From Wailea you'll follow Highway 311 to Kahului and then take Highway 37 and the Haleakalā Highway as noted. The GPS address is 30,000 Haleakalā Hwy., Kula.

There's no place to fuel up a conventional automobile or charge an electric vehicle in the national park, so if you're driving in, note that the town of Pukalani is the last spot for gas. The National Park Service warns that "electric vehicles with a full charge have been unable to make it to the summit," and with no charging station at the summit, that's quite the problem. Plan accordingly.

BEST NEARBY

Silversword Loop

When you arrive at Hōlua Cabin, you can either turn back and hike to the trailhead or tack on another 1 mi (1.6 km) to get to Silversword Loop. This short loop trail on the crater floor is known and named for the abundant 'āhinahina, or silversword plants. These endangered plants will count among the rarest plants you'll ever see. The rounded, mound-like plants have a dense rosette of silvery gray-green leaves, and when they bloom—a process that can take decades—the stalk and its head of purple flowers rises 6 ft (1.8 m) or more. Once they bloom, they die. Take plenty of pictures—especially if they're in bloom—but be sure not to step off trail for your shot, as these plants are endangered and grow only here on Maui and on the Island of Hawai'i (the Big Island).

NEED TO KNOW

Info: Headquarters Visitor Center, www.nps.gov/hale

Passes and Reservations: Entry into the park is $30/vehicle ($25/motorcycle, $15/pedestrian or cyclist). If you plan on seeing sunrise in the Summit District or if you're hitting Halemau'u Trail before 7 am, you'll need to secure a Sunrise Reservation ($1). Passes and reservations are available in advance at www.recreation.gov.

Weather Considerations: Weather on the volcano and at elevation can be unpredictable, with conditions quickly going from clear and sunny to cloudy and rainy (and back again) in minutes. The summit is around 30°F (17°C) cooler than the coast. Be sure to pack a rain shell or rainproof poncho, a good insulating layer, and a wide-brimmed hat. Also be sure to bring plenty of water, hiking poles, and a pair of gaiters (to keep dirt and scree out of your boots) along with your usual sunscreen and snacks.

Facilities: Restrooms are available at the trailhead. For more extensive facilities and offerings, stop by the Haleakalā Visitor Center 5 mi (8 km) southwest.

▼ HALEAKALĀ CRATER

▲ HALEAKALĀ CRATER

32

PIPIWAI TRAIL AND WAIMOKU FALLS

HALEAKALĀ NATIONAL PARK, HAWAI'I

Hike to an impressive pair of waterfalls, passing through a dense bamboo forest along one of Maui's most beautiful trails.

- **Distance:** 3.4 mi (5.5 km) round-trip
- **Duration:** 2-2.5 hours
- **Elevation Gain:** 909 ft (277 m)
- **Effort:** Moderate
- **When:** Year-round
- **Trailhead:** Pipiwai Trailhead near Kīpahulu Visitor Center

HIGHLIGHT: Soaking in views of the 400-ft (122-m) Waimoku Falls

Many visitors regard Pipiwai Trail as the best on Maui, and it's certainly a stunner. The trail explores the upper portion of the 'Ohe'o Gulch above the Seven Sacred Pools, leading you through thick bamboo groves to a pair of huge waterfalls. Along the way you'll see and hear plenty of birds, so be sure to grab info on our feathered friends when you stop by the visitor center.

▲ BANYAN TREE

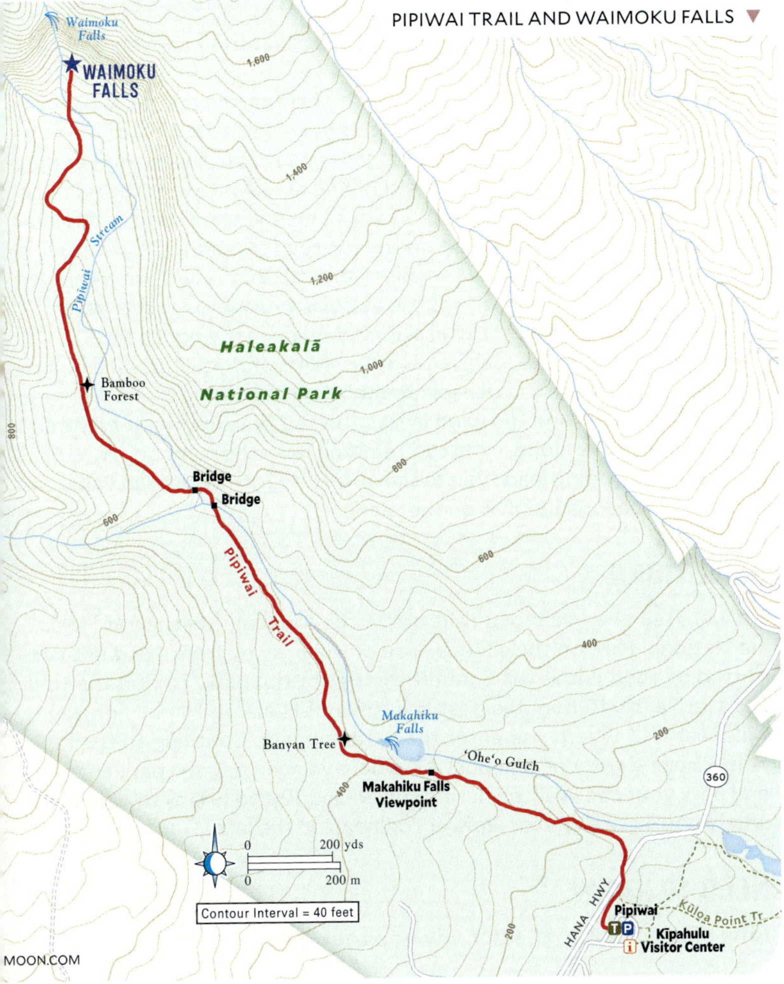

START THE HIKE

From the trailhead the path climbs steeply up a rock-strewn slope to a sign noting trail distances. Much of the Pipiwai Trail parallels **'Ohe'o Gulch,** and you can hear the rush of water as you make your way upstream (and uphill) toward the falls. As tempting as it may be, it's not safe to access the pools or the waterfalls along this stretch of trail. Over the years a number of people have, cutting social trails through the foliage to reach the water, but people have been swept to their deaths by flash floods, so take heed of the signs and the warnings issued by the National Park Service.

After only 10 minutes on the trail, you'll reach a viewpoint for **Makahiku Falls,** a 200-ft (61-m) plunge that ranges from barely a trickle in dry months to a violent torrent. As you pass the falls the trail climbs again, soon reaching the shade of a massive **banyan tree.** From here to the first bridge, there are several spur trails leading to waterfall, canyon, and pool viewpoints.

Ten minutes beyond the tree you reach a **bridge,** the first of two crossing the stream. It's a great photo spot, as you can snap shots of Makahiku Falls and the first bamboo forest. When you cross the second bridge, the trail converts to a set of stairs climbing steeply toward the bamboo forest. An opening in the railing on your left follows a path to **Pipiwai Stream.** Here you can rock-hop up the riverbed (for about 15 minutes; it can be slippery and tiring) to a smaller waterfall that few visitors lay eyes on. If you do go this way, make a little noise as you approach the waterfall, as some visitors like to do a little skinny-dipping in the pool here.

Back on the main trail, continue up the stairs and you'll reach a boardwalk leading through the densest **bamboo forest** on the island. The trail is tunnel-like here, and the wind sways the bamboo, making it creak and groan as you move along. When you emerge from the bamboo, a few minutes of rock-hopping leads you to the 400-ft (122-m) **Waimoku Falls,** one of the most beautiful sights on the island.

DIRECTIONS

Pipiwai Trail and Waimoku Falls are in the Kīpahulu District of Haleakalā National Park on the eastern side of Maui, away from—and not connected by road with—the Summit District of the park. To find the trailhead, drive 30-40 minutes past the town of Hana on Hana Highway to Milepost 41.7, where you enter the national park. Continue to the Kīpahulu Visitor Center at Milepost 42, where you can pay the park entry fee and park your car. Walk back to the road and 100 yd (91 m) toward Hana, where you'll see signs for Pipiwai Trailhead on the left.

NEED TO KNOW

Info: Kīpahulu Visitor Center, www.nps.gov/hale

BEST NEARBY

Kūola Point Trail

▶ *Adjacent to the Kīpahulu Visitor Center*

This short trail (0.5 mi/0.8 km with 75 ft/23 m of elevation gain) leads from the Kīpahulu Visitor Center through lush vegetation to the ocean, where the view of waves crashing against the cliffs mesmerizes visitors. From here the trail circles back to the visitor center, but not before passing a waterfall and the sacred pools in ʻOheʻo Gulch. As tempting as they seem, do not swim in the pools—the danger of flash floods is high. Due to this trail's proximity to the ocean, its verdant jungle foliage, and nearby food sources, it's a hotbed for birdwatching. Many photographers and sunrise/sunset admirers find their way here for a look at the scenery during these dramatic times of day.

Passes and Reservations: Entry into the park is $30/vehicle ($25/motorcycle, $15/pedestrian or cyclist). Passes are available in advance at www.recreation.gov.

Weather Considerations: The Kīpahulu District of Haleakalā National Park sits on the eastern (windward) side of Maui, where the weather is mild, breezy, and wet. In typical Hawai'i fashion, you can count on an afternoon rain shower, but this part of the island receives, on average, 187 in (475 cm) of rain annually, so bring a breathable rain jacket. Temperatures range from 70-80°F (21-27°C) in the day with nighttime lows in the 65-75°F (18-24°C) range.

Facilities: Restrooms and a water station are available at the trailhead.

▼ BAMBOO GROVES ALONG THE PIPIWAI TRAIL

33

KĪLAUEA IKI AND CRATER RIM TRAIL

HAWAI'I VOLCANOES NATIONAL PARK, HAWAI'I

Pass steam vents and walk through a lava tube on this hike through an alien landscape.

- **Distance:** 3.2 mi (5.1 km) round-trip
- **Duration:** 2-3 hours
- **Elevation Gain:** 741 ft (226 m)
- **Effort:** Moderate
- **When:** Year-round
- **Trailhead:** Kīlauea Iki Overlook

HIGHLIGHT: Hiking across the crater floor

Kīlauea Iki Trail takes you from the top of the crater—a landscape of lush tropical rain forest filled with native vegetation and birds—to the crater floor, an area devoid of vegetation where volcanic steam rises in ominous curls. There's a bit of a descent—around 400 ft (122 m) from the rim to the floor—giving this trail a moderate rating. The descent and ascent aside, it's an easy hike through an environment that's strange and beautiful. Pick up one of the trail guides, as it has a simple map and includes notes corresponding to markers along the way.

Along the route you'll notice stacks of stones, known as cairns elsewhere but called ahu ("stacked rocks") here. Park staff have established

VIEW OF THE CALDERA FLOOR

NARROW, ROCKY PORTION OF THE KĪLAUEA IKI TRAIL

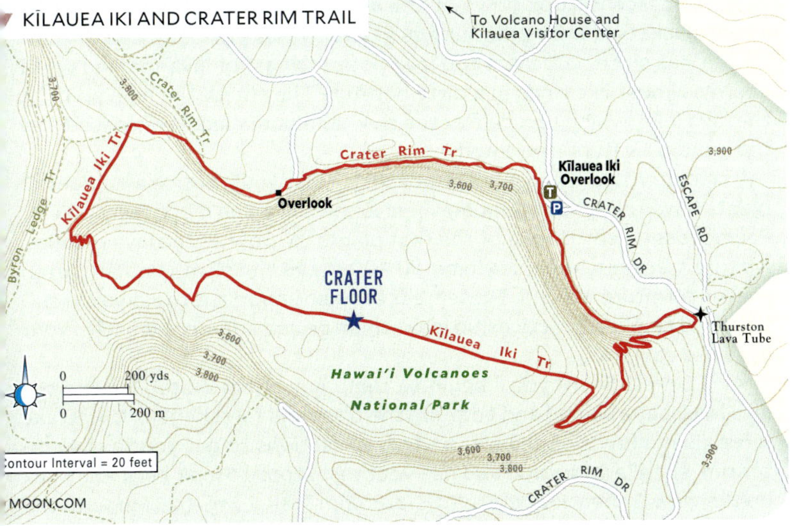

these ahu to mark the trail and ensure visitor safety. Please don't take these apart or build new ones. Here in Hawai'i the ahu have significant cultural importance, and though you may think stacking a few stones just for a picture might be harmless, or even "helpful" to other park visitors, you may inadvertently be culturally offensive or disorient other hikers.

The best time to do this hike is first thing in the morning, for several reasons. First: sunrise. Catching the sunrise from the crater rim is a must when visiting this park. Next, it's cooler in the morning and a more pleasant hike in the floor of the crater. When it's cooler it's also easier to spot all the steam vents, which are an active reminder that the crater could erupt again at any time. Finally, the birds are much more active in the morning. Look for them along the crater rim as they search for insects to keep their bellies filled.

START THE HIKE

Park at the **Kīlauea Iki Overlook** and turn right, following the Kīlauea Iki sign, which will direct you to the left and a counterclockwise loop. Here you're on a section of **Crater Rim Trail,** a much longer walk that leads along the crater rim and stops at various overlooks and interest points. Look down and to your left, beyond the railed-off lookouts, and you'll see the crater floor, your destination. Snap your pictures, give the route a good look, and get ready to descend into this 1-mi-wide (1.6-km) crater.

Around 0.5 mi (0.8 km) into the hike, an **overlook** offers a great view of Pu'upua'i, a cinder-and-spatter cone formed by ongoing eruptions decades ago. It's hard to believe, but when a vent opened on the other side of the crater, powerful lava fountains sent molten rock flying to this side of the rim. At 0.7 mi (1.1 km), Crater Rim Trail departs to the right and you will stay to the left, keeping to the left again and descending along **Kīlauea Iki Trail** at the junction a few steps down the trail. The steady descent grows wildly steep at the 1-mi (1.6-km) mark, where switchbacks ease the descent. Look down at the **crater floor** here and you'll notice it's all black rock. That's the surface of the lava lake that flooded the crater but has since hardened. You may notice "rings" of lava-marked earth nearby, almost like rings in a dirty bathtub. They mark the high point of the lava lake, which receded as the flow of magma and lava ceased and the molten "waters" retreated.

The crater floor is an inhospitable place, but you'll notice a number of plants have taken root. Among them is the ʻōhiʻa, the mountain apple or Pacific rosewood; it's one of the first plants to grow as the lava recedes. Mature trees are huge, reaching 60-100 ft tall (18-30 m), and are often used in furniture making. These trees are also important to Hawaiian cultural and spiritual practices, so leave them be and admire them with your eyes and camera.

At 2.2 mi (3.5 km) you'll begin to climb out of the crater, leaving the lava landscape behind and entering the trees and forest again. It will take more than a few switchbacks and steep sections to get you to the crater rim, so take your time and use your rest stops to look back and soak up the view. When you return to Crater Rim Trail, 2.7 mi (4.3 km) into the hike, you'll find the **Thurston Lava Tube.** If you're not pressed for time, take a few minutes to explore. Lava tubes like this are the remains of the channels that molten rock made and took to the surface, sort of like a subway system for magma. The lava tube is lit 8am-8pm. Flashlights are recommended outside of those hours.

It's a short jaunt from the Lava Tube parking area to where you parked, so enjoy the last looks at the trail as you head back to your ride.

DIRECTIONS

Kīlauea Iki and Crater Rim Trail is in the Kīlauea summit area of Hawaiʻi Volcanoes National Park. From Volcano, head west on Highway 11 (Hawaiʻi Belt Road) for 1.5 mi (2.4 km). Turn left on Crater Rim Drive and drive 1.6 mi (2.6 km) to Kīlauea Iki Overlook. The parking area is on your right.

BEST NEARBY

Volcano House

▶ *1 Crater Rim Dr., Hawaiʻi Volcanoes National Park; 808/756-9625; www.hawaiivolcanohouse.com; camper cabins from $80, rooms from $285*

Why wake up in a beachside hotel when you can welcome the day from the rim of an active volcano? Volcano House lets you do just that, offering both standard hotel rooms, 10 cabins, and 16 campsites. A pair of restaurants—The Rim at Volcano House (breakfast 7am-10:30am, lunch 11am-2:30pm, dinner 5pm-8:30pm; breakfast buffet $24 adults, $14 kids; lunch and dinner $13-50) and Uncle George's Lounge (11am-9:30pm; $12-28)—serve up tasty local fare that includes outstanding fresh seafood, slow-roasted kalua pork, chicken katsu, and more. The hotel is adjacent to the Kīlauea Visitor Center, and not far from the trailhead.

▲ LUSH FOLIAGE ALONG CRATER RIM TRAIL

NEED TO KNOW

Info: Kīlauea Visitor Center (closed for renovation), temporary visitor contact station 1.2 mi (1.9 km) west at the historic ball field near Kīlauea Military Camp, www.nps.gov/havo

Passes and Reservations: Entry into the park is $30/vehicle ($25/motorcycle, $15/pedestrian or cyclist). Passes are available in advance at www.recreation.gov.

Weather Considerations: Temperatures vary as altitude increases, and it can be 12-15 degrees cooler on the top of Kīlauea than the rest of the park. Be aware that there's little shade in and around the craters, so wear your sun shirt, wide-brimmed hat, sunglasses, and sunscreen. Pack at least 2 quarts or liters of water per person (but bring more if you're planning a longer hike), and because the weather can change in an instant, bring your rain gear and be ready to don it at a moment's notice. Always follow the advice of park rangers, volunteers, and notices about trail and weather conditions.

Facilities: The parking situation at the Kīlauea Iki Overlook is terrible and extremely limited, so if you arrive during peak hours, you may be in for a long wait or you may never get a parking spot at all. Arrive early to ensure you have a space, or be prepared for a much longer hike as you may need to park at the visitor center (1.6 mi/2.6 km northwest) or the Devastation Trailhead (1.8 mi/2.9 km southwest).

Other: Safety is a real concern with Hawai'i Volcanoes National Park. Volcanic conditions can change at any time, and an otherwise tame bit of park can turn to a hell of spewing magma and flowing lava with little or no notice. For that reason, stay on marked trails and avoid closed areas. Steam vents and cracks can release superheated water or gasses, so don't go peeking into any cracks or holes you find in the earth.

34

PU'ULOA PETROGLYPHS TRAIL

HAWAI'I VOLCANOES NATIONAL PARK, HAWAI'I

This easy boardwalk hike leads to a field filled with more than 20,000 petroglyphs in mounds of hardened lava.

- **Distance:** 1.2 mi (1.9 km) round-trip
- **Duration:** 1-1.5 hours
- **Elevation Gain:** 85 ft (26 m)
- **Effort:** Moderate
- **When:** Year-round
- **Trailhead:** Pu'uloa parking area

HIGHLIGHT: Admiring kiʻi pōhaku (petroglyphs)

At the foot of Kīlauea, a boardwalk trail leads across a 500-year-old lava field to mounds of stone incised with nearly 23,000 petroglyphs called kiʻi pōhaku (meaning "images carved into stone"). The boardwalk serves two purposes: keeping your feet off the ground where a stream of tourist traffic might damage both the kiʻi pōhaku we can see and the ones still buried under a layer of dirt and foliage, and to give you a better look at the kiʻi pōhaku.

▲ PU'ULOA PETROGLYPHS TRAIL

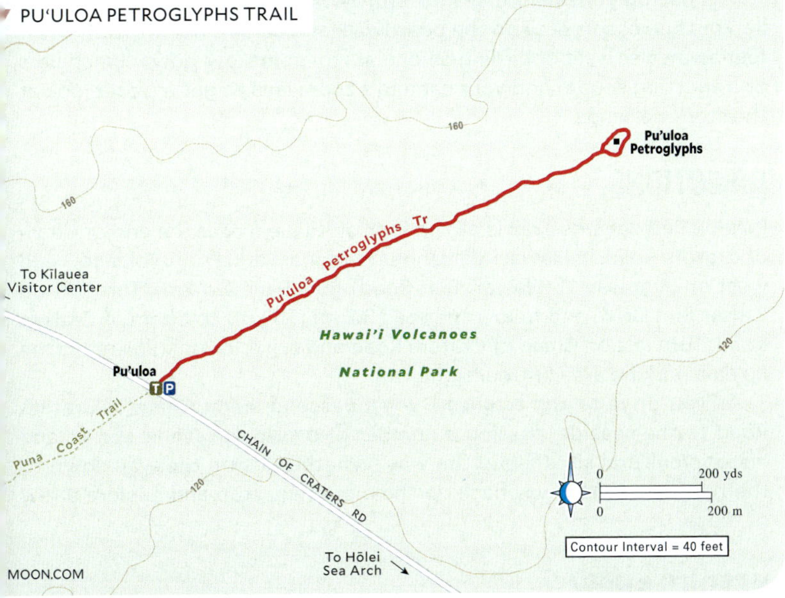

START THE HIKE

Near the end of Chain of Craters Road, park in the **Pu'uloa parking area** on the right side of the road and cross to the **Pu'uloa Trailhead.** The trail begins by the information placard and the emergency callbox as a stone and dirt path, but within a few hundred yards you'll join the boardwalk. The hike itself is unremarkable—follow the boardwalk to the end, turn around, come back—but hikers aren't drawn here for the challenge of the trail; instead they come to experience the lava landscape and to see the amazing **ki'i pōhaku.**

At several points on the hike, you'll be in a great position to see these rock carvings. They show the life and culture of native Hawaiian people, containing geometric patterns and anthropomorphic (human and human-like) forms and canoes. Since study of the ki'i pōhaku began in the early 1800s, anthropologists have made both observations and interpretations of some of the symbols here. Through interviews, anthropologist Martha Beckwith determined that some of the stone holes were ceremonial, containing a piece of the umbilical cord of a newborn (a rite symbolizing both good fortune and a long life). Earlier researchers determined some of the etched figures tell the stories of trips taken to circumambulate (encircling the island on foot) or circumnavigate (encircling the island by canoe/water) the island. Seeing something so old and culturally important in a place as elastic as the slopes of a volcano is a humbling experience, and it draws tight the connection between past and present. There are other petroglyphs in Hawai'i Volcanoes National Park (single images, a few small panels), but this is the most extensive collection, and it's the only place you can see petroglyphs carved into the lava substrate itself.

The petroglyphs here may look sturdy, but they're actually very fragile. For this reason, stay on the boardwalk and admire the art from a few feet away. Use a set of birding binoculars (or some low-power binoculars or a spotting scope) and your camera's zoom lens to get a closer look at the stone carvings.

DIRECTIONS

Pu'uloa Petroglyphs Trail is at the foot of Kīlauea, near the end of Chain of Craters Road, in Hawai'i Volcanoes National Park. From Volcano, head west on Highway 11 (Hawai'i Belt Road) for 1.5 mi (2.4 km). Turn left on Crater Rim Drive and follow the road 3.2 mi (5.1 km) to Chain of Craters Road. Turn left on Chain of Craters Road and drive 16.2 mi (26 km) to the Pu'uloa parking area on your right.

As you drive to the trailhead, you'll descend along Chain of Craters Road to the seaside, passing a number of overlooks, scenic vistas, and historic/cultural sites along the way. Whether it's on the way down to the trailhead or the way back up the mountain, stop and explore a few of these.

NEED TO KNOW

Info: Kīlauea Visitor Center (closed for renovation), temporary visitor contact station 1.2 mi (1.9 km) west at the historic ball field near Kīlauea Military Camp, www.nps.gov/havo

Passes and Reservations: Entry into the park is $30/vehicle ($25/motorcycle, $15/pedestrian or cyclist). Passes are available in advance at www.recreation.gov.

Weather Considerations: As you descend Chain of Craters Road, the environment grows windier, drier, and hotter. Be sure to bring a sun hat and sun protection (like a sun shirt or sunscreen) and at least 1 quart or liter of water per person. Always follow the advice of park rangers, volunteers, and notices about trail and weather conditions.

BEST NEARBY

Hōlei Sea Arch

▶ *At the end of Chain of Craters Road, 2.4 mi (3.9 km) from the Pu'uloa parking area*

After you've checked out the petroglyphs of Pu'uloa, follow Chain of Craters Road to the end (where there's a turnaround and small parking area) for a walk along the sea cliffs. Head east, passing the gate at the end of Chain of Craters Road and following the emergency evacuation route, where a viewpoint gives you a look at the Hōlei Sea Arch, a 90-ft-high (27-m) arch that looks like a flying buttress holding up the cliffs. Though it's made of sturdy stone, the sea arch won't last forever, and eventually waves will erode the arch, causing it to fall into the sea.

Facilities: None at the trailhead.

Other: Safety is a real concern with Hawai'i Volcanoes National Park. Volcanic conditions can change at any time, and an otherwise tame bit of park can turn to a hell of spewing magma and flowing lava with little or no notice. For that reason, stay on marked trails and avoid closed areas. Steam vents and cracks can release superheated water or gasses, so don't go peeking into any cracks or holes you find in the earth.

▼ PU'ULOA PETROGLYPHS

NORTH RIM OF THE GRAND CANYON

SOUTHWEST

Across the Southwest, trails lead to the fantastic. In this iconic region known for its arid deserts and red-rock landscapes, you can choose your own adventure. Are you looking for an epic journey—trekking through time on the Rim-to-Rim hike in the Grand Canyon? Or are you in the mood for simple and scenic—escaping to the lovely year-round views of Landscape Arch in Arches?

To reach Angels Landing in Zion, you traverse a long stone fin, earning a breathtaking look at canyons stretching to the horizon. At Bryce Canyon, snow crowns the hoodoos along Fairyland Loop Trail, turning stone pillars into sentinels that watch you delve deeper into a fantastical landscape. Petroglyphs hidden at the end of Canyonlands' lonely Great Gallery Trail have an otherworldly look, and dinosaur footprints in the rock speak of a long history. In Mesa Verde, Colorado, scrub trees give way at an overlook on Soda Canyon where stone villages lie hidden beneath the canyon rim.

SOUTHWEST
GRAND TETON NP
IDAHO
WYOMING
BADLANDS
NEVADA
UTAH
ROCKY MOUNTAIN NP
49-50
ARCHES NP
CAPITOL REEF NP
BLACK CANYON OF THE GUNNISON NP
41-44
45-47
51-53
ZION NP
BRYCE CANYON NP
CANYON-LANDS NP
COLORADO
GREAT SAND DUNES NP
48
MESA VERDE NP
35-38
56
54-55
GRAND CANYON NP
ARIZONA
NEW MEXICO
SAGUARO NP
39-40
57-59
BIG BEND NP
MEXICO
MOON
0
200 mi
0
200 km
© MOON.COM

GRAND CANYON

SAGUARO

ZION

BRYCE CANYON

CAPITOL REEF

ARCHES

CANYONLANDS

MESA VERDE

GREAT SAND DUNES

BIG BEND

35

RIM TRAIL (BRIGHT ANGEL LODGE TO MATHER POINT)

GRAND CANYON NATIONAL PARK, ARIZONA

This walk passes historic lodges, shops, viewpoints, and museums—with the Grand Canyon spreading out at your side the whole way.

- **Distance:** 6 mi (9.7 km) round-trip
- **Duration:** 1.5-2.5 hours
- **Elevation Gain:** 338 ft (103 m)
- **Effort:** Easy
- **When:** Year-round
- **Trailhead:** Bright Angel Lodge

HIGHLIGHT: Marveling at the Grand Canyon from Mather Point

Rim Trail offers the best way to see the Grand Canyon's South Rim, so if you find yourself short on time and can only do one hike, put this one at the top of your list. This section of Rim Trail is accessible, enabling visitors and hikers of all ability levels to get a taste of the Grand Canyon.

▲ RIM TRAIL

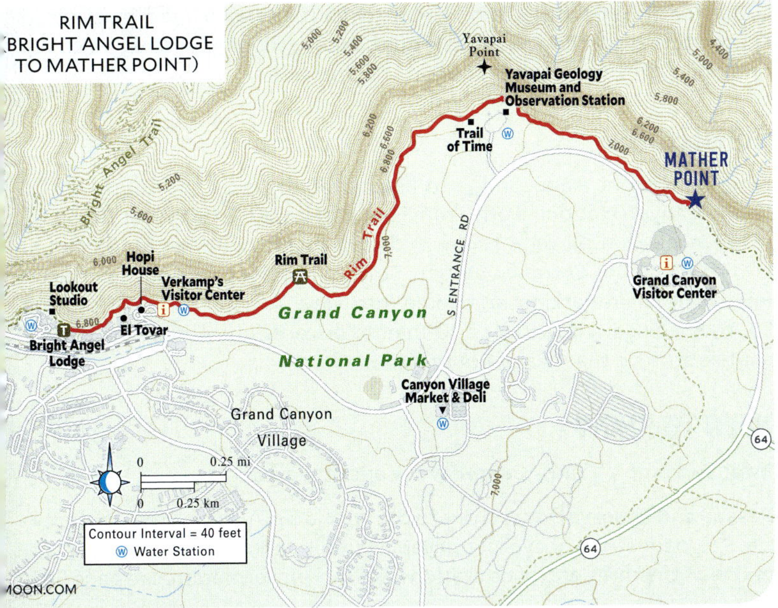

START THE HIKE

Start at **Bright Angel Lodge,** built in the 1930s to serve travelers lured to the Grand Canyon by the Santa Fe Railroad, and head east on Rim Trail where you'll be treated to the essential sights in **Grand Canyon Village; El Tovar,** one of the most distinctive hotels in Arizona, stands out as one of the not-a-natural-wonder sights to see (it really is something). Next door is **Hopi House,** designed by Mary Jane Colter in 1905 to look like traditional structures still standing on the Hopi Mesa (east of the Grand Canyon); Hopi workers used local materials to build this gift shop and gallery dedicated to Native American art.

As you continue on toward the Yavapai Geology Museum and Observation Station (1.8 mi/2.9 km from the lodge), Rim Trail follows the **Trail of Time.** The Trail of Time helps you grasp the temporal scale of the Grand Canyon, with markers measuring one million years of time as they tell the story of the formation of the canyon. Rocks and stones from within the canyon illustrate the eras of development, viewing devices give you a closer look into the canyon, and exhibits provide additional details on the formation of the canyon. Stop by the **Yavapai Geology Museum and Observation Station** as it tells the geological story of the Grand Canyon in greater detail. This spot—**Yavapai Point**—was handpicked by geologists as the best place to view the rock strata and receive a rim-side lesson on the geological history and present state of the Grand Canyon.

Continue east and enter a forested—and blissfully shady—stretch of Rim Trail leading to **Mather Point** (0.7 mi/1.1 km east of Yavapai). Mather Point has an astounding view of the canyon; it's a near-perfect rendition of what you imagine when you picture the Grand Canyon, so expect crowds here as others seek to satisfy their curiosity and take in the view. From here you can turn around and make your way back to Bright Angel

Lodge for the full 6-mi (9.7-km) circuit, or you can wait a few minutes for a shuttle bus. Note that the shuttle bus cannot accommodate wheelchairs or mobility devices more than 30 in (76 cm) wide.

DIRECTIONS

Rim Trail (Bright Angel Lodge to Mather Point) is on the South Rim of Grand Canyon National Park. From Flagstaff, take US 180 West for 50 mi (815 km). Turn right onto Highway 64 North and continue for 22 mi (35 km) to the South Entrance Station. Stay on Highway 64/South Entrance Road. The main parking lots come into view 4.8 mi (7.7 km) from the South Entrance, a little over a 10-minute drive. Bright Angel Lodge has a shuttle stop on the Village Route (Blue).

NEED TO KNOW

Info: Verkamp's Visitor Center, www.nps.gov/grca

Passes and Reservations: Entry to the park is $35/vehicle ($30/motorcycle, $25/pedestrian or cyclist), payable (credit or debit card only, no cash) at one of the three entrance stations. For more information, see page 502.

Weather Considerations: The South Rim has milder conditions than you'll find elsewhere in the park. In spring and summer, you may experience a thunderstorm, and fall and winter may bring ice, snow, or sleet; always follow warnings from rangers and play it safe.

Facilities: Many of the sights along the Rim Trail have restrooms.

Other: This stretch of the Rim Trail is paved and wheelchair accessible. Dogs are allowed on the Rim Trail on a leash, but you can't take them on the shuttle buses.

BEST NEARBY

El Tovar Dining Room

▶ *928/638-2631; www.grandcanyonlodges.com; 6:30am-10am, 11am-2:30pm, and 4:30pm-9pm daily, lounge 11am-10pm; reservations required for lunch and dinner*

A stay at El Tovar would be the secondary highlight—after the gorge itself—of any trip to the South Rim. Opened in 1905, the log-and-stone National Historic Landmark, standing about 20 ft (6 m) from the rim, has 78 rooms and suites. A mezzanine sitting area overlooks the log-cabin lobby, and a gift shop sells Native American art and crafts as well as canyon souvenirs.

The hotel's restaurant serves some of the best food in Arizona for breakfast ($7-14), lunch ($12-24), and dinner ($20-45). Fresh, creative, locally inspired and sourced dishes are served in a cozy, mural-lined dining room that has not been significantly altered from the way it looked back when Teddy Roosevelt and Zane Grey ate here. It's classic in that way, and in that it's an old-school fine dining experience, which means dress code: No jackets are required, but they discourage shorts and flip-flops, so try to look nice. There's also a comfortable cocktail lounge off the lobby with a window on the canyon.

▲ VIEW FROM YAVAPAI POINT

36

BRIGHT ANGEL TRAIL

GRAND CANYON NATIONAL PARK, ARIZONA

Introduce yourself to the inner canyon, passing through a rock tunnel and ending at a rest house along the trail.

- **Distance:** 3-9 mi (4.8-14.5 km) round-trip
- **Duration:** 2-8 hours
- **Elevation Gain:** 3,040 ft (927 m) for Havasupai Gardens option
- **Effort:** Moderate-strenuous
- **When:** Sept.-Mar.
- **Trailhead:** Just west of Bright Angel Lodge

HIGHLIGHT: Enjoying a lunch break at Havasupai Gardens

When you think "Grand Canyon hike," you think Bright Angel Trail. Switchbacks leading you below the rim; bright-eyed hikers heading down waving to weary hikers heading up; pack mules; the blissful shade of trailside resthouses. Bright Angel has all this and more. This is a great way to experience the inner canyon, though you should know that the difficulty of this hike is relative to the

◂ ROCKY PROMONTORY ON BRIGHT ANGEL TRAIL

▾ LOOKOUT STUDIO

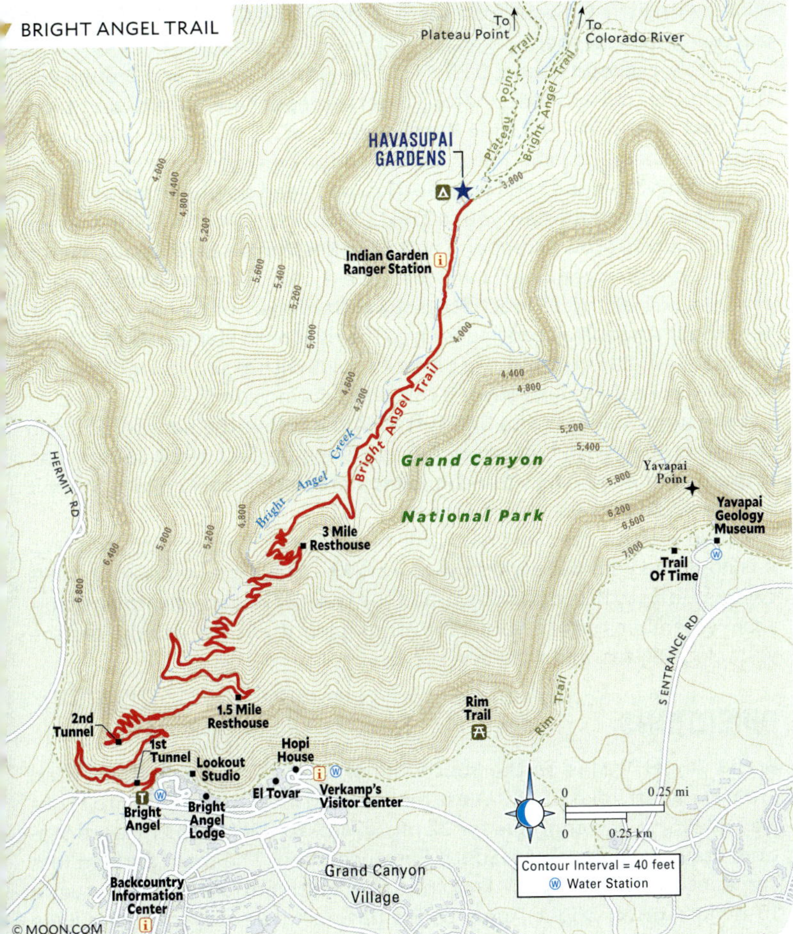

weather: When it's the hottest part of summer, it's unbelievably difficult; in mid-autumn when the weather is pleasant, it's hard but not "Why did I do this?" hard.

START THE HIKE

Almost as soon as you set boots on the trail, you'll leave the piney rim behind and descend into a rocky, dry, alien landscape that delivers exceptional views nearly every step of the way. Look below you and you'll see the switchbacks winding deeper into the canyon, but don't take your eyes off the trail for too long—the steady stream of mule trains leaves droppings everywhere. You'll reach your first landmark—a **tunnel**—at 0.2 mi (0.3 km) into the trail. If you're here to hike to the nearest great photo opportunity, this is it; snap a few shots and head back up. At 0.5 mi (0.8 km) you'll reach the first switchback, a great point to turn back if you're hiking with little kids out for a taste of the Grand Canyon. From here on, the trail grows steeper.

There's a **second tunnel** 0.75 mi (1.2 km) into the hike, and though you thought the trail was steep before, it gets steeper here, so take your time. The first resthouse—**1.5 Mile Resthouse**—is at 1.5 mi (2.4 km), and here you'll find shade, potable water, toilets, and an emergency phone. Rest up, have some water and refill your bottles, and head down. A sign at 2 Mile Switchback lets you know you're 2 mi (3.2 km) in and marks another place where the trail grows steeper. The **3 Mile Resthouse** (with shade, water, and an emergency phone) is another mile (1.6 km) down the trail. Finally, at 4.5 mi (7.2 km) you'll reach **Havasupai Gardens,** our turnaround point. Yes, Bright Angel Trail continues on to the river or to Plateau Point (an additional 3 mi/4.8 km round-trip), a rocky point with grand views of the river, but it's unsafe to hike beyond this point during summer.

Havasupai Gardens sits 3,000 ft (914 m) below the canyon rim, and this oasis lined with cottonwood trees is the perfect place to rest, eat, hydrate, and head back. You can **camp** here with a backcountry permit and backcountry reservation (see page 507).

When you're rested and ready, hit the trail. You'll really feel how steep it is now, and your pace will slow to a crawl—a hiking axiom says it takes twice as long to hike up as down, and the trek to the top will prove it true. Just remember to take your time, drink plenty, eat something, restore your electrolytes, and enjoy the scenery.

DIRECTIONS

Bright Angel Trail is on the South Rim of Grand Canyon National Park. From Flagstaff, take US 180 West for 50 mi (81 km). Turn right onto Highway 64 North and continue for 22 mi (35 km) to the South Entrance Station. Stay on Highway 64/South Entrance Road. The main parking lots come into view 4.8 mi (7.7 km) from the South Entrance, a little over a 10-minute drive. Bright Angel Lodge has a shuttle stop on the Village Route (Blue).

BEST NEARBY

Lookout Studio

▶ *9am-5pm daily; free*

Mary Jane Colter, the architect and designer who helped create the distinctive aesthetic here on the South Rim, designed Lookout Studio. This stacked-stone watch house appears to be part of the canyon rim itself, rising from the rocks around it and offering several excellent viewpoints and photo opportunities. The Lookout was built in 1914 exactly for that purpose: to provide a comfortable but "indigenous" building and deck where visitors could take in the sights of the inner canyon and take some magnificent photos. Inside you'll find a bookstore, Grand Canyon souvenirs, and more.

▲ SWITCHBACKS ON BRIGHT ANGEL TRAIL

NEED TO KNOW

Info: Verkamp's Visitor Center, www.nps.gov/grca

Passes and Reservations: Entry to the park is $35/vehicle ($30/motorcycle, $25/pedestrian or cyclist), payable (credit or debit card only, no cash) at one of the three entrance stations. To stay overnight at Havasupai Gardens or other campsites below the rim, you must obtain a permit from the Backcountry Information Center (www.recreation.gov; $10 plus $14 pp per night). For more information, see page 507.

Weather Considerations: In summer (May-Sept.), any hiking in the inner canyon should be done before 10am. It will be 100-120°F (38-49°C) inside the canyon during the day and stay in the 80s (27-32°C) and 90s (32-37°C) once the sun goes down. Remember to eat salty snacks and drink water or an electrolyte-rich sports drink; everyone in your party should carry ample water.

Facilities: Both the 1.5-Mile Resthouse and 3-Mile Resthouse have water available mid-May-mid-October. Havasupai Gardens has water year-round. All three have toilet facilities; there are also restrooms in Grand Canyon Village around the trailhead.

Other: A note on mules: Be wary of the mules. When you encounter a mule train, step off the hill on the uphill side (not the side with the edge and drop-off). Get quiet and listen to the mule wrangler. Don't return to the trail until the last mule in the train is 50 ft (15 m) past you. Oh, and watch for their droppings—it's not the kind of Grand Canyon keepsake you'll want to bring home.

37

WIDFORSS TRAIL

GRAND CANYON NATIONAL PARK, ARIZONA

Get to know the forests of the North Rim on this hike among pines, firs, and aspens, ending at a spectacular viewpoint.

- **Distance:** 10 mi (16.1 km) round-trip
- **Duration:** 4-6 hours
- **Elevation Gain:** 1,000 ft (305 m)
- **Effort:** Easy-moderate
- **When:** May-Oct.
- **Trailhead:** Widforss Trailhead, on dirt road off Highway 67

HIGHLIGHT: Wandering among wildflowers and wildlife

This hike gives you a double dose of Grand Canyon landscapes and scenery as it leads you through an evergreen and aspen forest to views of the inner canyon. Don't let the 10-mi (16.1-km) round-trip distance discourage you; this is the kind of hike where the distance is the primary challenge, so either set a pace you can sustain for a day of hiking or cut the hike short and turn around 2.5 mi (4 km) in for a round-trip of 5 mi (8 km). In spring and part of summer, there are plenty of wildflowers blooming along the trail and in nearby pocket meadows, and you have a good chance of spotting wildlife on this trail, so keep an eye out for the Kaibab squirrel (you'll know it by the tufted ears) and other small mammals and birds.

WIDFORSS TRAIL

Named for Gunnar Widforss, a lauded Grand Canyon painter in the 1920s and 1930s, this trail is loaded with views that inspire the inner artist in all of us. If you're handy with a paintbrush, drawing implement, or your camera, you'll find dozens of frame-worthy views, and if you're not artistically inclined, you'll find that these inspiring views urge you on to the next bend and the next view. The trail begins in Harvey Meadow, home to one of the early North Rim tourist camps. Check out the cave across the meadow (it's got a locked door, so no going inside). This is where Uncle Jim Owens, a game warden who killed more than 500 mountain lions in a misguided attempt to help the mule deer population nearby, lived. His is a strange legacy, but worth mentioning.

START THE HIKE

The trail follows the rim of **Transept Canyon** through a mixed forest of ponderosa pine, fir, and spruce trees, with a few stands of aspen thrown in for good measure. Ponderosa pines have thick, mostly fire-resistant bark, so if you see spots scarred by wildfire, you'll often find ponderosa pines standing relatively unharmed. Around 1.3 mi (2.1 km) into the hike, you'll be near **one of the largest ponderosa pine trees** on the whole trail. It's a whopper, measuring 13 ft (4 m) in circumference, and park rangers believe it's between 300 and 500 years old. Soon the view will open up and you'll be looking down the length of Transept Canyon into the **Grand Canyon proper,** and this view is outstanding. You can turn back here or nearby for a hike of approximately 5 mi (8 km), or press on to **Widforss Point** where you'll have an even better look at the Grand Canyon and be able to gaze back across Transept Canyon for another dramatic bit of landscape.

DIRECTIONS

Widforss Trail is on the North Rim of Grand Canyon National Park. From Jacob Lake, take Highway 67 South for 31 mi (50 km) to the North Rim Entrance Station. Continue south on Highway 67 for 10 mi (16.1 km), about a 15-minute drive. Turn right onto Point Sublime Road (a dirt road) and follow signs to Widforss Trailhead.

NEED TO KNOW

Info: North Rim Visitor Center, www.nps.gov/grca

Passes and Reservations: Entry to the park is $35/vehicle ($30/motorcycle, $25/pedestrian or cyclist), payable (credit or debit card only, no cash) at one of the three entrance stations. For more information, see page 502.

Weather Considerations: The North Rim is typically closed November-mid-May, with the only road leading to the area, Highway 67, closed December-mid-May. Check the Grand Canyon website (www.nps.gov/grca) for up-to-date trail and road closures and conditions.

BEST NEARBY

Grand Canyon Lodge

▶ *866/499-2574; www.grandcanyonrimnorth.com; mid-May-mid-Oct.*

The historic Grand Canyon Lodge rises from the North Rim at the end of Highway 67, a rustic masterpiece of local sandstone and pine gloriously isolated at 8,000 ft (2,438 m) on what feels like the very edge of the known world. Even if you aren't staying here, spend some time in the enchanting sunroom and on the lodge's terrace, both of which are essential North Rim experiences.

With its native stone walls and picture windows framing the impossible vastness of the canyon, the **Grand Canyon Lodge Dining Room** must be seen even if you don't eat here. Its high ceilings, wrought-iron chandeliers, Native American symbols, and exposed wood rafters give this large, bright, and open space an unforgettable atmosphere and represent the height of the National Park Service Rustic style. For more casual bites, try **Deli in the Pines** or the **Roughrider Saloon,** both found at the lodge.

Facilities: There are toilets at the trailhead. There is no water available along this trail, so come prepared.

▼ WIDFORSS TRAIL

38

RIM-TO-RIM

GRAND CANYON NATIONAL PARK, ARIZONA

On this four-day trek from the North Rim to the South Rim, you'll journey through dramatic landscapes, camp in the canyon, and check a legendary achievement off your bucket list.

- **Distance:** 24.6 mi (39.6 km) one-way
- **Duration:** 2-4 days
- **Elevation Gain:** 5,570 ft (1,698 m)
- **When:** Mar.-Apr. or Oct.
- **Effort:** Strenuous
- **Trailhead:** North Kaibab Trailhead

HIGHLIGHT: Camping in the Grand Canyon

One of the most epic ways to experience the Grand Canyon is with this Rim-to-Rim hike, trekking from the North Rim to the South Rim over four days of hiking on the North Kaibab and Bright Angel Trails. It's strenuous, it's challenging, and it's totally doable for most hikers, so, with a little training and planning, you can be trail fit and ready to complete your first rim-to-rim hike pretty quickly.

SOUTH KAIBAB TRAIL

RIM-TO-RIM
To North Rim Entrance Station
67
North Kaibab
Coconino Overlook
Supai Tunnel
Bridge in the Redwall
North Rim Visitor Center
Grand Canyon Lodge
Roaring Springs
Bright Angel Point
Pumphouse Residence
Manzanita Resthouse
Manzanita Point
Cottonwood
Komo Point
North Rim
Widforss Trail
Tiyo Point
Widforss Point
Grand Canyon
National Park
Ribbon Falls
North Kaibab Trail
Bright Angel Creek
Johnson Point
Jones Point
Brahma Temple
Zoroaster Temple
Sumner Point
Phantom Ranch
CAMPING IN THE CANYON
Bright Angel
Demaray Point
Colorado River
River Trail
Bright Angel Trail
Havasupai Gardens
Mather Point
Grand Canyon Visitor Center
Bright Angel
Backcountry Information Center
Grand Canyon Village
South Rim
0 1 mi
0 1 km
Contour Interval = 40 feet
© MOON.COM

Other options for a rim-to-rim hike include hiking the same route in reverse, from the South Rim to the North Rim, or hiking via the **South Kaibab Trail** (20 mi/32 km), a faster, more direct route to the river than the Bright Angel Trail. While shorter, the South Kaibab is a good deal steeper than the Bright Angel, and there is no water available.

Some power-hikers will tackle this trail in one marathon-length push, but unless you're an ultra-hiker, any rim-to-rim hike will be a multiday affair. Most hikers do this on a four-day itinerary, logging around 6 mi (9.7 km) each day (some days are slightly more, some are slightly less) and camping at Cottonwood, Bright Angel (or staying at Phantom Ranch), and Havasupai Gardens.

START THE HIKE

From the trailhead on the North Rim, follow **North Kaibab Trail** as it weaves among coniferous trees, transitions to a red-rock desert, and leads you deeper and deeper into the canyon. In addition to the staggering beauty of the views, several highlights await on the trail down. **Coconino Overlook** (0.7 mi/1.1 km from the trailhead) offers great views and photo opportunities; **Supai Tunnel** (2 mi/3.2 km), opened up out of the red rock in the 1930s by the Civilian Conservation Corps, is an interesting bit of trail engineering; and the **Bridge in the Redwall** (2.6 mi/4.2 km), built in 1966 after a flood ruined this portion of the trail, provides an interesting man-made element to your views of the Grand Canyon.

About 5 mi (8 km) from the rim, you'll pass the wet greenery of **Roaring Springs;** just beyond is the old **Pumphouse Residence,** now a ranger station, and the **Manzanita Resthouse** near the creek, where there's seasonal drinking water and shade.

At around the halfway point, 6.8 mi (10.9 km) from the rim, you'll reach the creekside **Cottonwood Campground,** a great place to spend the night. Another 1.5 mi (2.4 km) or so down the trail is **Ribbon Falls,**

◄ BRIDGE IN THE REDWALL

▼ RIBBON FALLS ON THE NORTH KAIBAB TRAIL

▲ DESCENDING ON THE RIM-TO-RIM HIKE

a wonderful spot with falling water and moss and other shocking greenery on the dry red land.

For another night in the canyon, 14 mi (22.5 km) from the rim, there's **Bright Angel Campground** and **Phantom Ranch.** Designed by Mary Jane Colter for the Fred Harvey Company in 1922, Phantom Ranch is the only noncamping accommodation inside the canyon. It has rustic, air-conditioned cabins, hiker-only dormitories, and a canteen.

From there, cross the **Colorado River** via suspension bridge, and climb 5 mi (8 km) up to reach **Havasupai Gardens;** follow the **Bright Angel Trail** (page 202) up to the South Rim to complete the hike.

DIRECTIONS

This Rim-to-Rim hike begins on the North Rim of Grand Canyon National Park. From Jacob Lake, take Highway 67 South for 31 mi (50 km) to the North Rim Entrance Station. Continue south on Highway 67 for 10.5 mi (16.9 km) to the North Kaibab Trailhead, about a 15-minute drive. The North Kaibab Trailhead has a decent-sized parking lot, though it fills up during the high season, so the earlier you get here the better. You can also arrange for a shuttle from Grand Canyon Lodge, or walk 1.5 mi (2.4 km) from the lodge to the trailhead via the Bridle Trail.

Unless you want to turn around and do it all over again, you'll need to stage cars before hiking, leaving a vehicle at the South Rim's main parking lot that can take you back to your car at the North Kaibab Trailhead. You can also arrange for rim-to-rim transportation with **Trans Canyon Shuttle** (www.trans-canyonshuttle.com; $120 pp one-way; reservations required).

NEED TO KNOW

Info: North Rim Visitor Center, www.nps.gov/grca

Passes and Reservations: Entry to the park is $35/vehicle ($30/motorcycle, $25/pedestrian or cyclist), payable (credit or debit card only, no cash) at one of the three entrance stations. To stay overnight at any campsite below the rim, you must obtain a permit from the **Backcountry Information Center** (928/638-7875; $10 plus $14 pp per night). For more information, see page 507.

Weather Considerations: The North Rim is typically closed November-mid-May, with the only road leading to the area, Highway 67, closed December-mid-May. The best times to hike in the inner canyon are April or October—but these are also some of the most difficult times to get permits. Summer is not a good time; it will be 100-120°F (38-49°C) inside the canyon during the day and stay in the 80s (27-32°C) and 90s (32-37°C) once the sun goes down.

Facilities: There's drinking water available along the trail, but don't rely on it. May 15-October 14, you can refill your water bottle at the North Kaibab Trailhead, Supai Tunnel, Roaring Springs, Manzanita Resthouse, Cottonwood Campground, and Bright Angel Campground/Phantom Ranch; these locations also have toilets. All the water stations along the trail are turned off October 15-May 14. Along the Bright Angel Trail, the 1.5-Mile Resthouse and 3-Mile Resthouse have water available mid-May-mid-October. Havasupai Gardens has water year-round. All three have toilet facilities; there are also restrooms in Grand Canyon Village around the Bright Angel Trailhead. There are no showers along the trail; coin-operated shower facilities are available at the North Rim Campground ($1.50/6 minutes) and at Camper Services in Market Plaza on the South Rim ($2.50/5 minutes).

Other: For $86 each way, you can hire a mule to carry up to 30 lb (13.6 kg) of gear for you, so all you have to bring is a day pack with water and snacks.

BEST NEARBY

Phantom Ranch

▶ *888/297-2757; www.grandcanyonlodges.com; year-round*

Phantom Ranch, the only noncamping accommodations found below the rim of the Grand Canyon, is a stunner. This collection of cabins and buildings were built using local materials, making each one appear as if it's grown out of the landscape (this style of architecture, found here and across the park system, is called National Park Service Rustic). You can reach Phantom Ranch one of three ways: hiking, riding a mule in, or arriving by river raft (and hiking up to Phantom Ranch). Because so many hikers, mule riders, rafters, and national park enthusiasts clamor to stay here, it's said Phantom Ranch is one of the most difficult, exclusive reservations to get, and when you consider that booking windows open 15 months in advance, it's handled by lottery, and specific dates are difficult to get (be flexible with your trip timing to maximize your chance of securing a bed), I'd say those rumors are accurate. Accommodations include cabins for two ($214) and group cabins ($355), as well as dormitories ($70); if you need food they have breakfast ($38), a sack lunch ($25), and dinner options from steak to stew to veggie-friendly dishes ($41-61).

▲ RIM-TO-RIM HIKE

39

LOMA VERDE LOOP

SAGUARO NATIONAL PARK, ARIZONA

Experience the Sonoran Desert, from mesquite and creosote groves to cactus forests, desert wildflowers, and what remains of a onetime gold and copper mine.

- **Distance:** 3.7 mi (6 km) round-trip
- **Duration:** 1-1.5 hours
- **Elevation Gain:** 154 ft (47 m)
- **Effort:** Easy
- **When:** Mar.-May and Sept.-Nov.
- **Trailhead:** Loma Verde Trailhead

HIGHLIGHT: Taking in grand views from the slopes of the Rincon Mountains

This loop trail serves as an excellent introduction to the Sonoran Desert landscape of Saguaro National Park and this part of Arizona. You'll pass through patches of mesquite trees, gaze upon a cactus forest, pass an abandoned mine, and, if your timing is right, see plenty of desert wildflowers in bloom. To see the bloom, plan to hike in March for flowers like the wild zinnia, gold poppy, and desert lupine; in April and May you'll find plenty of cacti in bloom including the saguaro, prickly pear, and strawberry hedgehog; and during the hot stretch from June to September—when we recommend hiking as early in the day as possible—you'll find century plant, sotol, and the night-blooming cereus in flower.

STRAWBERRY HEDGEHOG CACTUS

START THE HIKE

Loma Verde Trail heads almost due north from the **parking area,** immediately entering a stand of mature mesquite trees. These trees have a distinct and recognizable smell, familiar to anyone who's done any live-fire cooking—like barbecue—in this part of the United States. Soon into the hike, at 0.2 mi (0.3 km), you'll cross a seasonal stream and meet the intersection with Squeeze

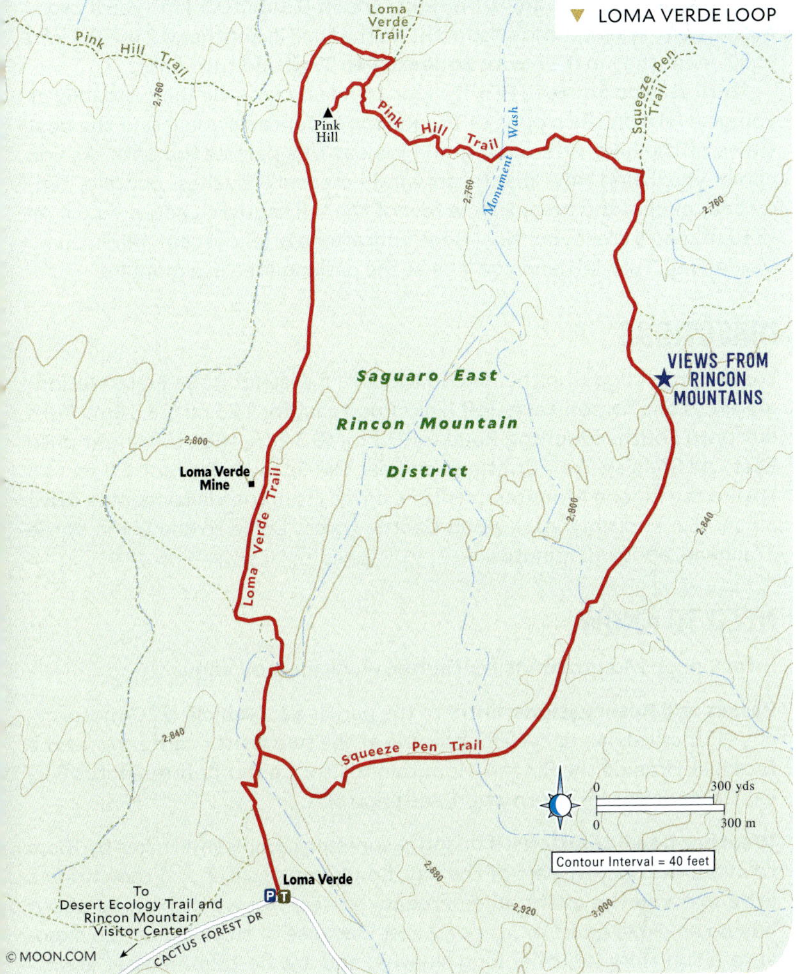

Pen Trail to the right (we'll return to this spot at the end of the loop). Keep to the left and cross the seasonal stream again (it's generally flowing in spring), then climb up the bluff onto a bajada—the Spanish word for a gravel plain at the base of a mountain—where you'll see a junction with the Cholla Trail; stay to the right and follow the trail on a long, gentle descent.

In 0.2 mi (0.3 km) you'll be near the **Loma Verde Mine,** sitting to your left among the cacti and mesquite. This onetime copper and gold mine was active in the early 1900s, but the Civilian Conservation Corps filled it in during work here in the 1930s. Continue along Loma Verde Trail another 0.7 mi (1.1 km) and you'll find a spur trail to the right leading to **Pink Hill.** The Pink Hill Trail leads to a low **summit** where you'll have panoramic views of the Catalina and Rincon Mountains and a carpet of cacti: cholla, prickly pear, barrel, and hedgehog, even a few saguaros (the saguaros are most abundant in the Tucson Mountain District/West Unit of the park). Rejoin the trail and turn right, and in 0.3 mi (0.5 km) you'll cross **Monument Wash,** the lowest point on the trail; in another 0.2 mi (0.3 km) you'll meet the junction with **Squeeze Pen Trail** and turn right.

You'll stay on Squeeze Pen Trail for 1.5 mi (2.4 km), climbing steadily as you go. Here on the slopes of the Rincon Mountains you'll find the best views of the hike, offering a grand look at this part of the park. As you climb, you'll find new plants growing—creosote bushes, ocotillo, teddy bear cholla, and more than a few of the tall saguaro cactus. At 3.4 mi (5.5 km) you'll crest your final ridge and, after a brief descent, rejoin Loma Verde Trail. Turn left and you'll be at the parking area in a moment.

DIRECTIONS

Loma Verde Loop is in the Rincon Mountain District of Saguaro National Park. From Tucson, take Golf Links Road east for 14.5 mi (23.3 km). Turn left onto South Houghton Road for 0.3 mi (0.5 km), then turn right onto East Old Spanish Trail. Continue on East Old Spanish Trail for 2.8 mi (4.5 km) to the Rincon Mountain Visitor Center. From the visitor center, drive 3.5 mi (5.6 km) northeast along Cactus Forest Drive to the Loma Verde Trailhead, about 10 minutes.

NEED TO KNOW

Info: Rincon Mountain Visitor Center, www.nps.gov/sagu

Passes and Reservations: Entry to the park is $25/vehicle ($20/motorcycle, $15/pedestrian or cyclist), payable at the two visitor centers or at the fee kiosk outside the Rincon Mountain Visitor Center before Cactus Forest Drive. For more information, see page 502.

Weather Considerations: If hiking in summer, complete all hikes by 10am to avoid the hottest part of the day. Bring ample water and then bring a little extra; in the event an emergency arises, you won't be mad about having an extra quart or liter of water. Because of the intense sun exposure, a sun shirt (or other long sleeves) and a wide-brimmed hat are essential, as is quality sunscreen and sunglasses.

Facilities: There are no facilities at the trailhead.

BEST NEARBY

Desert Ecology Trail

This 0.25-mi (0.4-km) paved trail provides an accessible way to experience the ecology of the Sonoran Desert. With little elevation gain—only 9 ft (2.7 m)—it's an easy jaunt into this foreign-to-most-of-us environment. Here you'll find a collection of cacti, shrubs, bushes, and trees typical to the area. March-September, various wildflowers, trees, and cacti will be in bloom. It's especially impressive to see the bright flowers on the prickly cacti. The Desert Ecology Trail is the type of short trail that I love: Densely packed with plants, it invites introspection and close examination of the world around you.

▲ SAGUARO CACTUS FOREST

40

GARWOOD DAM AND WILDHORSE TANK

SAGUARO NATIONAL PARK, ARIZONA

Hike through a cactus forest past the Garwood Dam to one of the only constant water sources in the park.

- **Distance:** 6.3 mi (10.1 km) round-trip
- **Duration:** 3 hours
- **Elevation Gain:** 889 ft (271 m)
- **Effort:** Moderate
- **When:** Mar.-May and Sept.-Nov.
- **Trailhead:** Douglas Spring Trailhead

HIGHLIGHT: Wildlife watching at Little Wildhorse Tank

Make your way through towering saguaro cactus forests and past blooming plants like the prickly pear and ocotillo on your way to this desert watering hole and haven for wildlife. Stay alert for signs of wildlife—birdsong; the tracks of sidewinders, tarantulas, and desert tortoises; lizards darting from shade to shade—as you hike in, then get quiet while you wait for larger critters to appear at Wildhorse Tank.

◀ GARWOOD DAM TRAIL

▼ LITTLE WILDHORSE TANK

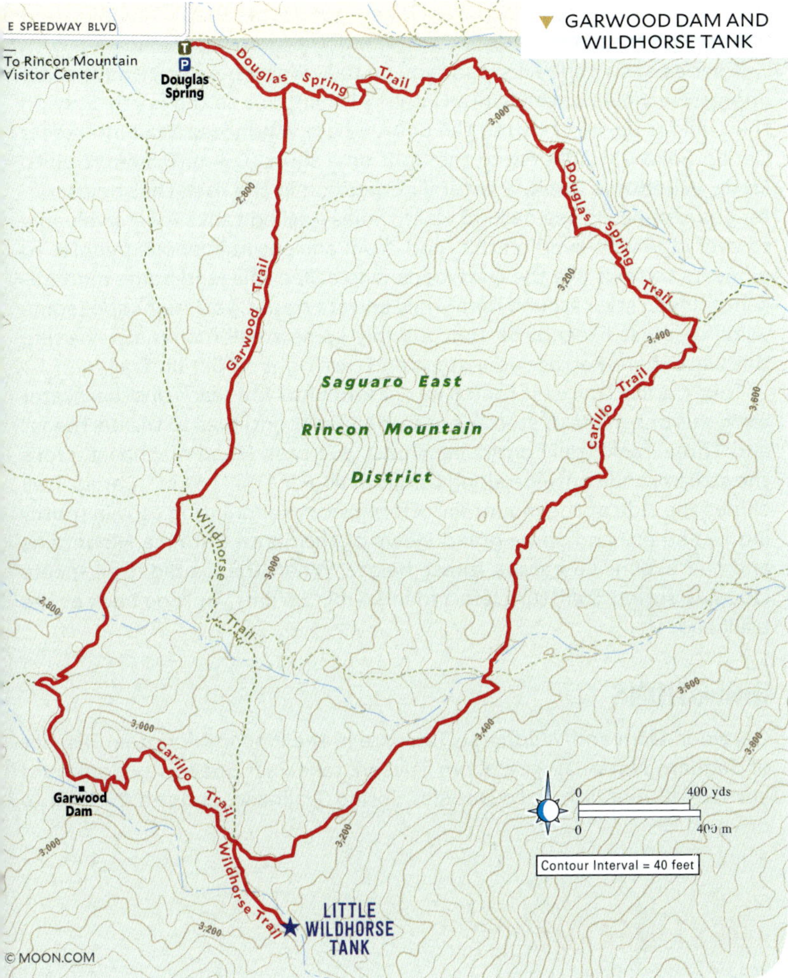

START THE HIKE

The hike to Garwood Dam and Wildhorse Tank starts in the northwestern corner of the park at the **Douglas Spring Trailhead** and leads to a rare sight in the desert: a consistent water source. Begin on **Douglas Spring Trail** and in 0.2 mi (0.3 km) you'll take a right on **Garwood Trail** as it enters a cactus forest. Take your time here and observe the saguaro, other plants, and the wildlife. These cactus forests—whether huge or pocket forests—inspired the creation of this national park back in 1933, and this vast collection of saguaro is exactly why: These majestic cacti are unlike any other in the park.

At 1.1 mi (1.8 km), Wildhorse Trail cuts across Garwood; stay on Garwood Trail until you reach the T junction with **Carillo Trail** at 1.4 mi (2.3 km). Turn left on Carillo and descend this steep portion of trail for 0.3 mi (0.5 km). Off to your right you'll see a semicircular concrete dam, the remains of **Garwood Dam.** Nelson Garwood built this dam back in the

1950s but the structure endures. Take a good look, snap a few pics, and get back on the trail.

A series of switchbacks leads you up to a ridge where you'll have some impressive views of the Santa Catalina Mountains to the north. Stay on this trail for 0.6 mi (1 km) to the point where **Wildhorse Trail** intersects Carillo. Follow Wildhorse to the right on a short (0.3 mi/0.5 km) trail to **Little Wildhorse Tank,** a natural depression in the rock that holds water year-round. These natural water holes—called tanks—were valuable to everyone who lived on this land, from ancient Indigenous peoples to pioneers to folks like the Garwoods who called this land home more recently. If you stick around for a while and stay quiet, you might spot some wildlife—most likely birds, but possibly some small mammals—visiting this water hole. Retrace your steps and turn right on Carillo Trail.

Take Carillo Trail east for 0.8 mi (1.3 km) until you reach another water tank, this one made of steel. Here, Carillo Trail continues to the northeast and Three Tank Trail continues almost due east. Head northeast, cross the stream, and continue along Carillo Trail. For 1 mi (1.6 km), Carillo Trail climbs the side of the mountain, offering some undulating terrain (nothing too steep) and some grand views of the Santa Catalina Mountains and the expansive cactus forest below. When the Carillo Trail meets Douglas Spring Trail, turn left and in 1.6 mi (2.6 km) you'll be back at the trailhead.

DIRECTIONS

Garwood Dam and Wildhorse Tank are in the Rincon Mountain District of Saguaro National Park. From Tucson, take East Speedway Boulevard east for 18 mi (29 km) to Douglas Spring Trailhead, about a 40-minute drive.

BEST NEARBY

Tanque Verde Falls

▶ *Coronado National Forest; 520/749-8700; www.fs.usda.gov/coronado; free (no entrance or parking fee)*

For a rare sight in the desert southwest, head to Tanque Verde Falls, only 6.8 mi (10.9 km) from the Douglas Spring Trailhead (which you used for the Garwood-Wildhorse hike). This 1.9-mi (3.1-km) round-trip hike in the Coronado National Forest is dog-friendly and popular with locals for the mountain scenery and the 80-ft (24-m) waterfall at the end. Smaller waterfalls, cascades, and pools by the trail make interesting habitats for desert flora and fauna. Due to the desert temperatures, this hike is best October-April.

To reach this trailhead from the trailhead for Garwood Dam and Wildhorse Tank, turn left (west) on East Speedway Boulevard, right (north) on North Wentworth Boulevard, and then right (east) again on East Reddington Road. Follow East Reddington for 3.7 mi (6 km) and the trailhead will be on your left. Note that the last section of this drive is on a gravel road generally suitable for sedans, no 4WD required. There are picnic tables and restrooms (but no water) available at the second parking area.

NEED TO KNOW

Info: Rincon Mountain Visitor Center, www.nps.gov/sagu

Passes and Reservations: Though there is no pay station at the trailhead, you're still responsible for acquiring an entrance pass, so you'll need to add a little time to your trip if you need to get your pass. Entry to the park is $25/vehicle ($20/motorcycle, $15/pedestrian or cyclist), payable at the two visitor centers or at the fee kiosk outside the Rincon Mountain Visitor Center before Cactus Forest Drive. For more information, see page 502.

Weather Considerations: If hiking in summer, complete all hikes by 10am to avoid the hottest part of the day. Bring ample water and then bring a little extra; in the event an emergency arises, you won't be mad about having an extra quart or liter of water. Because of the intense sun exposure, a sun shirt (or other long sleeves) and a wide-brimmed hat are essential, as is quality sunscreen and sunglasses.

Facilities: There are no facilities at the trailhead.

▼ SANTA CATALINA MOUNTAINS IN THE DISTANCE

▲ CACTUS IN SAGUARO NATIONAL PARK

41

PA'RUS TRAIL

ZION NATIONAL PARK, UTAH

This all-season trail offers hikers of all abilities the chance to immerse themselves in nature and soak up the scenery in a place where a bubbling river rushes beneath high, rocky peaks

- **Distance:** 3 mi (4.8 km) round-trip
- **Duration:** 2-2.5 hours
- **Elevation Gain:** 50 ft (15 m)
- **Effort:** Easy
- **When:** Year-round
- **Trailhead:** Zion Canyon Visitor Center

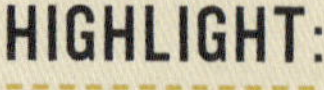

Immersing yourself in dramatic mountain and river views year-round

Pa'rus Trail draws its name from the Virgin River, which runs alongside the trail for its entire length. Pa'rus, a Paiute word meaning "bubbling, tumbling water," is an apt name, as the river offers a lovely sonic background for a hike. The trail is paved; accessible for those with mobility needs; bike-, stroller-, and pet-friendly (though we don't advise bringing your pet; see the note below); and absolutely

▲ FALL IN ZION

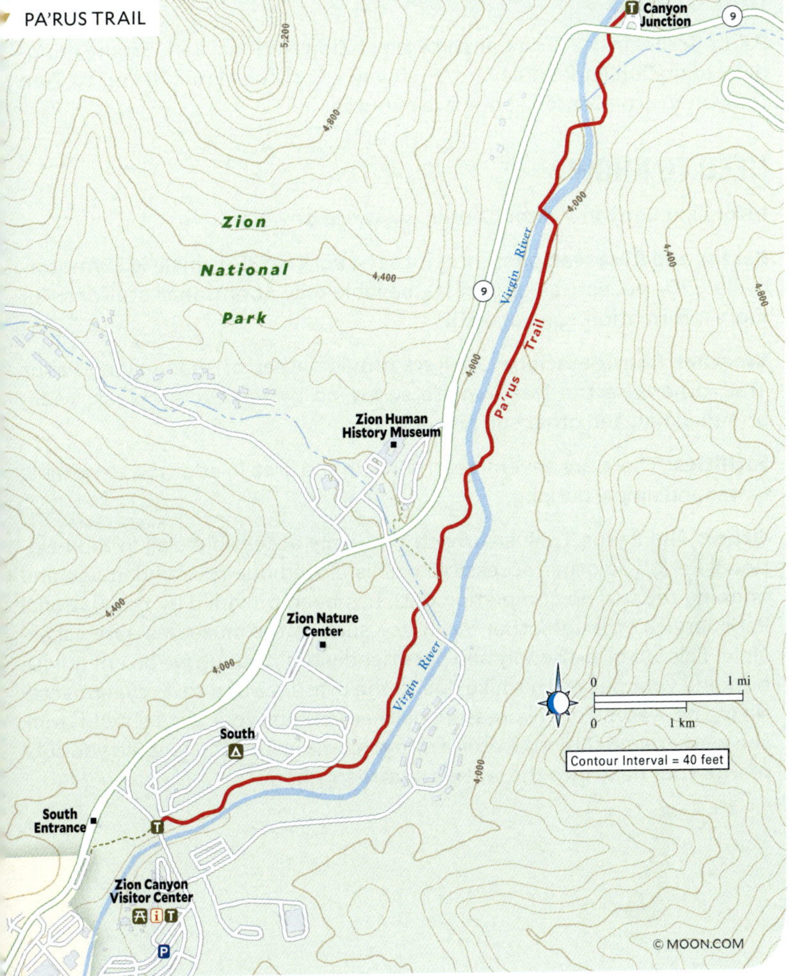

ideal for an early-morning or evening stroll. As you hike, you'll hear those bubbling, tumbling waters, but listen for the trill and song of the canyon wren and see if you can spot one of the tiny, elusive birds in trailside trees and bushes.

START THE HIKE

The trail runs between the **Zion Canyon Visitor Center** and **Canyon Junction,** passing the **South Campground, Zion Nature Center,** and **Zion Human History Museum** along the way. The view is great here, with excellent looks at the river and the peaks towering above: The Watchman, West Temple, Bee Hive, and others make dramatic backgrounds for any photos you take. Due to the ease of this trail, it's excellent in every season. During autumn the cottonwood, ash, and maple trees fill the canyon with color, and in winter, snow on the highest peaks adds drama to this rocky desert landscape.

DIRECTIONS

Pa'rus Trail is in the Zion Canyon area of Zion National Park. From Springdale, take Zion Park Boulevard/Highway 9 East for 1.1 mi (1.8 km) to Zion Canyon Visitor Center, about five minutes.

NEED TO KNOW

Info: Zion Canyon Visitor Center, www.nps.gov/zion

Passes and Reservations: Entry into the park is $35/vehicle ($30/motorcycle, $20/ pedestrian or cyclist), payable only at entrance stations. For more information, see page 502.

Weather Considerations: Shelters provide areas of shade along Pa'rus Trail; otherwise the trail is quite sunny, so bring your sunblock, wide-brimmed hat, and other sun protection.

Facilities: There are several restrooms in the area in addition to potable water and ample parking.

Other: The Pa'rus Trail is currently the only accessible trail in Zion National Park (the other accessible trail is closed due to trail damage and ongoing repairs; no completion date has been provided by the National Park Service), though other facilities—such as the museums—are accessible. This is a bike-friendly and pet-friendly trail, though we do not advise bringing your pet on this hike due to the presence of a toxic cyanobacteria in the water. For this reason, neither you nor your pets should drink the water (even filtered water) from streams in Zion, nor should you submerge your head into the waters or streams here.

BEST NEARBY

Zion Human History Museum

▶ *Shuttle stop: Zion Human History Museum; 9am-6pm daily mid-Apr.-late May, 9am-7pm daily late May-early Sept., 9am-6pm daily early Sept.-early Oct., 10am-5pm Sat.-Sun. early Oct.-mid-Apr.; entry included in park admission fee*

Through artifacts, archival material, and film, the Zion Human History Museum offers insights into the Indigenous peoples and settlers—largely Latter-day Saints—who lived in the region. Whether you're curious about the human presence in the park, it's time for a break from the trail, or the weather forces you inside, the museum offers insights, shade, and air-conditioning. From the back patio you can take in the sunrise (it's an excellent spot for sunrise watching) and two peaks: West Temple and the Altar of Sacrifice, so named for the iron-rich, red-streaked cliff face.

▲ VIEW FROM ZION HUMAN HISTORY MUSEUM

42

CANYON OVERLOOK TRAIL

ZION NATIONAL PARK, UTAH

Regarded as one of the gems of Zion National Park, this short, easy trail offers awe-inspiring views of Zion Canyon.

- **Distance:** 1 mi (1.6 km) round-trip
- **Duration:** 1 hour
- **Elevation Gain:** 157 ft (48 m)
- **Effort:** Easy
- **When:** Year-round
- **Trailhead:** Canyon Overlook Trailhead

HIGHLIGHT: Enjoying an expansive panoramic view of Zion Canyon

This hike is short, easy, and fun, making it a great introduction to hiking in Zion National Park whether it's your first trail ever or just the first trail of the day. You'll get a double-dose of landscape views thanks to the sights of Zion Canyon and the impressive natural skyline. The best thing about these views: You don't have to work too hard to earn them.

◄ CANYON OVERLOOK

▼ PINE CREEK NARROWS

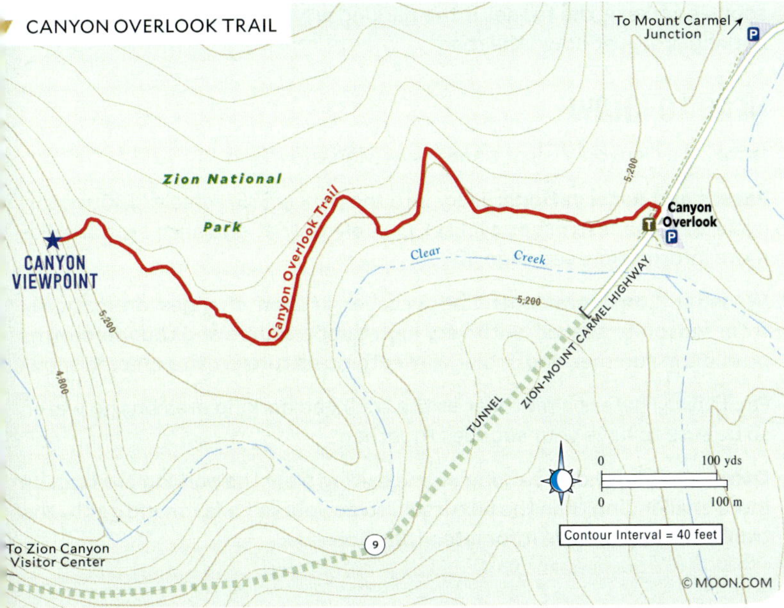

START THE HIKE

A set of stone steps ascends from the trailhead, leading you up a steady but not-too-steep slope. In places the trail is carved from the sandstone cliffs, offering deep, shady alcoves to one side and views of Pine Creek Canyon and the Pine Creek Narrows below. Soon you'll see Pine Creek Canyon open into a huge valley and reach the edge of the canyon where you'll have an expansive panoramic view of Zion Canyon.

This marks the toughest point in the trail: the 200-ft (61-m) descent to the **viewpoint** proper and the 200-ft (61-m) climb back out. From the viewpoint you'll have a spectacular skyline of stony peaks and spires. A sign at the viewpoint identifies the landmarks: Bridge Mountain, Streaked Wall, Towers of the Virgins, Beehives, and more. Below is a feature you can see from the road: the Great Arch of Zion, a "blind arch" open on only one side. The arch is truly impressive: 580 ft (177 m) high, 720 ft (219 m) long, and 90 ft (27 m) deep. If you want to see the Great Arch when it's an open, proper arch, set your alarm clock for around 30,000,000 years from now and come back.

From here, reverse course to return to the trailhead.

DIRECTIONS

Canyon Overlook Trail is in the Zion Canyon area of Zion National Park. From Springdale, take Zion Park Boulevard/Highway 9 East for 1.1 mi (1.8 km) to Zion Canyon Visitor Center, about 5 minutes. From the visitor center, drive 6 mi (9.7 km) northeast along Zion-Mount Carmel Highway/ Highway 9 East, about 15 minutes. The Canyon Overlook parking area is east of the Mount Carmel Tunnel on the Zion-Mount Carmel Highway as soon as you exit the tunnel. If the parking area is full, there's a secondary parking area just down the road.

NEED TO KNOW

Info: Zion Canyon Visitor Center, www.nps.gov/zion

Passes and Reservations: Entry into the park is $35/vehicle ($30/motorcycle, $20/ pedestrian or cyclist), payable only at entrance stations. For more information, see page 502.

Weather Considerations: The weather in Zion changes dramatically from season to season, with very high temperatures and thunderstorms possible in summer, and cooler winter temperatures with expected snow.

Facilities: There is a pit toilet at the trailhead parking area but no water, so be sure to have your supplies together.

Other: On a busy day, parking at and exiting from the parking area can be more challenging than the hike itself, so do yourself a favor and get to the trailhead early or save it for late afternoon.

BEST NEARBY

Zion-Mount Carmel Highway

▶ *Highway 9*

The east section of Zion National Park is a wild land of hoodoos, narrow canyons, and sandstone slickrock, a place impossible to see without being moved. This dramatic scenery unrolls before you along the Zion-Mount Carmel Highway (Highway 9), between Mount Carmel Junction and Zion Canyon Visitor Center, a 24.5-mi (39.4-km) drive that takes about 2 hours. As you ride, feel free to stop at overlooks and points of interest like Zion Canyon Overlook Trail and the Great Arch of Zion, the bizarre Checkerboard Mesa, and other natural wonders.

▲ GAZING ACROSS PINE CREEK NARROWS

43

WEST RIM TRAIL TO ANGELS LANDING

ZION NATIONAL PARK, UTAH

Climb a series of switchbacks, then grab hold of a chain to traverse the final stretch to a 360-degree view of Zion canyon.

- **Distance:** 5.4 mi (8.7 km) round-trip
- **Duration:** 4 hours
- **Elevation Gain:** 1,488 ft (454 m)
- **Effort:** Strenuous
- **When:** Mar.-Sept.
- **Trailhead:** Across the road from Grotto Picnic Area

HIGHLIGHT: Rewarding yourself with stunning summit views atop Angels Landing

This monster hike will test your strength and fortitude on the trail, through steep sections and dangerous drop-offs, as you follow the path to one of the best views of Zion Canyon. The challenge of the trail and the exceptional views along the way make this one of the most popular hikes in the park (be prepared to share the trail with others unless you get a very early start).

◂ ANGELS LANDING

▾ SWITCHBACKS TO ANGELS LANDING

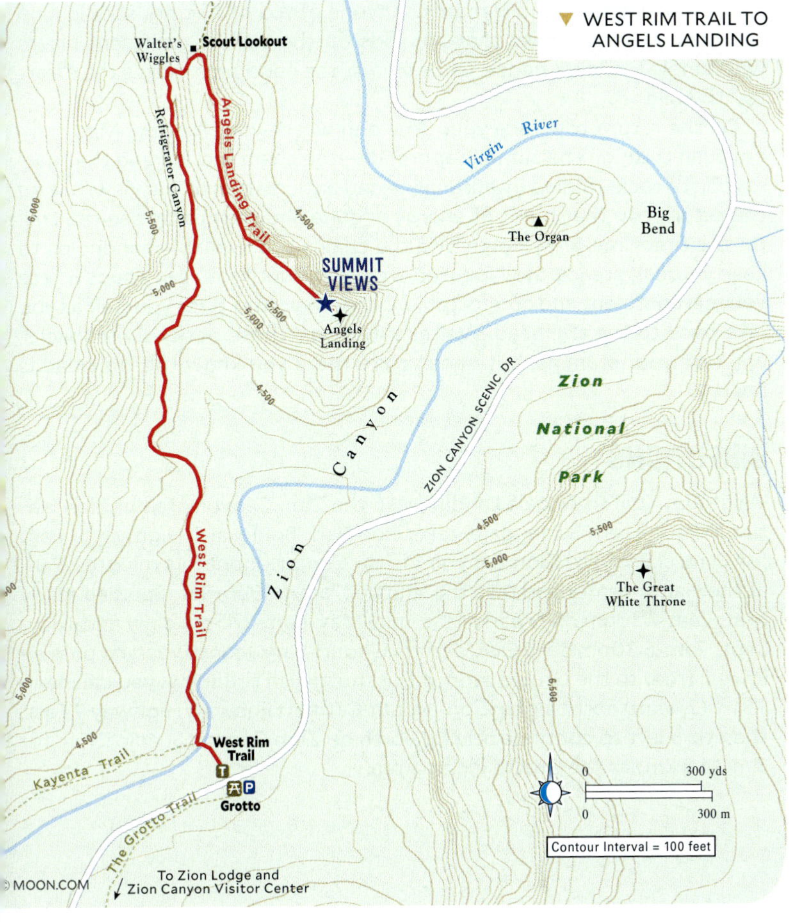

START THE HIKE

Your hike begins at the Grotto (elev. 4,300 ft/1,311 m), where you'll cross a footbridge, then turn right along the river. The trail, blasted out of the cliffside by the Civilian Conservation Corps back in the 1930s, climbs into the shady depths of the aptly named **Refrigerator Canyon. Walter's Wiggles,** a series of 21 closely spaced switchbacks, wind up to a trail junction and **Scout Lookout,** where you'll have excellent canyon views. Many hikers turn around here, satisfied with the view and wary of the narrow, fin-like trail to the summit of **Angels Landing.** If you turn back here, your hike will be 4 mi (6.4 km) round-trip and gain 1,050 ft (320 m) in elevation. If you continue, it's a hair-raising 0.5 mi (0.8 km) to the summit of **Angels Landing.**

Angels Landing itself is a sheer-walled monolith towering 1,500 ft (457 m) above the North Fork of the Virgin River. Although the trail to the summit is rough and very narrow, chains provide security on the sections with high exposure. Hike this final approach to Angels Landing carefully and only in good weather; don't go if the trail is covered with snow or ice or if thunderstorms threaten. Anyone afraid of heights should skip this trail, and we advise that any kids on the trail be confident hikers with ample trail experience. Once on top, the panorama makes the effort worthwhile.

On the return trip, take your time and watch your footing. Many hikers push through the summit approach—the chain section and that narrow fin of rock—fueled by adrenaline and anticipation of the view, but on the return trip that burst of energy is gone and they really see the trail for the first time. Slow down. Use the chains and available handholds to keep yourself steady. Stay focused on the trail until you're in a spot where you feel confident and comfortable. Other than that, pace yourself as you hike back to the trailhead. Walter's Wiggles, those pesky switchbacks, will test your stamina, but once you're there you know the trailhead is nearby.

DIRECTIONS

West Rim Trail to Angels Landing is in the Zion Canyon area of Zion National Park. From Springdale, take Zion Park Boulevard/Highway 9 East for 1.1 mi (1.8 km) to Zion Canyon Visitor Center, about five minutes. Park at the visitor center and take the shuttle (7am-6:15pm Sat.-Sun. Feb.-early Mar., 7am-7:30pm daily early Mar.-mid-May, 6am-8:15pm daily mid-May-Sept., 7am-6:30pm daily Oct.; seasonal hours vary year to year; no pets allowed; free) to the Grotto stop. If the shuttle isn't running, you can head 1.5 mi (2.4 km) north along Zion-Mount Carmel Highway/Highway 9 East, then turn left to continue driving north on Zion Canyon Scenic Drive for 3 mi (4.8 km) to the Grotto Picnic Area.

BEST NEARBY

Zion Lodge

▶ *Shuttle stop: Zion Lodge; 435/772-7700 or 888/297-2757; www.zionlodge.com*

Rustic Zion Lodge is in the heart of Zion Canyon, 3 mi (4.8 km) up Zion Canyon Scenic Drive. Open year-round, Zion Lodge provides the only accommodations (aside from camping) and dining options within the park. Dine inside the lodge at the Red Rock Grill (435/772-7760; 7am-8pm daily; dinner reservations required; dinner entrées $13-21), featuring a Southwest- and Native American-influenced menu for breakfast (7am-11am), lunch (11:30am-4pm), and dinner (4:30pm-8pm) daily. There's also a snack bar called the Castle Dome Café (breakfast and lunch daily spring-fall) with fast food and a patio beer garden cart. The lodge also has evening programs, a gift shop, Wi-Fi in the lobby (it's not very fast), and accessible public restrooms.

NEED TO KNOW

Info: Zion Canyon Visitor Center, www.nps.gov/zion

Passes and Reservations: Entry into the park is $35/vehicle ($30/motorcycle, $20/ pedestrian or cyclist), payable only at entrance stations. A permit is required to hike any part of the West Rim Trail to Angels Landing. For more information, see page 506.

Weather Considerations: It's best to do this steep hike during the cooler morning hours. Start extra early to avoid the crowds, which can make the final stretch all the more frightening.

Facilities: There is a restroom at the Grotto Picnic Area.

Other: Due to the steep and dangerous drop-offs along the trail, we don't recommend this hike for kids, those who experience issues with heights and exposure, or those absolutely new to hiking.

▼ ANGELS LANDING

44

THE NARROWS

ZION NATIONAL PARK, UTAH

On this unique and adventurous trek through the Virgin River, wade and sometimes swim upstream between canyon walls, surrounded by dramatic scenery.

- **Distance:** 5.2-10.2 mi (8.4-16.4 km) round-trip
- **Duration:** 5-9 hours
- **Elevation Gain:** 200 ft (61 m)
- **Effort:** Strenuous
- **When:** Mid-June-mid-July and mid-Sept.-mid-Oct.
- **Trailheads:** Riverside Walk Trailhead at Temple of Sinawava

HIGHLIGHT: Hiking in the Virgin River

Upper Zion Canyon is doubtless the most famous backcountry area in the park, and the hike here is among the most strenuous you'll encounter. There's no trail per se; instead you follow the Virgin River and the incredible course it's carved over millions of years. As you're following the river, significant wading and even swimming is required: At times the river is knee-deep, at other points it's chest-deep. The canyon ranges from broad to narrow, and at its most-narrow point, the high, fluted walls are a mere 20 ft (6 m) apart, and only a little sunlight reaches the floor of the Narrows. Side canyons full of mystery and the promise of discovery branch off from the main route. Bring your sense of adventure as you hike and you'll be left in awe at the plants growing high on the canyon walls and the haunting way the light filters through canyon and leaf to reach the river below.

▲ HIKING IN THE VIRGIN RIVER

The Narrows is a "bottom-up" hike. What exactly does "bottom up" mean? Hiking the Narrows this way means navigating it south to north, starting from the main Zion Canyon and following the river upstream. The benefits of doing so are easy access, no permit required, few technical challenges, and a

THE NARROWS
Big Springs
The Narrows
Zion National Park
Virgin River
Wynopits Mountain
Orderville Canyon
HIKING IN THE VIRGIN RIVER
Mountain of Mystery
End of Paved Trail
Riverside Walk
Temple of Sinawava
To Zion Canyon Visitor Center
West Rim Trail
0 500 yds
0 500 m
Contour Interval = 80 feet
© MOON.COM

length that can be knocked out in a day; you can make this a true daylong hike or simply wade a short distance for some photos and the experience before turning back. The downside is that most people hike the Narrows this way, so you'll deal with more crowds, especially toward the beginning. Hiking the Narrows from the top down is a two-day adventure requiring an overnight permit. Top-down access is via a remote road, and you may need to book a guide if you lack the navigation skills to confidently execute this adventure independently. Trust me, unless you're experienced with canyoneering and map-and-compass route-finding, you'll want a guide.

START THE HIKE

From the **Temple of Sinawava** shuttle stop and parking area, head north to the **Riverside Walk Trailhead** and enjoy the pleasant 1.1-mi (1.8 km) Riverside Walk, the first 0.4 mi (0.6 km) of which is accessible. The end of the paved trail is the gateway to The Narrows hike, during which you'll be walking, wading, and occasionally swimming in the **Virgin River.** For a half-day trip, follow the Narrows 1.5 mi (2.4 km, about 2 hours) upstream from the end of the Riverside Walk to **Orderville Canyon,** then back the same way. Day hikers without permits can continue hiking all the way to **Big Springs,** about 2.5 mi (4 km, 3 hours) past Orderville, before turning around.

DIRECTIONS

The Narrows is in the Zion Canyon area of Zion National Park. From Springdale, take Zion Park Blvd/Highway 9 East for 1.1 mi (1.8 km) to Zion Canyon Visitor Center, about five minutes. Park at the visitor center and take the shuttle (7am-6:15pm Sat.-Sun. Feb.-early Mar., 7am-7:30pm daily early Mar.-mid May, 6am-8:15pm daily mid-May-Sept., 7am-6:30pm daily Oct.; seasonal hours vary year to year; no pets allowed; free) to the Temple of Sinawava stop. If the shuttle isn't running, you can head 1.5 mi (2.4 km) north along Zion-Mount Carmel Highway/Highway 9 East, then turn left to continue driving north on Zion Canyon Scenic Drive for 6 mi (9.7 km) to the Temple of Sinawava parking area.

BEST NEARBY

Temple of Sinawava

▶ *Shuttle stop: Temple of Sinawava*

The last shuttle stop is at this sandstone amphitheater—named for Sinawava, a Paiute coyote spirit—that precedes the most drastic narrowing of Zion Canyon's 2,000-ft (610-m) walls. The paved, wheelchair-accessible Riverside Walk (1 mi/1.6 km one-way) hugs the eastern side of the Virgin River up the canyon alongside hanging gardens and birds nesting in holes in the cliffs. This path terminates at the Narrows.

▲ HIKING THE NARROWS

NEED TO KNOW

Info: Zion Canyon Visitor Center, www.nps.gov/zion

Passes and Reservations: Entry into the park is $35/vehicle ($30/motorcycle, $20/ pedestrian or cyclist), payable only at entrance stations. No permit is needed if you're not going farther than Big Springs. For more information, see page 506.

Weather Considerations: Hazards include flash floods and hypothermia; expect water temperatures of about 68°F (20°C) even in summer, and around 38°F (3°C) in winter. Finding the best time to go can be tricky. In spring, runoff is often too high. Summer thunderstorms bring flash flood risks that can temporarily close the hike, and summer temperatures bring toxic cyanobacteria blooms (which means keeping water away from your face, or avoiding contact altogether if toxicity is too high). In winter the water is too cold, unless you're in a dry suit. Early summer (mid-June-mid-July) and early autumn (mid-Sept.-mid-Oct.) are the best windows.

Before your hike, check conditions and the forecast with rangers at the Zion Canyon Visitor Center—they can also provide pointers and a handout with useful information.

Facilities: There is a restroom at the trailhead.

Other: Hikers should be well outfitted and in good shape—river hiking is more tiring than land hiking. Don't be tempted to wear river sandals or sneakers up the Narrows; it's easy to twist an ankle on the slippery rocks. You can use hiking boots you don't mind drenching, but the ideal solution is available from Zion Adventures (36 Lion Blvd., Springdale; 435/772-1001; www.zionadventures.com) and other Springdale outfitters. They rent specialized river-hiking boots, along with neoprene socks, hiking poles, and, in cool weather, dry pants and dry suits. Boots, socks, and sticks rent for $29; with a dry suit the package costs $59. They also offer guidance on hiking the Narrows and lead tours of the section below Orderville Canyon ($279-309 pp, varies by season). Zion Outfitter (7 Zion Park Blvd., Springdale; 435/772-5090; www.zionoutfitter.com), located just outside the park entrance, and Zion Guru (1013 Zion Park Blvd., Springdale; 435/632-0432; www.zionguru.com) provide similar services at comparable prices.

45

RIM TRAIL

BRYCE CANYON NATIONAL PARK, UTAH

Hike along the rim of the canyon to take in amazing scenery, from nearby rock formations to distant peaks.

- **Distance:** 11 mi (17.7 km) round-trip
- **Duration:** 5-7 hours
- **Elevation Gain:** 540 ft (165 m)
- **Effort:** Easy
- **When:** Apr.-Oct.
- **Trailhead:** Fairyland Point

HIGHLIGHT: Catching a sunrise from Sunrise Point

Rim Trail follows the edge of Bryce Amphitheater, providing jaw-dropping views nearly every step of the way. The whole hike is 11 mi (17.7 km) round-trip from Fairyland Point to Bryce Point (or vice versa), but if you're pressed for time or just want to stick to one area, you can follow Rim Trail as far as you want, taking on the full 11 mi (17.7 km) or satisfying your hiking itch with a mile (1.6 km) or less. If you're sticking to the highlights, the three Inspiration Point viewpoints—Upper, Middle, and Lower Inspiration Points—or the hike between Sunrise and Sunset Points offer maximum views for minimal effort. But this whole trail requires minimal effort: It's well maintained, mostly flat, and easy to follow. Several trails lead into the canyon and explore the area beneath the rim, so if you have the time and the inclination, there's more to discover here.

▲ FAIRYLAND POINT

START THE HIKE

Starting from the north, **Fairyland Point** provides views to wild and whimsical rock formations lining Fairyland Canyon a short distance below. As you walk southwest, the canyon is on your left. About 3 mi (4.8 km) after Fairyland Point, you'll find **Sunrise Point,**

RIM TRAIL
Dixie National Forest
Park Entrance Sign
63
Fairyland Point
Fairyland Canyon
Rim Trail
Boat Mesa
Bryce Canyon Visitor Center
Entrance Station
North
Fairyland Loop Trail
Bryce Canyon National Park
Campbell Canyon
General Store
SUNRISE POINT
Queen's Garden Trail
PAVED
Lodge at Bryce Canyon
Thors Hammer
Queen's Garden
Sunset Point
Navajo Loop
Sunset
BRYCE AMPHITHEATER
Tropic Trail
Inspiration Point
Peekaboo Loop Trail
BRYCE POINT RD
Bryce Point
500 yds
500 m
Contour Interval = 50 feet
© MOON.COM

connected to **Sunset Point** by a 0.5-mi (0.8-km) paved and mobility-accessible section of the trail. As you can imagine, sunrise and sunset are spectacular from both of these viewpoints, and panoramas from each point take in swaths of Bryce Amphitheater and beyond, including the Aquarius and Table Cliff Plateaus to the northeast, and the colorful cliffs rising 2,000 ft (610 m) or higher. As most of the amphitheater faces east, sunrise is especially breathtaking, as the first light of day illuminates the park's iconic hoodoos and red rocks in brilliant shades of orange, pink, and gold.

It's well worth the 0.75-mi (1.2-km) walk from Sunset Point south along the Rim Trail to see a fantastic maze of hoodoos in the "Silent City" from **Inspiration Point.** Weathering along vertical joints has cut rows of narrow gullies, some more than 200 ft (61 m) deep. It's a short but steep 0.2-mi (0.3-km) walk to Upper Inspiration Point.

Finally, Bryce Point (1.4 mi/2.3 km from Inspiration Point), an overlook at the south end of Bryce Amphitheater, takes in expansive views to the north and east. Reverse course to return to your car at the Fairyland parking area.

You can also start this hike from the south end—at Bryce Point—and head to Fairyland Point if you like.

DIRECTIONS

Rim Trail is in the Bryce Amphitheater area of Bryce Canyon National Park. From Panguitch, take US 89 South for 6 mi (9.7 km), then turn left onto Highway 12 East. Continue for 13.6 mi (21.9 km). The turnoff for Fairyland Point is just inside the park boundary, right before you get to the booth where payment is required; go north 0.8 mi (1.3 km) from the visitor center, then east 1 mi (1.6 km).

NEED TO KNOW

Info: Bryce Canyon Visitor Center, www.nps.gov/brca

BEST NEARBY

Stone Hearth Grille

▶ *1380 W. Stone Canyon Ln., Tropic; 435/679-8923; www.stonehearthgrille.com; 5pm-9pm daily Mar.-Oct.; reservations advised; $28-47*

The Stone Canyon Inn (www.stonecanyoninn.com; rooms from $200), located east of the park a couple of miles outside of downtown Tropic, offers the most luxurious lodging in the region inside a striking modern building and a collection of bungalows, cabins, and tree houses. The inn's restaurant, Stone Hearth Grille, has an upscale atmosphere and menu. The food is the best for miles around, featuring local, grass-fed beef; great salads and starters; and near-perfect desserts. In good weather, have your meal on the terrace and enjoy the lovely off-the-beaten-path setting. Reservations are recommended, as is changing out of your trail clothes and into something date-night-appropriate—it is a nice place after all.

Passes and Reservations: Entry into the park is $35/vehicle ($30/motorcycles, $20/pedestrian or cyclist). Passes are available in advance at www.recreation.gov. For more information, see page 502.

Weather Considerations: Winter can be harsh in Bryce Canyon, and snowfall can force road and trail closures. If you come in winter, know that sections of the main scenic drive may be closed, and sections of the Rim Trail (often the 1.5-mi/2.4-km section between Bryce Point and Inspiration Point) are closed.

Facilities: Restrooms and refreshments are available at the General Store near Sunrise and Sunset Points.

Other: The 0.5-mi (0.8-km) section of trail between Sunrise and Sunset Points is paved and wheelchair accessible; this part of the trail is also open to pets.

▼ SUNRISE FROM BRYCE POINT

46

QUEEN'S GARDEN-NAVAJO LOOP

BRYCE CANYON NATIONAL PARK, UTAH

From the rim, descend past sweeping views of Bryce Amphitheater into a hoodoo-filled basin.

- **Distance:** 3.2 mi (5.1 km) round-trip
- **Duration:** 1.5 hours
- **Elevation Gain:** 636 ft (194 m)
- **Effort:** Moderate
- **When:** Apr.-Oct.
- **Trailhead:** Sunset Point

HIGHLIGHT: Hiking among hoodoos in the Queen's Garden

The Queen's Garden-Navajo Loop is the most popular hike in the park, and for good reason: It's awesome, iconic, and a trail most hikers and national park visitors can and will enjoy. It begins at Sunset Point—where you'll have spectacular views even if you go no farther—and immediately drops below the rim of the canon to explore the features in Bryce Amphitheater, including a hoodoo that resembles a portly Queen Victoria.

▲ WALL STREET

▼ QUEEN'S GARDEN-NAVAJO LOOP

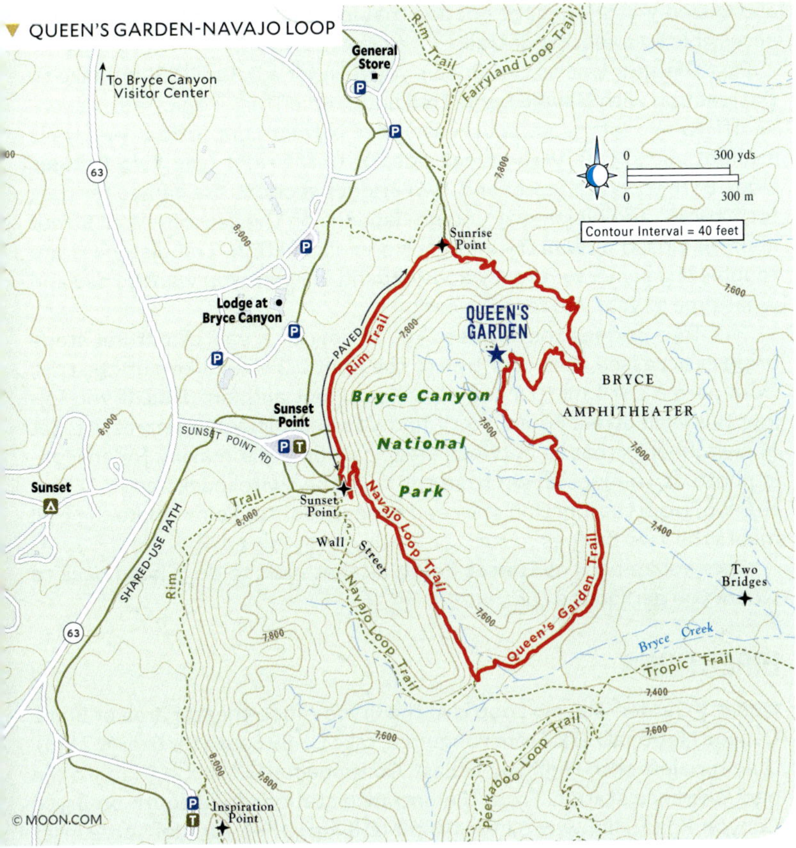

© MOON.COM

START THE HIKE

Park near **Bryce Canyon Lodge** at the **Sunset Point parking area** (or wherever there's a spot) and take the short spur trail to **Rim Trail;** turn left (northeast) toward **Sunrise Point.** Admire the view and then follow the trail below the canyon rim and into Bryce Amphitheater along **Queen's Garden Trail.** As you enter the **amphitheater** you'll find yourself surrounded by rock fins, wild-looking hoodoos and spires, and an otherworldly landscape. Begin your hike near sunrise and this first section will be awash in golden morning light, making the landscape that much more impressive. Around 0.3 mi (0.5 km) into the hike you'll be able to climb a small rise and gaze down into Queen's Garden.

Keep descending into the amphitheater, ignoring the trail branching off to the left (southeast) at the 0.6-mi (1-km) mark and staying on the trail to the right. In 0.2 mi (0.3 km), you'll enter the **Queen's Garden** proper and find yourself surrounded by multicolored hoodoos. Hoodoos are stone spires shaped and twisted by geological pressures and by ages of wind and water; the ones here are multicolored, appearing at times as if they were formed by gigantic hands. Two features in the Queen's Garden make it noteworthy: first, the Hole in the Wall, a literal hole in the wall;

and Queen Victoria, a huge hoodoo that looks like a queen on her throne, accessible by a short spur trail.

Past the spur trail to the Queen, you're in for a 0.8-mi (1.3-km) hike to the junction with **Navajo Loop Trail** and Tropic Trail. Tropic Trail branches off to the left (east/southeast), but Navajo Loop offers you trails straight ahead (the **Wall Street** side) or to the right (the **Two Bridges** side). Both the Wall Street and Two Bridges sections are named for rock formations, and which way you go depends on the season—Wall Street is often closed in winter—and your own inclination. The distances are roughly the same, so it really does depend on what you want to see and what time of year you're in the park.

The Two Bridges route offers you a view of a pair of natural stone bridges, accessed via a spur trail to the right 0.2 mi (0.3 km) up the trail; from here it's 0.4 mi (0.6 km) to Sunset Point and Rim Trail. If you follow the Wall Street route, you'll find yourself facing an impressive set of switchbacks that lie between steep canyon walls, making for an iconic photo as you look down from the top. The switchbacks begin 0.5 mi (0.8 km) from the junction; they end beneath Sunset Point where the trail meets the Two Bridges route.

Once you're back at **Sunset Point,** all that's left to do is head back to where you parked the car.

DIRECTIONS

Queen's Garden-Navajo Loop is in the Bryce Amphitheater area of Bryce Canyon National Park. From Panguitch, take US 89 South for 6 mi (9.7 km), then turn left onto Highway 12 East. Continue for 13.6 mi (21.9 km) to the park entrance station. From the entrance station, drive south on Bryce Canyon Road/Highway 63 for 0.5 mi (0.8 km), then turn left on Sunset Point Road, where you'll find the parking lot.

BEST NEARBY

Lodge at Bryce Canyon

▶ *435/834-8700 or 855/765-0255; www.visitbrycecanyon.com; late Mar.-early Nov.*

Set among ponderosa pines a short walk from the rim, the Lodge at Bryce Canyon was built in 1923 by a division of the Union Pacific Railroad; a spur line once terminated at the front entrance. Listed in the National Register of Historic Places, this is the only lodging in the park itself, and it's heavy on charm. With that yesteryear charm comes a yesteryear stay: You'll find no Wi-Fi, air-conditioning, or in-room televisions here, so come prepared to focus on the park. The dining room at the Lodge at Bryce Canyon (7am-10am, 11:30am-3pm, and 5pm-10pm daily late Mar.-early Nov.; $16-46) is classy and atmospheric, with a large stone fireplace and white tablecloths. The food is better than other options in the area. The General Store (generally 8am-8pm late Mar.-early Nov.) at the lodge provides groceries, including fresh, frozen, and canned foods and soda, beer, and water, but it also offers grab-and-go hot and cold foods. The General Store has seasonal laundry and shower facilities too, as well as a gift shop full of park goodies.

The summer shuttle (every 15-20 minutes 8am-8pm daily mid-Apr.-mid-Oct., shorter hours early and late in season; free) stops at Sunrise Point and Sunset Point.

NEED TO KNOW

Info: Bryce Canyon Visitor Center, www.nps.gov/brca

Passes and Reservations: Entry into the park is $35/vehicle ($30/motorcycles, $20/pedestrian or cyclist). Passes are available in advance at www.recreation.gov. For more information, see page 502.

Weather Considerations: Sections of Bryce's main scenic drive may be closed in winter. During winter, the Wall Street side of Navajo Trail closes.

Facilities: Restrooms and drinking fountains are available at the General Store at Sunrise Point and at Sunset Point.

Other: Of all the trails in the park, this is the most prone to rockfall, so watch for slides or the sounds of falling rocks; it's not uncommon for at least part of the trail to be closed for rockfall.

▼ TWO BRIDGES

▲ NAVAJO LOOP, BRYCE CANYON NATIONAL PARK

47

FAIRYLAND LOOP TRAIL

BRYCE CANYON NATIONAL PARK, UTAH

This long hike immerses you in the wild landscape of hoodoos and multicolored rock characteristic of Bryce Canyon.

- **Distance:** 8 mi (12.9 km) round-trip
- **Duration:** 4-5 hours
- **Elevation Gain:** 2,300 ft (701 m)
- **Effort:** Strenuous
- **When:** Apr.-Oct.
- **Trailheads:** Fairyland Point

HIGHLIGHT: Taking in the panoramic views of Bryce Amphitheater

This meandering 8-mi (12.9-km) trail leads through colorful rock spires and formations in the northern part of Bryce Amphitheater. Though this part of the park is less visited than other areas, expect to find a few folks here, as the challenge of this hike and the incredible scenery here draw intrepid hikers such as yourself. If you have two cars and want to shave 3 mi (4.8 km) of trail from this hike, you can park one car at Sunrise Point and another at Fairyland Point, and hike car-to-car, enjoying the great outdoors along the way.

TOWER BRIDGE

START THE HIKE

Begin at Fairyland Point in the northern section of Bryce Canyon National Park and descend immediately into **Bryce Amphitheater.** The descent is gentle at first, but soon grows steep, and for the first 1 mi (1.6 km) you'll be pointed firmly downhill. Adjust your boots at the stream crossing, then descend a little more. Take note of the scenery as you climb down into the canyon—it's a showstopper. The stone fins, the hoodoos, and the multicolored rock dazzle with an otherworldly beauty. A handful of short spur trails lead to overlooks of interesting hoodoo formations and other photogenic sites; feel free to explore them or stick to the main trail.

At the 4-mi (6.4-km) mark you'll find a trail leading to **Tower Bridge,** a hoodoo and arch formation that looks like a castle torn from the pages of *A Song of Ice and Fire* or its TV adaptation *Game of Thrones.* From here, you're in for an uphill climb with little relief until you're back at Rim Trail and headed toward your car. Readjust your laces, fix your hiking poles to climbing length, and get started. Fortunately, the scenery offers plenty of mystery and discovery to pull you forward.

Once you reach **Rim Trail,** you'll follow it right toward Fairyland Point and your vehicle. If you need to make a pit stop at the **General Store** for a restroom break or a snack, go for it.

DIRECTIONS

Fairyland Loop Trail is in the Fairyland Canyon area of Bryce Canyon National Park. From Panguitch, take US 89 South for 6 mi (9.7 km), then turn left onto Highway 12 East. Continue for 13.6 mi (21.9 km). The turnoff for Fairyland Point is just inside the park boundary, right before you get to the booth where payment is required; go north 0.8 mi (1.3 km) from the visitor center, then east 1 mi (1.6 km).

NEED TO KNOW

Info: Bryce Canyon Visitor Center, www.nps.gov/brca

Passes and Reservations: Entry into the park is $35/vehicle ($30/motorcycles, $20/pedestrian or cyclist). Passes are available in advance at www.recreation.gov. For more information, see page 502.

Weather Considerations: This trail is very sunny and exposed during summer, so bring sunscreen, a sun shirt, and a wide-brimmed hat. Plan to bring at least 1 quart or liter of water per person for every 2-3 hours of hiking (2-3 quarts/liters for this hike). Sections of Bryce's main scenic drive may be closed in winter.

Facilities: Restrooms, water fountains, and grab-and-go dining items are available at the General Store near Sunrise Point.

Other: Pets are not permitted on this trail.

BEST NEARBY

Mossy Cave Trail

This easy, 1-mi (1.6-km) round-trip trail is just off Highway 12 near the east edge of the park (meaning no park entrance fee is required) and takes about an hour or less. Hike up Water Canyon to a cool alcove of dripping water and moss. Sheets of ice and icicles appear in winter. Just before the cave, a side trail branches right a short distance to a little waterfall. Look for several small arches in the colorful canyon walls above. Although the park lacks perennial natural streams, the stream in Water Canyon flows even during dry spells. Latter-day Saints pioneers labored for three years to channel water from the East Fork of the Sevier River through a canal and down this wash to the town of Tropic. Without this irrigation, the town might not exist. To reach the trailhead from the visitor center, return to Highway 12 and turn east, then travel 3.7 mi (6 km) toward Escalante; the parking area is on the right just after a bridge, between Mileposts 17 and 18.

▲ BRYCE AMPHITHEATER

48

CASSIDY ARCH TRAIL

CAPITOL REEF NATIONAL PARK, UTAH

Hike to a spectacular arch where Butch Cassidy is said to have once hidden among this spectacular desert landscape.

- **Distance:** 3.1 mi (5 km) round-trip
- **Duration:** 3 hours
- **Elevation Gain:** 686 ft (209 m)
- **Effort:** Moderate-strenuous
- **When:** Apr.-June or Sept.-Oct.
- **Trailhead:** End of drivable section of Grand Wash Road

HIGHLIGHT: Taking a dramatic picture on Cassidy Arch

Our national parks preserve places of great beauty, important natural history, and places that reveal our human history; Capitol Reef is no exception. Here, a vast wrinkle of rock called the Waterpocket Fold stretches across more than 100 mi (161 km) of the Utah desert. In the park you'll find soaring rock formations, canyons, ancient petroglyphs, and orchards planted by pioneers. Highway 24 and the paved Scenic Drive offer easy glimpses at the landscape, but to truly explore, park the car and hit the trail.

◀ CASSIDY ARCH
▼ GRAND WASH TRAIL

Cassidy Arch Trail—named for the famed outlaw Butch Cassidy, not the Grateful Dead tune "Cassidy"—begins on Grand Wash Road, a gravel track through a narrow sandstone canyon, and leads to this impressive arch on the canyon rim some 400 ft (122 m) above. The trail is simple, straightforward, and marked with stone cairns, but as cell service is spotty in this remote park, be sure to download your map or bring a paper copy with you.

START THE HIKE

From the **parking area,** head northeast along **Grand Wash Trail** for 0.2 mi (0.3 km) and then turn left (west) onto **Cassidy Arch Trail** and begin your uphill climb. This is where you put in the work for the trail. The next 0.25 mi (0.4 km) is steep and the trail has several switchbacks to make the climb easier. As soon as you finish the switchback section, the trail grows easier and the views of Grand Wash Road open up to your right. As you continue to climb, the views open even more, at times reminding me of scenes from *Raiders of the Lost Ark* or *Star Wars Episode IV*. Soon you'll see Cassidy Arch in the distance.

The trail splits 1.2 mi (1.9 km) into the hike. Left leads to Cassidy Arch; right leads across the slickrock along Frying Pan Trail to Cohab Canyon. When the trail splits, it grows a little more difficult to follow. The slickrock doesn't reveal the trail and cairns marking the route are spaced far apart. Take your time, study the landscape in front of you, and continue working toward Cassidy Arch. As you walk uphill across huge sandstone slabs, you'll come upon what looks like a giant hole in the ground, but give it a moment and **Cassidy Arch** will reveal itself.

The arch is wide and stable, so feel free to walk across it; pictures of you on the arch will make a dramatic shot to send to friends and family.

While you take in the scenery and catch your breath, you'll wonder, "Did Butch Cassidy really come here?" Maybe so, maybe not. We know he had a hideout in Grand Wash Canyon, so it's likely he saw or even camped here at the arch. Regardless, it's a good name. When it's time to return, simply retrace your steps.

DIRECTIONS

Cassidy Arch Trail is in the northern area of Capitol Reef National Park, near the Fruita Historic District. From Torrey, take Highway 24 East for 10.7 mi (17.2 km) to the visitor center. From the visitor center, turn right onto Scenic Drive and continue for 3.4 mi (5.5 km). Turn left onto Grand Wash Road and follow it all the way to its end at the trailhead.

NEED TO KNOW

Info: Capitol Reef National Park Visitor Center, www.nps.gov/care

Passes and Reservations: Entry into the park is $20/vehicle ($15/motorcycle, $10/pedestrian or cyclist). Passes are available in advance at www.recreation.gov. For more information, see page 502.

Weather Considerations: Expect hot summer days, with highs in the upper 80s and low 90s (30-34°C) and cool nights. Late-afternoon thunderstorms are common in July-August; be alert for impending storms, which can bring flash flooding. In winter, snow accents the colored rocks and rarely hinders traffic on the main highway. Winter travel on the back roads and trails may be halted by snow, but it melts when the sun comes out.

Facilities: Toilets are at the trailhead. There are no dining options in the park.

BEST NEARBY

Fremont Petroglyphs

Petroglyphs offer a rare glimpse into cultures long past, and several panels of Fremont petroglyphs are easy to get to along Highway 24. On the north side of Highway 24 are several panels of Fremont petroglyphs—the best in the park. The artwork was created 600-1300 CE, when the Indigenous Fremont people called this area home. The Fremont people were primarily hunter-gatherers who dwelled in pit houses in this valley.

To see the petroglyphs, follow Highway 24 1.2 mi (1.9 km) east from the visitor center and park in the designated area. You'll find petroglyphs of bighorn mountain sheep and human figures (some wearing headdresses) on the cliff nearby. For the best viewing, bring your binoculars. There are more petroglyphs here, and to see them, wander along the boardwalk to the left and right of the cliff face and see what you find.

▲ STONE SLABS ALONG CASSIDY ARCH TRAIL

TOP EXPERIENCE

49

DELICATE ARCH TRAIL

ARCHES NATIONAL PARK, UTAH

Hike up a slickrock trail past desert wildflowers to the most iconic site in Utah (as seen on state license plates).

- **Distance:** 3 mi (4.8 km) round-trip
- **Duration:** 2 hours
- **Elevation Gain:** 500 ft (152 m)
- **Effort:** Moderate-strenuous
- **When:** Year-round; Mar.-Oct. is most crowded
- **Trailhead:** Wolfe Ranch

HIGHLIGHT: Watching the sunset at Delicate Arch

It's likely you've seen Delicate Arch before hitting the trail: It's the arch featured on Utah's license plates. With a little effort you can snap your own license plate-worthy shot of Delicate Arch, but before we hit the trail, let's talk about the name. One glimpse of the arch and you'll know why it's called "delicate," but it's had other, more colorful names before Delicate Arch came into wide use in 1934. Those names include Salt Wash Arch, Cowboy's Chaps, and Old Maid's Bloomers. As creative as the other names may be, Delicate Arch seems fitting, so head to Wolfe Ranch and get on the trail.

◄ WOLFE RANCH CABIN

▼ PETROGLYPHS NEAR WOLFE RANCH

▼ DELICATE ARCH TRAIL

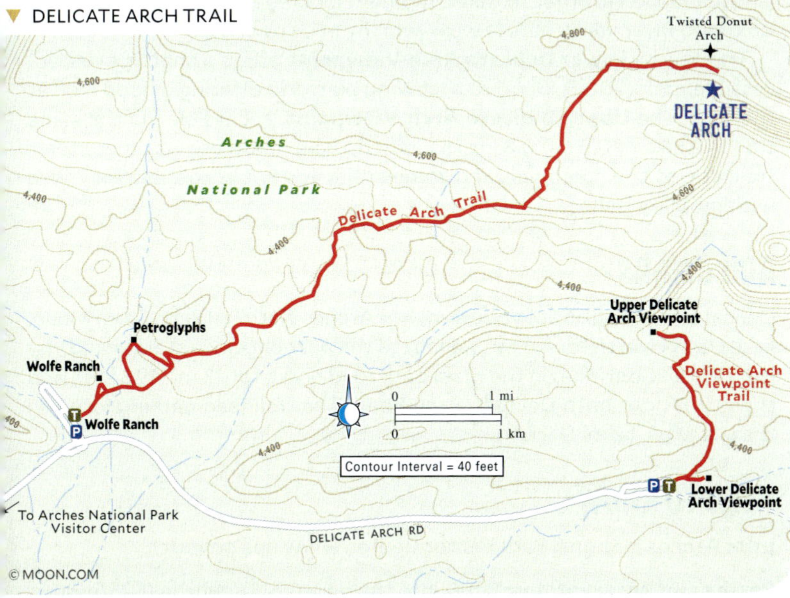

START THE HIKE

Delicate Arch Trail begins at **Wolfe Ranch,** but we're going to take a pair of detours before hitting the trail proper. The first detour is a few paces up the trail where a spur trail on the left leads to what remains of Wolfe Ranch, a onetime ranch and sheep station. The second detour is not much farther on; this spur—again on your left—leads to a gallery of **petroglyphs** (rock art) created in the mid-late 1600s by the Ute people showing bighorn sheep and human figures riding horses. After you've seen it, continue along the spur trail and rejoin **Delicate Arch Trail.**

The beginning section of the trail is easy: broad, flat, and, frankly, lacking a little in the dramatic scenery department; in spring, wildflowers add some color and interest to this part of the trail. Keep hiking as the payoff is coming up. After 30 minutes, the trail begins a steep climb, heading up the slickrock face to the rocky summit. The higher you climb, the better the view becomes, so take your time and soak up the views. Up here on the slickrock, it's easy to lose the trail, so keep an eye on the rock cairns marking the route.

As you near Delicate Arch, keep an eye on the scenery to the right, where you'll spot a small arch called Twisted Donut Arch by some, Frame Arch by others. Detour off trail over to **Twisted Donut Arch** and peer through for a fabulously framed look at Delicate Arch. Snap a few shots and rejoin the trail. Soon you'll round the bend to Delicate Arch.

At **Delicate Arch** you'll be tempted to stay all day (or night, depending on when you arrive) because there's something mesmerizing about this place. If you want to take the classic Delicate Arch photo, plan to arrive in late afternoon or early evening, times when the setting sun makes the sandstone glow golden. Spend a little time hiking around the arch, looking for other angles for a photo and exploring what interests you in the landscape. Don't forget to take a moment looking at the long view, as the Colorado River valley here is wow-worthy in its own right.

The nearby **Lower Delicate Arch Viewpoint** offers a short, paved, accessible path (200 ft/61 m) to a viewing platform offering a good look at the arch. The **Upper Delicate Arch Viewpoint,** accessible via the same trail, is a hike of 0.5 mi (0.8 km) round-trip up a moderate, at times steep, trail; due to the steepness and some stairs, it's not accessible for those with mobility issues.

DIRECTIONS

Delicate Arch Trail is at Wolfe Ranch in Arches National Park. From Moab, take US 191 North for 4.6 mi (7.4 km) to the park entrance station and visitor center. Continue on the main park road north for 12 mi (19.3 km), and then turn right onto Delicate Arch Road. The trailhead parking lot is on the left after 1.2 mi (1.9 km).

NEED TO KNOW

Info: Arches National Park Visitor Center, www.nps.gov/arch

Passes and Reservations: Entry into the park is $30/vehicle ($25/motorcycle, $15/pedestrian or cyclist). Passes are available in advance at www.recreation.gov. Timed entry tickets ($2) are required April 1–October 31. For more information, see page 503.

Weather Considerations: Sudden storms in late spring-fall can whip up flash floods and draw lightning to the park, so watch the sky and the forecast and avoid getting caught up in some nasty weather. During winter, mind the ice and snow as they can make the trail slippery. During summer, or whenever it's hot and sunny, be careful: This hike has little shade and you'll want to bring extra water to account for the heat.

BEST NEARBY

Wolfe Ranch

Pioneer history lives on at Wolfe Ranch, where Civil War veteran John Wesley Wolfe settled in 1888, hoping the desert climate would help his health problems and old injuries. He picked this spot because of a spring found high in the rocks, grass to feed his herd of cattle, and water enough to irrigate a small garden. Wolfe and his family lived here for more than 20 years, and after their departure, cattle ranchers used it as a line ranch. Though the grass in the area survived cattle ranching, when sheepherders arrived, their animals overgrazed the range so badly, the grass has yet to recover.

A weather-beaten cabin built in 1906 still survives, and a short trail leads to petroglyphs above Wolfe Ranch. Here you'll see figures of bighorn sheep and people riding horses, indicating that the Ute people, rather than earlier inhabitants, did the artwork. Park staff can give directions to other rock-art sites nearby—take great care not to touch the fragile artwork.

Facilities: There are toilets at the trailhead. There are no accommodations or restaurants inside the park.

Other: To avoid crowds, try visiting for sunrise, when the crowds are a little thin (not everyone wants to get up early on vacation), or at sunset, when you'll have a few more partners on the trail, but not as many as a midday hike.

▼ SUNSET AT DELICATE ARCH

50

LANDSCAPE ARCH TRAIL

ARCHES NATIONAL PARK, UTAH

Follow this easy trail through the desert and rock of Devils Garden to the largest arch in the United States.

- **Distance:** 2.4 mi (3.9 km) round-trip
- **Duration:** 1 hour
- **Elevation Gain:** 348 ft (106 m)
- **Effort:** Easy
- **When:** Year-round; Mar.-Oct. is most crowded
- **Trailhead:** Devils Garden Trailhead

HIGHLIGHT: Stretching your arms beneath Landscape Arch

Landscape Arch is located in the Devils Garden section of the park. Devils Garden has a fierce name, but it's fitting for a landscape full of narrow rock walls, tall fins of stone, spires, arches, and more. The hike to Landscape Arch is one of several in this section, and if you were to hike to each of the six arches and on each of the spur trails here, you'd face 7.9 mi (12.7 km) of hiking and nearly a full day on the trail. This hike to Landscape is the easiest of the bunch—and it has a big payoff

TUNNEL ARCH

with a view of the largest arch in the United States. If you do decide to press on and hike all or most of the trails here, know that the section between the trailhead and Landscape Arch is the easiest, so prepare for a more difficult trail as you go deeper into the Devils Garden.

START THE HIKE

Join the crowd at the trailhead (it's a popular hike, so you're going to have some companions on the trail, though not nearly as many as on Delicate Arch Trail) and make your way along the packed sand path. At 0.2 mi (0.3 km), a spur trail to the right leads to **Pine Tree Arch** and **Tunnel Arch.** Tunnel Arch, accessed via a second spur trail on the right, has a fairly symmetrical opening: 22 ft (6.7 m) high and 27 ft (8.2 m) wide, and is worth the visit. Pine Tree Arch has a similar symmetry with an opening that's 48 ft (15 m) high and 46 ft (14 m) wide, though a pinyon pine that once grew inside the arch gave it a great name.

After you've visited this pair of arches, rejoin the trail and head to Landscape Arch, which is dead ahead.

Landscape Arch is incredible. The 306-ft (93-m) span—6 ft (1.8 m) longer than a football field—is one of the longest unsupported rock spans in the world. The size makes it precarious, and the thin arch looks like it's ready to collapse at the slightest tremor or breeze. Indeed, parts of it have fallen off over the years, notably a big rockfall in 1991 that led park rangers to fence off the area directly beneath the arch.

If you're interested in extending the hike, a trio of trailheads near Landscape Arch will set you on the Devils Garden Primitive Trail Loop. Whether you circle the Primitive Trail Loop clockwise or counterclockwise, you'll encounter four spur trails leading to viewpoints and arches and another 4.5 mi (7.2 km) of trail.

DIRECTIONS

Landscape Arch Trail is in the Devils Garden section of Aches National Park. From Moab, take US 191 North for 4.6 mi (7.4 km) to the park entrance station and visitor center. Continue north on the main park road for 18 mi (29 km) until it terminates at the Devils Garden Trailhead, about a 30-minute drive.

NEED TO KNOW

Info: Arches National Park Visitor Center, www.nps.gov/arch

Passes and Reservations: Entry into the park is $30/vehicle ($25/motorcycle, $15/pedestrian or cyclist). Passes are available in advance at www.recreation.gov. Timed entry tickets ($2) are required April 1–October 31. For more information, see page 503.

Weather Considerations: Sudden storms late spring-fall can whip up flash floods and draw lightning to the park, so watch the sky and the forecast and avoid getting caught up in some nasty weather. During winter, mind the ice and snow as they can make the trail slippery. During summer, or whenever it's hot and sunny, be careful: This hike has little shade and you'll want to bring extra water to account for the heat.

Facilities: There are toilets at the trailhead. There are no accommodations or restaurants inside the park.

BEST NEARBY

Balanced Rock

I love a weird natural wonder, and few things defy visual logic like a balancing rock. Arches' gravity-defying formation is on the right side of the park road, 8.5 mi (13.7 km) from the visitor center. A boulder more than 55 ft (17 m) high rests precariously atop a 73-ft (22-m) pedestal. Chip Off the Old Block, a much smaller version of Balanced Rock, stood nearby until it collapsed in the winter of 1975-1976. For a closer look at Balanced Rock, take the 0.3-mi (0.5-km) trail encircling it. There's a picnic area across the road. Author Edward Abbey lived in a trailer near Balanced Rock for a season as a park ranger in the 1950s, and his journal became the basis for the classic novel *Desert Solitaire*.

▲ BALANCED ROCK

51

MURPHY POINT TRAIL

CANYONLANDS NATIONAL PARK, UTAH

This easy hike through the high desert delivers you to an overlook where sunrise, sunset, and stargazing compete for the best time of day (or night) to visit.

- **Distance:** 3.4 mi (5.5 km) round-trip
- **Duration:** 1 hour
- **Elevation Gain:** 177 ft (54 m)
- **Effort:** Easy
- **When:** Mar.-Dec.
- **Trailhead:** Murphy Point

HIGHLIGHT: Catching a sunrise or sunset at Murphy Point

You won't be on the trail long when you make the short trek to Murphy Point, but the hour you're on the move is an hour well spent, as this trail ends with an amazing view from the mesa top. When you arrive at the end—you'll know it by the mesa rim—you'll be met with panoramic views of the Utah desert and canyonlands: Candlestick Tower, the Green River, and the ribbon or White Canyon Rim Road lending the landscape texture and depth.

▲ VIEW ALONG MURPHY POINT TRAIL

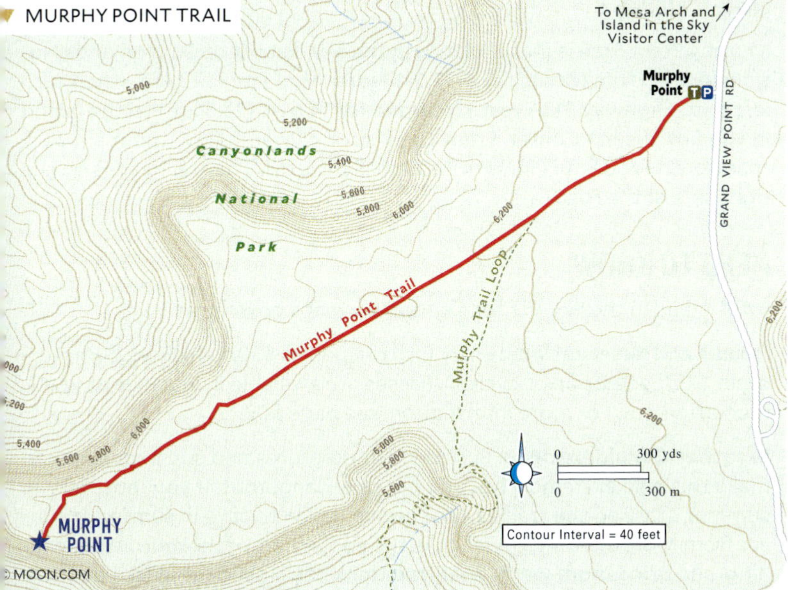

START THE HIKE

The hike is straightforward. From the trailhead, hike southwest for 0.4 mi (0.6 km) and stay to the right (the trail to the left leads to the long, 10.1-mi/16.2-km **Murphy Trail Loop,** which descends into the canyon, leads you near the summit of Murphy's Hogback, and then loops back to return to the starting point). This trail, the **Murphy Point Trail,** is wide and easy to follow, with a slight uphill grade as you climb. As you near the endpoint, it might seem you've lost the trail. You haven't. Here the trail is marked with stone cairns, and it's easy to miss these subtle stone stacks if you've never encountered them before. Soon you'll reach the mesa's edge and have an enormous view from **Murphy Point.** The hike back out is easier than the hike in—you know your route and how to look for the cairns, so all you have to do is enjoy the scenery. When you reach the junction with Murphy's Hogback Trail (1.2 m/1.9 km from Murphy Point proper), the parking area is only 0.4 mi (0.6 km) away.

The view here really wows, but in that perfect golden-hour light near dawn and dusk, it's something special. I can't decide which is better, sunrise or sunset. Trekking through the high desert under the soft morning light is a peaceful experience, and the long shadows and soft pastel glow bring the desert to life. But a sunset hike is especially good as you're facing west and can witness quite a dramatic sky, plus those lengthening shadows in the canyon below. And I can't say enough about night here. It's dark in this corner of Utah, and that means the stargazing is out of this world.

DIRECTIONS

Murphy Point Trail is in the Islands in the Sky district of Canyonlands National Park. From Moab, take US 191 North for 11 mi (17.7 km), then turn left onto Highway 313 West. Continue for 14.6 mi (23.5 km) to the Island in the Sky Visitor Center. From the visitor center, follow the main park road south for 8.8 mi (14.2 km), about 15 minutes. The trailhead is on the right side of the road.

NEED TO KNOW

Info: Island in the Sky Visitor Center, www.nps.gov/cany

Passes and Reservations: Entry into the park is $30/vehicle ($25/motorcycle, $15/pedestrian or cyclist). Passes are available in advance at www.recreation.gov. For more information, see page 502.

Weather Considerations: Summer temperatures and sun exposure can make this hike extremely hot and possibly dangerous. If you must hike in summer, start on the trail early or late and plan to take in sunrise or sunset from Murphy Point, traveling in the cooler part of the morning or evening, and bring more water than you think you'll need (at least 1 quart or liter per person per hour). There's a chance that sudden thunderstorms might bring lightning strikes to the ridges and mesas around the area, so be mindful of the weather and forecast. In winter, ice and snow can obscure the trail and make it slippery, so take your time and come with the proper equipment (like strap-on ice spikes for your boots).

Facilities: Canyonlands is a large, remote park in a wilderness-filled pocket of Utah, and there are few facilities or conveniences inside the park. There are no amenities at the Murphy Point Trailhead, and within the park there are no restaurants or accommodations (aside from camping) available; water is available at the Island in the Sky and The Needles Visitor Centers.

BEST NEARBY

Mesa Arch

Take an easy trail (0.25 mi/0.4 km, 15 minutes) to a spectacular arch on the mesa rim. On the way, the trail crosses the arid grasslands and scattered juniper trees. The rather barren, undramatic trail climbs gently until it suddenly descends toward the edge of an 800-ft (244-m) precipice, topped by a sandstone arch. The arch frames views of rock formations below and the La Sal Mountains in the distance. Photographers come here to catch the sun or the moon rising through the arch; time your visit right and the sun or moon will fill the arch, making it look very much like an eye.

▲ VIEW FROM MURPHY POINT

52

GREAT GALLERY TRAIL

CANYONLANDS NATIONAL PARK, UTAH

With ancient life-size drawings, the Great Gallery in the Horseshoe Canyon district of the park is one of the best destinations for rock art in the country.

- **Distance:** 7-10.6 mi (11.3-17.1 km) round-trip
- **Duration:** 4-6.5 hours
- **Elevation Gain:** 1,654 ft (504 m)
- **Effort:** Moderate-strenuous
- **When:** Mar.-May and Sept.-Dec.
- **Trailhead:** Horseshoe Canyon parking area

HIGHLIGHT: Admiring the petroglyphs and pictographs at the Great Gallery

Horseshoe Canyon sits to the northwest of the main body of Canyonlands National Park; it's a noncontiguous element of the park (meaning it sits out on its own like an island) that contains exceptional prehistoric rock art. In The Great Gallery, life-size pictographs and petroglyphs stand like ghosts in the rock. These figures are believed to have held religious importance, though that's just a theory and the true meaning behind and reason for the figures is unknown.

▲ HIKING THROUGH HORSESHOE CANYON TO THE GREAT GALLERY

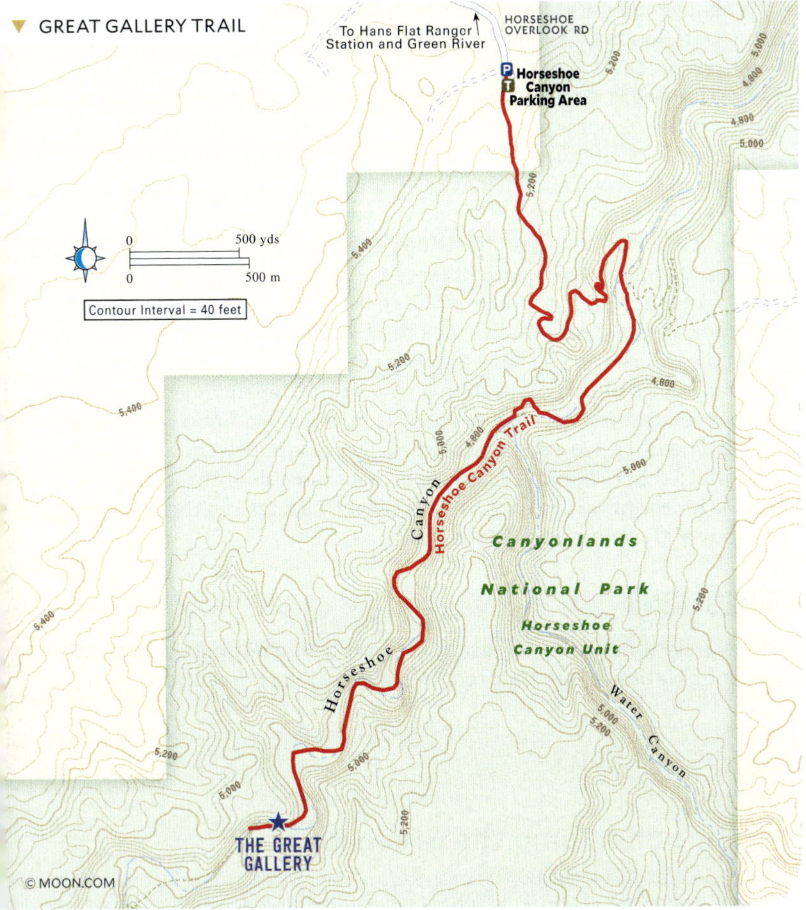

This has led to some fun speculation, from the reasonable (they held religious significance) to the out-of-this-world (they depict alien visitors). Theories and speculation aside, archaeologists believe the Barrier Canyon Style of these drawings dates back to an ancient culture beginning at least 8,000 years ago and lasting until around 450 CE. They are truly a sight to behold and make the effort of this hike worth every step.

START THE HIKE

The trail is simple and straightforward, but by no means easy. From the **Horseshoe Canyon parking area,** you'll descent some 800 ft (244 m) along an old jeep road that's now closed to vehicle traffic. At the bottom of the canyon, turn right and continue upstream for 2 mi (3.2 km). A short spur trail leads to The Great Gallery. There's no shade available on the mesa rim or on the climb in/out, but scattered trees provide shade on the canyon floor. The canyon floor is sandy and typically dry, so you may want some gaiters to keep the sand out, or you may have to stop a few times to empty your shoes. If it's been raining, the route can vary between difficult (the sandy mud gets sticky and can build up on your boots) and dangerous (flash floods and canyons aren't a good mix), so keep an eye on the weather forecast.

At **The Great Gallery,** take all the photos and video you want, but please observe, admire, and film from a distance and do not touch the petroglyphs or pictographs. Oil from your hands can remove the pigment from the rock and invite water and dirt to gather, further eroding this precious prehistoric art. Along the way you'll find spur trails leading to scenic points and other collections of pictographs and petroglyphs. If you join a park ranger- or volunteer-led hike here you'll discover more secrets, like dinosaur footprints in the rock (one is midway down the trail into the canyon, if you want to look for it yourself).

On the return trip you have the chance to observe the landscape, wildlife, and plants of this place from a new angle. Depending on timing and resources—Did you eat all your food? How much water do you have left? What time is it?—you can explore nearby areas a little, but if you return straight to the trailhead, it's an easy go. Just remember to look for that dinosaur footprint on the way out (it's 0.8 mi/1.3 km from the spur road at the foot of the climb back to the trailhead).

DIRECTIONS

Great Gallery Trail is in Horseshoe Canyon, a noncontiguous unit of Canyonlands National Park that requires quite a bit of driving to reach. The

BEST NEARBY

Canoe and Camp the Green River

This part of Canyonlands National Park is remote and, frankly, there isn't much nearby, but if you're up for big adventure—several nights of canoeing and camping on the Green River as it makes its way south through Labyrinth Canyon on its way to the national park—you'll find it in the town of Green River. Green River sits 66 mi (106 km) northeast of Horseshoe Canyon along Highway 24 and I-70, a 1.5-hour drive. There you can put in your canoe—loaded with camping supplies and plenty of water—at a state park for a canoeing, camping, and hiking trip (complete with shuttle back) that'll have you in the wilderness for 3-10 days.

Fortunately, you don't have to do all the planning yourself. Moab-based **Canyonlands by Night & Day** (1861 N. Hwy. 191, Moab; 800/394-9978 or 435/259-2628; www.canyonlandsbynight.com) offers a variety of tours (camping, climbing, jeep tours, and more) in Canyonlands, Arches, and across the region, but its Canyonlands Self-Guided Trip with Jet Boat Shuttle is one for the ages. Imagine up to 120 mi (193 km) of flatwater paddling through desert and canyon landscapes, camping by night on sandbars and beaches, and hiking through canyons and along ridges in an isolated segment of Bureau of Land Management land. That's this tour. You'll need to rent a canoe (from $35/day), a backcountry fire pan ($3/day), and toilet system (from $10/first day, $6/day after), and then there's the jet boat shuttle ($240 adults, $145 ages 3 and under), and you'll need a free permit from the BLM (www.blm.gov). You'll also need supplies (food, water, maps, coolers, etc.), so this can be a pricey trip to add on to a national park visit, but if you've got the time and the funds, it's an epic adventure.

▲ THE GREAT GALLERY

dirt access road (signed) across from the entrance to Goblin Valley State Park turns east from Highway 24 between Hanksville (14 mi/22.5 km south) and I-70 exit 149 (19 mi/31 km north). Travel 30 mi (48 km) east to Horseshoe Canyon, keeping left at the Hans Flat Ranger Station and at the Horseshoe Canyon turnoff 25 mi (40 km) in. In good weather, the road is passable by most cars, though it has many washboard sections, and blowing sand can be a hazard. Allow an hour to make the journey in from Highway 24 to the Horseshoe Canyon parking area.

NEED TO KNOW

Info: Hans Flat Ranger Station, www.nps.gov/cany

Passes and Reservations: Entry into the park is $30/vehicle ($25/motorcycle, $15/pedestrian or cyclist). Passes are available in advance at www.recreation.gov. Call the **Hans Flat Ranger Station** (435/259-2652) to inquire about ranger-led hikes to the Great Gallery (Sat.-Sun. spring and fall). For more information, see page 502.

Weather Considerations: This hike can be "**dangerously** hot in summer!" (that's a direct quote and emphasis from the National Park Service), so plan to hit the trail in the pre-dawn hours so you're finished before midday or start after 4pm (bring your headlamp if you're hiking late in the day).

Facilities: There is a vault toilet at the trailhead. There's no water station, however, so come prepared with at least 1 gallon (4 liters) per person (I always bring more).

53

CHESLER PARK AND THE JOINT

CANYONLANDS NATIONAL PARK, UTAH

This hike leads you to something unexpected in the desert: a pocket grassland. Along the way you'll pass through rocky fins and outcroppings and an unusual slot canyon, and have the option to visit a towering arch.

- **Distance:** 10.2 mi (16.4 km) round-trip
- **Duration:** 5-6 hours
- **Elevation Gain:** 1,794 ft (547 m)
- **Effort:** Strenuous
- **When:** Mar.-Dec.
- **Trailhead:** Elephant Hill parking area

HIGHLIGHT: Passing through The Joint, a unique slot canyon

Chesler Park offers Canyonlands visitors a rare sight in this rocky desert: a flat, roughly circular grassland meadow ringed by towering needles of sandstone, the namesake feature in this section of the national park. I've rated this as a strenuous trail due to the length, but the trail itself is moderate and only a few sections demand extra care. Along the way you're likely to see mule deer, desert cottontails, and tracks from creatures like the kangaroo mouse and the gopher snake.

▲ A HIKER IN CHESLER PARK

START THE HIKE

The trail begins at the **Elephant Hill parking area's southwestern corner.** It can be tough to find a spot here, so arrive early or park at one of the two pullouts a short ways back down Elephant Hill Road. As you start the hike—heading south on **Chesler Park Trail**—you may be serenaded by the sound of revving engines as vehicles attempt the difficult 4WD road that begins near the picnic area. Don't worry; with 10 minutes of hiking you'll leave the engine noise behind.

The first 0.5 mi (0.8 km) of the trail are steep, ascending sharply and giving

you an introduction to the trail ahead: rock fins, slot canyons, sandy trails, brushy areas, and grassy meadows. At 1.8 mi (2.9 km) into the hike, you'll cross **Elephant Creek** and a trail to your left headed due south. This is Druid Arch Trail; take note of it as you can extend the hike by visiting Druid Arch and you'll return to Chesler Park Trail at this spot.

Continue through the sandstone fins and canyons another 0.6 mi (1 km) to where the trail forks: right leads to Devils Kitchen, but our trail heads left. In a few hundred yards you'll reach a **scenic viewpoint** and catch a glimpse of the grassy meadow that is Chesler Park. Another fork in the trail awaits 100 paces farther on; this trail loops the meadow, and you'll be taking a right and circling the meadow counterclockwise. As you circle the meadow, headed toward The Joint, you'll find three more trail junctions waiting; stay to the left and you'll be all set.

There's a primitive **restroom** 2.4 mi (3.9 km) down the trail. From here it's 0.5 mi (0.8 km) to **The Joint,** a narrow slot canyon that differs from other slot canyons in the park: Where others were formed by water erosion, The Joint is a fracture in the rock. Photo opportunities abound on this section and immediately after you exit. When you exit The Joint, a trail to the right leads 0.1 mi (0.2 km) to the Chesler Park Viewpoint; it's worth the extra effort.

A collection of backcountry campsites awaits another 0.7 mi (1.1 km) down the trail near a tall fin of stone. Take note of the trail to the right—Joint Trail continues east, connecting to Druid Arch Trail—because if you elect to extend by hiking to Druid Arch, you'll follow this trail (more on this side-quest hike in a moment).

To complete our loop and return to the parking area, skip the Joint-Druid side trail and continue forward. In 1 mi (1.6 km) you'll arrive at Chesler Park Trail near the viewpoint and the place where we began our counterclockwise trek. Follow Chesler Park Trail 2.6 mi (4.2 km) back to the parking area.

DIRECTIONS

Chesler Park and The Joint are in the Needles district of Canyonlands National Park. From Moab, take US 191 South for 39.6 mi (63.7 km), then turn right onto Highway 211 West. Drive for 34.4 mi (55.4 km) to the Needles Visitor Center. From the visitor center, continue southwest on Highway 211 for 3 mi (4.8 km). Turn left and drive another 3 mi (4.8 km) past the Needles Campground turnoff (on passable dirt roads) to the Elephant Hill picnic area and trailhead at the base of Elephant Hill.

NEED TO KNOW

Info: Needles Visitor Center, www.nps.gov/cany

Passes and Reservations: Entry into the park is $30/vehicle ($25/motorcycle, $15/pedestrian or cyclist). Passes are available in advance at www.recreation.gov. For more information, see page 502.

Weather Considerations: Summer heat and sun exposure can be dangerous, so bring plenty of drinking water and hike early or late in the day

BEST NEARBY

Druid Arch Trail

You can extend this hike and turn it into a 14-mi (22.5-km) monster that pays off with The Joint, the beautiful meadow at Chesler, and a good look at the towering Druid Arch. To add Druid Arch to the Chesler Park Loop, at 6.6 mi (10.6 km) into the hike, just past The Joint and the backcountry campsites, turn right (east) on Joint Trail. Follow Joint Trail 0.9 mi (1.5 km) to where it intersects with Druid Arch Trail. Turn right and head south toward Druid Arch. You'll reach the arch in 1.6 mi (2.6 km). Druid Arch is fantastic: The top stands some 450 ft (137 m) above the canyon floor, and a pair of keyhole arches—one larger than the other—gives it an impressive shape from nearly any angle.

Once you've had your fill of Druid Arch, reverse course and head north along Druid Arch Trail. From here it's 4.8 mi (7.7 km) back to the trailhead. At 2.7 mi (4.3 km) you'll reach the junction with Chesler Park Trail at the point where the trail crosses Elephant Creek; turn right to return to the parking area.

to dodge the worst of the heat. Winter snow and ice may make the trail slippery, so use caution on a late-season hike. Always check the forecast before you hit the trail.

Facilities: There is a toilet at the trailhead.

▼ CHESLER PARK

▲ CHESLER PARK

54

PETROGLYPH POINT TRAIL

MESA VERDE NATIONAL PARK, COLORADO

This trail clings to the wall of the canyon, then delivers a sublime petroglyph panel (and other archaeological wonders) before circling back on the flat top of the mesa.

- **Distance:** 2.4-mi (3.9-km) loop
- **Duration:** 2 hours
- **Elevation Gain:** 330 ft (101 m)
- **Effort:** Moderate-strenuous
- **When:** Apr.-Oct.
- **Trailhead:** Chapin Mesa Archeological Museum

HIGHLIGHT: Studying the park's largest petroglyph panel at Petroglyph Point

From the mesa rim it's hard to get a feel for the size and nature of the cliff dwellings and life here before modern conveniences; that's why this trail is important. You descend from the mesa tops into the canyons where you'll get a closer look at the cliff dwellings (you'll need to join an official tour if you want to go inside and experience them further) and the incredible mesa landscape before you reach petroglyph-filled rock panels that will astound you.

SPRUCE TREE HOUSE IN WINTER

VIEW OF THE MAIN CANYON

START THE HIKE

The loop begins next to the **Chapin Mesa Archeological Museum,** immediately descending a paved set of switchbacks where you'll have views across the canyon to **Spruce Tree House,** one of the largest cliff dwellings in the park. This site, containing 130 rooms and 8 kivas, or ceremonial pits, was built by Ancestral Puebloans between 1211 and 1278 CE.

At the bottom of the paved switchbacks, turn right as the trail turns to dirt and continue to the trail register, where you'll sign your name and proceed into the canyon. Soon after, the trail splits. Climb the stairs on your left to travel counterclockwise on the **Petroglyph Point Trail;** you'll return via the other trail.

At 0.7 mi (1.1 km), look for an archaeological site on the rock above the trail to the left. There is a spur trail leading up to it for a better view, but you're not allowed to enter, so view it from below. Just beyond the spur trail, look for an 800-year-old tool sharpening stone on your left, with a series of grooves carved out of a boulder. At about 0.8 mi (1.3 km), as the trail follows the contour back toward the main canyon, you'll get a view of the way you just came. At 1.2 mi (1.9 km), stone stairs lead to a level bit of trail along a multicolored wall. Finally, at 1.6 mi (2.6 km), the park's largest petroglyph panel, **Petroglyph Point,** appears on the cliff. No one is sure exactly what the petroglyphs mean, though one interpretive sign offers the idea that the spirals represent migration or movement and the animal figures could be different clans of people.

At the next trail junction, turn left up a stone staircase, following the museum signs (another trail continues straight down to the canyon bottom but is closed). This first little ascent involves a few rock scrambles on what's probably the steepest section of the loop. Continue up the hill until you are on the top of the mesa. From there it's a wide, easy path through the scrubby pinyon-juniper forest back to the Chapin Mesa Museum to close the loop.

You can combine Petroglyph Point Trail with nearby Spruce Canyon Trail, making a figure-8 (or double bunny ears) loop.

DIRECTIONS

Petroglyph Point Trail is in the Chapin Mesa area of Mesa Verde National Park. From Cortez, take US 160 East 10.9 mi (17.5 km) to the park entrance station and visitor center. Continue on the main park road southwest for 19 mi (31 km), then turn right toward the Chapin Mesa Archeological Museum and Spruce Tree House, about a 40-minute drive.

NEED TO KNOW

Info: Mesa Verde Visitor and Research Center, www.nps.gov/meve

BEST NEARBY

Far View Terrace Café

▶ *Milepost 15; 970/529-4465; www.visitmesaverde.com; 7am-10am and 11am-3pm daily mid-Apr.-mid-May, 7am-10am and 11am-4pm daily mid-May-late Oct.*

Far View Terrace Café is your closest pre-hike breakfast spot or post-hike lunchroom located inside the national park. For breakfast they have made-to-order omelets and espresso drinks, and for lunch it's burgers and the like. Nothing will set you back more than $10.

If you're hiking later in the day, head to Far View Lodge (Milepost 15; 800/449-2288; visitmesaverde.com; mid-Apr.-late Oct.; from $125), a unique, upscale accommodation inside the national park that lives up to its name. Splurge on a fine meal at the lodge's restaurant, the Metate Room, or have a beer on their rooftop.

Passes and Reservations: Entry into the park is $30/vehicle ($25/motorcycle, $15/pedestrian or cyclist) May 1-October 22, and $20/vehicle ($15/motorcycle, pedestrian, or cyclist) October 23-April 30. Passes are available in advance at www.recreation.gov. For more information, see page 502.

Weather Considerations: Be mindful of spring and summer thunderstorms, as the wind and the possibility for lightning can pose a threat to hikers. Otherwise, monitor the forecast, bring extra water if the temperatures are high, and enjoy.

Facilities: There are restrooms at the trailhead/museum parking lot.

Other: As the NPS website reminds us, "All of Mesa Verde is an ancestral home that is sacred to 26 tribes. Please visit with respect by staying on trails and leaving cultural and natural resources where you find them." That means being extra strict about leave-no-trace principles, including no snacking on the trail (this rule helps avoid crumb-chasing rodents infesting the archaeological sites).

▼ SPRUCE TREE HOUSE

55

SODA CANYON OVERLOOK

MESA VERDE NATIONAL PARK, COLORADO

This easy hike gives you a good view of Balcony House and smaller cliff dwellings clinging to the walls of Soda Canyon.

- **Distance:** 1.2 mi (1.9 km) round-trip
- **Duration:** 30-40 minutes
- **Elevation Gain:** 60 ft (18 m)
- **Effort:** Easy
- **When:** Apr.-Oct.
- **Trailhead:** 1 mi (1.6 km) past the Balcony House parking area, along Cliff Palace Loop Road

HIGHLIGHT: Marveling at the architectural wonders of Balcony House

Mesa Verde National Park is known for two things: the cliff houses and the petroglyphs that mark the area's onetime Indigenous populations. On this short, easy hike (it's more of a jaunt through the woods to a beautiful overlook than a true hike), you'll be treated to views of Colorado's canyon country with the added bonus of the impressive Balcony House. Balcony House is not one structure but

SODA CANYON

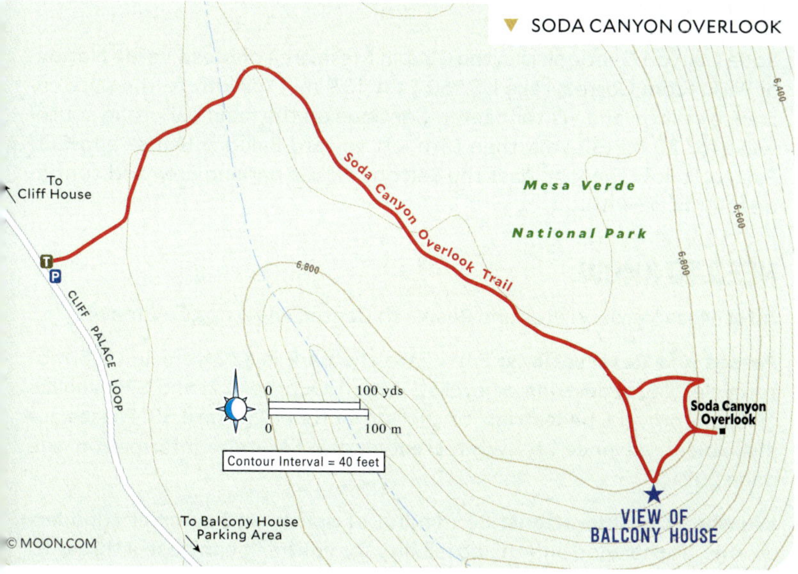

a complex of structures encompassing 40 rooms built originally by the Ancestral Puebloans around 1200 CE and excavated by the National Park Service in 1910. You can tour Balcony House, but be aware you'll climb ladders to enter the structures (just like those Ancestral Puebloans), crawl through a tunnel 18 in (46 cm) wide, and traverse a number of narrow passageways on the tour. Note that this hike is the only way to see Balcony House without joining a guided tour.

START THE HIKE

This trail stays in a forest of pinyon pine and Utah juniper trees for nearly the entire distance until you arrive at the canyon rim where the scenery unfolds before you. On the way in, note the pinyon pines; many of the mature pinyons are centuries old, which seems impossible given their gnarled, stunted look. Watch for mule deer, desert cottontails, black-tailed jackrabbits, and turkeys as you hike; they like the forest for the shade, protection, and food supply. You may spot birds like American kestrels, ravens, turkey vultures, white-throated swifts, and violet-green swallows.

You'll leave the forest as you wrap up the final approach to the trio of overlooks perched on a rocky promontory at the edge of **Soda Canyon. Balcony House** is almost due south, and if you have binoculars you'll be able to spot several smaller cliff dwellings with ease. Take a moment to study Soda Canyon though. The canyon gets its name from the stark white calcium carbonate mineral deposits below the rim. These deposits are what remains of seep springs once used by the Ancestral Puebloan peoples.

When you've had your fill, follow the trail back to the trailhead.

DIRECTIONS

Soda Canyon Overlook is in the Chapin Mesa area of Mesa Verde National Park. From Cortez, take US 160 East 10.9 mi (17.5 km) to the park entrance station and visitor center. Continue on the main park road southwest for 20 mi (32 km), then turn left toward Balcony House and Cliff Palace. Follow the loop past the Balcony House parking area and continue for 1 mi (1.6 km).

NEED TO KNOW

Info: Mesa Verde Visitor and Research Center, www.nps.gov/meve

Passes and Reservations: Entry into the park is $30/vehicle ($25/motorcycle, $15/pedestrian or cyclist) May 1-October 22, and $20/vehicle ($15/motorcycle, pedestrian, or cyclist) October 23-April 30. Passes are available in advance at www.recreation.gov. For more information, see page 502.

Weather Considerations: Be mindful of spring and summer thunderstorms, as the wind and the possibility for lightning can pose a threat to hikers. Otherwise, monitor the forecast, bring extra water if the temperatures are high, and enjoy.

Facilities: There are no amenities at the trailhead.

Other: As the NPS website reminds us, "All of Mesa Verde is an ancestral home that is sacred to 26 tribes. Please visit with respect by staying on trails and leaving cultural and natural resources where you find them." That means being extra strict about leave-no-trace principles, including no snacking on the trail (this rule helps avoid crumb-chasing rodents infesting the archaeological sites).

BEST NEARBY

Cliff Palace and Balcony House

After living on the mesa top for nearly 600 years, the Ancestral Puebloans began building pueblos beneath the cliff overhangs, constructing structures from one-room storehouses to whole villages.

The largest is Cliff Palace ($8), with more than 150 rooms and 20 circular kivas (distinctive pits uses in rituals), far larger than the average 1-5-room cliff dwelling; an estimated 100 people lived here. Nearby Balcony House ($8) has 40 rooms. On the tour you'll find the rooms in each cramped, but Ancestral Puebloans were smaller than we are, standing around 5 ft (152 cm) for females and 5 ft 4 in (163 cm) for males.

Villagers used tall wooden ladders and hand- and footholds carved into the sandstone to reach mesa-top gardens. Visit Balcony House and you'll climb a 32-ft (10-m) modern version, a long staircase carved into the canyon, and traverse a 12-ft-long (3.7-m), 18-in-wide (46-cm) tunnel.

Cliff dwelling tours run mid-May through mid-October and must be reserved in advance at recreation.gov. Reservations become available 14 days in advance of the tour date.

▲ SODA CANYON

TOP EXPERIENCE

56

HIGH DUNE TRAIL

GREAT SAND DUNES NATIONAL PARK & PRESERVE, COLORADO

Trek over the shifting geography of this hike through mind-blowing mountains and valleys of sand.

- **Distance:** 4 mi (6.4 km) round-trip
- **Duration:** 3 hours
- **Elevation Gain:** 700 ft (213 m)
- **Effort:** Strenuous
- **When:** Mar.-June and Sept.-Dec.
- **Trailhead:** Great Sand Dunes parking lot

HIGHLIGHT: Stargazing from the dunes

Though this hike's freeform, unstructured nature is a departure from other hikes in this guide, don't let it deter you. The dune field at Great Sand Dunes National Park is a great place to explore. The dunes are huge and active, so maps and specific directions don't do much good. Instead, hikers and explorers here head to a few semi-fixed high points among the dunes. High Dune isn't the tallest, but from the parking area it seems to be. Climb to the top for a great view of the whole dune field; many visitors race to the top, take a look, and head back down.

◄ HIKING THE DUNE FIELD

▼ THE HIGH DUNE

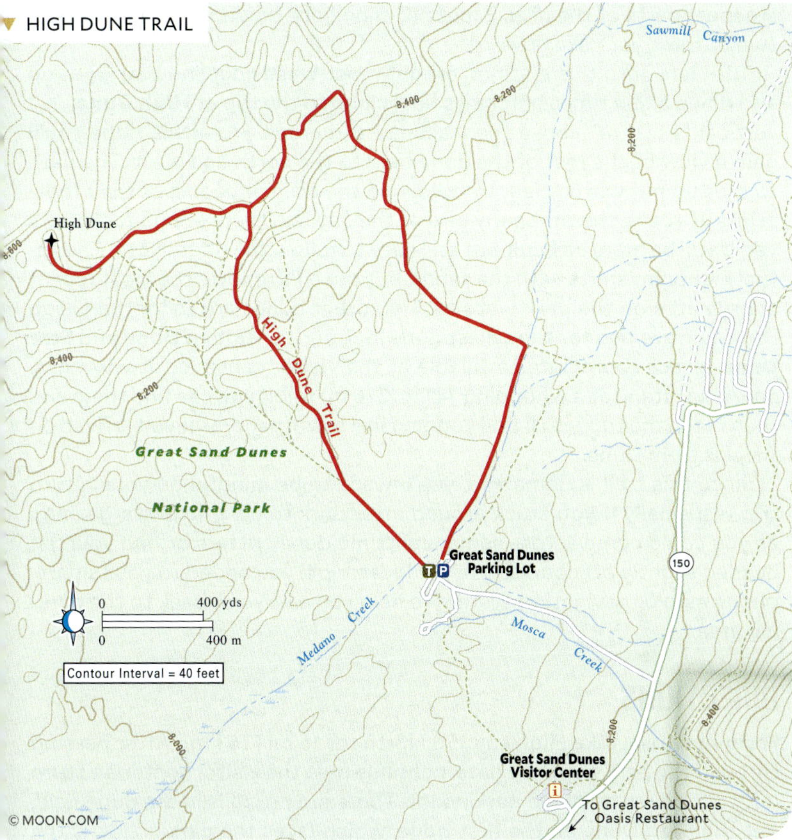

Great Sand Dunes is an **International Dark Sky Park,** so you know the stargazing is out of this world; bring your own telescopes or binoculars, or show up for a planned event like a full-moon hike, a park ranger-led stargazing outing, or the early August Dark Skies Celebration (check www.nps.gov/grsa for specific dates).

START THE HIKE

Before leaving your car, drop a pin on your smartphone map or navigation system—you can generally find a signal in the main visitor area, and you'll want the pin for your return trip. To get to the dune field from the main trailhead parking lot, walk through one of the openings to the dunes and see if you can spot High Dune, to the northwest, which is the highest point in the first ridgeline; note where it is, and keep an eye on it as you ascend. Your first step is to cross **Medano Creek,** a unique feature that only flows at certain times of the year. Sometimes it can be several hundred feet wide and only a couple of inches deep. Walk across the dry or flowing creek bed and continue northwest up the first set of dunes. Make your way to the top of the highest ridge and see if you can spot where it curves toward the high point. The last little section here is one of the steepest parts of the hike. Expect to slide back down one step for every two or three you take upward.

Turn left onto this distinct, roughly east-west ridgeline that goes up and down a few times before its final climb to the top of **High Dune,** 692 vertical ft (211 m) above the trailhead and creek. From this ridge you'll gain a view of the rest of the dune field to the north and west. The path to the summit will be clear by following the train of people or their footprints. If you're the first early bird of the day and there are no footprints yet, it will be more difficult but still easy to follow the ridge. Note: The actual highpoint shifts with the sands, but the NPS reports the most recent coordinates on the park website. Two other dunes are taller than High Dune and are tied for the tallest dune in America. **Hidden Dune** and **Star Dune** (exact coordinates available at the visitor center or at www.nps.gov/grsa) stand at a whopping 741 ft (226 m) tall. If you can find them and then reach the top, you'll find yourself in a sea of sand, as if you arrived on Arrakis from Dune.

Since this trail is unmarked, you'll want to be mindful on your return trip (especially if you stuck around after dark to do a little stargazing), as you could come across some nighttime dune critters or find yourself headed slightly off course. Use the locator pin you added to your smartphone map or navigation system to help you easily get back to the parking area.

DIRECTIONS

From Alamosa, take Highway 150 North for 16 mi (26 km). After passing through the park entrance gate, continue past the visitor center and turn left to the first trailhead parking lot. There are no trails in the dune field, but the High Dune on the first ridge, which faces the parking lot, is the most common destination for hikers at Great Sand Dunes National Park & Preserve.

BEST NEARBY

Great Sand Dunes Oasis Restaurant

▶ *7800 Hwy. 150, Mosca; 719/378-2222; www.greatdunes.com; seasonally mid-Mar.-Oct. 31, open daily 9am-4pm mid-Mar.-Apr., 8am-5pm Apr.-June and Sept.-Oct., 8am-8pm July-Aug.*

There's more to do than just wander like one of the Sand People on Tatooine. Arrive in the pre-dawn dark and watch the sunrise. Try your hand at sandboarding or sand sledding. You'll need to rent a board or sled, and the park keeps a list of nearby vendors. The closest is Great Sand Dunes Oasis, 4 mi (6.4 km) away; boards and sleds are $20 daily.

Great Sand Dunes Oasis also has a motel ($219), camping ($7-80), and a restaurant on-site. The restaurant has diner-style food, including a big ol' huevos rancheros plate and perfectly weak coffee.

▲ MEDANO CREEK CUTTING THROUGH GREAT SAND DUNES NATIONAL PARK & PRESERVE

NEED TO KNOW

Info: Great Sand Dunes Visitor Center, www.nps.gov/grsa

Passes and Reservations: Entry into the park is $25/vehicle ($20/motorcycle, $15/pedestrian or cyclist). Passes are available in advance at www.recreation.gov. For more information, see page 502.

Weather Considerations: Hiking in the dune field is best done early in the morning before the sand heats up to feet-burning temperatures (up to 150°F/66°C in summer), and before you are exposed to afternoon lightning storms. Medano Creek is typically dry October-March. By April the creek usually arrives as a trickle and may be a few inches deep by the end of the month. Flow increases through May, and late May-early June is the best opportunity to experience "surge flow," where waves flow down across the sand. July-September, Medano Creek continues to gently flow at 0.5-1 in (1.3-2.5 cm) deep.

Facilities: There are bathrooms and sand-washing-off stations at the main trailhead, plus more facilities at the visitor center.

Other: There's no marked trail system in the 30-sq-mi (78-sq-km) dune field; instead, you can wander as you wish (just be sure to mark the parking area on your phone's GPS). You'll want to be mindful of your footwear—opt for high-top boots or sneakers and long pants or gaiters; if visiting April-September, consider waterproof shoes for the creek crossing. Don't plan on walking barefoot in the sand or wearing sandals or flip-flops, as the sand can be extremely hot and you'll end up with blisters. For those with mobility needs, the visitor center has a small fleet of dunes-accessible wheelchairs (with balloon tires) you can borrow at no cost.

57

LOST MINE TRAIL

BIG BEND NATIONAL PARK, TEXAS

Combining moderate grades, extraordinary vantage points, and stupendous scenery, Lost Mine Trail is the ultimate Big Bend experience.

- **Distance:** 4.8 mi (7.7 km) round-trip
- **Duration:** 3 hours
- **Elevation Gain:** 1,131 ft (345 m)
- **Effort:** Moderate-strenuous
- **When:** Oct.-May
- **Trailhead:** Lost Mine Trailhead

HIGHLIGHT: Wandering among wildflowers and wildlife

Escape the desert heat with an alpine-ish trek along Lost Mine Trail. It's cooler, it's invigorating, and the scenery is stupendous, and that's why many consider this one of the ultimate Big Bend hikes. The trail isn't too steep, there's a real variety of flora and fauna here in the Chisos Mountains, the scenic viewpoints are amazing, and the interpretive brochure at the trailhead offers excellent insights (and a map) to the trail. Be here early, as the parking lot is small and the hike is popular; if you arrive around dawn, you'll get the double bonus of a parking spot and the experience of watching the desert awaken.

VIEW OF CHISOS MOUNTAINS FROM LOST MINE TRAIL

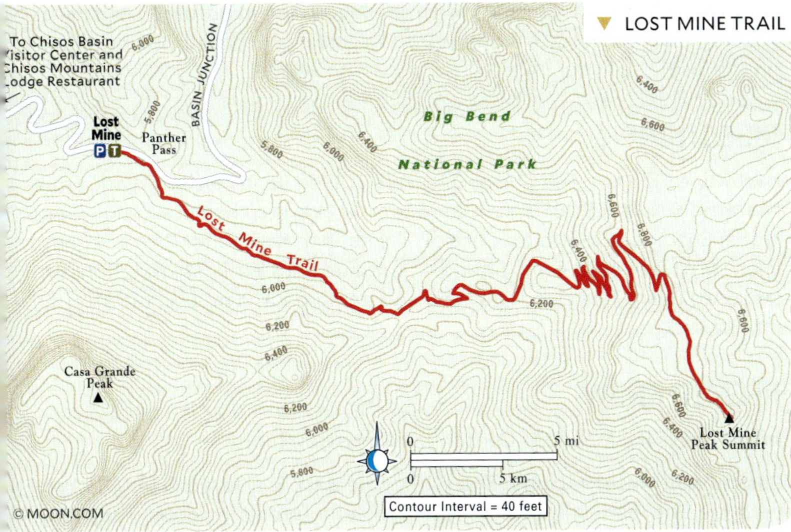

START THE HIKE

My granddad would say that this trail is uphill one way, downhill the other. It's true. Once you leave the parking area it's a steady climb for 2.1 mi (3.4 km) through scrubby desert trees until you reach the mostly flat ridge near **Lost Mine Peak.** Then you get to go back down. Along the way there are no real landmarks or waypoints aside from the ridge 1 mi (1.6 km) into the hike (it's marker #10 if you're using the trail brochure you picked up at the trailhead). Here you'll find the second-most incredible view on the trail—and one of the best views in the park. As you hike up and crest a little rise, you'll have magnificent, far-reaching views of Juniper Canyon, Casa Grande, and the Chisos Basin. I say it's the second-most incredible view on the trail because the real payoff is at the **summit.** Here the vista is grand: hundreds of miles of undulating terrain that's offered the same bit of beauty to visitors and viewers for thousands of years.

As you hike and when you're lounging at the summit, soaking up the view, get quiet and observant and see what wildlife appears. You're likely to see white-tailed deer, rock squirrels, and maybe a gray fox. If you're lucky, you'll spot a black bear. If you're really lucky, you'll see a mountain lion in the distance or even some mountain lion tracks in the sand and dust on the trail.

If you happen to be at the park in late summer or early fall (following the summertime rains), you'll get the bonus experience of seeing the Lost Mine Trail's environs in a mini growth spurt with plenty of subtle colors and emerging flora. Look for red, yellow, orange, and blue blossoms on bushes, trees, cacti, and stems around every bend. Be sure to take a few minutes to stop hiking and do a 360-degree turn, absorbing all the fresh green growth of new leaves and blooming cacti. If you look (and listen) closely, you'll identify unfamiliar insects buzzing over new flowers, completely unaware of your presence.

On the return trip you have superb views. That valley you hiked up is now open before you. And thanks to the low, relatively sparse vegetation, you'll find plenty of views. As with the hike in, be mindful of the trail as you hike out—no need to stumble upon a snake or other surprising animal on the last leg of your hike.

DIRECTIONS

Lost Mine Trail is in the Chisos Basin area of Big Bend National Park. From Marathon, take US 385 South for 42 mi (68 km) to the Persimmon Gap/ North Entrance. Continue south on the main park road for 26 mi (42 km), then turn right onto Gano Springs. Continue for 3.2 mi (5.1 km), then turn left onto Basin Junction. The trailhead parking lot is on the left after 5.1 mi (8.2 km).

NEED TO KNOW

Info: Chisos Basin Visitor Center, www.nps.gov/bibe

Passes and Reservations: Entry into the park is $30/vehicle ($25/motorcycle, $15/pedestrian or cyclist), payable (credit or debit card only, no cash) at one of the four entrance stations. For more information, see page 502.

Weather Considerations: The weather in this part of the park can be volatile, so prepare for anything. In April, you may experience sunny, short-sleeved weather while ascending the trail, then, after basking in the warmth and scenery, you may turn a corner while descending and encounter a wall of surreal snow flurries.

Facilities: There are no amenities at the trailhead.

Other: Be sure to get to the trailhead before 9am—the small parking lot fills up quickly.

BEST NEARBY

Chisos Mountains Lodge Restaurant

▶ *432/477-2291; www.chisosmountainslodge.com; 7am-10am, 11am-3pm, and 4:30pm-8:30pm daily; breakfast buffet $12, lunch and dinner $12-47*

The only place to order a meal in Big Bend National Park is the Chisos Mountains Lodge Restaurant. Fortunately, the food here is much better than expected for a remote national park, with a surprisingly varied menu offering regional fare (Tex-Mex, prickly pear cactus sauces, etc.), the expected dishes (sandwiches, pastas), and hearty breakfasts to fuel a long morning trek. "Hikers lunches" are also available as to-go options. The views of the mountains (particularly The Window formation) are stunning through the floor-to-ceiling windows, and it's always nice to know a decent meal is available daily with enough variety (along with beer and wine) to make things interesting for several days' worth of eating.

▲ LOST MINE TRAIL

58

BALANCED ROCK VIA GRAPEVINE HILLS TRAIL

BIG BEND NATIONAL PARK, TEXAS

Hike across a boulder field to stunning mountain views and get a good look at Balanced Rock.

- **Distance:** 1.9 mi (3 km) round-trip
- **Duration:** 1-2 hours
- **Elevation Gain:** 246 ft (75 m)
- **Effort:** Easy-moderate
- **When:** Year-round, best Sept.-Apr.
- **Trailhead:** 6.5 mi (10.5 km) down Grapevine Hills Road (dirt road)

HIGHLIGHT: Checking out Balanced Rock from all angles

Balanced Rock is one of those "is this real?" rock formations. Unlike other Balanced Rocks where there's a boulder standing atop a column of rock like some giant golf ball on its tee, this Balanced Rock features a huge boulder hanging suspended between a "Y" of vertical stones. It's more like a slingshot loaded and ready to be pulled back.

▲ DEER BELOW BOULDERS OF GRAPEVINE HILLS

START THE HIKE

From the trailhead parking area you're a dozen paces from the start of this hike. You may be headed to Balanced Rock, but you're following Grapevine Hills Trail; it can get confusing as the National Park Service and services like AllTrails disagree on the hike's name. Regardless, the end destination—Balanced Rock—is the same. When you have your gear together, you'll have a short hike—only 0.9 mi (1.4 km)—along a gravel wash and boulder field before you reach Balanced Rock. That **boulder field** is challenging: The slope is steep, the bedrock is rough, and a scree of sand and small pebbles covers much of the rock, making for slippery

footing. Additionally, a few of the park's resident reptiles—yes, that includes snakes—frequent the sun-warmed rock and the protective shade, so be sure you can see where you put your hand or foot before you place it. This also means no climbing the boulders. As tempting as they are, they're not worth a snakebite.

In the boulder field you'll find directional arrows painted onto the rocks, indicating the direction to Balanced Rock. Like the old Sesame Street song said, "Follow the arrows, they'll show you where to go," and soon you'll reach the destination. Check out **Balanced Rock** from all angles, find one that suits you, and enjoy. If you've got the time and the inclination, explore the area a little. Hike among the boulders to the top of the rise where you'll have views of the Grapevine Hills and Chisos Mountains. Sit still and quiet and listen for birds (the park is home to 450 species of birds) and other animals; you never know what you'll see or hear.

To return to the trailhead, go back downhill and follow the gravel wash to the parking area.

DIRECTIONS

Balanced Rock is in the Chisos Basin area of Big Bend National Park. From Marathon, take US 385 South for 42 mi (68 km) to the Persimmon Gap/ North Entrance. Continue south on the main park road for 26 mi (42 km), then turn right onto Gano Springs. The turnoff onto Grapevine Hills Road is on the right after 3.5 mi (5.6 km).

NEED TO KNOW

Info: Chisos Basin Visitor Center, www.nps.gov/bibe

Passes and Reservations: Entry into the park is $30/vehicle ($25/motorcycle, $15/pedestrian or cyclist), payable (credit or debit card only, no cash) at one of the four entrance stations. For more information, see page 502.

Weather Considerations: From September-April, the sweet spot for this hike, temperatures range from 37-80°F (3-27°C). Though Big Bend is a desert park, this hike is in the mountains, which stay cooler year-round and see little precipitation.

Facilities: There are no amenities at the trailhead.

Other: Be careful on this trail as the rocky surface is covered with a thin layer of rock and sand, making it slick. Big Bend park rangers regularly respond to twists and sprains on this trail, so be mindful of your footing and rely on your hiking poles for added dexterity.

BEST NEARBY

Fossil Discovery Center

▶ *8 mi (12.9 km) north of Panther Junction on Highway 835; http://fossildiscoveryexhibit.com; daily dawn-dusk; free*

The Fossil Discovery Center is a surprising find in Big Bend National Park. This area was once a huge, shallow sea full of creatures from mosasaurs (swimming reptiles) to sharks and fish, and a load of "sea shells" like oysters, clams, snails, and urchins. As the sea receded, the region became a swampy, coastal environment more like today's Texas coast, and dinosaurs and giant alligators roamed the marshy land. Later still, the region was forested, and dinosaurs and pterosaurs ruled the land and air. Fossils, dioramas, interactive exhibits, and other displays tell the stories of these creatures and reveal the ways we use geology to tell part of that tale. Whether you're a dinosaur-obsessed kid or just want to gain a new appreciation on this place, stop by for a while.

▲ BALANCED ROCK

▲ SANTA ELENA CANYON

59

SANTA ELENA CANYON

BIG BEND NATIONAL PARK, TEXAS

Descending into Santa Elena Canyon's sheer 1,500-ft (457-m) cliffs along the Rio Grande is a mesmerizing journey.

- **Distance:** 1.6 mi (2.6 km) round-trip
- **Duration:** 1 hour
- **Elevation Gain:** 220 ft (67 m)
- **Effort:** Easy
- **When:** Nov.-Apr.
- **Trailhead:** Parking lot at end of Ross Maxwell Scenic Drive

HIGHLIGHT: Swimming in Santa Elena Canyon

Santa Elena Canyon delivers drama from the moment you spot the cleft in the cliffs that is the trail to the moment it disappears from your rearview mirror. You can see the massive walls from miles away, but once you're in Santa Elena Canyon, with 1,500-ft-high (457-m) walls to either side, it's mesmerizing (and it only gets better the farther you go). Though the Rio Grande River flows through the

▲ HIKING NARROW PATHS ON THE RIVERBANK

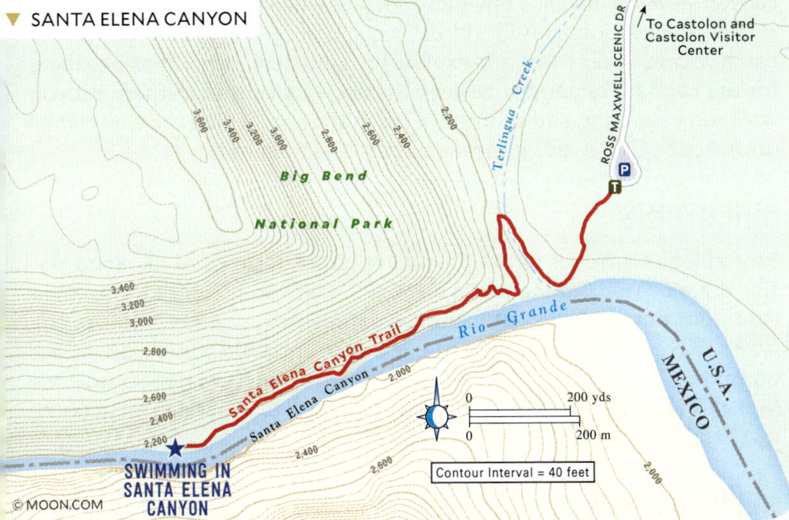

canyon, the canyon was formed by the Terlingua Fault Line rather than the river's erosion. Since the Rio Grande marks the official border between the United States and Mexico, you're walking a tightrope between the two nations.

START THE HIKE

You might think the wide swath of the **Rio Grande** flowing from the massive canyon walls marks the trail, but the difficult-to-find trail begins off to your right. It's marked by a crude stone pathway across the shallow **Terlingua Creek.** Depending on the season, the creek could be high and impassible (in which case, no hike here today, time for Plan B), gently flowing, or muddy; in any case plan to get your feet wet. Cross the creek and you'll find a series of tight switchbacks and concrete steps that ascend a rocky trail and eventually descend into the canyon.

Hike, watch, enjoy. The cliff walls are wild, and in a way will remind you of slot canyons found in Utah's Zion National Park. Keep an eye open for birds—more than 450 species call Big Bend home—and listen for frogs and toads; you may be surprised to learn they like the permanent pools and cool mud of the Rio Grande.

When you reach the end of the trail, you'll be surrounded by the stunning vertical cliff walls, which echo with the sounds of kids (even adults) playing in the water. This is one of the few places in the park where swimming is safe and generally tolerated. **Santa Elena Canyon** is truly a magical place where you can sit and absorb the surroundings for hours, so plan accordingly. Find a riverside rock and soak up the sounds and sights of the stunning canyon, from borderland birds soaring among the walls, to people on the riverbank tossing beer cans to passing paddlers. It's like no other place.

When it's time to return, it's easy: Head downstream. All kidding aside, as you walk downstream and back toward the trailhead, take note of the canyon, as it will reveal a few more secrets when you see it from this direction. Pockets of plant life, birds' nests, or interesting bits of rock will catch your eye—let them, and explore for a moment rather than beelining for the car. Just remember to keep Mexico—that's the southern canyon wall—on your right, and soon you'll reach the spot where the trail climbs up and out of the river's path and back to the trailhead.

DIRECTIONS

Santa Elena Canyon is in the Castolon Historic District of Big Bend National Park. From Terlingua, take FM 170 east for 4.5 mi (7.2 km), then turn right onto Highway 118 South. Continue for 2.9 mi (4.7 km) to the park's Maverick Junction entrance. From the entrance station, drive east on Panther Junction Road for 7.6 mi (12.2 km), then turn right onto Ross Maxwell Scenic Drive. The road ends at the trailhead parking lot after 22 mi (35 km).

NEED TO KNOW

Info: Castolon Visitor Center, www.nps.gov/bibe

Passes and Reservations: Entry into the park is $30/vehicle ($25/motorcycle, $15/pedestrian or cyclist), payable (credit or debit card only, no cash) at one of the four entrance stations. For more information, see page 502.

Weather Considerations: In late summer/early fall (after the rainy season drops up to a foot of moisture on the park), there will be more water in the Rio Grande, which affects access to the Santa Elena Canyon Trail. Instead of being able to walk across Terlingua Creek on a stone pathway, you'll be faced with the not-very-recommended option of wading through several feet of murky water to get to the trail. Depending on the

BEST NEARBY

Castolon

Be sure to drop by the historic village of Castolon, located about 8 mi (13 km) east of the trailhead for Santa Elena Canyon, to check out the museum exhibits and military structures that date back to the early decades of the 1900s. This spot is rich in recent history, starting with the turn of the 20th century when farmers began to raise crops on the banks of the Rio Grande. In 1901 the first store opened in the home of Cipriano Hernandez; the site is now known as the Alvino House, named for a later occupant. From 1912 to 1920, Mexico was caught up in revolution and many families fled north to escape the fighting; in response the National Guard established camps along the border, including Camp Santa Helena here at Castolon. By the time Camp Santa Helena's permanent structures were built and cavalry soldiers were about to move out of their tents, the Mexican Revolution was over. There are other structures to explore, including another store, several adobe ruins, and a pair of cemeteries. The Alvino House is the oldest-standing adobe structure in the national park. This is a great place to grab a snack and a cold drink.

water level, you may be able to walk down the shoreline and cross around to the trailhead. Regardless, you can still get a sense of wonder just from being at the base of the canyon, but you won't get the full experience of being within its sheer cliff walls.

Facilities: There are toilets at the trailhead.

▼ SANTA ELENA CANYON

GRAND TETON NATIONAL PARK

ROCKY MOUNTAINS

Boasting a breathtaking landscape of rugged peaks, alpine meadows, dense forests, and glacial lakes, the Rocky Mountains region is a haven for outdoor enthusiasts—and for wildlife, including elk, bears, and bighorn sheep. Each season brings unique beauty, from snow-covered peaks in winter to vibrant wildflower blooms in summer, making the Rockies a year-round spectacle of natural wonder.

An alpine swim awaits at Lake Haiyaha, at the end of a wildflower-lined trail high in Rocky Mountain; this hike is a preview of tomorrow when you pack your tent and set out for Longs Peak and the Keyhole Route. At Yellowstone, you're awestruck by the sight of Fairy Falls, but truth be told, the turquoise pool and vibrant coloring of Grand Prismatic Spring had you marveling from the minute you set foot on this trail. After four days on Grand Teton's Teton Crest Trail, you've gazed at the stars, watched grizzlies from afar, and heard bull elk bugle at dusk, but it's the wildflowers and altitude and alpine mornings that you'll remember. The short hike to The Notch led you through and above South Dakota's Badlands and you arrived in time for a blazing prairie sunset. Now the only thing to do is wait for summer's biggest meteor shower to send sparks across the sky.

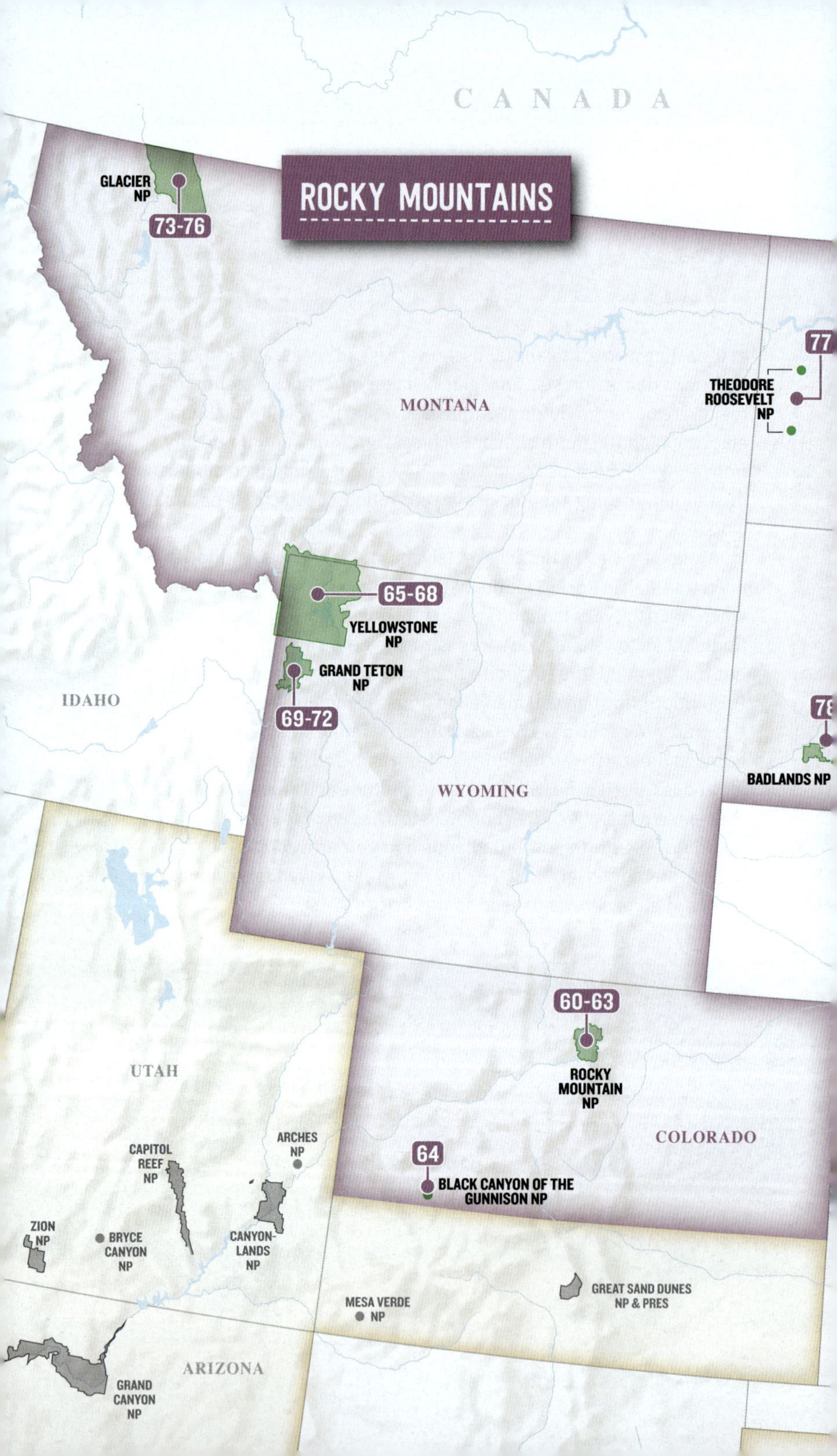

ROCKY MOUNTAINS

CANADA

GLACIER NP
73-76

MONTANA

THEODORE ROOSEVELT NP
77

YELLOWSTONE NP
65-68

GRAND TETON NP
69-72

IDAHO

WYOMING

BADLANDS NP
78

60-63
ROCKY MOUNTAIN NP

COLORADO

UTAH

ARCHES NP

CAPITOL REEF NP

64
BLACK CANYON OF THE GUNNISON NP

ZION NP

BRYCE CANYON NP

CANYON-LANDS NP

GREAT SAND DUNES NP & PRES

MESA VERDE NP

ARIZONA

GRAND CANYON NP

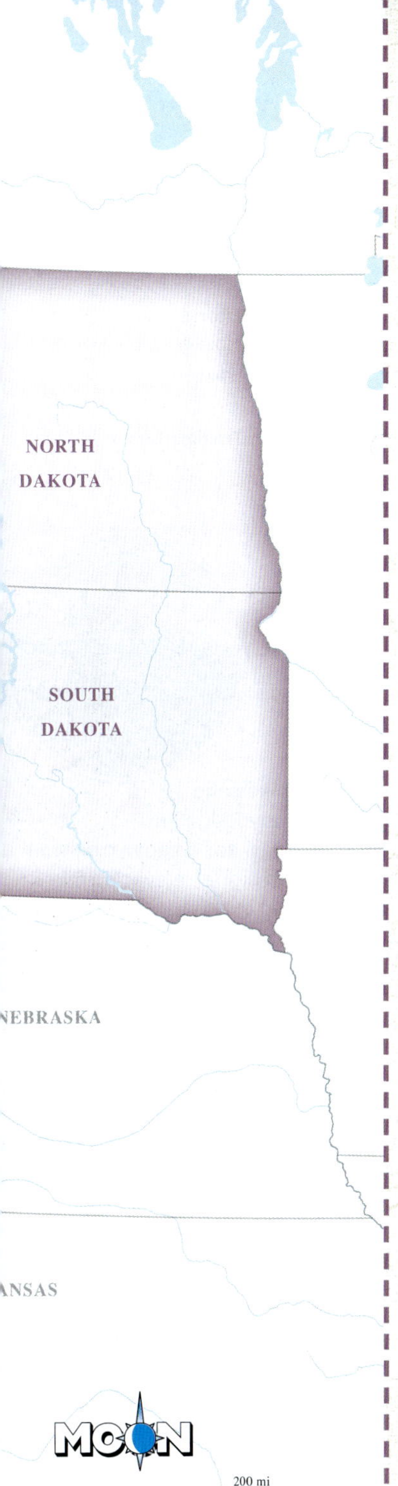

ROCKY MOUNTAIN

BLACK CANYON OF THE GUNNISON

YELLOWSTONE

GRAND TETON

GLACIER

THEODORE ROOSEVELT

BADLANDS

60

LUMPY RIDGE AND GEM LAKE

ROCKY MOUNTAIN NATIONAL PARK, COLORADO

This short, year-round hike leads you through a forest and ice-carved rocks to the picturesque Gem Lake.

- **Distance:** 3.8 mi (6.1 km) round-trip
- **Duration:** 2.5 hours
- **Elevation Gain:** 1,085 ft (331 m)
- **Effort:** Moderate
- **When:** Year-round
- **Trailhead:** Lumpy Ridge Trailhead

HIGHLIGHT: Crossing through the aspen grove in autumn

Sitting at a lower elevation than many of the hikes and ridges in Rocky Mountain National Park, Lumpy Ridge and the hike to Gem Lake offers hikers a longer window for a snow-free trail from September to June. When early snows fall on higher-elevation hikes, Lumpy Ridge may only receive a light dusting, and in the heart of winter, the trail here is passable with the proper equipment, making for a beautiful year-round hike.

Along the way you'll find some great views—Rocky Mountain seems to be filled with great views—of the mountains above, but also of the famous Twin Owls Rock formations. These rocks, and others along the way, are popular with climbers, so if you're hiking in the warmer months, you'll share part of the trail with climbers loaded with gear.

▲ TWIN OWLS

START THE HIKE

From the trailhead, go left and ascend at the foot of **Twin Owls.** When you reach the main trail, a right turn takes you below the Owls and past the next junction, where you'll cross through an **aspen grove** (that is absolutely stunning in autumn). As you climb up Lumpy Ridge,

LUMPY RIDGE AND GEM LAKE

you pass through evergreen forest and the ancient granite boulders and knobs that lend the ridge its funny name. The land here was sculpted by ice, wind, and rain over millions of years, so in many ways you're hiking through time as you pass through the forest.

Ascend via a set of small switchbacks and you'll reach a notable rock formation: **Paul Bunyan's Boot** (see if you can find the hole in the "sole" while you're there). Finally, you're in for a steep climb to **Gem Lake,** along the way enjoying distant views of Longs Peak, Mount Meeker, and the town of Estes Park. When you reach Gem Lake you'll find several great spots to stop for lunch or a rest on the rocky outcrops and small sandy beach. On the return trip, retrace your steps back to the trailhead and parking area. Or, to shorten the hike a little, turn left at the first junction to complete a circumnavigation of Twin Owls.

DIRECTIONS

Lumpy Ridge and Gem Lake are in the northeastern region of Rocky Mountain National Park. From the intersection of US 34 and MacGregor

Avenue in Estes Park, take MacGregor Avenue northeast for 1.3 mi (2.1 km) to the turnoff for the Lumpy Ridge Trailhead.

NEED TO KNOW

Info: Fall River Visitor Center, www.nps.gov/romo

Passes and Reservations: Entry into the park is $30/vehicles ($25/motorcycle, $15/pedestrian or cyclist). Passes are available in advance at www.recreation.gov. Timed entry reservations ($2) are required May 24-mid-October. For more information, see page 504.

Weather Considerations: If you come to hike during wintry weather, be aware the trail can grow icy; you won't need full-on crampons, but a pair of microspikes will do the trick. On the rare occasion the trail is snowy—snow seldom reaches a notable depth here—you can don a pair of snowshoes or slow down and take turns breaking trail with your companions. One of my favorite things to bring with me on a winter hike is a thermos filled with coffee, tea, hot cocoa, or something a little stronger, depending on my hiking companions. Driving to the trailhead in winter shouldn't present many issues as Estes Park does a good job with road upkeep.

Facilities: There are vault toilets at the trailhead.

BEST NEARBY

Trailborn Rocky Mountains

▶ *130 Stanley Ave., Estes Park; 970/586-4471; www.staytrailborn.com; from $225*

Only 10 minutes from Rocky Mountain National Park's Fall River or the Beaver Meadows Visitor Centers, Trailborn Rocky Mountains offers a hip, comfortable place to stay while you relive the highlights of your day's hikes and plan tomorrow. With a seasonal outdoor pool, fire pits, complimentary bikes (Estes Park is an easy bike or walk away), and an assortment of kid- and group-friendly activities (like sunrise hikes, snowshoeing trips, and even in-room "camping," among others), this is the type of hotel you'll stay at again and again. An on-site café and restaurant serves a small but tasty breakfast and dinner menu ($4-11). The hotel is pet-friendly (pets up to 40 lb/18 kg welcome, $35/day), and they even put a branded bandanna in the room for your furry friend. They have a sister hotel—Trailborn Rocky Mountains Outpost (1040 Big Thompson Ave., Estes Park)—nearby.

▲ GEM LAKE WITH LONGS PEAK IN THE DISTANCE

61

LAKE HAIYAHA

ROCKY MOUNTAIN NATIONAL PARK, COLORADO

Hike past four or more lakes to a rugged, boulder-strewn lake in a glacial couloir above 10,000 ft (3,048 m)—you'll feel like you've arrived on another planet.

- **Distance:** 4.2 mi (6.8 km) round-trip
- **Duration:** 2-3 hours
- **Elevation Gain:** 767 ft (234 m)
- **Effort:** Moderate
- **When:** May-Sept.
- **Trailhead:** Bear Lake Trailhead

HIGHLIGHT: Circling Nymph Lake among wildflowers in spring or early summer

Haiyaha is the perfect name for this lake as this Indigenous word means "rock," "lake of rocks," or "big rocks," depending on the translation. This out-and-back hike is a popular one in spring and summer for the wildflowers and on the warmest days for those bold enough for a summertime polar plunge (the water's cold year-round). You can make this hike longer by continuing on to The Loch and Mills Lake, or make it just a little longer by circling Bear Lake as you return to the trailhead.

◀ LAKE HAIYAHA

▼ NYMPH LAKE

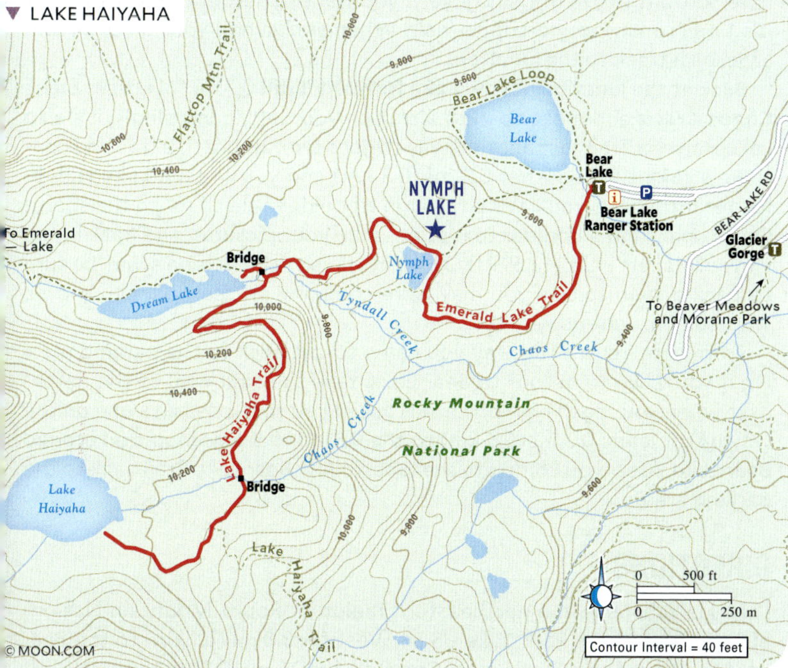

START THE HIKE

Beginning at the massive **Bear Lake parking lot,** look for the trailhead directly behind the **ranger station.** Bypass the first trail on your right, but turn left when you reach the junction with Bear Lake/Emerald Lake Trails. Almost immediately you'll cross the creek and find another intersection; bear right here to stay on **Emerald Lake Trail,** which ascends steadily for the next 0.4 mi (0.6 km) until it reaches **Nymph Lake.**

At Nymph Lake you'll have views and reflections of Hallett Peak and a choice to make: circle the lake along the eastern shore or head uphill and continue west. For this hike, circle Nymph Lake on its eastern shore, staying on Emerald Lake Trail. You'll pass a spur trail leading to Bear Lake on the right as you round the corner of the lake and begin to climb again. This section is especially pretty in spring and early summer as it's a riot of **wildflowers,** including shooting star, salsify, Nelson's larkspur, mariposa lily, and snowball saxifrage, among others.

In areas where wildflowers grow the thickest, you stand a good chance of spotting some of the park's elusive bighorn sheep; watch the cliffs and scree slopes, and along the edges of vegetation, and you might see them browsing for breakfast or lunch. Elk, a bucket-list Rocky Mountain wildlife sighting, are more likely to be spotted in nearby Moraine Park, though you could spot a lone bull elk wandering far from the herd.

Just before you reach Dream Lake, you'll cross **Tyndall Creek** and come to a junction where Emerald Lake Trail splits off to the right and Lake Haiyaha Trail breaks to the left. We're going right for a moment so we can get a good look at **Dream Lake** and take a breather—the elevation here, 9,900 ft (3,018 m), is no joke. If you want to detour to Emerald Lake, it's 1 mi (1.6 km) round-trip to visit. When you've had your fill of Dream Lake, backtrack to the junction.

Back at the junction, follow **Lake Haiyaha Trail** 0.7 mi (1.1 km) to cross **Chaos Creek** and meet up with a trail on your left (confusingly, it's also Lake Haiyaha Trail, just another way to get here); ignore this trail and continue straight for another 0.2 mi (0.3 km) and you'll reach **Lake Haiyaha.** Near the lake, you'll wind through a boulder field to reach the shoreline proper. Find a boulder to rest on, snap your pictures, and bask in the view of Hallett Peak (12,599 ft/3,840 m). If you're keen for a swim, be sure to pack a swimsuit as you may have company on the trail. Oh, and be warned: The water's very cold.

From here, return the way you came to get back to the parking area. Or, if you'd like to detour to Bear Lake, take the spur trail to the northeast when you reach Nymph Lake (I asked you to bypass this one on the way up); it leads 0.3 mi (0.5 km) to the 0.5-mi (0.8-km) loop trail around Bear Lake. After you complete the loop, follow Bear Lake Trail back to the parking area.

DIRECTIONS

Lake Haiyaha is in the northeastern region of Rocky Mountain National Park. From Estes Park, take US 36 West for 3.8 mi (6.1 km) to the Beaver Meadows Entrance Station. Continue for 0.2 mi (0.3 km) and turn left on the Bear Lake Road. It's another 9 mi (14.5 km) to Bear Lake Trailhead.

NEED TO KNOW

Info: Beaver Meadows Visitor Center or Bear Lake Ranger Station, www.nps.gov/romo

Passes and Reservations: Entry into the park is $30/vehicles ($25/motorcycle, $15/pedestrian or cyclist). Passes are available in advance at

BEST NEARBY

Moraine Park

The easy-to-get-to and popular Moraine Park is a must-see for the wildlife-viewing opportunities, the postcard-worthy views of the Rockies, and the natural history. Geologists consider this area to be one of the best exposures of glacial moraines—areas where glaciers have deposited tons of material like soil, stones, and boulders—in the Rocky Mountains. It doesn't matter which season you visit Moraine Park because it's a year-round treat. Wildflowers and a sea of verdant grass welcome you in summer, when the Big Thompson River cuts a fine figure through the fields. Throughout fall, the changing of the leaves and the snowcapped mountains give you a beautiful backdrop where you can watch huge herds of elk graze and even see a few bull elk clash with rivals as they look for mates. Hearty campers show up in winter and spring, braving seasonal snows for a bit of solitude. Whether you stop for a picnic lunch, watch some wildlife, hit one of the trails meandering through the area, or cast a line into the Big Thompson River, you'll be glad you paid a visit to Moraine Park.

▲ LAKE HAIYAHA TRAIL

www.recreation.gov. Timed entry reservations ($2) are required May 24-mid-October; permit options include timed entry or timed entry + Bear Lake Road (required for access to the Bear Lake Corridor). For more information, see page 504.

Weather Considerations: From spring through early fall, you'll find temperatures pleasant, ranging from 40°F (4°C) at night to a daytime high of 77°F (25°C). Though it's unlikely, you could experience a late-spring, early-fall, or even mid-July dusting of snow in this part of the park.

Facilities: Bear Lake Trailhead has a ranger station and restrooms.

Other: The elevation of Rocky Mountain National Park is no joke. Take it easy and give yourself time to acclimate to the altitude. Pack extra water and stay vigilant for signs of acute mountain sickness (symptoms include dizziness, nausea, sudden or unrelenting headache, and shortness of breath, among others) in yourself and your hiking partners; be prepared to call it quits if you or a companion begins to feel ill. Often, altitude-related issues can be resolved with a long rest, plenty of water, and a change of pace, but if this doesn't resolve any issues you're experiencing, it's best to head back down to lower altitudes, possibly seeking the aid of a ranger or emergency services.

Keep at least 75 ft (23 m) between you and any elk or bighorn sheep, and 120 ft (37 m) between you and any bear or moose you spot. If you see a mountain lion, maintain eye contact and make yourself large (raise your arms, lift your pack overhead) and, if the mountain lion approaches, make noise, wave your arms, and let that lion know you're not food. Report any mountain lion sighting or wildlife incident to rangers at the first opportunity.

62

SKY POND VIA GLACIER GORGE TRAIL

ROCKY MOUNTAIN NATIONAL PARK, COLORADO

This scenic and challenging trek offers some of the park's most spectacular views, including forests, waterfalls, and alpine lakes.

- **Distance:** 8.6 mi (13.8 km) round-trip
- **Duration:** 6 hours
- **Elevation Gain:** 1,771 ft (540 m)
- **Effort:** Strenuous
- **When:** May-Oct.
- **Trailhead:** Glacier Gorge Trailhead

HIGHLIGHT: Seeing the jagged edges of The Sharkstooth from Sky Pond

Spectacular scenery awaits on the journey to Sky Pond, and adventurous souls will enjoy the final push toward the end of this hike, which includes a few fun minutes of rock scrambling.

START THE HIKE

Begin on **Glacier Gorge Trail** and you'll reach your first waterfall—**Alberta Falls**—after 0.8 mi (1.3 km). Admire the falls and cascades, then continue along the path until the trail intersects with the North Longs

◀ LAKE OF GLASS

▼ ALBERTA FALLS

Peak Trail; go right toward Mills Lake and Loch Vale (that's Scottish for "lake valley") and, almost immediately, the landscape opens up to breathtaking views. After a relatively flat section there's a brief descent and the trail splits off again; stay right on **Loch Vale Trail.** Slog through a set of steep switchbacks and arrive at **The Loch.** Wind around this stunningly gorgeous lake, where there are plenty of nice spots to eat a snack or lunch, go fishing, or recharge with a quick nap.

When you have had your fill, continue on the Loch Vale Trail to Sky Pond. After crossing two small bridges, hike past the trail split on your right for **Andrews Glacier Trail.** Here you reach a marshy environment; to protect this sensitive area there are several wooden planks set up to help you cross. After climbing some steep rock steps you'll find yourself in the middle of a wide-open boulder field surrounded by exceptional views. Continue hiking to a small wooden sign for Sky Pond that points to the right. Before you head to Sky Pond, take a moment to admire the cascade that is **Timberline Falls.**

Your next move is a rock scramble. Don't sweat it; it's not too hard and the reward is worth it. At the top of the scramble is pretty **Lake of Glass.** Continue following cairns along rocky terrain and you will reach your final destination, **Sky Pond,** at 10,900 ft (3,322 m). The cliffs surrounding this lake, including the jagged edges of **The Sharkstooth,** are the most impressive feature at the end of this memorable hike. Return the way you came.

DIRECTIONS

Sky Pond is in the northeastern region of Rocky Mountain National Park. From Estes Park, take US 36 West for 3.8 mi (6.1 km) to the Beaver Meadows Entrance Station. Continue for 0.2 mi (0.3 km) and turn left on the Bear Lake Road. Continue another 8.5 mi (13.7 km) to Glacier Gorge Trailhead.

The Glacier Gorge parking lot fills by 6am in the summer. If the lot is full, you can park at the Park & Ride (Bear Lake Rd., across from Glacier Basin Campground) to take the hiker shuttle (daily summer, Sat.-Sun. Sept.-Oct.; $2, must reserve in advance), which stops at Glacier Gorge Trailhead (last shuttle departs the Glacier Gorge stop at 7:30pm).

NEED TO KNOW

Info: Beaver Meadows Visitor Center, www.nps.gov/romo

Passes and Reservations: Entry into the park is $30/vehicles ($25/motorcycle, $15/pedestrian or cyclist). Passes are available in advance at www.recreation.gov. Timed entry reservations ($2) are required May 24-mid-October. For more information, see page 504.

Weather Considerations: The final scramble up to Sky Pond is tricky, especially because the rocks can be wet in late spring and fall and icy

BEST NEARBY

The Barrel: Beer, Wine & Spirits Garden

▶ *251 Moraine Ave., Estes Park; 970/616-2090; https://thebarrel.beer; noon-9pm Mon.-Wed., 11am-10pm Thurs.-Sat., 10:30am-9pm Sun.*

There are several great breweries in Estes Park, and as a beer fan with wide-ranging tastes, I find myself returning to The Barrel on every visit. The Barrel offers up a rotating selection of craft beer and cider as well as spirits, wines, and nonalcoholic drinks from craft sodas to NA beers to kombucha. I can always find a sour beer, creative seasonal brews, a crisp lager, or a refreshing IPA on draft, and with most of their selection coming from Colorado breweries, I come away with another place to explore (when I'm not on the trail). Food trucks stop by most nights, ensuring you don't go hungry, and the place is both kid and pet friendly (provided both are well behaved).

throughout winter. If you can, especially on the way down, remove your backpack and hand it to someone below for better balance. It's possible to do a winter hike here, but it's not recommended: You'll need to come equipped with the proper gear, and with some winter hiking and backcountry experience under your belt. Depending on conditions, you'll require equipment ranging from snowshoes to microspikes to full-size crampons. And if you're out hiking in winter, keep a close eye on avalanche and weather conditions.

Facilities: The trailhead has vault toilets.

▼ LOCH VALE

63

LONGS PEAK: KEYHOLE ROUTE

ROCKY MOUNTAIN NATIONAL PARK, COLORADO

This popular but challenging route takes you through switchbacks and boulder fields to the summit of the highest peak in Rocky Mountain National Park.

- **Distance:** 15 mi (24 km) round-trip
- **Duration:** 10-15 hours
- **Elevation Gain:** 5,000 ft (1,524 m)
- **Effort:** Very strenuous
- **When:** Late Aug.-early Sept.
- **Trailhead:** Longs Peak Trailhead

HIGHLIGHT: Admiring the views from the Longs Peak summit

The Keyhole Route is by far the most popular path to the summit of 14,259-ft (4,346-m) Longs Peak, a trail that's more of a mountaineering route than a hiking trail. A distinctive notch in the ridgeline extending from the north side of the peak lends this route its name, and though it's considered the least difficult way to the top, don't underestimate it; before you hit the trail, check and double-check current conditions on the park's website or at the **Longs Peak Ranger Station.**

▲ LONGS PEAK CLIFFS

START THE HIKE

The first part of the trail is steep, but after a brief break at **Goblins Forest,** a wilderness campsite with a spooky name, you're in for even more climbing via some steep switchbacks. Keep climbing to **Lightning Bridge,** a footbridge with a well-documented sign warning hikers about lightning dangers ahead.

Tishma's Corner—a massive switchback named after Walter Tishma, a local who climbed this peak more than 100 times—is your next landmark; here, subalpine and alpine environments meet. Soon you'll be above the tree line.

▲ THE KEYHOLE

Your next landmark is a little less glorious: At **Chasm Junction** you'll find a small meadow and a vault toilet that, admittedly, has the best views of any I've visited.

The landscape is rockier here, and at 6 mi (9.7 km) into the hike you'll reach the **Boulderfield,** a spot full of stop-you-in-your-tracks views, ptarmigan, and campsites. The wilderness campsites here are perfect if you're splitting this hike into two or three days and are lucky enough to land a reservation; these sites fill fast, so reserve yours well in advance. Near the equestrian **hitching posts** and the privies you'll find a sign to the Keyhole Route; the trail is marked with cairns from here on out.

This next part is a challenge. The **Keyhole,** the long north ridge of Longs Peak, offers up rock ledges; the trough, a gully that's 0.3 mi (0.5 km) long; the narrows, a sidewalk-wide stretch of trail; and the **homestretch,** a bit of Class 2 rock leading to the summit.

The summit is spectacular. It's wide—the size of several football fields (no matter which type of footie you play)—and you could spend hours admiring the view. Celebrate, snap your summit shots, and fuel up to head back: It's 7.5 mi (12.1 km) back to the trailhead.

DIRECTIONS

Longs Peak is in the heart of Rocky Mountain National Park. From Estes Park, take Highway 7 south for 9 mi (14.5 km). Turn right at the National Park Service sign and drive about 1 mi (1.6 km) up Longs Peak Road to arrive at the main Longs Peak Trailhead parking lot on the left.

NEED TO KNOW

Info: Longs Peak Ranger Station, www.nps.gov/romo

LONGS PEAK: KEYHOLE ROUTE

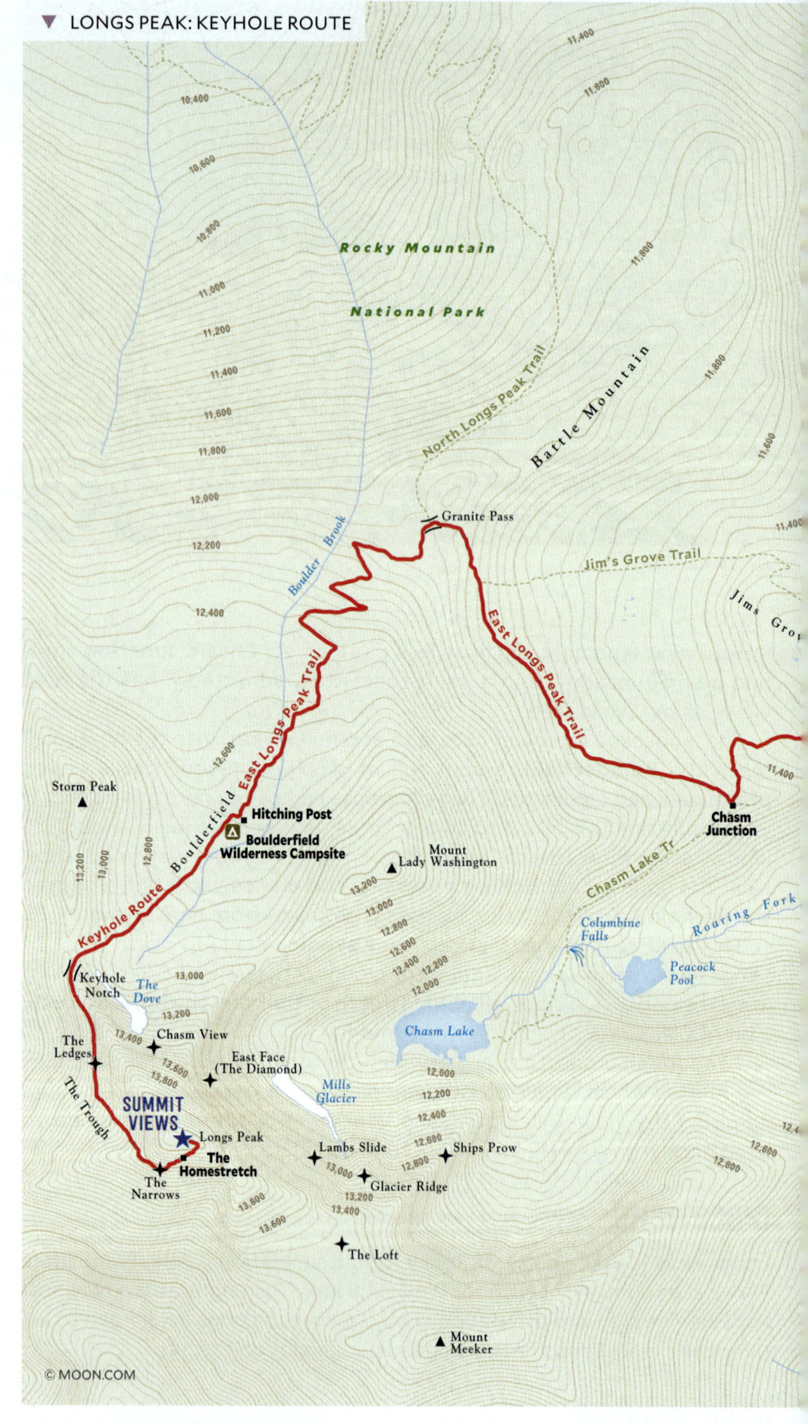

Storm Pass Trail
GOBLINS CASTLE ROAD
Inn Brook
Eugena Mine Trail
Pine Ridge
Larkspur Creek
East Longs Peak Trail
Lightning Bridge
Alpine Brook
Goblins Forest
Alpine Brook
Longs Peak
Longs Peak
LONGS PEAK RD
Longs Peak Ranger Station
To Lily Lake
Tishma's Corner
Mills Moraine
Roaring Fork
Rocky Mountain
National Park
0
0.25 mi
0
0.25 km
Contour Interval = 40 feet

Passes and Reservations: Entry into the park is $30/vehicles ($25/motorcycle, $15/pedestrian or cyclist). Passes are available in advance at www.recreation.gov. Timed entry reservations ($2) are required May 24-mid-October. You can make this hike a two- or three-day affair by reserving wilderness campsites at Boulderfield or Goblins Forest. For more information, see page 504.

Weather Considerations: The climbing season gains momentum at a slightly different time each year, depending on the amount of snowfall the previous winter and on how long the snow sticks to the mountain. June-August also often sees afternoon thunderstorms. Thus, late August-early September is considered the most ideal time to attempt Longs.

Since completing the trip as a day hike usually takes 10-15 hours, the safest time to start the trek is 1am-3am. (If you're camping and making this a 1-2-night affair, time your summit push so you'll be descending the peak by noon.) An early start time and a headlamp packed with fresh batteries are essential, as you will want to be on your way down from the peak at or before noon, when foul weather can start to develop. Many people aim to arrive at the Keyhole around sunrise.

Facilities: There's a seasonal ranger station (closed winter) adjacent to the Longs Peak Trailhead. Toilets are available at Chasm Junction and the Boulderfield campsite, but not at Goblins Forest. Water is available from Alpine Brook at Goblin Forest, though you'll need to filter, treat, or boil it prior to use; at Chasm Junction and Boulderfield you'll also rely on nearby streams, so your water will require treatment before use. When backcountry camping, always check with park rangers or the backcountry office for water availability.

Other: If possible, schedule your Longs Peak trip for a weekday, when the trails are less crowded.

BEST NEARBY

Lily Lake

▶ *Highway 7, 6.3 mi (10.1 km) south of the junction of Highway 7 and US 36 in Estes Park*

Lily Lake stands at 8,880 ft (2,707 m), between the subalpine and montane ecosystems. It makes for an interesting place to observe wildlife and see a variety of flora. Along the north side of the lake you'll find thick stands of ponderosa pines, fragrant year-round; to the south you'll find wetlands full of birds and heavy with wildflowers throughout summer. In the pond you may spot muskrats, and in the shallows tiger salamanders, garter snakes, and other critters. The trail here—0.8 mi (1.3 km) encircling the lake—is flat and composed of crushed gravel, and is accessible. There's also an accessible fishing pier, restrooms (though they're accessible, they are pit toilets), and picnic facilities.

▲ HIKING TO LONGS PEAK

64

NORTH VISTA TO EXCLAMATION POINT

BLACK CANYON OF THE GUNNISON NATIONAL PARK, COLORADO

This easy hike along the north rim of one of the lesser-visited parks delivers vistas of an incredible canyon.

- **Distance:** 3 mi (4.8 km) round-trip
- **Duration:** 1 hour 15 minutes
- **Elevation Gain:** 360 ft (110 m)
- **Effort:** Easy
- **When:** Apr.-mid-Nov.
- **Trailhead:** North Rim Ranger Station

HIGHLIGHT: Taking in wow-worthy canyon views at Exclamation Point

Black Canyon of the Gunnison is nothing short of spectacular. The comparisons to the Grand Canyon are obvious and warranted—a powerful river carved this canyon over millions of erosive years, leaving behind a jaw-dropping landscape—but the canyons differ significantly. Where the Grand Canyon is broad, Black Canyon of the Gunnison is narrow. Here, the Gunnison River carved a channel through incredibly hard metamorphic rock, creating a deep canyon with sheer walls (they're higher than Chicago's Willis Tower) and an inner gorge so narrow it sees only minutes of sunlight each day. The national

▲ PLAINS AND ROLLING HILLS NEAR BLACK CANYON OF THE GUNNISON

▼ NORTH VISTA TO EXCLAMATION POINT

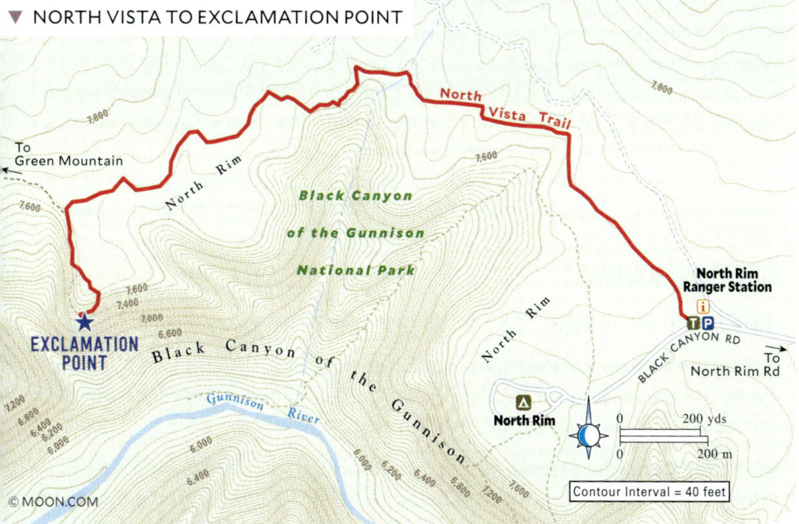

park preserves the gorge's 12 most incredible miles (19.3 km), and nearly every hike in the park leads you to the canyon rim where you'll peer over the edge of the abyss to the glittering river below.

START THE HIKE

North Vista Trail leads 1.5 mi (2.4 km) along the North Rim to Exclamation Point along an easy, well-maintained, mostly flat trail. As you hike, you'll find the trail leads you to the canyon rim—where you'll have many opportunities to slow down, take in the view, and snap a few pics—and into the scrubby woods nearby. The only real climb comes at **Exclamation Point,** an aptly named rocky outcrop where the inner-canyon views are definitely exclamation worthy. Take your time here, and once you've had your fill of the view, reverse course and return to the trailhead past the small, often unstaffed **North Rim Ranger Station.** It's likely you'll have the trail to yourself, and a few moments of trail solitude.

Many hikers are hungry for more of this landscape and add on another 2 mi (3.2 km) by hiking to **Green Mountain.** The hike to the summit of Green Mountain isn't too steep—you'll gain 918 ft (280 m) in 2 mi (3.2 km)—and offers a few welcome patches of shade, but the real payoff is up top. From the summit you'll have 360-degree views of Grand Mesa, the Uncompahgre Plateau, and the San Juan Mountains in addition to an aerial view of the canyon and surrounding lands. This makes the hike a 7-mi (11.3-km) round-trip trek that will take a little more than three hours to complete. If you think you'll extend your hike to Green Mountain, bring a couple of extra liters of water.

DIRECTIONS

North Vista Trail is on the North Rim of Black Canyon of the Gunnison National Park. From Grand Junction, follow US 50 East to its junction with Highway 92 in the town of Delta. Turn left and follow Highway 92 east for about 31 mi (50 km) to the town of Crawford. At the junction with Fruitland Mesa Road, turn right and follow this road for 3.3 mi (5.3 km), then continue straight on Road 7745 for 1.2 mi (1.9 km) until the junction with Black Canyon Road. Turn right to follow Black Canyon Road for about 5 mi (8 km) to the North Rim Ranger Station.

The last 7 mi (11.3 km) of Black Canyon Road are unpaved, so drive with care, especially if you're not in a vehicle with a higher ground clearance.

NEED TO KNOW

Info: North Rim Ranger Station, www.nps.gov/blca

Passes and Reservations: Entry into the park is $30/vehicle ($25/motorcycle, $15/pedestrian or cyclist). Passes are available in advance at www.recreation.gov. For more information, see page 502.

Weather Considerations: North Rim Road—also called G74 Road—is an unpaved track that follows the North Rim of the canyon for a few miles between the North Rim Ranger Station and Kneeling Camel View; it closes during winter, usually from late November to mid-late April. Black Canyon Road has similar seasonal closures. Temperatures get very cold here in winter, and it would be difficult for rangers, rescue volunteers, or other services to reach you in an emergency situation. I recommend tackling this hike only while North Rim Road is open.

Facilities: Though there are vault toilets at the trailhead, water is very limited; in fact, late fall-early summer, drinking water is not available in the park, and for the rest of the year, most drinking water is trucked in.

Other: Along the North Rim there are a few areas where cattle grazing is permitted; if you encounter any cattle gates, please close them. There are bears in the area, so do your part to secure your trail snacks and food waste (including wrappers and containers) in something airtight.

BEST NEARBY

North Rim Road

Since you've trekked all the way to the North Rim, you might as well spend a couple of hours exploring North Rim Road (marked on some maps at G74 Road), where you'll find six overlooks offering impressive views. This 5-mi-long (8-km) road is unpaved, so the going will be a little slow, but since the canyon walls here on the north side are nearly vertical, the views you'll enjoy are of the "I can't believe it" variety. One of the best overlooks is The Narrows View, overlooking the canyon's narrowest point: a measly 40 ft (12 m) wide at river level. Balanced Rock Overlook has both big canyon views and an improbably perched boulder, and Kneeling Camel Overlook—the turnaround point on this scenic drive—will leave you in awe of this park. And if you still have a hankering for a trail, Deadhorse Trail (5 mi/8 km with 560 ft/171 m in elevation gain) begins in the Kneeling Camel Overlook parking area and heads into the wilderness area along an old service road that you might share with equestrians.

▲ BLACK CANYON OF THE GUNNISON

65

FAIRY FALLS AND GRAND PRISMATIC SPRING OVERLOOK

YELLOWSTONE NATIONAL PARK, WYOMING

En route to the gossamer Fairy Falls, pass through a lodgepole forest, peek at a colorful hot spring, and take in the seasonal delights: In summer the falls plunge into a deep pool, but in winter the falls are draped in ice.

- **Distance:** 6.8 mi (10.9 km) round-trip
- **Duration:** 3.5 hours
- **Elevation Gain:** 88-129 ft (27-39 m)
- **Effort:** Easy-moderate
- **When:** June-Mar.
- **Trailhead:** Fairy Falls parking area

HIGHLIGHT: Admiring the colorful rainbow of Grand Prismatic Spring Overlook

Fairy Falls, the park's fourth-highest waterfall, drops some 197 ft (60 m) into a picturesque plunge pool, making a great year-round destination for hikers, bikers, and skiers. Add in the short spur loop to the Grand Prismatic Spring overlook, where the view of the cobalt waters and fiery arms of thermophiles give you yet another reason to love this hike.

◀ GRAND PRISMATIC SPRING OVERLOOK

▼ FOOTBRIDGE OVER THE FIREHOLE RIVER

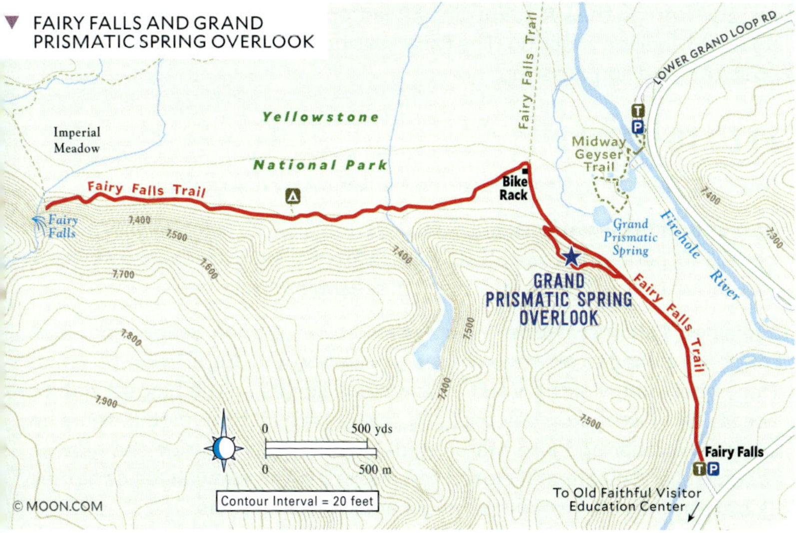

START THE HIKE

From **Fairy Falls Trailhead,** cross the **Firehole River** and follow the abandoned road. In 0.5 mi (0.8 km), climb the spur trail 105 ft (32 m) to the overlook of **Grand Prismatic Spring.** From there, descend westward to reach another junction on the main **Fairy Falls Trail.** Continue west 0.2 mi (0.3 km) on the main trail to the signed junction for **the falls.** Take the trail 1.5 mi (2.4 km) through a young lodgepole forest to the base of the falls. Throughout summer, the ribbon-like falls plunges into a pool; in winter, ice turns it into an abstract sculpture. Once you've admired the falls, return the way you came.

This trail is easy, but what pushes it to that "moderate" category is the length. Take your time on the return trip; a slower pace gives you the opportunity to both conserve your energy (6.8 mi/10.9 km is no joke) and grow observant of the natural world. See a trailside flower that intrigues you? Investigate. Time for a water break? Sit down and enjoy, and while you're at it, get quiet and notice the sounds of the forest returning. The lodgepole forest near the falls makes for a great wildlife habitat and provides some interesting photo opportunities, so look out for both. And when you arrive back at Grand Prismatic Spring Overlook, really take in the sights—note how the wild and vivid color bands stretch across the steaming pools, observe the way the colors change depending on the time of day and the cloud cover, and listen to the other visitors at the overlook as they gaze down in awe. When you've had your fill, the parking area and trailhead are not far off.

DIRECTIONS

Fairy Falls and Grand Prismatic Spring are in the Midway Geyser Basin area of Yellowstone National Park. From Bozeman, Montana, take US 191 South for 82 mi (132 km) to the West Entrance Station. Head east for 13 mi (20.9 km) on the West Entrance Road, and then turn onto Grand Loop Road at Madison Junction. The Fairy Falls parking area is 11.5 mi (18.5 km) south of Madison Junction.

NEED TO KNOW

Info: Old Faithful Visitor Education Center, www.nps.gov/yell

Passes and Reservations: Entry into the park is $35/vehicle ($30/motorcycle, $20/pedestrian or cyclist). Passes are available in advance at www.recreation.gov. For more information, see page 502.

Weather Considerations: West Yellowstone is open year-round. Park roads are closed to private vehicles November-mid-April. In winter (mid-December-mid-March), West Yellowstone serves as the biggest hub to access Old Faithful on day trips via snowcoach or snowmobile tours. In early November and late March-mid-April, cyclists can ride the plowed roads while they are still closed to cars. In winter, snowshoes or Nordic skis are advised, depending on snow and trail conditions.

Facilities: There are no facilities at the trailhead.

Other: Bears close this trail in spring until late May. Bicyclists should lock their bikes at the bike rack at the Fairy Falls junction as only hikers are allowed on the narrow spur trail to the falls.

BEST NEARBY

Grand Prismatic Spring

At 370 ft (113 m) across and 121 ft (37 m) deep, Grand Prismatic Spring is the largest hot spring in Yellowstone and the third largest in the world. Enjoy the glorious hues: fiery arms of orange, gold, and brown thermophiles that radiate in a full circle from the yellow-rimmed, blue hot pool. Its 160°F (71°C) water discharges in all directions at 560 gallons per minute. To get even closer than the overlook, see it from the boardwalk loop, accessible from the Midway Geyser Basin parking area. Please be a responsible visitor when you stop by Grand Prismatic Spring. In recent years, badly behaved visitors have injured themselves in the hot and caustic waters of Yellowstone's hot springs and geysers, and damaged the sensitive environments here. Stay on the boardwalk and marked trails, heed the signage and rangers' guidance, and enjoy.

▲ FAIRY FALLS

▲ BISON IN YELLOWSTONE NATIONAL PARK

66

LONE STAR GEYSER TRAIL

YELLOWSTONE NATIONAL PARK, WYOMING

This easy, accessible (with the right equipment) hike leads through piney woods and wildlife-filled meadows to reveal a geyser that's picturesque in any season.

- **Distance:** 5.3 mi (8.5 km) round-trip
- **Duration:** 3-5 hours
- **Elevation Gain:** 127 ft (39 m)
- **Effort:** Easy
- **When:** June-Mar.
- **Trailhead:** Lone Star Geyser Trailhead

HIGHLIGHT: Logging the date and time of Lone Star Geyser's eruption

Hiking—or cycling or skiing—to Lone Star Geyser offers a few moments of quiet meditation as you follow an old service road along the banks of the Firehole River through a conifer forest. Plenty of folks hit this trail to see Lone Star Geyser erupt every three hours or so, spewing superheated water up to 45 ft (14 m) into the air from a wild-looking 12-ft (3.7-m) sinter cone. The path is partially paved, though the pavement runs out around 100 ft (31 m) from the geyser.

▲ FIREHOLE RIVER ALONG LONE STAR GEYSER TRAIL

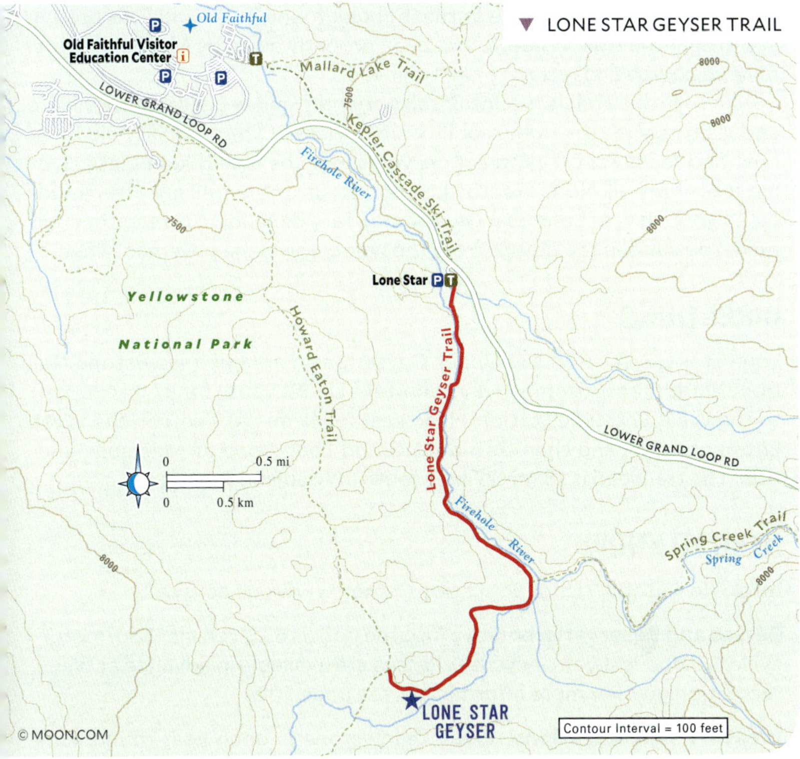

Old Faithful
Old Faithful Visitor Education Center
LOWER GRAND LOOP RD
Mallard Lake Trail
Kepler Cascade Ski Trail
Firehole River
Lone Star
Yellowstone National Park
Howard Eaton Trail
Lone Star Geyser Trail
LOWER GRAND LOOP RD
Firehole River
Spring Creek Trail
Spring Creek
LONE STAR GEYSER
0 0.5 mi
0 0.5 km
Contour Interval = 100 feet

START THE HIKE

Almost immediately after starting the trail, a spur leads to the **Firehole River;** several spur trails do the same along the way, so feel free to take a look or stick to the main trail as you move toward Lone Star Geyser. At 0.8 mi (1.3 km) in, there are two small geysers near the trail that are worth checking out. As you hike along, keep an eye out for wildlife as deer, bears, owls, coyotes, and other small mammals are frequently spotted on and near the trail. When you reach the 1.5-mi (2.4-km) mark, Spring Creek Trail branches off to the left; stick to **Lone Star Geyser Trail.** Here, the space opens up a little and you'll find a large meadow as you ascend a gentle hill to the geyser basin.

Nestled there in the geyser basin is **Lone Star Geyser,** which erupts from a 12-ft-tall (3.7-m) pink and gray sinter cone every three hours. Some of its spurts last an incredible 30 minutes, so stick around and watch the show. If you're there when the geyser goes off, do a bit of citizen science and make

▲ GRIZZLY BEAR IN YELLOWSTONE NATIONAL PARK

a note of the date and time in the logbook found in the old interpretive stand near the trail. When you've been properly awed by Mother Nature, reverse course and return to the trailhead.

Much of this trail is mountain-bike friendly and is passable for hikers and visitors with the right mobility aid devices. If your mobility aid is robust and ready for off-road action, you should be able to complete all or most of this trail. Note that the last few yards of the trail are often muddy, so your view of Lone Star Geyser may vary depending on weather and mud. You can see the geyser from the point where the pavement ends.

DIRECTIONS

Lone Star Geyser is in the Upper Geyser Basin area of Yellowstone National Park. From Bozeman, Montana, take US 191 South for 82 mi (132 km) to the West Entrance Station. Head east for 13 mi (20.9 km) on the West Entrance Road, and then turn onto Grand Loop Road at Madison Junction. The trailhead is 18 mi (29 km) south of Madison Junction.

NEED TO KNOW

Info: Old Faithful Visitor Education Center, www.nps.gov/yell

Passes and Reservations: Entry into the park is $35/vehicle ($30/motorcycle, $20/pedestrian or cyclist). Passes are available in advance at www.recreation.gov. For more information, see page 502.

Weather Considerations: West Yellowstone is open year-round. Park roads are closed to private vehicles November-mid-April. In winter (mid-December-mid-March), West Yellowstone serves as the biggest hub to access Old Faithful on day trips via snowcoach or snowmobile tours. In early November and late March-mid-April, cyclists can ride the plowed roads while they are still closed to cars. In winter, snowshoes or Nordic skis are advised, depending on snow and trail conditions.

Facilities: There are vault toilets at Lone Star Geyser Trailhead.

Other: This trail also makes for a great bike ride.

BEST NEARBY

Old Faithful Geyser

Hands down the most famous geyser anywhere is Old Faithful, and no trip to Yellowstone is complete without attending at least one of the geyser's eruptions. Old Faithful has a well-earned name: On average it erupts once every 88 minutes, since 2013 (though eruption intervals can vary by 45-120 minutes, so plan to stick around for a bit). The area around Old Faithful, the Upper Geyser Basin, has 410 active geysers, the most in the park. There are many accessible boardwalks and viewing areas in this part of the park, so everyone can enjoy the geyser show regardless of their hiking abilities.

▲ LONE STAR GEYSER ERUPTING

67

SILVER CORD CASCADE

YELLOWSTONE NATIONAL PARK, WYOMING

This short, flat hike provides an easy way to get a look at Yellowstone's tallest waterfall and enjoy views of the Grand Canyon of the Yellowstone.

- **Distance:** 2 mi (3.2 km) round-trip
- **Duration:** 1 hour
- **Elevation Gain:** 223 ft (68 m)
- **Effort:** Easy
- **When:** Summer (June-Sept.) is peak season; fall (Oct.-Nov.) has fewer crowds
- **Trailhead:** Seven Mile Hole Trailhead/Glacial Boulder Trailhead

HIGHLIGHT: Enjoying a direct look at Silver Cord Cascade

Waterfall fans, take note: This short hike leads you to exceptional views of Silver Cord Cascade, a horsetail waterfall that falls 1,200 ft (366 m) from the canyon rim to the Yellowstone River below. It's the tallest waterfall in the park, and this easy, nearly flat trail leads you to a series of viewpoints where you'll have an unobstructed look at the cascade and at the immense Grand Canyon of the Yellowstone.

◄ GRAND CANYON OF THE YELLOWSTONE

▼ BANKS OF THE YELLOWSTONE RIVER BEYOND THE VIEW OF SILVER CORD CASCADE

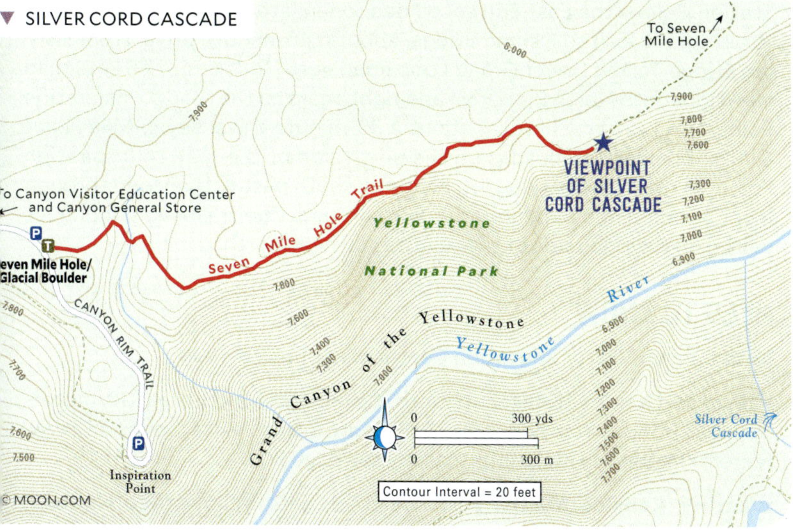

START THE HIKE

Start this hike at the **Seven Mile Hole Trail Trailhead,** sometimes called **Glacial Boulder Trailhead** (thanks to the giant boulder, deposited by a glacier, naturally, right by the trailhead), and hike east. The trail is relatively flat—there's little elevation gain or loss on this portion of the trail—and well maintained, but given the lack of guardrails or fencing on the canyon rim, watch your footing and stay aware of your surroundings as you admire and photograph the view.

After 0.3 mi (0.5 km) on the trail, the path draws close to the canyon rim, providing those jaw-dropping views of the canyon interior, the **Yellowstone River** far below, and the steep cliffs on the canyon's south side. At around 0.7 mi (1.1 km) you'll catch glimpses of Silver Cord Cascade as it tumbles over the lip of the canyon. Your view of the cascade grows better as you proceed farther down the trail, and once you're parallel with **Silver Cord** (around 1 mi/1.6 km), you'll have the best views. When you've had your fill of watching the wispy thread of Silver Cord Cascade spill over the canyon rim on the south side, simply return to the parking area.

You can extend this hike into an absolutely huge day hike that will challenge your endurance by hiking from the trailhead to **Seven Mile Hole** at the edge of the Yellowstone River. This turns an easy stroll into a strenuous 9.7-mi (15.6-km) hike with 2,043 ft (623 m) in elevation gain as you descend to the river and climb back to the rim on the return. The views never stop on this hike, so if you've got the time and the inclination, spend the day here and immerse yourself in this impressive landscape.

DIRECTIONS

Silver Cord Cascade is in the Canyon Area of Yellowstone National Park. From Cody, Wyoming, take US 14 West 52 mi (84 km) to the East Entrance

Station. Follow the East Entrance Road (open late May-early November) for 27 mi (43 km) to Fishing Bridge, about a 40-minute drive. From Fishing Bridge, follow Lower Grand Loop Road north for 14 mi (22.5 km), then turn right onto North Rim Drive and right again on the road to Inspiration Point, 17 mi (27 km) in total, about a 30-minute drive. Seven Mile Hole/ Glacial Boulder Trailhead is on the north side of the road to Inspiration Point. To reach the parking lot, continue south past it, then loop through Inspiration Point's parking lot to turn around. The trailhead parking lot will be on the right side of the road as you head north.

NEED TO KNOW

Info: Canyon Visitor Education Center, www.nps.gov/yell

Passes and Reservations: Entry into the park is $35/vehicle ($30/motorcycle, $20/pedestrian or cyclist). Passes are available in advance at www.recreation.gov. For more information, see page 502.

Weather Considerations: Entrance roads into Yellowstone National Park are generally open late May-early November, though unexpected weather can cause intermittent closures, especially during the extreme ends of the season. Most roads close to cars in winter (mid-December-early March) but remain open for commercially guided snowcoach and snowmobile tours. The road between the North and Northeast Entrances stays open for ordinary vehicles year-round.

This trail is open year-round (pending weather conditions), but in winter, you'll need snowshoes, Nordic skis, or crampons, depending on snow and ice on the trail. Even a dusting of snow can make footing on this trail questionable, so exercise additional caution near the canyon rim.

Facilities: There are no facilities at the trailhead.

BEST NEARBY

Canyon General Store

▶ *2 Canyon Village Loop Rd.; 307/242-7377; www.yellowstonevacations.com; 7:30am-8:30pm daily mid-May-early Oct.; $5-20*

In addition to the usual gift shop goods, the Canyon General Store has a large soda fountain-style diner that delivers a tasty meal and a pleasant dose of yesteryear kitsch: Red stools line several peninsula counters, plus the 1950s and early '60s music makes good on that retro promise. Breakfast runs until 10:30am, then it's lunch and dinner: Burgers, sandwiches, fries, and salads are complemented nicely by soda fountain ice cream treats (using Wilcoxson's ice cream from Montana). They also server Junior Ranger meals for the kids. The store, restaurant, and facilities are accessible.

▲ SILVER CORD CASCADE

68

SOUTH RIM TRAIL TO POINT SUBLIME

YELLOWSTONE NATIONAL PARK, WYOMING

Get ready for more than 300 stair steps, the closest view of the Lower Falls, and unique canyon views along this incredible hike.

- **Distance:** 6.6 mi (10.6 km) round-trip
- **Duration:** 3 hours
- **Elevation Gain:** 250-790 ft (76-241 m)
- **Effort:** Easy-strenuous
- **When:** Summer (June-Sept.) is peak season; fall (Oct.-Nov.) has fewer crowds
- **Trailheads:** Wapiti Picnic Area or Artist Point parking lot

HIGHLIGHT: Taking in views of colorful canyon walls and Lower Falls from Point Sublime

South Rim Trail offers multiple overlooks of the Grand Canyon of the Yellowstone, and as you head east to Point Sublime, you'll be dazzled by the scenery.

START THE HIKE

From the **Wapiti Picnic Area,** a 0.4-mi (0.6-km) walk through the forest heads northeast, following the Yellowstone River to the first viewpoint of **Upper Falls.** Here, a short spur trail descends to a **viewpoint,** offering

▲ HIKING WITH AN OFF-ROAD WHEELCHAIR ON POINT SUBLIME TRAIL

▼ SOUTH RIM TRAIL TO POINT SUBLIME

you a closer look with only a little more effort. Continue on to the junction with **Uncle Tom's Trail.** If it's open (it sometimes closes for repairs), follow this short (500 ft/152 m), strenuous trail down (and back up) 328 metal stairs to an **overlook** with wow-worthy views. If you prefer an easier walk, you can skip this spur trail.

Beyond the junction with Uncle Tom's Trail, the route continues through the forest, with several side trails to overlooks and openings in the forest providing viewpoints along the canyon rim, eventually coming to the **Artist Point Trailhead and parking area.** If you want to detour down the short spur to **Artist Point,** go for it. From here, the dirt trail continues east 1.5 mi (2.4 km) to **Point Sublime.** This area is a little dicey—the overlooks are totally exposed (no railings), so exercise caution as you move around and take photos here. The view is indeed sublime. The canyon walls and hoodoos are colorful—smeared with reds and pinks—above the frothy blue water at the **Lower Falls** plunge pool. When you've had your fill, simply turn around and head back.

▲ LOWER FALLS

DIRECTIONS

South Rim Trail is in the Canyon Area of Yellowstone National Park. From Cody, Wyoming, take US 14 West 52 mi (84 km) to the East Entrance Station. Follow the East Entrance Road (open late May-early November) for 27 mi (43 km) to Fishing Bridge, about a 40-minute drive. From Fishing Bridge, follow Lower Grand Loop Road north for 13 mi (20.9 km) and turn onto South Rim Drive. The south trailhead, Wapiti Picnic Area, is on the east side of the bridge over the Yellowstone River. The north trailhead, Artist Point parking lot, is 1.5 mi (2.4 km) farther down South Rim Drive, at the terminus of the road.

NEED TO KNOW

Info: Canyon Visitor Education Center, www.nps.gov/yell

Passes and Reservations: Entry into the park is $35/vehicle ($30/motorcycle, $20/pedestrian or cyclist). Passes are available in advance at www.recreation.gov. For more information, see page 502.

Weather Considerations: Entrance roads into Yellowstone National Park are generally open late May-early November, though unexpected weather can cause intermittent closures, especially during the extreme ends of the season. Most roads close to cars in winter (mid-December-early March) but remain open for commercially guided snowcoach and snowmobile tours. The road between the North and Northeast Entrances stays open for ordinary vehicles year-round.

This trail is open year-round (pending weather conditions), but in winter, you'll need snowshoes, Nordic skis, or crampons, depending on snow and ice on the trail. Even a dusting of snow can make footing on this trail questionable, so exercise additional caution near the canyon rim.

Facilities: Both trailheads have vault toilets.

BEST NEARBY

Wildlife Watching in Hayden Valley

Hayden Valley is an unusual spot. Full of wildlife—loads of bison, hordes of Canada geese, and more coyotes, moose, elk, grizzly bears, wolves, and other creatures than you'd believe—this verdant spot between Canyon Village and Fishing Bridge was once an arm of Yellowstone Lake. The Yellowstone River wanders through the 50 sq mi (130 sq km) sagebrush and grass valley, lending it a sleepy, bucolic feel. As you drive through, stop at the pullovers for wildlife and scenery admiration, but stick to marked trails; this environment is sensitive, so no off-trail travel or fishing is permitted. Be sure to bring your binoculars or spotting scope, and your camera.

▲ COLORFUL CANYON WALL SEEN FROM ARTIST POINT

69

HIDDEN FALLS AND INSPIRATION POINT

GRAND TETON NATIONAL PARK, WYOMING

The most popular hike in Grand Teton starts with a boat shuttle across Jenny Lake and takes in Hidden Falls before summiting Lower Inspiration Point, a rocky outcrop with impressive views of Jackson Hole.

- **Distance:** 2 mi (3.2 km) round-trip
- **Duration:** 2 hours, including boat rides
- **Elevation Gain:** 443 ft (135 m)
- **Effort:** Moderate
- **When:** May-Oct.
- **Trailhead:** Jenny Lake Visitor Center

HIGHLIGHT: Enjoying a stunning panorama of Jenny Lake and Jackson Hole from Lower Inspiration Point

Tucked into a narrow chute between Mount Teewinot and Mount St. John, Cascade Canyon is home to Hidden Falls, a 100-ft (30-m) cascading waterfall that, along with Lower Inspiration Point, make the perfect destination for a moderate hike. In addition to the waterfall views, you'll have a stunning panorama that includes the blue waters of Jenny Lake, the peaks to either side, and the Gros Ventre Mountains, across the lake behind Jackson Hole.

◀ INSPIRATION POINT WITH A VIEW OF JENNY LAKE

▼ TRAIL TO INSPIRATION POINT

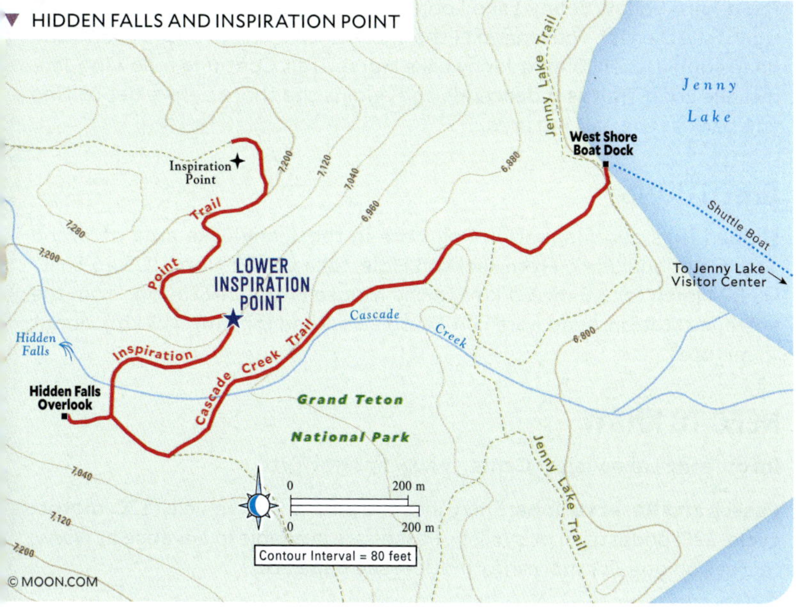

START THE HIKE

Start the hike by taking the boat shuttle near the **Jenny Lake Visitor Center,** crossing the lake to the **west shore boat dock;** head up the trail to the signed junction. Turn left and immediately begin an uphill climb. At junctions, follow the signs for Hidden Falls as the trail climbs along the north side of **Cascade Creek,** a photo-friendly, frothing stream. At a junction for Hidden Falls, turn left to ascend Cascade Creek to the bridge crossing to the south side of the creek. Continue to the junction with the **Hidden Falls Overlook** spur. Be careful as you jockey for position on getting a photo-friendly angle of **Hidden Falls;** summertime crowds can make capturing your perfect shot a little tricky, but be patient and enjoy the scenery while you wait.

To continue to Inspiration Point from the junction with the Hidden Falls spur, cross the two upper bridges over Cascade Creek, then climb a sweeping traverse cut into the rock along the flanks of **Lower Inspiration Point.** This is the steepest part of the trail, with most of the elevation gain taking place between Cascade Creek and **Inspiration Point** above, but the views start off great and get better with every few steps. The trail is exposed here, with a sheer drop to one side, so be cautious, and if you're not good with heights, be extra careful, take your time, and know your abilities (there's no shame in sitting it out). This part of the trail can get hot in midsummer, so if you're visiting then, hit the trail early and try to be here by mid-morning. Enjoy the view before retracing your steps back to the west boat-shuttle dock.

If you'd rather buy a one-way ticket for the boat shuttle, the hike back is 2.5 mi (4 km), starting from the junction of the Hidden Falls Overlook spur and Inspiration Point Trail where the trail crosses Cascade Creek.

From here, follow Jenny Lake Loop Trail back to the lakeshore and turn right (southeast); you'll parallel the shore until the trail ducks inland and heads uphill, soon joining Jenny Lake Horse Trail. Continue following Jenny Lake Loop Trail as it descends and rejoins the shore before depositing you back at the parking area.

DIRECTIONS

Hidden Falls and Inspiration Point are in the Jenny Lake area of Grand Teton National Park. From Jackson Hole, take US 191 North/US 26 East/ US 89 North for 3.8 mi (6.1 km) to the Moose Entrance Station. From the entrance station, head north on Teton Park Road for 7 mi (11.3 km), about 15 minutes.

NEED TO KNOW

Info: Jenny Lake Visitor Center, www.nps.gov/grte

Passes and Reservations: Entry into the park is $35/vehicle ($30/motorcycle, $20/pedestrian or cyclist). Passes are available in advance at www.recreation.gov. For more information, see page 502.

Weather Considerations: Grand Teton National Park experiences extreme winter weather, and November-April there are widespread closures in the park. Some roads, all campgrounds, and most visitor-facing facilities are closed or operate under reduced hours. During winter, a number of the roads—like Teton Park Roa and several lesser-traveled routes—are groomed for cross-country skiing and snowshoeing. For up-to-date information on conditions and seasonal operating hours, check the park's website.

Facilities: There are restrooms at the Jenny Lake Visitor Center.

Other: Jenny Lake Boating (307/734-9227; www.jennylakeboating.com; 7am-7pm daily early June-early Sept., 10am-4pm daily mid-May-early

BEST NEARBY

Jenny Lake

Tucked below the Grand Teton, Jenny Lake is a placid place of beauty backdropped by jagged peaks. The 2-mi-long (3.2-km), 250-ft-deep (76-m) lake was created behind a moraine in a glacial depression. Visitors can lodge or camp and spend days hiking, biking, boating, paddling, fishing, swimming, climbing, backpacking, and wildlife watching.

The 0.5-mi (0.8-km) paved, mobility-accessible Discovery Loop leads from the plaza to the lakeshore, providing visitors of all ability levels with a beautiful view of Jenny Lake snuggled in at the feet of the Tetons. The path leads to three boulder-rimmed overlooks with seating for soaking up the scenery. Stairways and a curved ramp lead to a shoreside beach for wading, swimming, and further reflection on this magnificent place.

June and mid-late Sept.; $12 adults one-way, $20 adults round-trip) runs the boat shuttle across Jenny Lake. Shuttles run every 10-15 minutes throughout the day, but be prepared to wait if you're here during high visitation periods. The last boat leaves the dock at the posted closing time. Reservations are not required.

▼ SUNSET OVER HIDDEN FALLS

70

PAINTBRUSH CANYON-CASCADE CANYON LOOP

GRAND TETON NATIONAL PARK, WYOMING

Hike through two canyons via a high-elevation pass over Paintbrush Divide and enjoy alpine lake views, waterfalls, and more along the way.

- **Distance:** 19.2 mi (30.9 km) round-trip
- **Duration:** 13 hours
- **Elevation Gain:** 4,124 ft (1,257 m)
- **Effort:** Very strenuous
- **When:** Late July-mid-Sept.
- **Trailhead:** String Lake Trailhead

HIGHLIGHT: Cresting Paintbrush Divide for unbelievable mountain views

The Paintbrush Canyon-Cascade Canyon Loop offers long-distance hikers and backpackers the chance to explore Grand Teton National Park on a multi-night hike filled with stargazing, alpine lakes, and the challenge of hiking a long loop at altitude. The wildlife watching and stargazing are incomparable on this loop, and the in-your-face views of Grand Teton will keep you talking about this hike for ages. If you're not up for the full 19.2-mi (30.9-km) loop, shorten it with a loop around Holly Lake (13 mi/20.9 km round-trip, 2,600 ft/792 m elevation gain).

▲ LAKE SOLITUDE HIGH IN THE TETONS

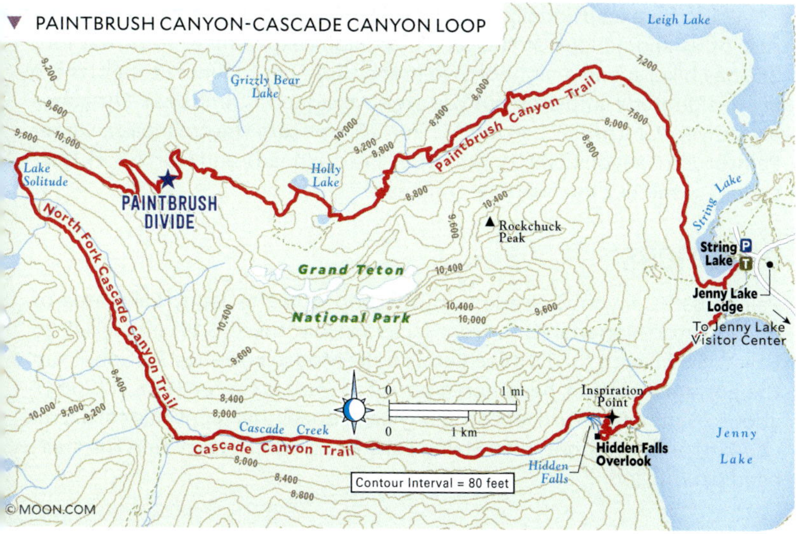

START THE HIKE

From the trailhead, skirt the east side of **String Lake.** Circle around the north side of **Rockchuck Peak** and begin the climb into **Paintbrush Canyon.** The trail leads through conifer forests, occasionally interrupted by giant talus fields and avalanche paths, before a series of switchbacks carry you through wildflower-filled meadows and impressive boulders. Keep an ear open for the "eep" of pikas, adorable little rodents that live around the boulders.

The next trail junction leads to **Holly Lake** (to the right) or straight for a direct route to Paintbrush Divide. Don't skip Holly Lake: The meadow and idyllic alpine lake in this small cirque is lovely, with wildflowers all over and the talus slopes letting you know you're in the mountains. From the lake, an unmarked path leads directly to the main trail to Paintbrush Divide.

Climb steadily upward out of the forest into the alpine landscape of scree slopes and snows that linger into summer. Pass the junction to **Grizzly Bear Lake** (keeping an eye out for those same bears), and follow the trail north across a switchback-filled slope that leads to the crest of **Paintbrush Divide.** Here you'll have unbelievable views in any direction.

For the full loop to Cascade Canyon, descend along 2.4 mi (3.9 km) of switchbacks to **Lake Solitude,** a turquoise beauty rimmed with wildflowers throughout August. To the south you'll have views of the Grand Teton, and the trail heads straight for this peak for 2.4 mi (3.9 km), leading through broad meadows before descending into the forest. Once in the forest you'll find the fork to Cascade Canyon, where you'll descend another 6.8 mi (10.9 km) and 1,950 ft (594 m) via **Cascade Canyon Trail.** You'll visit **Inspiration Point** and have the chance to take the short spur trail to **Hidden Falls** before you skirt the north side of **Jenny Lake** and return to the **String Lake parking area.**

While the exceptionally fit can tackle this trail in one brutal day, the rest of us should look at this as a multinight experience. To turn it into 2-3-day hike, spend a night or two in the three backcountry zones (there are designated campsites, but you aren't assigned a campsite). The zones are Lower Paintbrush Canyon (3.7 mi/5.9 km from the trailhead), Upper Paintbrush Canyon (7 mi/11.2 km from the trailhead), and North Fork Cascade (11.3 mi/18.2 km from the trailhead).

DIRECTIONS

Paintbrush Canyon-Cascade Canyon Loop is in the Jenny Lake area of Grand Teton National Park. From Jackson Hole, take US 191 North/US 26 East/US 89 North for 3.8 mi (6.1 km) to the Moose Entrance Station. From the entrance station, head north on Teton Park Road for 11 mi (17.7 km), about 20 minutes. Turn left on Jenny Lake Road, then continue for 1.5 mi (2.4 km) and turn right onto String Lake Road, where you'll find the trailhead parking lot.

NEED TO KNOW

Info: Jenny Lake Visitor Center, www.nps.gov/grte

Passes and Reservations: Entry into the park is $35/vehicle ($30/motorcycle, $20/pedestrian or cyclist). Passes are available in advance at www.recreation.gov. All backpackers are required to carry food in an approved **bear canister** (permit offices have loaners) and have a **wilderness camping permit.** For more information, see page 507.

BEST NEARBY

Jenny Lake Lodge

▶ *400 Jenny Lake Loop; 307/543-3100; www.gtlc.com; daily early June-early Oct.*

If you want to stay overnight, Jenny Lake Lodge offers a bit of log-cabin luxury that comes at an incredible price—in fact, it's the most expensive in Grand Teton National Park ($950-1,700). But it's so charming. The log cabins, built in the 1920s, have been revamped and updated with modern amenities (like Wi-Fi and refrigerators) while retaining their cabin charm, including rocking chairs on the front porch.

Most likely, you'll stop by for a meal, and the dining room here is worth experiencing. The restaurant offers brilliant looks at the peaks for astounding, and romantic, views. Serving breakfast, lunch, and dinner, the dining room uses foods from local suppliers and purveyors from across Wyoming, delivering a true taste of the place on each plate. Breakfast is a gourmet prix fixe menu but lunch features burgers, sandwiches, trout, salads, and more. Dinner is the most lavish meal, with a five-course prix fixe menu ($125) that rotates regularly. Reservations are recommended for breakfast and lunch, and are required for dinner. Also required for dinner: dressy attire. Bring your dresses, jackets, and slacks if you want to try that five-course feast.

Weather Considerations: Teton Park Road, along with several lesser roads, closes November-April but is groomed for cross-country skiing and snowshoeing. Most in-park facilities are closed November-April, too. Until late July, you may need an ice ax for crossing Paintbrush Divide.

Facilities: There are no amenities at the trailhead, but there is a restroom at the nearby Leigh Lake Trailhead. Backcountry campsites are primitive and have neither potable water nor restroom facilities. Campers are required to properly dispose of all trash and waste (including human waste) and to source and purify their own water.

Other: For hiking the full loop in one day, plan to depart at dawn for maximum daylight.

▼ ON THE TRAIL IN CASCADE CANYON

▲ WILDFLOWERS ON PAINTBRUSH DIVIDE

TOP EXPERIENCE

71

TAGGART AND BRADLEY LAKES

GRAND TETON NATIONAL PARK, WYOMING

This loop takes you to two lakes at the base of Avalanche and Garnet Canyons. At Bradley Lake, you can stare straight up at the Grand Teton.

- **Distance:** 3-6 mi (4.8-9.7 km) round-trip
- **Duration:** 2-4 hours
- **Elevation Gain:** 400-900 ft (122-274 m)
- **Effort:** Easy-moderate
- **When:** Year-round
- **Trailhead:** Taggart Lake Trailhead

HIGHLIGHT: Walking along the beaches of Bradley Lake's eastern shore

Taggart and Bradley Lakes huddle at the base of Avalanche and Garnet Canyons at around 7,000 ft (2,134 m) in elevation, and on this hike you'll have the option of visiting both lakes or cutting it short and taking in views of Taggart Lake, the larger of the pair. If you hike only to Taggart Lake, you're in for a 3-mi (4.8-km) hike, but I recommend the very scenic, longer hike to Bradley Lake (for the full 6-mi/9.7-km experience) where you can gaze up at Grand Teton in a

◀ BRADLEY LAKE

▼ TAGGART AND BRADLEY LAKES TRAIL

▼ TAGGART AND BRADLEY LAKES

jaw-dropping view. Anglers love both lakes (so get your permit and bring your fishing gear), and on hot days you'll find plenty of places to go for a swim in both lakes.

START THE HIKE

From the trailhead, the trail curves north and crosses a tumbling stream before ascending glacial moraines full of conifers and wildlife-filled meadows. At 1.1 mi (1.8 km) you'll reach a signed junction; if you are planning to hike both lakes, you will loop back to this junction. Start by heading to **Taggart,** turning left to hike 0.5 mi (0.8 km) to the lake. Explore the small peninsula and bridge to the south for a place to enjoy the water and views.

To continue the loop to Bradley Lake, circle north around the shore of Taggart Lake to climb a pair of switchbacks that crest a forested glacial moraine. After dropping to a signed junction, turn left to visit **Bradley Lake.** Beaches flank the east shore, while the north side contains a **footbridge** crossing the outlet. After the lake, retrace your steps back to the last junction and take the fork heading left to climb over the moraine again and complete the loop to the first junction to return to the trailhead.

Whether you pick the shorter, Taggart-only loop or the full Taggard-and-Bradley loop, pack a lunch and spend some time absorbing the sights and sounds of this breathtaking place before you return to the trailhead.

DIRECTIONS

Taggart and Bradley Lakes are in the Moose area of Grand Teton National Park. From Jackson Hole, take US 191 North/US 26 East/US 89 North for 3.8 mi (6.1 km) to the Moose Entrance Station. From the entrance station, head north along Teton Park Road for 2.5 mi (4 km) to Taggart Lake Trailhead.

NEED TO KNOW

Info: Craig Thomas Discovery & Visitor Center, www.nps.gov/grte

Passes and Reservations: Entry into the park is $35/vehicle ($30/motorcycle, $20/pedestrian or cyclist). Passes are available in advance at www.recreation.gov. For more information, see page 502.

Weather Considerations: Teton Park Road, along with several lesser roads, closes November-April but is groomed for cross-country skiing and snowshoeing. Most in-park facilities are closed November-April, too. In winter, the road makes a fine trail for snowshoeing or cross-country skiing. For up-to-date information on conditions and seasonal operating hours, check the park's website.

Facilities: There is a vault toilet at the trailhead.

BEST NEARBY

Mormon Row

▶ *Off Antelope Flats Road*

I'm sure you've seen the iconic photos of the Teton Range glowing pink in the sunset, an absolutely picture-perfect barn in the foreground. That's Mormon Row, and it's a treat for photographers, history buffs, and wildlife lovers. This tract was originally a ranch established by members of the Church of Jesus Christ of Latter-day Saints (LDS) back in the 1890s, growing to an impressive 27 homesteads. Today it's called "Mormon Row," and the remaining six clusters of buildings, the ruins of another, and the famous **Moulton Barn** are on the National Register of Historic Places. At the moment, the old hay fields are being converted to native plants, an act that's drawing wildlife—sage grouse, elk, pronghorn, bison, and other critters—back to the area. A self-guided tour brochure and a free audio tour (on the NPS app) offer deeper insights into this beautiful spot.

▲ HIKING THE TAGGART LAKE TRAIL

72

TETON CREST TRAIL

GRAND TETON NATIONAL PARK, WYOMING

This rugged, high-elevation trek, tripping through thin air along the mountain spines, is one of the best in the Rockies.

- **Distance:** 31.5-40 mi (50.7-64 km) one-way
- **Duration:** 3-5 days
- **Elevation Gain:** 6,253-9,140 ft (1,906-2,786 m)
- **Effort:** Very strenuous
- **When:** Late July-early Sept.
- **Trailhead:** Granite Canyon Trailhead

HIGHLIGHT: Watching wildlife and camping under the stars

For the most epic of backpacking trips in this park, look no further than the Teton Crest Trail. This high-elevation exploration is as demanding as it is beautiful. While you're on the trail, expect to see wildlife (from grizzly bears to elk to the tiny pika), be challenged by the elevation gains and descents, do some camping under the stars, and spend time high in the mountains. Teton Crest Trail crosses Fox Creek Pass, Death Canyon Shelf, Mount Meek Pass, Alaska Basin, Hurricane Pass, and Paintbrush Divide at 9,600-10,720 ft (2,926-3,267 m), with the central Tetons providing most of the scenery. We recommend taking on this trail headed north.

▲ A BACKPACKER ON TETON CREST TRAIL

▼ TETON CREST TRAIL

START THE HIKE

There are several ways to approach this hike, and most are point-to-point, so you'll need to arrange for a shuttle between trailheads, unless you want to add on more miles by hiking a shorter route back to your starting trailhead. The shortest route is 31.5 mi (50.7 km) between Granite Canyon and Jenny Lake. This hike begins in the park at the **Granite Canyon Trailhead,** following **Granite Canyon Trail** uphill for 7.3 mi (11.7 km) to join **South Fork Granite Canyon Trail, South Fork Cut Off,** and **Middle Fork Trail** to **Fox Creek Trail,** which leads, finally, to **Teton Crest South Trail.** Follow this for a day until you reach **Hurricane Pass Trail,** which connects to **Cascade Canyon Trail** and leads to the shores of **Jenny Lake.**

For the 40-mi (64-km) point-to-point trip (five days), follow the same route as above, and plan to camp at **Marian Lake** (use Upper Granite as an alternative), **Death Canyon Shelf, South Fork Cascade,** and **Upper Paintbrush,** before descending to the northern trailhead near **Jenny Lake Lodge.** You can save a few miles by taking the Aerial Tram (fee) at **Jackson Hole Mountain Resort,** bypassing Granite Canyon and joining the Teton Crest Trail 3.8 mi (6.1 km) from Rendezvous Mountain. Taking the tram reduces the mileage to 34 mi (55 km).

DIRECTIONS

Teton Crest Trail is in the Laurance S. Rockefeller Preserve area of Grand Teton National Park. From Jackson, take US 191 South/US 26 West/US 89 South for 1.5 mi (2.4 km). Turn right onto Highway 22 West and continue for 4 mi (6.4 km). Turn right onto Moose-Wilson Road for 7.7 mi (12.4 km) to the Granite Canyon Entrance Station. From the entrance station, Granite Canyon Trailhead is a 3-minute drive (1 mi/1.6 km) northeast along Moose-Wilson Road.

BEST NEARBY

Laurance S. Rockefeller Preserve Center

▶ *9am-5pm daily June-late Sept.*

Near the midpoint of Moose-Wilson Road, the Laurance S. Rockefeller Preserve Center anchors a 1,000-acre (405-ha) preserve that was once a Rockefeller family ranch. The Rockefellers were influential in the development of our national park system, using the family's political sway, considerable wealth, and landholdings to the benefit of all Americans and park visitors. The Rockefeller Preserve Center is loaded with exhibits that engage all your senses to tell the story of this place. Rangers lead daily hikes and talks, kids can check out a backpack filled with ways to engage with nature and enrich their on-trail experiences, and there's more to discover when you visit.

Plan to visit early in the morning or late in the afternoon as the small parking area here (space for about 50 cars, no RVs or trailers) gets crowded; during busy times you'll have a 30-90-minute wait for a parking space. If you stop by and the visitor center is closed, know the preserve is still open for hiking, cross-country skiing, and snowshoeing, unless signage says otherwise.

▲ WILDFLOWERS ALONG THE TETON CREST TRAIL

NEED TO KNOW

Info: Craig Thomas Discovery & Visitor Center, www.nps.gov/grte

Passes and Reservations: Entry into the park is $35/vehicle ($30/motorcycle, $20/pedestrian or cyclist). Passes are available in advance at www.recreation.gov. All backpackers are required to carry food in an approved **bear canister** (permit offices have loaners) and have a wilderness **camping permit.** For more information, see page 507.

Weather Considerations: June-September, you'll find the best conditions for hiking with warm days and cool nights (a little cooler at high elevations) and little precipitation. There is a chance for thunderstorms in the afternoons during July and August, and as you push into September and later in the season, you could experience a snowstorm. Bring rain gear for summer and fall hikes, and due to the cool nights and cooler temperatures at elevation, bring insulating layers, a warm sleeping bag, and a tent suited for cold nights. As you hike along the Teton Crest you'll have a lot of sun exposure, so a wide-brimmed hat, long sleeves, and sunscreen are advised.

Facilities: You'll find pit toilets at the trailhead but no water, so bring your own for drinking and sanitation purposes. Along the trail, there are no water stations, so the streams and lakes are your water source. There are also no toilets at the backcountry campsites along the trail; bring a trowel and toilet paper, which you must pack out.

Other: Portions of Moose-Wilson Road are closed for construction in 2022-2025, but the preserve can still be reached via the open half. In 2024-2025, the northern half is closed while the southern Granite Canyon Entrance will be open as far as the preserve. Check online or at visitor centers for details.

TOP EXPERIENCE

73

TRAIL OF THE CEDARS AND AVALANCHE LAKE

GLACIER NATIONAL PARK, MONTANA

Walk through the easternmost Pacific rain forest in the United States and then venture to a scenic subalpine lake.

- **Distance:** 0.9-mi (1.5-km) loop-5.9 mi (9.5 km) round-trip
- **Duration:** 0.5-3 hours
- **Elevation Gain:** 0-730 ft (0-223 m)
- **Effort:** Easy-moderate
- **When:** June-mid-Oct.
- **Trailhead:** Trail of the Cedars

HIGHLIGHT: Casting a line into the crystalline waters of Avalanche Lake

This two-part hike offers an accessible experience along Trail of the Cedars' 0.9-mi (1.5-km) loop with the option to follow the remainder of the trail along Avalanche Creek to Avalanche Lake. It's the second-busiest trail in the park, with some 1,500

AVALANCHE LAKE

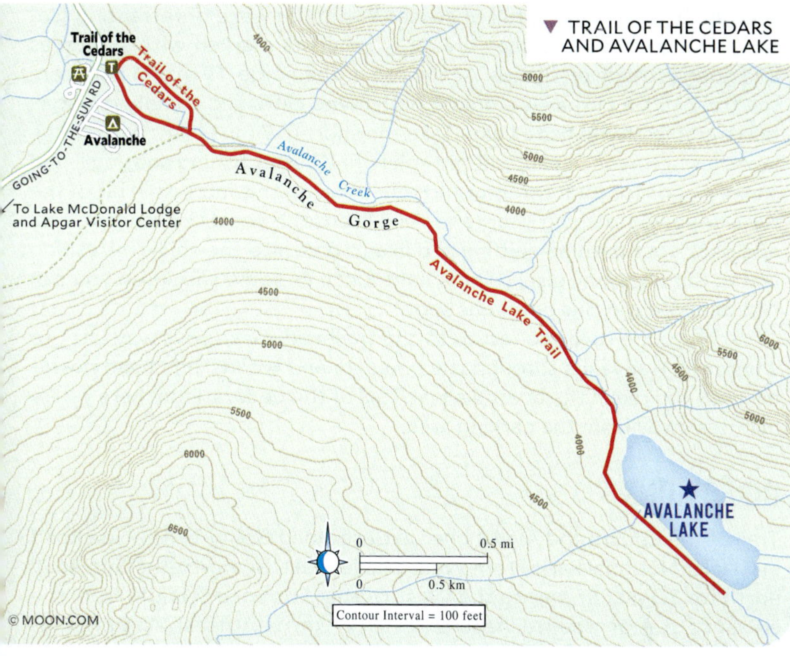

people on the trail each day in summer. The parking area can grow quite crowded quite early, so come very early or be prepared to wait a bit for a parking spot to open.

START THE HIKE

Lined with interpretive signs, the **Trail of the Cedars boardwalk** leads walkers and wheelchair users on a loop that twice crosses **Avalanche Creek.** The path winds through a lush rain forest where fallen trees become nurse logs—fertile habitats for the growth of fungi, mosses, hemlocks, and tiny foamflowers. Huge black cottonwoods and their deeply furrowed bark, as well as enormous western red cedars—some 500 years old—dominate the forest. At Avalanche Gorge, the creek took eons to slice through the red rocks. To finish the boardwalk loop, continue along the hard-surface walkway back to the trailhead.

At the midway point around Trail of the Cedars you'll find the trail to Avalanche Lake. Follow the trail uphill to the top of **Avalanche Gorge,** which was etched into the rock over millions of years. Exercise caution: It's beautiful, but there have been far too many fatal accidents here when a hiker slipped, so stay aware of your footing. From the gorge the trail climbs

▲ TRAIL OF THE CEDARS

steadily through woods full of stones left in the wake of retreating glaciers. Some of these stones are large boulders marked with scratches and gouges made by the ice. At the top of the gorge, 1.9 mi (3.1 km) from the trailhead, a cirque—complete with steep cliffs and tumbling waterfalls—cradles **Avalanche Lake.** Take the short (0.7 mi/1.1 km) path to the lake's less-crowded head, where anglers find better fishing and you'll find a lovely spot for photography and reflection on this incredible bit of nature. Bring your fishing gear (and valid license) if you'd like to wet a line, and pack your bathing suit if you'd like to dive into the chilly, refreshing water. But above all else, bring a light lunch or some snacks so you can rest and refuel in this gorgeous spot.

When you're ready to return to the trailhead, make your way back to where the trail leads through the boulders and woods, and head downhill until you reach the boardwalk at Trail of the Cedars. From here you're minutes away from the parking area.

DIRECTIONS

Trail of the Cedars and Avalanche Lake are along Going-to-the-Sun Road in Glacier National Park. From West Glacier, take Going-to-the-Sun Road north for 2.3 mi (3.7 km) to the West Glacier Entrance Station. From the entrance station, the trailhead is 17 mi (27 km) northeast along Going-to-the-Sun Road, about a 40-minute drive. Parking spots at the trailhead typically fill up by 7am in peak season.

The west-side shuttle (7am-7pm daily July-Labor Day, 9am-5pm daily early- to mid-Sept.) also goes to Avalanche. West-side shuttles stop at the Apgar Visitor Center, Sprague Creek Campground, Lake McDonald Lodge, Avalanche Creek, The Loop, and Logan Pass.

BEST NEARBY

Lake McDonald Lodge

▶ *288 Lake McDonald Lodge Loop; reservations 855/733-4522, front desk 303/265-7010; www.glaciernationalparklodges.com; mid-May-late Sept.*

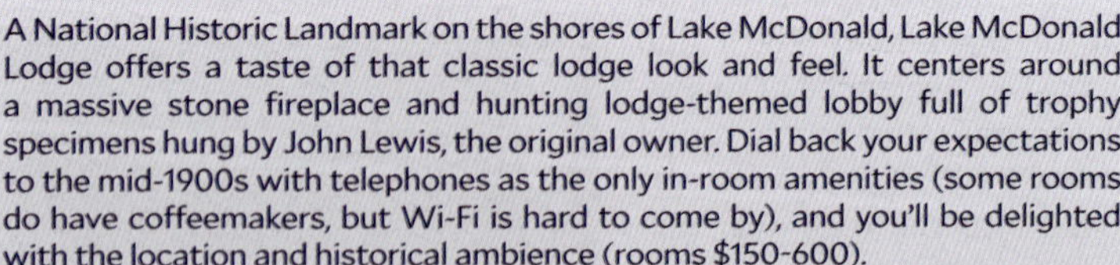

A National Historic Landmark on the shores of Lake McDonald, Lake McDonald Lodge offers a taste of that classic lodge look and feel. It centers around a massive stone fireplace and hunting lodge-themed lobby full of trophy specimens hung by John Lewis, the original owner. Dial back your expectations to the mid-1900s with telephones as the only in-room amenities (some rooms do have coffeemakers, but Wi-Fi is hard to come by), and you'll be delighted with the location and historical ambience (rooms $150-600).

The headliner restaurant is Russell's Fireside Dining Room, decorated with painted Native American chandeliers and full of historical ambience. Breakfast (6:30am-10am daily; $14-21 buffet, $5-13 à la carte), lunch (11:30am-2:30pm daily; $10-18), and dinner (5pm-9:30pm daily; $17-50) are served. Additionally, Lucke's Lounge and Jammer Joe's Grill and Pizzeria offer more casual spots to hang out for a drink or chow down on some pizza.

NEED TO KNOW

Info: Apgar Visitor Center, www.nps.gov/glac

Passes and Reservations: Entry into the park is $35/vehicle ($30/motorcycle, $20/pedestrian or cyclist). Passes are available in advance at www.recreation.gov. In addition to park entry fees, you'll need a vehicle ticket reservation for Going-to-the-Sun Road 6am-3pm daily late May-early September. For more information, see page 503.

Weather Considerations: Going-to-the-Sun Road is generally open mid-June-mid-October.

Facilities: There are vault toilets at the adjacent Avalanche Picnic Area. There is a pit toilet located on the northwestern end of Avalanche Lake, on the approach trail about 500 ft (152 m) from the lake.

▼ AVALANCHE GORGE

74

HIGHLINE TRAIL AND GRANITE PARK CHALET

GLACIER NATIONAL PARK, MONTANA

Tiptoe along the Continental Divide on a vertigo-inducing path where the views will stun you into silence. Hikers often spot mountain goats and bighorn sheep on this trail.

- **Distance:** 7.4-11.4 mi (11.9-18.3 km) one-way
- **Duration:** 3.5-6 hours
- **Elevation Gain:** 1,400-2,500 ft (427-762 m)
- **Effort:** Strenuous
- **When:** Mid-July-mid-Oct.
- **Trailhead:** Across Going-to-the-Sun Road from the Logan Pass parking lot and shuttle stop

HIGHLIGHT: Taking in spectacular mountain views—and the occasional wildlife

You'll be tempted to stop every dozen paces to take a photo or two, and I can't blame you, but I can offer some advice: Bring a camera and your phone. Set your phone to shoot video or time lapse and use your camera for still images; that way you can focus on the trail, which will give some hikers a case of the willies as there are several exposed sections with thousand-foot drop-offs.

◄ GRANITE PARK CHALET

▼ HIKER ON THE HIGHLINE TRAIL

START THE HIKE

Start the trail at **Logan Pass** with a walk along the cliff above Going-to-the-Sun Road before crossing a flower-filled section that gives the Garden Wall arête its name. At 3 mi (4.8 km) in you'll encounter one of the few noticeable inclines on this relatively flat hike as you ascend to **Haystack Saddle.** This might look like the end of the steep stuff, but there's a little more. Once you hit the Haystack high point, descend into several large bowls before you pass into Bear Valley to reach **Granite Park Chalet** perched atop a knoll at 6,680 ft (2,036 m). This will wrap up the steep inclines until you make the return trip. This section of trail between Logan Pass and Granite Park Chalet is typically closed until early July, if not later, due to avalanche risk and deep snow. Once it dries out, expect some dusty hiking here as the traffic—as many as 900 hikers a day—keeps things stirred up.

Some hikers stop here at the 7.4-mi (11.9-km) mark and stay overnight at the Granite Park Chalet, or turn back for a 14.8-mi (23.8-km) trek.

Others push on to The Loop, descending another 4 mi (6.4 km) along Granite Park Trail to a parking area where the shuttle can carry you back to the trailhead. You can also reverse course here for a huge 22.8-mi (36.7-km) day on the trail.

DIRECTIONS

Highline Trail and Granite Park Chalet are in the Logan Pass area of Glacier National Park. From St. Mary, take Going-to-the-Sun Road northwest for 0.7 mi (1.1 km) to the St. Mary Entrance Station. From the entrance station, the trailhead is 18 mi (29 km) along Going-to-the-Sun Road, about a 30-minute drive. During high season (mid-June-Aug.), the Logan Pass parking lot fills around 6am.

NEED TO KNOW

Info: Logan Pass Visitor Center, www.nps.gov/glac

Passes and Reservations: Entry into the park is $35/vehicle ($30/motorcycle, $20/pedestrian or cyclist). Passes are available in advance at www.recreation.gov. In addition to park entry fees, you'll need a vehicle ticket reservation for Going-to-the-Sun Road 6am-3pm daily late May-early September if you are approaching from the west. Vehicle reservations are not needed if you are approaching from the eastern St. Mary Entrance. You can overnight at the rustic **Granite Park Chalet** (Belton Chalets; 888/345-2649; www.graniteparkchalet.com; July-early Sept.; $140 first guest, $95 pp after, bedding service $40 pp); reservations are required and online bookings for the upcoming summer go fast, starting in early January. For more information, see page 507.

Weather Considerations: Do not underestimate this trail: Hikers have high incidents of dehydration and hypothermia here due to exposure to the sun, wind, rain, and snow. Carry 2 quarts or liters of water and extra layers for surprise changes in weather.

BEST NEARBY

Logan Pass

▶ *32 mi (52 km) from the West Entrance*

Logan Pass sits atop the **Continental Divide** at 6,646 ft (2,026 m) and rules an alpine wonderland of wildflower meadows and snowfields. Weather can be chilly and windy even in midsummer.

Take a selfie at the Continental Divide sign. Explore the visitor center and scan surrounding slopes for mountain goats, bighorn sheep, and bears. In late July the pink alpine laurel, paintbrush, and monkeyflower reach their prime. Meadows at this elevation are fragile, with short-lived flora, so stick to the paths.

In addition to the Highline Trail, another must-do hike departs from Logan Pass: Hidden Lake Overlook (2.6 mi/4.2 km round-trip to overlook, 5 mi/8 km round-trip to lake; 2-4 hours; moderate) is the most popular hike in the park.

Facilities: There are restrooms at Logan Pass and vault toilets at Granite Park Chalet and The Loop. Granite Park Chalet does not have running water, but it does have bottled water and snacks for purchase. Day hikers may also use the outdoor picnic tables at the chalet.

▼ BEARGRASS ALONG HIGHLINE TRAIL

75

GRINNELL GLACIER TRAIL

GLACIER NATIONAL PARK, MONTANA

This stunning trail leads hikers through picturesque alpine scenery and pristine lakes to reach breathtaking views of Grinnell Glacier.

- **Distance:** 11 mi (17.7 km) round-trip
- **Duration:** 6 hours
- **Elevation Gain:** 1,619 ft (493 m)
- **Effort:** Moderate-strenuous
- **When:** July-mid-Oct.
- **Trailhead:** Grinnell Glacier Trailhead or Many Glacier Hotel

HIGHLIGHT: Seeing Grinnell Glacier, the lake, and the ring of peaks above

Catch a glimpse of the closest trail-accessible glacier in the park for a hike you'll wish you could do twice a week. The trek to Grinnell Glacier requires stamina for two reasons: It's 11 mi (17.7 km) round-trip, and most of the 1,600-ft (488-m) elevation gain is jam-packed into a 2-mi (3.2-km) segment of the trail.

START THE HIKE

To hike from the picnic area at the **Grinnell Glacier Trailhead,** follow **Swiftcurrent Lake's** shore to the west boat dock. If you're starting from

▲ GRINNELL GLACIER

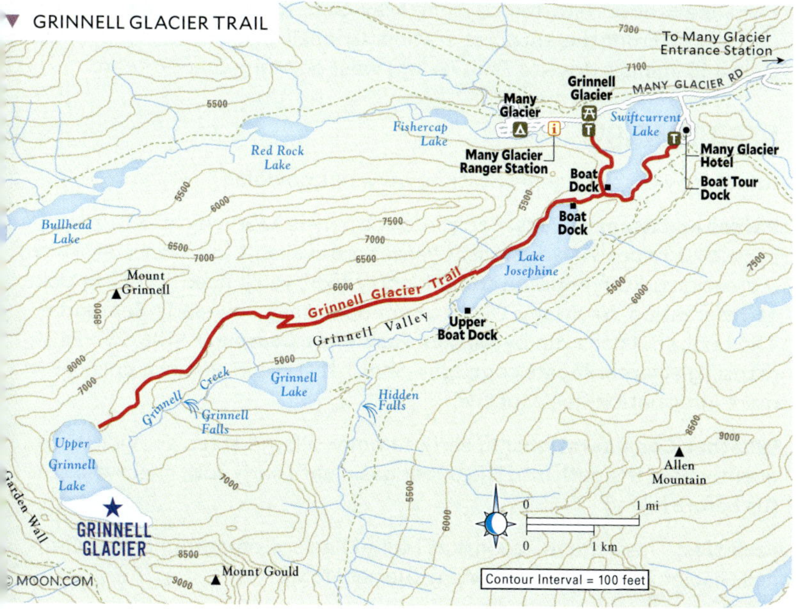

Many Glacier Hotel, just follow the trail along the southern shore to the same dock on the west side of the lake.

Crest the short hill and hike along **Lake Josephine's** north shore. As you near the lake's west end, **Grinnell Glacier Trail** breaks off and heads uphill. As you climb through the rocks—their multicolored strata are quite the sight—you'll see the milky turquoise waters of glacier-fed Grinnell Lake flowing past. High above you can spot what remains of two other glaciers—Gem and Salamander Glaciers—though both have shrunken back to large snowfields. Here, the trail ascends along a cliff stairway and an icy waterfall gives you a bit of a baptism as you hike along. Continue on the path and you'll skirt cliffs and steep ravines, eventually reaching a rest stop where a few outhouses enjoy remarkable views. With one final, steep climb up the moraine you'll find the view you've been waiting for: the glacier, the lake, and the ring of peaks above. Soak it in for a moment before making your way through the labyrinth of paths leading to **Upper Grinnell Lake's** shore. As tempted as you may be to walk out onto the glacier, do not. Hidden beneath the ice and snow are crevasses, deep and often deadly cracks in the glacier that you won't know are there until it's too late, so enjoy the view from afar.

Many hikers make reservations for the boat shuttle and take it both ways, cutting 5 mi (8 km) off the length for a hike of 6 mi (9.7 km) round-trip.

DIRECTIONS

Grinnell Glacier Trail is in the Many Glacier area of Glacier National Park. From St. Mary, take US 89 North for 8.6 mi (13.8 km), then turn left on Many Glacier Road. Continue for 16.2 mi (26 km) to the Many Glacier

Entrance Station (staffed daytime May-Oct., when unstaffed use self-pay kiosk). From the entrance station, Grinnell Glacier Trailhead is less than a 10-minute drive (4.7 mi/7.6 km) west on Many Glacier Road.

NEED TO KNOW

Info: Many Glacier Ranger Station, www.nps.gov/glac

Passes and Reservations: Entry into the park is $35/vehicle ($30/motorcycle, $20/pedestrian or cyclist). Passes are available in advance at www.recreation.gov. In addition to park entry fees, you'll need a vehicle ticket reservation for Many Glacier 6am-3pm daily July-early September. The boat shuttle is run by **Glacier Park Boat Company** (406/257-2426; https://glacierparkboats.com; June-Sept.); reserve in advance online. For more information, see page 517.

Weather Considerations: In early summer, a large steep snowdrift frequently bars the path into the upper basin until early July; check the status before hiking.

Facilities: There are restrooms at Many Glacier Campground near Grinnell Glacier Trailhead and at Many Glacier Hotel.

BEST NEARBY

Many Glacier Hotel

▶ *Milepost 11.5, Many Glacier Road; reservations 855/733-4522, front desk 406/732-4411; www.glaciernationalparklodges.com; early June-mid-Sept.; $250-650*

A National Historic Landmark, Many Glacier Hotel is the largest of the park's lodges and the most popular due to its stunning location. Set on Swiftcurrent Lake, the immense hotel cowers below surrounding peaks, looking very much like it belongs in the Swiss Alps. The lodge centers around its massive four-story lobby and colossal fireplace. A Swiss theme pervades the hotel, with bellhops dressed in lederhosen and elaborate woodwork called gingerbread adorning deck railings (rooms $260-660).

The hotel's restaurant, the **Ptarmigan Dining Room,** has massive windows that look out on Swiftcurrent Lake, Grinnell Point, and Mount Wilbur. The restaurant serves breakfast (6:30am-10am daily; $13-20 buffet, $3-13 à la carte), lunch (11:30am-2:30pm daily; $8-22), and dinner (5pm-9pm daily; $26-45), or grab small plates, sandwiches, salads, and pasta in the adjacent **Swiss Lounge** (noon-3pm and 5pm-8pm daily; $13-22). If you just need a coffee and pastry, Heidi's Snack Shop & Espresso Stand (6:30am-9pm daily) has you covered.

▲ GRINNELL LAKE

76

SWIFTCURRENT PASS AND LOOKOUT TRAIL

GLACIER NATIONAL PARK, MONTANA

This hike atop the Continental Divide climbs through lush valleys and past alpine lakes, and offers sweeping views of surrounding peaks.

- **Distance:** 3.6-16.2 mi (5.8-26 km) round-trip
- **Duration:** 2-8 hours
- **Elevation Gain:** 100-3,496 ft (30-1,066 m)
- **Effort:** Easy-strenuous
- **When:** June-mid-Oct.
- **Trailhead:** Swiftcurrent parking lot

HIGHLIGHT: Soaking up the views of glaciers, peaks, and distant plains from Swiftcurrent Lookout

This is one of those "it's got everything" trails: a scenic path dotted with lakes and waterfalls, full of wildlife from moose to bears to birds, trailside wildflowers, and even glaciers. Expect to share the trail with a crowd along the valley floor, but the farther you go, the more the crowd thins, meaning there's even more Mother Nature for you to enjoy.

◄ VIEW FROM SWIFTCURRENT PASS

▼ FISHERCAP LAKE

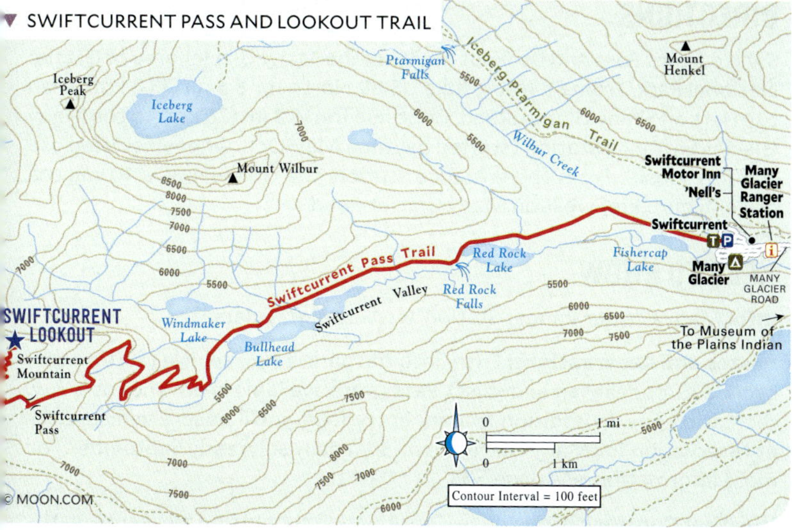

START THE HIKE

As the trail begins, it winds through pines and aspen groves, and a spur to **Fishercap Lake** offers the opportunity to look for moose as they browse for lunch along the lake's edge. The trail makes a gentle ascent to **Redrock Lake and Falls** (1.8 mi/2.9 km up the trail) and skirts the shoreline for some views you'll doubtless immortalize as a phone or desktop background (I know I'm guilty of this). If you're satisfied with the views, you can turn around here and return the way you came for an easy 3.6-mi (5.8-km) round-trip hike. If you're up for more hiking—and more incredible vistas—continue along the trail and you'll reach meadows full of wildflowers, notably Sitka valerian in July, before reaching **Bullhead Lake** at 3.9 mi (6.3 km) into the hike. If you have a keen eye or some good binoculars you might spot bighorn sheep as they patrol the scree slopes nearby.

Here the trail departs the valley floor and the view opens up. Follow the switchbacks uphill and take in the view of the waterfall in front of you, but also take time to admire the view behind you—it's incredible. As you climb, you'll reach **Swiftcurrent Pass** at 6.6 mi (10.6 km). Keep on hiking until you reach the sign-marked junction where you'll proceed north for 1.4 mi (2.3 km) of switchbacks (ugh, more switchbacks; don't even try to count them, just endure them) leading to **Swiftcurrent Lookout.** The view here is somehow better than spectacular. The valley opens before you and you can see it all: glaciers, peaks, wild landscapes and panoramas, and in the distance, the plains. Far below you'll spot the monumental Many Glacier Hotel, but from here it looks like a model. Take a while to soak up the view, get some food and water, and visit the outhouse, which might just have the best view of any toilet anywhere on earth. Return by following the trail back down to the trailhead.

Or, if you want a different challenge, at Swiftcurrent Pass, drop downhill 0.9 mi (1.5 km) to Granite Park Chalet and connect with Granite Park Trail (The Loop) or Highline Trail to catch the west-side shuttle at The Loop on Going-to-the-Sun Road.

DIRECTIONS

Swiftcurrent Pass and Lookout Trail is in the Many Glacier area of Glacier National Park. From St. Mary, take US 89 North for 8.6 mi (13.8 km), then turn left on Many Glacier Road. Continue for 16.2 mi (26 km) to the Many Glacier Entrance Station (staffed daytime May-Oct., when unstaffed use self-pay kiosk). From the entrance station, the trailhead is a 10-minute drive (5 mi/8 km) west on Many Glacier Road.

NEED TO KNOW

Info: Many Glacier Ranger Station, www.nps.gov/glac

Passes and Reservations: Entry into the park is $35/vehicle ($30/motorcycle, $20/pedestrian or cyclist). Passes are available in advance at www.recreation.gov. In addition to park entry fees, you'll need a vehicle ticket reservation for Many Glacier 6am-3pm daily July-early September. For more information, see page 503.

Weather Considerations: June-October, you should find pleasant weather in the park and along this hike's high-altitude path. Temperatures will be warm during the day and cooler at night, with the coldest temperatures coming later in the season and at the highest elevations. Much of the trail is exposed to the sun, so you'll want to add sun protection—sunscreen, a wide-brimmed hat, a UV-blocking shirt—to your kit along with warm layers to combat early morning or evening chill. There is a chance of afternoon thunderstorms and lightning, so time your hike according to the local weather forecasts and avoid stormy days. It's possible you'll encounter some residual snow in June, but only at the highest elevations and then only in pockets, but you could run into snowy or icy conditions the later you hike into October.

Facilities: There are restrooms at Many Glacier Campground and Swiftcurrent Motor Inn.

BEST NEARBY

Museum of the Plains Indian

▶ *19 Museum Loop, Browning; 406/338-2230; www.doi.gov; 9am-4:45pm Tues.-Sat. June-Sept., 10am-4pm Tues.-Fri. Oct.-May; $6 adults, $5 ages 65 and up, $2 ages 6-16, free ages 5 and under and Blackfeet Tribal Members with tribal ID card*

Founded in 1941, the Museum of the Plains Indian has an impressive display of decorative and functional arts from Northern Plains Tribal groups including the Blackfeet, Crow, Sioux, Assiniboine, Arapahoe, Nez Perce, Flathead, Cree, Chippewa, and Northern Cheyenne. Exhibits include historic clothing, weapons, and tack (saddles, blankets, and horse-related gear) as well as an assortment of household implements and tools, toys, and baby carriers. Exhibitions include single-artist displays; themed showcases focused on Plains Indian horse culture and community scenes; and bold modern art exhibitions by Plains Indian artists.

▲ REDROCK FALLS

77

BIG PLATEAU AND EKBLOM TRAIL LOOP

THEODORE ROOSEVELT NATIONAL PARK, NORTH DAKOTA

Hike in one of Teddy Roosevelt's favorite parts of the United States and spot wildlife—mule deer, bison, feral horses, prairie dogs, and more—as you explore this remarkable landscape.

- **Distance:** 5.3 mi (8.5 km) round-trip
- **Duration:** 2-2.5 hours
- **Elevation Gain:** 534 ft (163 m)
- **Effort:** Moderate
- **When:** Apr.-Oct.
- **Trailhead:** Peaceful Valley Ranch

HIGHLIGHT: Seeing bison, wild horses, elk, and other wildlife roaming the park's grasslands

Here in Theodore Roosevelt National Park, you can hike to cool rock formations, explore a patch of petrified forest, even pay a visit to a prairie dog metropolis, but on the Big Plateau and Ekblom Trail Loop you're in for one of Teddy's favorite sights: wildlife. As you hike across Big Plateau and along Ekblom Trail, you'll see plenty of wildlife signs, from tracks to scat (that's a polite but outdoorsy word for poop), and you'll hear everything from birdcall to the bark of prairie dogs, but the real treat comes when you spot mule deer, feral horses, bison (people think they're buffalo, but they're bison), prairie dogs,

▲ LITTLE MISSOURI RIVER

coyotes, maybe even a badger or pronghorn near the trail and golden eagles circling above.

START THE HIKE

This lollipop hike works from either direction, but I recommend hiking counterclockwise as it puts the only strenuous uphill climb—the ascension to the top of Big Plateau—early in the hike when you're full of energy. From the **parking area,** join **Ekblom Trail/Lone Tree Loop/Big Plateau Loop** and follow it through a small patch of forest to the **Little Missouri River,** which you'll have to cross. There's no bridge, but often a series of stepping-stones stand in the river; if it's there, cross with care, but if it's not, time to slip off your boots and wade across. You'll be doing the same on the return trip, but by then the cool water will be a refreshing treat for your tired feet. Once you cross, proceed until you reach the junction with **Big Plateau Trail.** Turn right and start climbing. The trail begins on a moderate slope but soon grows steep; keep climbing and soon you'll be at the top of the plateau. Up here, keep an eye out for feral horses, coyotes, and deer.

As you cross the plateau the trail is relatively flat, until you reach the end. Near the junction with Maah Daah Hey Trail you'll climb again, with a few steep uphills before you reach one short, steep downhill and turn left along Maah Daah Hey, where you'll begin a moderate downhill section. At the point where the trail meets up with Lone Tree Trail, you'll cross **Knutson Creek** for the first time. In 0.4 mi (0.6 km), bear left onto Ekblom Trail and soon you'll cross Knutson Creek again. Watch and listen for prairie dogs here, and keep an eye open for bison, deer, and feral horses—they all love this area. Follow Ekblom back to the junction with Big Plateau and the Little Missouri River crossing, and in a few moments you'll be back at the trailhead.

You can extend this hike by following Big Plateau to Maah Daah Hey Trail, turning right (north), and continuing along South Petrified Forest Trail for 1.2 mi (1.9 km), then joining Lone Tree Trail for 3.8 mi (6.1 km) to the junction with Maah Daah Hey Trail, where you'll continue back to the parking area by following the trail as noted above. This makes the hike 9.1 mi (14.6 km), pushing it into the strenuous category (for the length) and taking closer to four hours to complete.

DIRECTIONS

Big Plateau and Ekblom Trail is in the South Unit of Theodore Roosevelt National Park. From Dickinson, take I-94 West 34 mi (55 km) to the South Unit entrance in Medora. Head north along East River Road for 7 mi (11.3 km) to the trailhead at Peaceful Valley Ranch.

NEED TO KNOW

Info: South Unit Visitor Center, www.nps.gov/thro

Passes and Reservations: Entry into the park is $30/vehicle ($25/motorcycle, $15/pedestrian or cyclist). Passes are available in advance at www.recreation.gov. For more information, see page 502.

BEST NEARBY

South Unit Scenic Drive

For the best way to see the dramatic badlands, tour the paved South Unit Scenic Drive. Watch for pronghorn, wild horses, and bison on the narrow road with steep, sharp curves, and stop at the several prairie dog towns that can be noisy with the animals' alarm call barks. Due to a landslide in 2019, the route is an out-and-back tour (44 mi/71 km round-trip, 2 hours) rather than a loop. But repairs are underway, with plans to reopen the full loop in summer 2025.

The route passes multiple interpretive stops. Views from the **Skyline Vista,** an accessible walkway, take in the Little Missouri River. The renovated **Peaceful Valley Ranch** is the only original remaining ranch house in the South Unit. At **Boicourt Overlook,** another accessible walkway, peer down on rugged eroded waterways that feed the Little Missouri. A spur road goes to the steep trail that leads you up **Buck Hill** (0.2 mi/0.3 km round-trip, 15 minutes, moderate) to stand at the top of the South Unit.

Weather Considerations: Summer (May-September) is high season here, with warm, pleasant weather and a relative abundance of visitors, but sudden thunderstorms will pop up several times a season, so be prepared with your foul-weather gear. In winter you'll find this place windwhipped and bitingly cold, so wear your warm layers; snowstorms and blizzards will occasionally close park roads.

Facilities: The trailhead for Big Plateau and Ekblom Trail Loop is at Peaceful Valley Ranch. There's little here beyond the trailhead and a pit toilet. There's no potable water or accessible facilities. For full facilities, trail maps, and park rangers, visit the South Unit Visitor Center in Medora, 20 minutes (7 mi/11.3 km) south.

Other: This park is divided into the North and South Unit, and each is (somehow) in a different time zone: The South Unit (where this hike is) observes Mountain Time and the North Unit is on Central Time; don't forget to factor this in if you're driving from one to the other.

▼ BIG PLATEAU

TOP EXPERIENCE

78

THE NOTCH

BADLANDS NATIONAL PARK, SOUTH DAKOTA

This hike leads through a landscape of canyons, stony domes, and rocky spires to a viewpoint as expansive as the sky itself.

- **Distance:** 1.5 mi (2.4 km) round-trip
- **Duration:** 2 hours
- **Elevation Gain:** 128 ft (39 m)
- **Effort:** Moderate-strenuous
- **When:** Apr.-June
- **Trailhead:** South end of the Door and Window parking lot

HIGHLIGHT: Climbing the ladder to the canyon rim

The mixed landscape of Badlands National Park provides a fascinating place to explore even if the name is a little less than inviting. That name comes from the Lakota, who called this region mako sica, literally translated to "bad lands," something French fur trappers—the first Europeans to visit the area—agreed with. The prairies, canyons, and buttes can make for rough travel, and the clay-rich soil here is both sticky and slick in the rain. On this hike to The Notch, you'll get

◀ STARGAZING AT BADLANDS NATIONAL PARK

▼ VIEW FROM NOTCH TRAIL

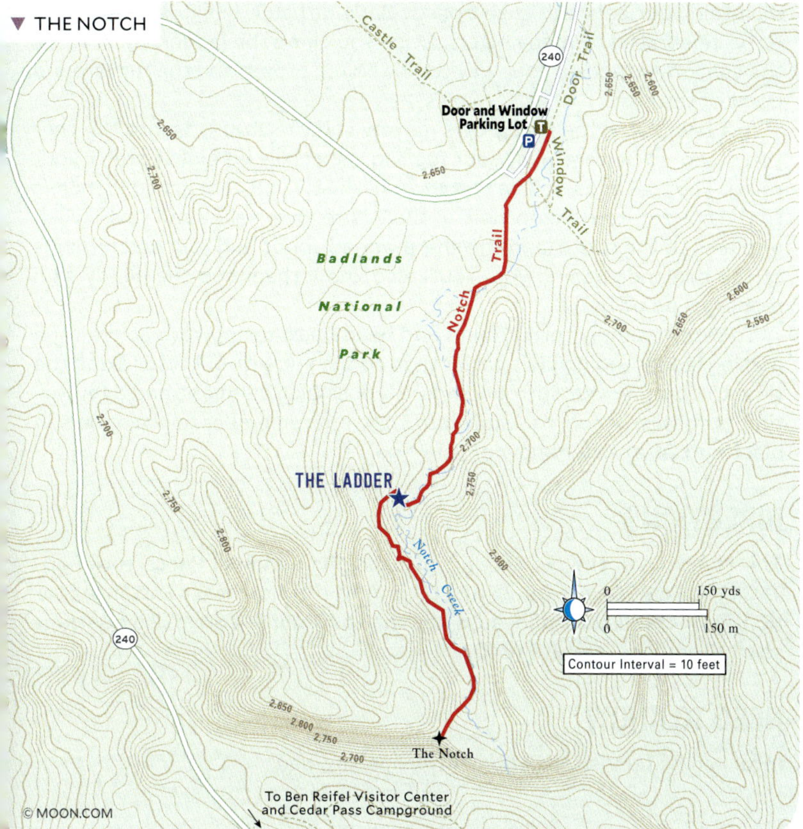

a feel for Badlands that'll tempt you to explore more by vehicle and on foot—there are plenty of trails and scenic drives throughout the park's various areas.

START THE HIKE

The trail begins in a **parking area** with three other trails: **Door Trail** (0.75 mi/1.2 km, the first 0.25 mi/0.4 km is accessible via boardwalk), **Window Trail** (0.25 mi/0.4 km), and **Castle Trail** (10 mi/16.1 km, the longest in the park). The Notch Trailhead sits at the south end of the parking area.

You'll start this hike in a canyon formed in part by Notch Creek. As you hike, you'll climb, switching between the canyon floor and trails that hug canyon walls and put the creek far below. If you're wary about heights, this might not be the hike for you.

When you're about halfway to The Notch and the view there, you'll reach a **rope and log ladder** that climbs some 40 ft (12 m) to the canyon rim. "Ladder" is a bit of a misnomer as this is no ladder like you'd use to climb onto the roof; it's a long lacing of rope and log, and for the first half you'll find that the "rungs" are more like footholds or steps, but once you reach the steep point, you'll be on all fours climbing the ladder to maintain your balance. It isn't particularly difficult, but it is a challenge to be celebrated by many hikers. Once you climb the ladder, you'll be on the canyon rim and on your way to The Notch proper and the turnaround point of the hike.

In a few places the trail grows narrow and the drop-offs into the canyon steep, so be careful of your footing, especially if heights aren't your thing. The trail ends at **The Notch.** You'll know you've reached it thanks to the horizon-to-horizon view of the White River valley and vast sweep of plains to the south, and the sharp-edged spires and rounded mounds of the badlands behind you. You'll also know thanks to the handy sign reading "End of Trail."

To return, simply turn around and head back, taking care at the rope and log ladder (going up is easier than coming down), but also taking the time to observe your surroundings. It's possible you might find a few artifacts, fossils, or cool rocks on your walk, but remember to leave them in place and let a ranger know of your find.

DIRECTIONS

The Notch is in the North Unit of Badlands National Park. From Rapid City, take I-90 East for 75 mi (121 km) to the Northeast Entrance Station. From there, the trailhead is less than a 10-minute drive (2.5 mi/4 km) southeast along Highway 240.

NEED TO KNOW

Info: Ben Reifel Visitor Center, www.nps.gov/badl

BEST NEARBY

Stargazing

▶ *Amphitheater at the Cedar Pass Campground; daily at sunset or shortly after from Memorial Day-Labor Day*

The night sky at Badlands is nothing short of incredible. Some 7,500 celestial bodies—stars, star clusters, nebulae, planets, moons, and even galaxies—are visible on clear nights, but the star of the show is our very own Milky Way Galaxy. After the **evening program,** rangers and volunteers deliver a stellar **Night Sky Viewing** session. Thanks to the Badlands Natural History Association and Celestron, there are plenty of telescopes on hand (but feel free to bring your own or bring along a good pair of binoculars), ensuring everyone can get a look at what lies beyond our planet. Night Sky Viewing sessions run about 40 minutes.

If your timing is right, you can take part in the **Badlands Astronomy Festival.** Over the course of three days and nights, rangers, volunteers, and space science professionals deliver a series of family-friendly talks, activities, events, and celestial viewing sessions. Activities vary year to year, but expect to view deep space, learn constellations and planets, and take part in a solar viewing for a peek at our nearest star. The festival takes place in July or August every year; check the schedule online or at the **Ben Reifel Visitor Center** for exact dates.

Passes and Reservations: Entry into the park is $30/vehicle ($25/motorcycle, $15/pedestrian or cyclist). Passes are available in advance at www.recreation.gov. For more information, see page 502.

Weather Considerations: Do not attempt this trail if there has been recent rainfall as the clay-rich soil here is slick, making this trail more difficult and even dangerous in places. Fire danger can be high in the prairie during hot, dry summers. Be sure to pack at least 2 quarts or liters of water per person and bring along your sunblock, sun hat, and hiking poles.

Facilities: There are restrooms at the trailhead parking lot.

Other: Bison roam free in the park and are to be avoided; admire them (and other wildlife) from a distance, and keep at least 100 yards (90 m) away from these dangerous and unpredictable animals.

▼ NOTCH TRAIL

▲ SUNRISE OVER BADLANDS NATIONAL PARK

OCEAN PATH, ACADIA NATIONAL PARK

GREAT LAKES AND NORTHEAST

Hiking in the Great Lakes and Northeast blends the wild and the urban, with hikes near Cleveland and Chicago, and challenging trails that crest the mountains of Maine and push your limits on a rocky isle miles from shore.

Acadia's Jordan Pond Path and South Bubble hike lives up to the hype—it's moderately tough—but all around you trees blaze with autumn color, and the views of Maine's rocky coastline make the climb worth the effort. For an easier, family-friendly, and mostly accessible trail, take a scenic stroll along Ocean Path, which hits all the highlights of the park. Not too far south of Cleveland, you can hike through a lush forest to Cuyahoga's 15-ft (4.6-m) Blue Hen Falls, a great choice for any season. From Indiana Dunes' West Beach Three-Loop Trail, which leads you through sand dunes and oaky savannahs, Chicago's noise and hustle sits on the horizon, visible yet far from this peaceful patch of nature.

GREAT LAKES AND NORTHEAST
CANADA
89
ISLE ROYALE NP
Lake Superior
MICHIGAN
WISCONSIN
Lake Michigan
MICHIGAN
Lake Huron
Lake Ontario
NEW YO
Lake Erie
PENNSYLVANI
INDIANA DUNES NP
86-88
CUYAHOGA VALLEY NP
83-85
OHIO
INDIANA
ILLINOIS
Washington D
WV
NEW RIVER GORGE NP
SHENANDOAH NP
VIRGINIA
KENTUCKY
MISSOURI
NORTH CAROLINA
GREAT SMOKY MOUNTAINS NP
TENNESSEE
SOUTH CAROLINA
CONGAREE NP

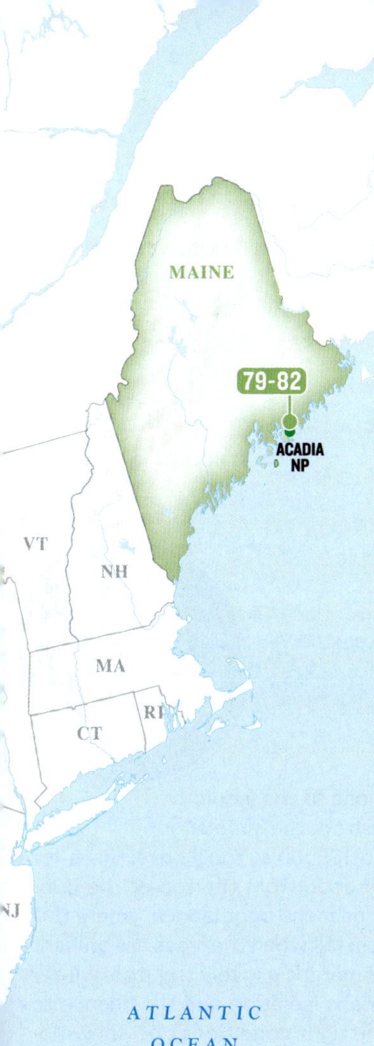

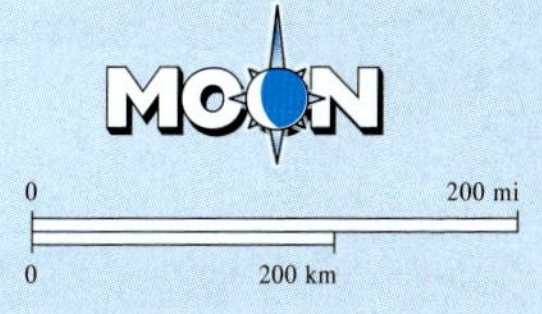

© MOON.COM

ACADIA

CUYAHOGA VALLEY

INDIANA DUNES

ISLE ROYALE

79

JORDAN POND PATH AND SOUTH BUBBLE

ACADIA NATIONAL PARK, MAINE

This pleasant stroll around one of Acadia's most well-loved lakes offers beautiful views and a summit challenge if you detour to South Bubble.

- **Distance:** 3.5 mi (5.6 km) round-trip
- **Duration:** 2-4 hours
- **Elevation Gain:** 508 ft (155 m)
- **Effort:** Moderate-strenuous
- **When:** May-Oct., Oct.-Dec. for Jordan Pond circuit
- **Trailhead:** Jordan Pond boat launch

HIGHLIGHT: Viewing Jordan Pond from the South Bubble summit

This trail loops around Jordan Pond—one of the iconic landscapes in Acadia—then detours from the simple loop for a thrilling hike to the top of the South Bubble. You'll have views for most of the hike, but they're especially good from the top of the Bubble and from the south end of the pond near the boat launch, where this hike begins. This hike is simply stunning in fall when the trees are brilliant with autumn color, but throughout summer it's a lovely trek too; winter is something else. Visiting in winter means isolation and the chance to snowshoe or cross-country ski (with the right conditions), go snowmobiling, or even ice-fish in the park; it also means you could spot the aurora

◀ BUBBLE ROCK

▼ JORDAN POND PATH

borealis reflecting in Jordan Pond and get a feel for Maine's coast during a time most visitors avoid.

Note that hikers of different experience and fitness levels will spend more or less time on the trail. The route is both strenuous and, frankly, a little scary, with exposed ledges, ladder rungs, and other technical elements.

START THE HIKE

Begin at the boat launch near the **parking area,** and absorb some of the jaw-dropping view: From the south end of the pond, you can take in all of Jordan Lake—carved by retreating glaciers—the steep valley to either side and the twin rounded peaks of the Bubbles. After snapping a few pics, proceed counterclockwise along the trail on the east side of Jordan Pond. The path—a mix of packed dirt and gravel—grows rocky and rooty in places, but not enough to interrupt a good walking, hiking, or jogging pace. Continue on this path for 1.1 mi (1.8 km) to where, near the northern end of the lake, a short spur trail leads you to **South Bubble Trail** and the

0.4-mi (0.6-km) path to the summit of the South Bubble. If you've brought your dog along for a hike, skip South Bubble as the path here is rugged and steep, in places requiring the use of the park's signature iron-rung ladders and handholds; instead, continue around the pond for a shorter, but no less beautiful, hike of 3.1 mi (5 km).

As you climb the trail up South Bubble, you'll find it grows steep—at times requiring rock scrambling, at other times exposing you to narrow ledges and points where handholds and ladders will lead the way. At two points you'll need to climb up and over some boulders to continue the trail; be careful in these sections and take your time. Near the summit, the views of Jordan Pond return and only get better. Atop the **summit,** take a look, stop for a rest, then head to Bubble Rock, a giant, mostly round boulder deposited in a precarious position by glaciers. Descend South Bubble until you reach **Bubbles Divide Trail,** where you'll turn left to return to Jordan Pond Path in 0.2 mi (0.3 km). Continue counterclockwise around Jordan Pond and you'll be back at the boat ramp in 1.5 mi (2.4 km). Reward yourself with a treat: one of the legendary popovers from **Jordan Pond House.**

DIRECTIONS

Jordan Pond and South Bubble are on the east side of Mount Desert Island in Acadia National Park. From Bar Harbor, head south on Highway 3 East for 8 mi (12.9 km). Turn right onto Stanley Brook Road, then continue onto Park Loop Road. Continue straight and remain on the two-way section of Loop Road. Signs lead you to Jordan Pond. Park in the North Lot, on the right near the Jordan Pond House. The trail crosses the boat launch.

NEED TO KNOW

Info: Hulls Cove Visitor Center, www.nps.gov/acad

BEST NEARBY

Galyn's

▶ *147 Main St., Bar Harbor; 207/288-9706; www.galynsbarharbor.com; 11am-9pm daily; $11-50*

The best of Maine seafood graces every table at Galyn's. Maine oysters—on the half shell and Rockefeller—lobster bisque, and New England clam chowder are great ways to start. Tuck into something hearty like the Frenchman Bay Stew (their spin on bouillabaisse) or a trio of massive crab cakes for dinner. But you come to Maine for the lobster, so lobster rolls, lobster tails, lobster combos with scallops and crab cakes and sauces, lobster enchiladas, and, of course, whole lobsters will give you something to think about. Since the seafood's fresh and these folks take pride in their food, you're in for a delicious dilemma when you're figuring out dinner.

▲ JORDAN POND AT SUNSET

Passes and Reservations: Entry to the park is $35/vehicle ($30/motorcycle, $20/pedestrian or cyclist). Passes are available in advance at www.recreation.gov. For more information, see page 502.

Weather Considerations: You can expect some snow squalls in early spring, but these are infrequent in late spring; muddy trails and hordes of black flies are a guarantee. Summer is very pleasant, with temperatures from 45-90°F (7-32°C). Winter brings solitude, snow, and the chance for spotting the aurora borealis.

Facilities: At the trailhead there's a seasonal restaurant (Jordan Pond House Restaurant is open mid-May-late Oct.), restrooms, and a stop for the free Island Explorer bus.

Other: Dogs are allowed on the Jordan Pond Loop portion of this hike, but it's not advisable to bring them along on the detour to South Bubble as that trail contains sets of iron ladders and handholds along risky sections of trail. While you can use the iron ladders and handholds, your pup cannot.

Other ponds in Acadia National Park are fine for a swim or to dip your feet in while you rest, but Jordan Pond is a municipal water source, so no swimming, dipping, dunking, or wading by you, your hiking party, or your pooch.

80

PRECIPICE TRAIL

ACADIA NATIONAL PARK, MAINE

This hike will challenge your nerves as you use iron ladders and handholds bolted into the mountain to ascend, but it all pays off with sweeping views of Acadia National Park, nearby islands, and the surrounding bays.

- **Distance:** 2 mi (3.2 km) round-trip
- **Duration:** 1.5-3 hours
- **Elevation Gain:** 1,060 ft (323 m)
- **Effort:** Very strenuous
- **When:** Sept.-Oct.; frequently closed mid-Apr.-Aug.
- **Trailhead:** Precipice Trailhead

Summitting Champlain Mountain via iron rungs, ladders, and handholds

The Precipice Trail is one of the most popular and challenging hikes in Acadia, lauded for the views along the way and the sense of accomplishment that fills hikers when they return. This trail combines traditional hiking with a via ferrata-like experience, leading you up the face of Champlain Mountain—gaining 1,000 ft (305 m) in 0.9 mi (1.5 km)—via stairs, iron rungs, ladders, handholds, and bridges. Unlike a true via ferrata, which sees hikers clipped into a safety line, there's

SUMMIT VIEWS

no such safety here, and the risk of falls is serious along the first leg of the hike. If you're doubtful of your ability to boulder scramble, or if you have a fear of heights, this hike is not for you. The Precipice Trail closes frequently during peregrine falcon nesting season (from early March into August), so double-check trail conditions before you set your heart on this hike.

START THE HIKE

Precipice Trail begins at the west side of the **parking area** with a relentless and immediate ascent through the pine and deciduous forest. You'll navigate over, under, and around boulders, rocks, and stairs carved into the granite, and soon encounter a wooden bridge and the iron handholds that lend this trail so much notoriety. At 0.3 mi (0.5 km) you'll meet the **Orange and Black Path** (leading to your right); head left and you'll be at the summit of Champlain Mountain in 0.5 mi (0.8 km). This last half mile involves more boulders, more ledges, and more exposure, but take your time and savor the view.

At the **summit** spend a few moments admiring the scenery. To your east is Frenchman's Bay and Schoodic Peninsula. Schoodic is part of Acadia, an hour's drive from here; in fall, Frenchman's Bay hosts the occasional cruise ship. The islands dotting the bay are called "porcupine islands" by locals, so named for the "quills"—spruce trees—rising from the islands.

Precipice Trail ends at the summit, and it's an easy walk back along the stony head of Champlain Mountain and the forested Orange and Black Path. Head north along Champlain North Ridge Trail for 0.6 mi (1 km), the connector with Orange and Black. Skip the Orange and Black trail leading east (left) and stay straight for 0.4 mi (0.6 km) to meet up with the Precipice Trail and the short, steep hike down to the parking lot.

DIRECTIONS

Precipice Trail is on the east side of Mount Desert Island in Acadia National Park. From Bar Harbor, take Ledgelawn Avenue south, which turns into Great Meadow Drive. Great Meadow Drive leads to Ocean Drive/Park Loop Road where you'll take a left. Stay on Ocean Drive/Park Loop Road for 2.7 mi (4.3 km) and the Precipice Trailhead will be on your right.

NEED TO KNOW

Info: Hulls Cove Visitor Center, www.nps.gov/acad

Passes and Reservations: Entry to the park is $35/vehicle ($30/motorcycle, $20/pedestrian or cyclist). Passes are available in advance at www.recreation.gov. For more information, see page 502.

Weather Considerations: November is the park's rainiest month, and ice and snow that fall and accumulate during winter make this trail more difficult and dangerous; I don't advise this trail under inclement conditions.

BEST NEARBY

Abbe Museum

▶ *26 Mt. Desert St., Bar Harbor; 207/288-3519; www.abbemuseum.org; 10am-5pm Mon.-Fri. May-Nov.; $10 adults, $7 seniors, $5 kids ages 11-17, free children ages 10 and under and military and tribal ID holders*

It's important to acknowledge our lands and the peoples who called our parks home before European settlers arrived. Here at the Abbe Museum they tell the story of the Wabanaki Nations, the People of the Dawn. It's the only Smithsonian Affiliate in Maine, and the permanent and rotating exhibitions here meet the Smithsonian's high standards for storytelling and proper handling of the artifacts and materials on view. You'll find traditional costuming and crafts, stories from the Wabanaki's myth cycle and history, and a number of engaging talks and activities for the family. There's a second part to the museum, at Sieur de Monts Spring in Acadia National Park proper, but at the time of publication, ongoing maintenance had the facility temporarily shuttered, though it should reopen soon.

Facilities: There are neither restroom facilities nor potable water at the trailhead.

Other: The Precipice Trail is not accessible. Pets are not permitted on this hike. Peregrine falcons nest on Champlain Mountain early March-August, causing periodic trail closures; check trail conditions and status before you go.

▼ IRON RUNGS ON PRECIPICE TRAIL

81

OCEAN PATH

ACADIA NATIONAL PARK, MAINE

This easy path is perfect for new hikers or folks seeking a scenic stroll that hits the highlights of the park. A good portion of this trail is accessible.

- **Distance:** 1.6-4.4 mi (2.6-7.1 km) round-trip
- **Duration:** 1.5-2 hours; 30-45 minutes for accessible portion
- **Elevation Gain:** 375 ft (114 m)
- **Effort:** Easy
- **When:** May-Oct.
- **Trailhead:** Sand Beach/Otter Cliff parking area

HIGHLIGHT: Enjoying scenic coastal views along the entire path

Ocean Path runs along the shore for the entirety of its length, offering unobstructed coastal views every step of the way. Those views include the highlights of Park Loop Road, like Sand Beach (the northern start/end point), Thunder Hole, Otter Cliff, the giant sea stack at Monument Cove, and Frenchman Bay and the bay's "porcupine islands" quilled with spruce trees. The path leads 2.2 mi (3.5 km) from Sand Beach (at the northern end) to Otter Point (at the southern end). The first mile (1.6 km) of Ocean Path, stretching from Sand Beach to Thunder Hole, is composed of packed gravel and paved sections, making it accessible for a number of mobility-assistance devices; unfortunately,

◀ THUNDER HOLE

▼ MONUMENT COVE

OCEAN PATH

the second half of the hike—from Thunder Hole to Otter Cliff—is not accessible due to uneven ground and granite stairs.

Because this hike is the ideal blend of beautiful and easy, it's quite popular, so you'll share the trail with many other visitors. At the height of summer Ocean Path can be a mob scene from 10am-3pm, so to avoid the crowds show up early for sunrise, late for sunset, or visit Acadia anytime but summer's peak.

START THE HIKE

From the **Sand Beach/Otter Cliff parking area,** head south along **Ocean Path.** As you walk along Ocean Path, you'll find dozens of spur trails leading down to secluded coves and rocky cliffs; feel free to follow these and explore, just mind your footing (and any kids or pets joining you) on any side trip. Many of these side trails lead to viewpoints where you can snap a great picture of the scenery; in fact, just south of Sand Beach, an overlook offers one of the best views back at the beach.

Thunder Hole is your first major stop on the trail. Here an underwater sea cave creates thunderous booms under the right conditions: high winds and two hours prior to high tide. Thunder Hole marks the end of the accessible portion of the hike. South of Thunder Hole, the trail grows rocky and uneven, in places requiring the park's signature granite stairs.

Your next landmark is **Monument Cove,** a small cove where a tall, thin granite rock formation stands like some sort of monument or ancient lighthouse. After that you'll reach **Boulder Beach,** where the shore is composed of smooth, roundish, bowling ball-size rocks; with the cliffs and pines rising in the background and the beach formed of these miniature boulders, it makes for a striking photo.

Finally, you reach **Otter Cliff** and the last leg of the hike at **Otter Point.** Otter Cliff stands 110 ft (34 m) high and offers rock climbers a stunning place for their sport, as well as a unique set of challenges that the climbing sort clamor for. When you've had your fill of the view and ocean air, turn back and head north to Sand Beach or catch the Island Explorer bus (stops at Otter Point and Thunder Hole) for a ride and a quicker return.

DIRECTIONS

Ocean Path is on the east side of Mount Desert Island in Acadia National Park. From Bar Harbor, follow Highway 3/Eden Street to Mt. Desert Street and turn left. Turn right on Main Street, then left on Schooner Head Road. At 6.5 mi (10.5 km), turn right to meet Park Loop Road. Turn left on Park Loop Road and follow it for 0.6 mi (1 km) and the parking area will be on the right.

NEED TO KNOW

Info: Hulls Cove Visitor Center, www.nps.gov/acad

BEST NEARBY

Acadia Mountain Guides Climbing School

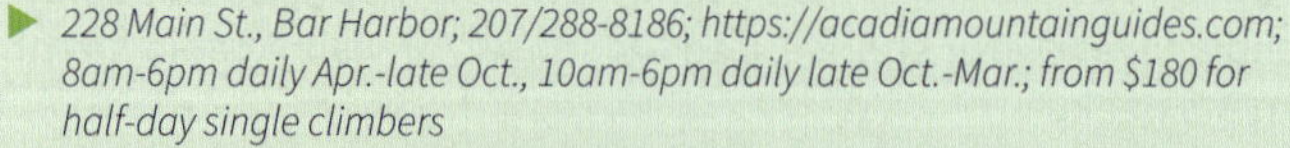

228 Main St., Bar Harbor; 207/288-8186; https://acadiamountainguides.com; 8am-6pm daily Apr.-late Oct., 10am-6pm daily late Oct.-Mar.; from $180 for half-day single climbers

Acadia Mountain Guides offers climbing and climbing instruction for solo climbers, families, and groups of up to 12 in Acadia National Park. Their seasoned guides know these rocks and routes and will help novices make their first climb or work with experienced rock climbers to hone their techniques or tackle the park's most challenging routes. They also offer guided hikes and canoe trips (from $150 half day, $250 full day) inside the park and ice climbing (from $500) at locations outside the national park. Guide clients meet at the retail shop in Bar Harbor.

Passes and Reservations: Entry to the park is $35/vehicle ($30/motorcycle, $20/pedestrian or cyclist). Passes are available in advance at www.recreation.gov. For more information, see page 502.

Weather Considerations: You can expect some snow squalls in early spring, and muddy trails and hordes of black flies are a guarantee. Summer is very pleasant, with temperatures from 45-90°F (7-32°C). In early fall—peak leaf-peeping time—the weather is quite pleasant, too.

Facilities: There are accessible parking spots as well as accessible restrooms at the trailhead.

Other: Pets are permitted on this trail provided they are on-leash. This path is for hiking only; bicycles are not allowed.

▼ OTTER CLIFF

82

GORHAM MOUNTAIN LOOP

ACADIA NATIONAL PARK, MAINE

This is one of the shortest peaks in the park, but your pictures from the top will be proof that you don't need to get high to have a great view.

- **Distance:** 3.5 mi (5.6 km) round-trip
- **Duration:** 1.5-2.5 hours
- **Elevation Gain:** 525 ft (160 m)
- **Effort:** Moderate with strenuous option
- **When:** May-Oct.
- **Trailhead:** Gorham Mountain parking area

HIGHLIGHT: Watching the sunrise or sunset atop Gorham Mountain summit

This popular hike to the summit of Gorham Mountain—one of the park's lowest peaks at 525 ft (160 m)—leads you through wooded slopes to the open-ledge granite peak, offering a taste of the park's signature iron ladders and granite staircases and serving up coastal views.

▲ GORHAM MOUNTAIN LOOP

The Bowl
Bowl Trail
Beehive Trail
The Beehive
To Hulls Cove Visitor Center
Bowl Trail
Kief Pond
Beehive Trail
Bowl Trail
Ocean Path
Sand Beach
Acadia National Park
Newport Cove
Gorham Mountain
GORHAM MOUNTAIN SUMMIT
Gorham Mountain Trail
ROAD
Ocean Path
LOOP
Thunder Hole Information Station
Thunder Hole
ATLANTIC OCEAN
To Beal's Lobster Pier
Cadillac Cliffs Trail
PARK
OTTER CLIFF RD
Otter Cove Trail
Monument Cove
Gorham Mountain
0 250 yds
0 250 m
Contour Interval = 20 feet
Otter Cove
Fabbri

START THE HIKE

The trail begins in the southwest corner of the **Gorham Mountain parking area** and climbs a series of granite ledges to a plaque commemorating Waldron Bates (the path maker responsible for the trail design, namely those granite stairs and iron ladders). Bear left and stay on **Gorham Mountain Trail,** continuing all the way to the summit. Here you'll have views of Sand Beach, Beehive Mountain, and miles of marvelous coastline. If you time your hike properly, this is an excellent summit to take in the sunrise or sunset.

From here, the trail descends. Stay straight at the first intersection; in 0.2 mi (0.3 km) the trail intersects with **Bowl Trail;** turn left and you'll reach the intersection with Beehive Trail and **the Bowl,** where you can rest pondside (I don't recommend swimming since it's popular with leeches). Retrace your steps along Bowl Trail, turn left at the first intersection, then stay to the right for two more trail intersections and Bowl Trail will lead you to Park Loop Road. Here, cross the road, turn right toward Sand Beach, and follow Ocean Path back to the Gorham Mountain parking area.

If you want to make this hike more strenuous, reverse direction. Park at Sand Beach, ascend Bowl Trail until it meets Beehive Trail. Beehive Trail—an Acadia classic—features those ingenious (and a little scary) ladders, steps, and iron handholds. If you have a fear of heights, this trail may not be for you. Stay on Beehive Trail until you reach the Bowl. From there, follow Bowl Trail to Gorham Mountain Trail, hike up to the summit, then back down to the parking area; it's a 3.5-mi (5.6-km) round-trip hike.

DIRECTIONS

Gorham Mountain Loop is on the east side of Mount Desert Island in Acadia National Park. From Bar Harbor, follow Highway 3/Eden Street to Mt. Desert Street and turn left. Turn right on Main Street, then left on Schooner Head Road. At 6.5 mi (10.5 km), turn right to meet Park Loop Road. Turn left on Park Loop Road and follow it for 1.6 mi (2.6 km) and the parking area will be on the right.

BEST NEARBY

Beal's Lobster Pier

▶ *182 Clark Point Rd., Southwest Harbor; 207/244-3202; https://bealslobster.com; 11am-8pm daily Memorial Day-mid-Oct.; $12-60*

You're in Maine, so you'd better crack open a fresh lobster or tuck into a dreamy lobster roll. Beal's offers that quintessential lobster experience from their dockside dining room. Steamed lobsters by the pound plus lobster rolls, bites, and bisque deliver your fill of this crustacean; fried seafood platters, burgers, and some spectacular blueberry pie give you more culinary options to consider.

NEED TO KNOW

Info: Hulls Cove Visitor Center, www.nps.gov/acad

Passes and Reservations: Entry to the park is $35/vehicle ($30/motorcycle, $20/pedestrian or cyclist). Passes are available in advance at www.recreation.gov. For more information, see page 502.

Weather Considerations: Wear heavy-soled boots and bring plenty of water, snacks, and sunscreen.

Facilities: Restroom facilities and potable water are not available at the trailhead.

Other: Gorham Mountain Loop is not accessible. Pets are allowed on the trail provided they are on-leash.

▼ GORHAM MOUNTAIN TRAIL

83

BLUE HEN FALLS TRAIL

CUYAHOGA VALLEY NATIONAL PARK, OHIO

This short but scenic hike leads you through a lush forest to a charming 15-ft (4.6-m) waterfall cascading over a sandstone ledge.

- **Distance:** 2.5 mi (4 km) round-trip
- **Duration:** 1-2 hours
- **Elevation Gain:** 498 ft (152 m)
- **Effort:** Easy
- **When:** Year-round
- **Trailhead:** Boston Mill Visitor Center

HIGHLIGHT: Taking a photo in front of Blue Hen Falls

Blue Hen Falls makes for a lovely destination on this easy, beginner-friendly hike not far south of Cleveland. You'll traverse woods dotted with wildflowers in spring and blazing with color in autumn, hike along a portion of Ohio's statewide Buckeye Trail, and arrive at the small but picturesque waterfall. It's a lovely hike in any season, and if you're willing to brave winter's chilly temperatures, you may find the waterfall iced in.

TRAIL MARKER TO BLUE HEN FALLS

START THE HIKE

From the **Boston Mill Visitor Center,** cross Riverview Road and make for the stone staircase and entrance to the **Buckeye Trail** (a statewide trail more than 1,400 mi/2,255 km long), marked with a blue blaze. Immediately, this trail begins to climb, gaining 200 ft (61 m) over the next 0.3 mi (0.5 km). When you reach the ridgeline, follow it and descend along the path and set of stairs to the ravine floor. You'll climb a second hill and emerge near a commercial business. Here, Buckeye Trail stays on the south side of the road for 650 ft (198 m) before ducking into the woods; follow the trail into the woods and you'll reach an emergency parking area. Cross the road via Buckeye Trail and you'll find Blue Hen Falls less than 1,000 ft (305 m) down the trail.

Blue Hen Falls only drops 15 ft (4.6 m), but with a consistent flow, the curving rock lip it flows over, and the verdant forest here, it's a fine sight. Fall photos are excellent, with the waterfall framed by colorful trees and the leaf litter a blaze of reds and orange on the rocks below. Spring is likewise lovely with a few wildflowers on the hike in, and in summer the coolness of the falls area can be a welcome respite from the periodic humidity. Winters can be cold here, so the falls can present an interesting sight: the rock face bearded in ice and jagged icicles hanging from the rocky lip.

BLUE HEN FALLS

When you've had your fill of the falls, reverse course and soon you'll be back at the trailhead, ready for your next adventure.

DIRECTIONS

Blue Hen Falls is in the central area of Cuyahoga Valley National Park. From Cleveland, take I-77 south to exit 147 (Highway 21 to Miller Road), turn left on Miller Road at the bottom of the exit, turn right on Brecksville Road, then left on Snowville Road. In 2.8 mi (4.5 km), turn right on Riverview Road. Follow Riverview Road for 1.8 mi (2.9 km), then turn left on Boston Mills Road. The visitor center is on the right just before the bridge.

NEED TO KNOW

Info: Boston Mill Visitor Center, www.nps.gov/cuva

Passes and Reservations: No fees or parking passes are required in Cuyahoga Valley National Park.

Weather Considerations: Ohio experiences all four seasons. Throughout spring, expect an abundance of wildflowers, as well as occasional rains and early season snows. Summer brings beautiful, sunny days, plus humidity and the chance for pop-up thunderstorms. Fall has generally good weather and seasonal colors. In winter, temperatures can range from frigid to cold, with occasional snows.

Facilities: Restrooms and a water bottle station are available adjacent to the Boston Mill Visitor Center.

Other: Pets are permitted on this trail provided they are on-leash.

BEST NEARBY

Cuyahoga Valley Scenic Railroad

▶ *Peninsula Depot, 1630 Mill St. West, Peninsula; 330/439-5708; www.cvsr.org; 9am-4pm daily; one-way rides $5, national park scenic excursions from $18*

Take a scenic train ride through the national park or use the train to transport you from Akron to the Blue Hen Falls Trailhead and back. The Cuyahoga Valley Scenic Railroad operates on a historic stretch of railroad track that dates back to the 1880s, offering an Explorer ticket (a $5 one-way ride intended to help hikers, bikers, and kayakers in the national park make an easy return to their cars) and specialty ticketed rides like the National Parks Explorer (a slow, scenic ride through the park), Ales (and Wine and Cocktails) on Rails trips, and family-themed excursions like the Day Out with Thomas and seasonal Polar Express-themed trips. Peninsula Depot is a six-minute drive south of the Boston Mill Visitor Center (south on Highway 9/Riverview Road, left on West Streetsboro Road, cross the river, left on Locust Street, and left on Mill Street). Alternately, you could walk (or bike) along the Ohio & Erie Canal Towpath Trail, a 2.6-mi (4.2-km) trek along a well-maintained trail; head north and turn left at Boston Mills Road to reach the visitor center.

▲ STAIRS ALONG BUCKEYE TRAIL

84

BRANDYWINE GORGE LOOP

CUYAHOGA VALLEY NATIONAL PARK, OHIO

This loop hike gets you close to Brandywine Falls and allows you to experience the gentle topography of north-central Ohio.

- **Distance:** 0.8-3.9 mi (1.3-6.3 km) round-trip
- **Duration:** 35 minutes-3 hours
- **Elevation Gain:** 463 ft (141 m)
- **Effort:** Moderate
- **When:** Year-round
- **Trailhead:** Brandywine Falls parking area

HIGHLIGHT: Viewing the 60-ft (18-m) Brandywine Falls from accessible platforms

Brandywide Gorge Loop offers hikers and walkers an easy-to-follow route through the Ohio countryside on a path that blends boardwalks, wooded paths, and a local multiuse trail. The highlight is the 60-ft (18-m) Brandywine Falls, viewable from accessible platforms on the trail.

For hikers with accessibility needs, note that only the first portion of the trail—the upper boardwalk leading to a viewpoint of Brandywine

▲ BRANDYWINE GORGE TRAIL

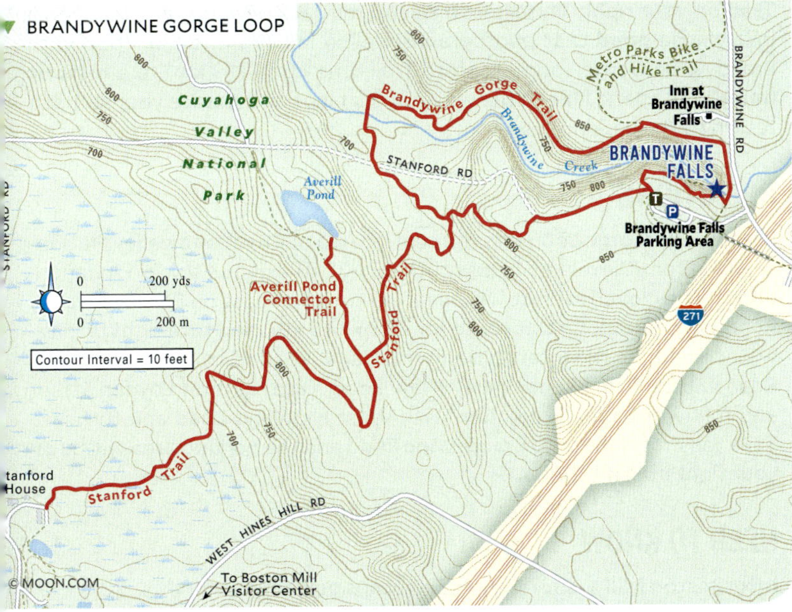

Falls—is accessible (stairs and uneven surfaces impede portions of the full trail), but the trailhead sits on the Summit Metro Parks Bike & Hike Trail, a 34-mi (55 km) rails-to-trails path that converted a large portion of the Lake Erie & Pittsburg Railroad's footprint into a wide, paved, accessible trail across Ohio's countryside.

START THE HIKE

The hike begins at the northwest corner of the **Brandywine Falls parking area.** Brandywine Gorge Loop follows the edge of the gorge and descends to the creek—a tributary of the Cuyahoga River—before making a short ascent back to the gorge rim. Follow this trail counterclockwise and head to the right to take in the sight of 60-ft (18-m) **Brandywine Falls** courtesy of the upper (accessible) and lower viewing areas. The accessible portion—0.8 mi (1.3 km) round-trip—includes views of the bridge from the upper viewing area following a path that's a combination of boardwalk and paved trail. Getting to the lower viewing area means navigating a short set of stairs.

After seeing the falls you'll briefly join the **Summit Metro Parks Bike & Hike Trail,** following its curving path around the falls to join **Brandywine Gorge Trail** 0.3 mi (0.5 km) into the hike. Here the loop leaves the paved Bike and Hike Trail and enters the woods, soon descending to the creek. Cross the creek via the bridge and the trail climbs, intersecting a bike-only trail at 0.9 mi (1.5 km).

At 1.2 mi (1.9 km) you'll meet up with **Stanford Trail.** Here, you can return to the parking lot and wrap up the Brandywine Gorge Loop with a last look at the waterfall, or you can lengthen your hike and turn right on Stanford Trail. In 0.4 mi (0.6 km) you'll find the **Averill Pond Connector**

Trail on your right. This short hike (0.5 mi/0.8 km round-trip) leads to a lovely little **pond** that photographs well in fall. From the junction with Brandywine Gorge Loop, Stanford Trail runs 1.2 mi (1.9 km) to a **historic home** in the park; hike to the western terminus and retrace your steps to return to the parking area.

DIRECTIONS

Brandywine Gorge Loop is in the central area of Cuyahoga Valley National Park. From Cleveland, head south on I-77 to exit 153 toward Independence. The cloverleaf exit will have you traveling east on Pleasant Valley Road; continue along this route for 2.7 mi (4.3 km) and turn right on Fitzwater Road. At the intersection with Canal Road, turn left. Soon Canal Road will be Canal Road/Valley View Road. Turn right on Boyden Street and follow it to the T junction with West Highland Road and turn left. Take the first right onto Brandywine Road and the parking area will be on your right in 1.1 mi (1.8 km).

NEED TO KNOW

Info: Boston Mill Visitor Center, www.nps.gov/cuva

Passes and Reservations: No fees or parking passes are required in Cuyahoga Valley National Park.

Weather Considerations: If the trail is muddy or conditions are iffy and you want to see the falls, a boardwalk leads to the upper falls viewing area (this section of the trail is the only accessible portion). A set of 80 or so steps lead to a lower viewing platform, making your waterfall souvenir pic an easy one to take.

Facilities: Accessible restrooms, flush toilets, drinking water, and a water bottle filling station are available in the parking area.

Other: Pets are allowed on this trail provided they are on-leash.

BEST NEARBY

The Inn at Brandywine Falls

▶ *8230 Brandywine Rd., Northfield; 330/467-1812; www.brandywinefallsinn.com; $179-355*

This historic property sits a short walk away from Brandywine Falls and was built in 1848 by the family who owned the surrounding 800 acres (324 ha) and Brandywine Mills. Rooms here range from traditional B&B rooms in the main house to lofts and suites in the property's converted barn to whole-property rentals (sleep 10, from $1,000).

▲ BRANDYWINE FALLS

85

LEDGES LOOP TRAIL

CUYAHOGA VALLEY NATIONAL PARK, OHIO

Get a glimpse into Ohio's geological past and take in some wow-worthy views on this short hike.

- **Distance:** 2.3 mi (3.7 km) round-trip
- **Duration:** 1 hour
- **Elevation Gain:** 203 ft (62 m)
- **Effort:** Easy-moderate
- **When:** Year-round
- **Trailhead:** Ledges Trailhead

HIGHLIGHT: Enjoying the park's most scenic view from Ledges Overlook

Ledges Loop Trail is a favorite of Cuyahoga Valley National Park fans for the elevation and the views, which are especially good at the Ledges Overlook on the southwest corner. From this plateau—one of the highest points in the park—the views are exceptional in fall when the woods are bright with color. The whole loop is fun to explore, with rocks and boulders to (carefully) climb on and plenty of places that make you feel remote, not like you're within 30 minutes of a city. The large open field here—ideal for a picnic or a game of Frisbee—gives you room to play or just hang out before or after your hike.

▲ LEDGES LOOP TRAIL

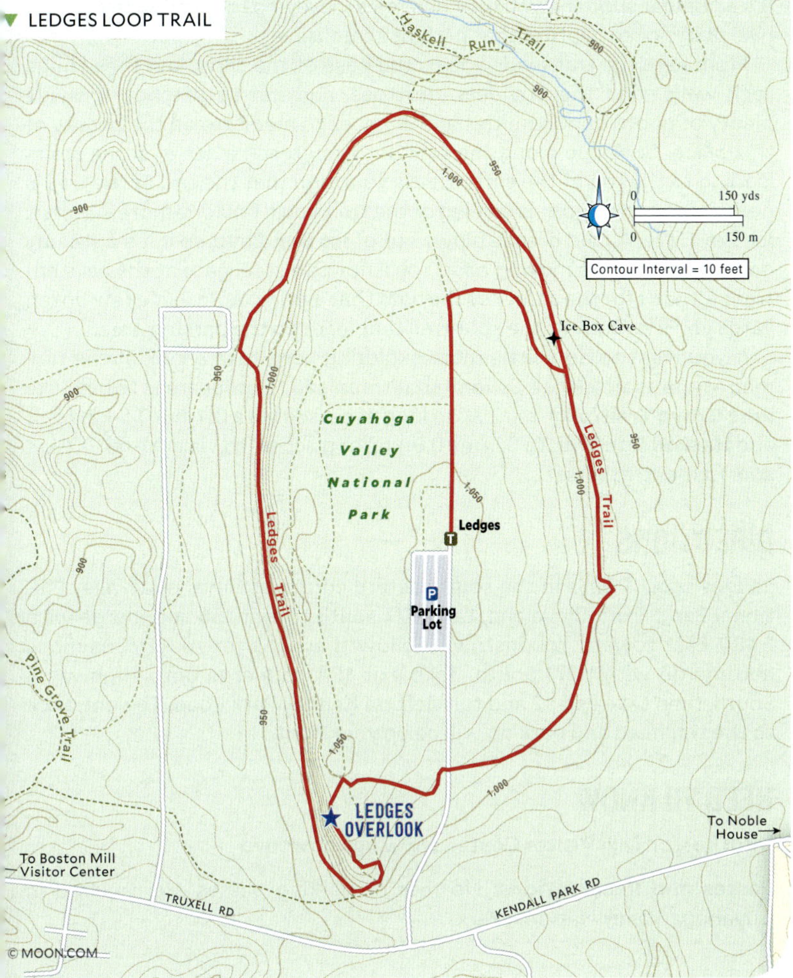

START THE HIKE

The hike begins in the **parking lot** as a paved road, but it quickly transitions to a wide, gravel path. When the "stick" of this lollipop loop hike meets Ledges Trail proper, the path grows a little rocky and rooty, but allows you to maintain as leisurely or as quick a pace as you'd like. When you meet **Ledges Trail** (marked by a metal sign), head to the right and hike the loop in a clockwise direction. Hiking in this direction gets the least exciting part of the trail—the short stretch between here and the Overlook—out of the way first.

At just under 1 mi (1.6 km) you'll reach **Ledges Overlook,** lauded as the most scenic in the national park. Trees in full leaf frame the view from late spring through summer, and in winter and early spring the bare branches reveal more of the landscape, giving you beautiful views at both times of year. But in fall, when the leaves are blazing with color here on the plateau and across the countryside, it's a place you'll want to linger. And folks do.

It's a popular spot and you may find folks jockeying for position for a mid-hike photo or to capture that perfect screensaver.

From here the trail leads you to the base of the cliffs, and these huge rock walls—and the boulders, grottoes, and mossy patches—provide plenty of photo opportunities and chances to meditate on the beauty of this place. Continue along the trail until you reach a set of stone stairs leading to the top of the cliffs; this is your sign that the end of the trail is near. As you wrap up this last leg of the trail, you'll find one more surprise: Ice Box Cave. A cold breeze blows out of **Ice Box Cave,** so if it's a steamy day, take your time moving past. You'll notice a steel gate at the cave entrance; that's for the safety of the bats that live inside. In just a few dozen yards you'll be back at the spur trail that leads to the parking area.

If you want to do a little more exploring here, take a look at the trail map at the nearby kiosk. Several spur trails lead to other areas to hike, like **Pine Grove Trail** (a 1.4-mi/2.3-km loop accessed via a 0.4-mi/0.6-km trail) and **Haskell Run Trail** (a 0.5-mi/0.8-km loop accessed via a 0.1-mi/0.2-km spur), among others.

DIRECTIONS

Ledges Loop Trail is in the southeastern corner of Cuyahoga Valley National Park. From Cleveland, take I-77 south to exit 156 and merge with I-480 East toward Youngstown. Follow the signs for Akron/Columbus and merge with I-271 South. Take exit 18A to merge onto Highway 8 South, then take exit 12 and turn left on Kendall Park Road. The entrance to the trailhead and parking will be on your right.

NEED TO KNOW

Info: Boston Mill Visitor Center, www.nps.gov/cuva

Passes and Reservations: No fees or parking passes are required in Cuyahoga Valley National Park.

BEST NEARBY

Noble House

▶ *60 W. Streetsboro St., Hudson; 330/655-9550; https://noblehouseinhudson.com; 11:30am-2:30pm and 4:30pm-9:30pm Mon.-Fri., 4:30pm-9:30pm Sat.-Sun.; $6-39*

There's great food in every corner of Ohio, so it's no surprise to find an excellent restaurant just a few minutes from Cuyahoga Valley National Park. Noble House is a longtime favorite in Hudson, and both locals and visitors love the Chinese American cuisine they dish up here. Whether you're going for a veggie-forward dish like eggplant yu sheng or maw paw tofu, the spicy kung bao chicken, or a classic like moo shu pork, you'll leave happy and ready to come back for another meal. Reservations recommended.

Weather Considerations: Ohio experiences all four seasons. Throughout spring, expect an abundance of wildflowers, as well as occasional rains and early season snows. Summer brings beautiful, sunny days, plus humidity and the chance for pop-up thunderstorms. Fall has generally good weather and seasonal colors. In winter, temperatures can range from frigid to cold, with occasional snows.

Facilities: This trailhead has restrooms and picnic tables, but no potable water.

Other: Pets are permitted on this trail provided they are on-leash. A large, grassy play field gives you plenty of space to spread out for a picnic or playtime with the kiddos.

▼ NARROW PASSAGE ON LEDGES LOOP TRAIL

▲ SUNSET AT LEDGES OVERLOOK

86

COWLES BOG TRAIL

INDIANA DUNES NATIONAL PARK, INDIANA

On this trail through a National Natural Landmark, with complex dune ecology, plant diversity, and varied terrain, you'll experience loads of natural beauty.

- **Distance:** 4.3 mi (6.9 km) round-trip
- **Duration:** 1.5-2 hours
- **Elevation Gain:** 216 ft (66 m)
- **Effort:** Moderate
- **When:** May-Nov.
- **Trailhead:** Cowles Bog Trailhead

HIGHLIGHT: Hiking through five different ecosystems

This hike is special. In 1965 this location was designated as a National Natural Landmark, thanks to the work of Dr. Henry Cowles, who studied the area's plant ecology and succession in depth in the early 1900s. Several distinct habitats mark this 4.3-mi (6.9 km) loop, and the ponds, marshes, swamps, black oak savannahs, and beaches gave Dr. Cowles plenty to study. In addition to being a beautiful, wildlife-filled hike, it's still an important area for environmental researchers today.

There are 4.8 mi (7.7 km) of trails here, but a 1-mi (1.6-km) stretch serves as a connector between the loop proper and the Greenbelt Trailhead; two other trails allow you to shorten or lengthen the loop hike as you will.

◀ COWLES BOG TRAIL

▼ COWLES BOG TRAIL

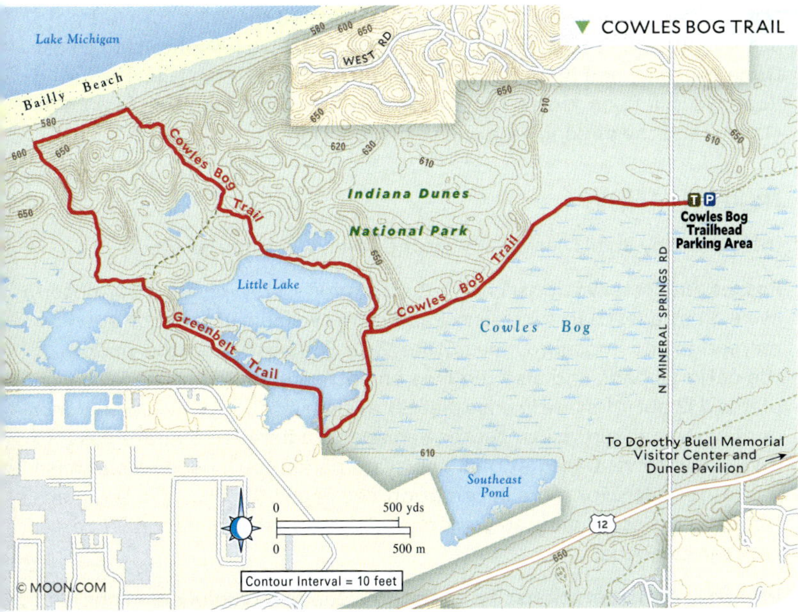

START THE HIKE

From the **Cowles Bog Trailhead parking area,** head west on the trail and walk along the north edge of a broad **marshy expanse** (the Greenbelt connector sits on the south side). After 0.8 mi (1.3 km) you'll reach a junction and turn right. From here we're going to move counterclockwise, weaving through the **woods** and **dunes** to spy on the wildlife. As you leave the marsh, you'll find yourself in a **black oak savannah** and several low dunes; interdunal ponds form here, and the largest stay filled with aquatic life. When you spot one of these ponds, stick around for a few minutes and see what wildlife shows up.

Soon you'll see a trail to the left; this will cut the hike short, so if you need to turn back, you can; otherwise proceed forward. As you draw closer to Lake Michigan, the dunes grow steeper. You'll climb a couple and finally reach the last one and some exceptional **views of Lake Michigan and Chicago** in the distance. Many hikers bring a lunch and linger here on or near the **beach** for a while, and I recommend you do the same, as it's a lovely spot.

Turn left and walk along the beach until you see the trail and signs leading south over the dunes and back into the woods. Enjoy the walk back, ignoring the first trail to your left, but taking the second trail to the left. This second trail skirts the edge of the marshy area you saw at the beginning of the hike. In 0.3 mi (0.5 km) you'll turn right and follow the first path you walked on back to the parking area.

DIRECTIONS

Cowles Bog Trail is in the central area of Indiana Dunes National Park, which runs for about 20 mi (32 km) along the southern shore of Lake

Michigan. From Chicago, take I-80/94 to exit 14B for Gary; turn left onto 5th Avenue/US 12 East/US 20. In 4 mi (6.4 km), turn left onto US 12/East Dune Highway and follow it for 9.8 mi (15.8 km) to North Mineral Spring Road. Turn left on North Mineral Spring Road and follow it for 0.7 mi (1.1 km) and the parking area will be on your right.

NEED TO KNOW

Info: Dorothy Buell Memorial Visitor Center, www.nps.gov/indu

Passes and Reservations: Entry into the park is $25/vehicle ($20/motorcycle, $15/pedestrian or cyclist). Passes are available in advance at www.recreation.gov. Indiana Dunes State Park lies nestled in the middle of the national park, and also requires an entrance fee ($7 in-state license plates, $12 out-of-state license plates), available online (www.in.gov/dnr) or in person at the visitor center. Each park requires a separate pass, so if you plan to visit the national and state parks, you'll need to purchase passes for each. For more information, see page 502. This hike is not adjacent to the state park, so you only need your national park pass to access the trailhead.

Weather Considerations: Temperatures can drop rapidly as night sets in, so if you plan on being out around sunset, be sure to have some warm layers to put on. Winters here can be especially cold and icy, with slushy waves and ice forming on and near the shore (it's quite a sight); if you're visiting during winter, remember to pack something warm and windproof.

Facilities: Restrooms are available at the Cowles Bog Trailhead, but there is no potable water.

BEST NEARBY

Dunes Pavilion

▶ *In Indiana Dunes State Park, 1600 N. 25 E, Chesterton; 219/250-2568; www.dunespavilion.com; restaurant 11am-9pm daily, general store 9am-6pm daily; $7-20*

Nestled inside Indiana Dunes State Park (you'll need to pay a $7 in-state/$12 out-of-state entrance fee to enter the state park), this 1930s building is home to a restaurant, seasonal rooftop bar, general store, ice cream shop, and wedding/meeting venue. The restaurant serves a small menu of salads, handhelds from burgers to tacos, and bowls, and in the general store you can pick up supplies you might have forgotten (like sunscreen), a souvenir, or bit of hiking kit. They also have a rooftop bar (4pm-10pm daily Memorial Day-Labor Day; $5-14) serving a Latin-themed menu of tacos, entrée-sized plates, and cocktails.

▲ COWLES BOG TRAIL

87

WEST BEACH THREE-LOOP TRAIL

INDIANA DUNES NATIONAL PARK, INDIANA

Hike among the dunes, pine groves and oak thickets, interdunal ponds, and the shore of Lake Michigan as you take in big views of Chicago and explore this surprising environment not far from the city's center.

- **Distance:** 3.6 mi (5.8 km) round-trip
- **Duration:** 3 hours
- **Elevation Gain:** 114 ft (35 m)
- **Effort:** Moderate
- **When:** May-Oct.
- **Trailhead:** West Beach parking lot

HIGHLIGHT: Taking in surprising views of Lake Michigan and Chicago

West Beach Three-Loop Trail joins three short hikes into one longer exploration of this surprising environment. The loops—Dune Succession Trail (0.9 mi/1.5 km), West Beach Trail (1.1 mi/1.8 km), and Long Lake Trail (1.7 mi/2.7 km)—provide three distinct looks at this place. Dune Succession Trail shows how dunes develop, and from the crest of the dune ridge the views are of the stop-you-in-your-tracks variety. West Beach Trail leads through a

▲ WEST BEACH

1920s-era sand mine undergoing reclamation efforts to turn it back into an oak savannah; this trail skirts Long Lake. Long Lake Loop takes you through the dunes to several spots where you can see the lake; along the way you can spot seasonal wildflowers and a number of native and migrating birds.

You can hike the loops here in any order, any distance, but I've combined them into one longer hike that eliminates a few of the connector trails and gives you one easy circuit.

START THE HIKE

We'll make this hike in something of a sloppy figure eight. Start at the north end of the **parking area,** take the spur trail to the right, and immediately begin climbing the quad-burning 270 stairs leading to the top of the dune ridge where **the views of Lake Michigan and Chicago** are surprising—how can you be in a dune-filled national park and have a view of Chicago? As you descend, you'll enter a **pinery** of jack pines; this is one of the southernmost patches of jack pines, and scientists believe they're here as a result of ice-age glaciers bringing seeds south. Once you exit the woods you'll be on the shore. At the **bathhouse,** loop back to the parking lot and make your way for those stairs. Don't worry, we're turning left at the foot of the stairs to join West Beach Trail.

West Beach Trail is sandy and soft. This partially bare patch of land is being restored to an oak savannah, and it's drawing lots of wildlife. Birds especially love this area as the young trees and the shoreline of **Long Lake** provide the habitats they need, and you'll often find groups of birders here. As the trail leaves the lake, it crosses West Beach Road—watch for cars—and meets Long Lake Loop; turn left at the T junction. This trail crosses West Beach Road twice before ducking back into the dunes and woods. The trail climbs, giving you a view of Long Lake and a good look at Lake Michigan, before emerging from the woods at the picnic area beside the parking lot.

DIRECTIONS

West Beach is in the western region of Indiana Dunes National Park, which runs for about 20 mi (32 km) along the southern shore of Lake Michigan. From Chicago, take I-90 southeast out of the city to exit 14B for Gary. Turn left onto 5th Avenue/US 12 East/US 20 East for 4 mi (6.4 km), then left onto US 12/East Dunes Highway for 2.3 mi (3.7 km), then right onto West Beach Road; this road terminates in the parking area.

NEED TO KNOW

Info: Paul H. Douglas Center for Environmental Education, www.nps.gov/indu

Passes and Reservations: Entry into the park is $25/vehicle ($20/motorcycle, $15/pedestrian or cyclist). Passes are available in advance at www.recreation.gov. Indiana Dunes State Park lies nestled in the middle of the national park, and also requires an entrance fee ($7 in-state license plates, $12 out-of-state license plates), available online (www.in.gov/dnr) or in person at the visitor center. Each park requires a separate pass, so if you plan to visit the national and state parks, you'll need to purchase passes for each. For more information, see page 502. This trailhead is outside the state park, meaning you only need your national park pass to access the trail.

Weather Considerations: Temperatures can drop rapidly as night sets in, so if you plan on being out around sunset, be sure to have some warm layers to put on. Winters here can be especially cold and icy, with slushy waves and ice forming on and near the shore (it's quite a sight); if you're visiting during winter, remember to pack something warm and windproof.

BEST NEARBY

Third Coast Spice Cafe

▶ *761 Indian Boundary Rd., Ste. 6, Chesterton; 219/926-5858; www.thirdcoastspice.com; 6am-2pm daily; $6-15*

This is the kind of diner you wish you had in your neighborhood: classic diner food made with local, organic products; vegetarian- and omnivore-friendly; cool local art on the walls. Grab a stack of flapjacks to fuel your hike or go for a veggie-filled omelet; post-hike, chow down on a Reuben, a hearty grilled cheese, or the vegetarian coconut curry.

▲ BOARDWALK AT INDIANA DUNES NATIONAL PARK

Facilities: The West Beach parking lot offers accessible parking, bathhouse access, and restrooms; some picnic shelters and a portion of the walkway to the beach are accessible as well. Potable water and restrooms are available at this trailhead, and a bathhouse, showers, and lockers are available seasonally. Lifeguards (on duty 10am-6pm daily Memorial Day-Labor Day) are stationed at the swimming area adjacent to the bathhouse. There are no concessions here, but cooking fires and portable grills are permitted as long as they follow posted guidelines.

Other: No special equipment or gear is required to hike in Indiana Dunes National Park, but if you're keen to spot birds, bring your binoculars, and if you're here for a little stargazing, you'll want those binoculars or a telescope. The trails here at West Beach are a mix of soft sand, packed dirt, and wooden stairs and boardwalks. The soft sand will slow you down, so plan on this hike taking longer than the mileage might suggest. Leashed pets are welcome.

88

PAUL H. DOUGLAS TRAIL

INDIANA DUNES NATIONAL PARK, INDIANA

This out-and-back hike leads through wetlands and dunes to the shores of Lake Michigan; along the way look for beavers, birds, and other wildlife in the dunes and marshy areas.

- **Distance:** 3.4 mi (5.5 km) round-trip
- **Duration:** 1-2 hours
- **Elevation Gain:** 124 ft (388 m)
- **Effort:** Moderate
- **When:** May-Sept.
- **Trailhead:** Paul H. Douglas Center parking area

HIGHLIGHT: Watching for wildflowers and wildlife

Traversing towering dunes, lush wetlands, a pond full of wildlife, and serene forestland, the Paul H. Douglas Trail shows off the diverse ecosystems found in Indiana Dunes. Birders will find a number of species along this trail, and wildlife from deer to small mammals may cross your path as you hike. Don't be surprised if you find artists and photographers here trying to capture the short and long views, and when you get to the shoreline, be ready for some swimming or wading in the chilly waters of Lake Michigan.

PAUL H. DOUGLAS CENTER FOR ENVIRONMENTAL EDUCATION

START THE HIKE

From the **parking area,** cross the street to the **Paul H. Douglas Center for Environmental Education** and follow the trail along the north side of the pond. Beavers frequent this pond and many of the interdunal ponds between here and Lake Michigan, so keep an eye out for wildlife. If you're here in spring or summer, there should be wildflowers along the length of the trail.

At the west end of the pond, a trail leads into the dunes and woods to the north. For the next mile (1.6 km), this trail leads through dunes and oak

savannahs, past interdunal ponds, and through patches of seasonal wildflowers. Deer, beavers, and dozens of species of birds are some of the wildlife you can spot along the way. This is a popular trail, but if you can find a few moments of solitude where you can sit and get quiet for a few minutes, do it—you'll be amazed at how much wildlife you'll observe. When the trail crosses the **Grand Calumet River,** the landscape changes to the complex of tall dunes that line the lakeshore.

The trail leads you through the dunes to the shoreline where you can play, go for a swim, beachcomb and explore, or catch your breath and head back. When you've had your fill of Lake Michigan, reverse course and make your way back to the parking area.

DIRECTIONS

Paul H. Douglas Trail is in the western region of Indiana Dunes National Park, which runs for about 20 mi (32 km) along the southern shore of Lake Michigan. From Chicago, take I-90 to exit 14B to Gary. Turn left onto 5th

Avenue/US 12 East/US 20 East for 4 mi (6.4 km), then left onto South Lake Street. The parking area is 0.7 mi (1.1 km) ahead on the right.

NEED TO KNOW

Info: Paul H. Douglas Center for Environmental Education, www.nps.gov/indu

Passes and Reservations: Entry into the park is $25/vehicle ($20/motorcycle, $15/pedestrian or cyclist). Passes are available in advance at www.recreation.gov. Indiana Dunes State Park lies nestled in the middle of the national park, and also requires an entrance fee ($7 in-state license plates, $12 out-of-state license plates), available online (www.in.gov/dnr) or in person at the visitor center. Each park requires a separate pass, so if you plan to visit the national and state parks, you'll need to purchase passes for each. For more information, see page 502. You won't need a state park pass to access this trailhead.

Weather Considerations: Temperatures can drop rapidly as night sets in, so if you plan on being out around sunset, be sure to have some warm layers to put on. Winters here can be especially cold and icy, with slushy waves and ice forming on and near the shore (it's quite a sight); if you're visiting during winter, remember to pack something warm and windproof.

Facilities: There are neither restrooms nor a water station in the parking area. Restrooms can be found at the Paul H. Douglas Center for Environmental Education but are only available when the center is open.

Other: Bring a pair of binoculars on this walk so you can scan the marshy areas and interdunal ponds for beavers and other wildlife.

BEST NEARBY

Riley's Railhouse

▶ *1232 N. 4th St., Chesterton; 219/395-9999; www.rileysrailhouse.com; $200-230*

Why opt for a boring old hotel when you can stay in a train car? Riley's Railhouse has five rooms—two in a onetime railroad freight station, two in refitted boxcars, and one in an updated caboose. The upstairs room sleeps five (perfect for families or close-knit groups), the boxcars sleep four, and the caboose sleeps two in comfort and style. They're right around the corner from several restaurants, so you can park the car once you've arrived.

▲ MARSHY AREA ON THE PAUL H. DOUGLAS TRAIL

89

GREENSTONE RIDGE TRAIL

ISLE ROYALE NATIONAL PARK, MICHIGAN

This spectacular hike through one of the most isolated national parks offers solitude, plenty of wildlife watching, and the chance to complete a 40-mi (64-km) trail in a few days' time.

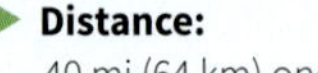

- **Distance:** 40 mi (64 km) one-way
- **Duration:** 2-4 days
- **Elevation Gain:** 4,088 ft (1,246 m)
- **Effort:** Moderate-strenuous
- **When:** June-Aug.
- **Trailhead:** Rock Harbor Visitor Center or Windigo Visitor Center

HIGHLIGHT: Wildlife watching along an epic long-distance hike

Isle Royale National Park is one of the least visited of the US national parks, in part because it's so difficult to reach. With private boats, ferries, or seaplanes being the only way to arrive on this 50- by 9-mi (81- by 14.5-km) island in the northwestern corner of Lake Superior, getting here can be an adventure in itself. But once you arrive you'll find a near pristine patch of wilderness where two visitor centers—Rock Harbor, at the northeast end of the park, and Windigo, at the southwest end of the park—bracket an island filled with 36 campsites and 165 mi (265 km) of trails to hike. Hikers tend to stick close to one of the visitor centers or campgrounds and do a series of day hikes, or they go on a trek from one end of the island to the other, which is our route.

PRICKLY WILD ROSE IN ISLE ROYALE NATIONAL PARK

This point-to-point hike leads along the Greenstone Ridge Trail from Rock Harbor to Windigo, but you could easily reverse the route by acquiring ferry or seaplane tickets to Windigo and heading north via the same trail. This path isn't especially technical, but it's long and you'll be self-reliant for food, water, medical help, and navigation along the way. Wildlife abound on this hike; expect to see beavers, foxes, and otters

▲ ROCK HARBOR, ISLE ROYALE

along the way, but keep an eye out for moose and listen carefully for the howl of the wolves that live here. The grasslands are a riot of wildflowers in spring, and throughout summer, wild raspberries and blueberries abound.

START THE HIKE

To get to Greenstone Ridge Trail—which runs almost arrow-straight from one end of the park to the other—head southwest out of **Rock Harbor** toward **Suzy's Cave** (an ancient sea cave) and **Three Mile Campground.** At Three Mile, follow the connector trail to **Mount Franklin** and the Greenstone Ridge Trail. Take in the view from Mount Franklin and make your way southwest. As you hike from one end of the island to the other, you'll follow the Greenstone Ridge, a ridge named for Michigan's state gem (yes, you'll find some lying around, but as with anything you find in a park, take a look, snap a pic, and leave it undisturbed), and pass through a number of environments. Forests of maple, aspen, and sometimes head-high ferns stand among grasslands and bogs; lakes dot the landscape. You'll climb to the top of Mount Desor (1,394 ft/425 m), the highest point in the park, and spend a little time admiring the view of Lake Michigan and the smaller, but no less lovely, Hatchet Lake and Lake Desor. On the hike you'll crest a total of six peaks, pass a pair of observation towers, and find campgrounds at **Chickenbone Lake, Hatchet Lake, Lake Desor,** and on the trail to **Island Mine,** then you'll reach **Windigo Visitor Center.** Most hikers take this on in four days, but it can be done in two if you're a power hiker.

If you're going to reverse this route, begin in Windigo where a short spur trail leads from the harbor past Washington Creek Campground and joins Greenstone Ridge Trail.

DIRECTIONS

Greenstone Ridge Trail spans the length of Isle Royale, the largest island in Isle Royale National Park. Isle Royale, along with over 450 smaller

Pie Island
Flatland Island
Thompson Island
Lake Superior
CANADA
UNITED STATES
Hatchet Lak
Minong Ridge Trail
Ishpeming Trail
Lake Desor
Lake Desor
Island Mine
Greenstone Ridge Trail
To Grand Portage, MN via *Sea Hunter III* & *Voyageur II*
Windigo Visitor Center
Washington Harbor
Carnelian Beach
Siskiwit Bay
Isle Royale National Park
Grace Harbor
Feldtmann Lake
Feldtmann Ridge Trail
© MOON.COM

Rock Harbor Visitor Center/ Rock Harbor Lodge
Duncan Bay
Tobin Harbor
Rock Harbor
Suzy's Cave
Mount Franklin
Three Mile
Greenstone Ridge Trail
Sargent Lake
Chickenbone Lake
Moskey Basin
Isle Royale National Park
Lake Richie
Siskiwit Lake
To Copper Harbor, MI via Isle Royale Queen II
Lake Superior
0
4 mi
0
4 km
Contour Interval = 100 feet
To Houghton, MI via Ranger III

surrounding islands, is in the northwest region of Lake Superior, near the border of Michigan and Canada, and essentially you have two options for getting to the park: boat or seaplane.

Boat

Four ferries—two from Michigan, two from Minnesota—will transport you between the mainland and the park.

Michigan ferries are *Ranger III,* which departs from **park headquarters** (800 E. Lakeshore Dr., Houghton, MI; 906/482-0984; www.nps.gov/isro; $80 adults, gear limited to 100 lb/45.3 kg per person) and *Isle Royale Queen II* (14 Waterfront Landing, Copper Harbor, MI; 906/289-4437; www.isleroyale.com; $80 adults, gear limited to 70 lb/31.7 kg).

Minnesota ferries are *Voyageur II* (402 Upper Rd., Grand Portage, MN; 218/600-0765; www.isleroyaleboats.com; from $87 adults, gear limited to 40 lb/18.1 kg per passenger) and *Sea Hunter III* (402 Upper Rd., Grand Portage, MN; 218/600-0765; www.isleroyaleboats.com; $87 adults, gear limited to 40 lb/18.1 kg per passenger).

You can also take a private boat to the park.

Seaplane

Isle Royale Seaplanes (906/483-4991; www.isleroyaleseaplanes.com; from $230 one-way) offers daily flights from **Hancock, Michigan** (Hancock Portage Canal Seaplane Base, 21205 Royce Rd., Hancock, MI) and **Grand Marais, Minnesota** (Cook County Airport, 123 Airport Rd., Grand Marais, MN); the trip takes 35-45 minutes. Seaplanes also offer inter-island flights (from $142) between the Rock Harbor and Windigo Visitor Centers.

BEST NEARBY

Rock Harbor Lodge

▶ *Rock Harbor, Isle Royale National Park; 877/841-1064; www.rockharborlodge.com; $245-315*

If you're visiting Isle Royale National Park, you're staying here, and if you're staying here, spend at least a night or two before or after your epic hike at the Rock Harbor Lodge. Located at the northeastern end of the park near the Rock Harbor Visitor Center, the lodge offers three kinds of stays: lodge rooms, suites, and cabins (called "housekeeping" cabins). Traditional rooms and suites are good for couples and groups of four, while the housekeeping cabins are suitable for up to six guests. There's a store here with a limited selection of groceries, freeze-dried backpacker food, camping fuel, toiletries, souvenirs, and sundries, as well as a pair of restaurants and a marina (where you can arrange for a fishing charter, your ferry back to the mainland, or a ferry to the other end of the island). **Greenstone Grill** ($6-18) serves breakfast burritos and a few grab-and-go breakfast goodies, and for lunch and dinner, burgers, sandwiches, pizzas, a kid's menu, and a few drinks (domestic beer and wine only). **Lighthouse Restaurant** ($12-36) dishes up a hearty breakfast buffet and a menu of appetizers and entrées—including fish-and-chips, steak, chicken, and pasta—that are a welcome break from a few days of backpacker grub.

NEED TO KNOW

Info: Rock Harbor Visitor Center or Windigo Visitor Center, www.nps.gov/isro

Passes and Reservations: Entry into the park is $7/day. Passes are available in advance at www.pay.gov. The park's 36 campgrounds are free after you pay the entrance fee, and are first-come, first-served (not reservable) for parties of six or fewer. Permits are required, regardless of group size, for all overnight stays at campgrounds, and are separate from campground reservations. For more information, see page 508.

Weather Considerations: Isle Royale National Park is open April 16-October 31 every year; it is closed November 1-April 15 because of the extreme temperatures and winter-weather conditions on this island.

Facilities: Rock Harbor has the Rock Harbor Lodge; a trading post; showers, laundry, and potable water; fuel and fishing charters; and a pair of seasonal restaurants. Windigo has seasonally available gasoline and fuel; showers, laundry, and potable water; and cabins. All campgrounds along the trail offer tent sites, a water source, and outhouses. Some campgrounds on Lake Superior offer shelters and picnic tables.

Other: Be careful planning your gear and food supplies before you leave, as goods and supplies in the park are limited; your essential supplies should include reliable bug repellent and bug netting as the insects can be brutal here. Note that sealable food storage containers are a must on the island; be sure to check for updated regulations on permitted storage containers.

Isle Royale is remote, so if you encounter a wilderness emergency, you'll likely have to wait for rangers or other emergency responders to reach you. Carry a robust first-aid kit and know how to use it. Cell phone service is spotty and unreliable in the park, so if you'll be hiking and camping here for an extended period, your best bet for emergency contact will be via marine radio or satellite phone.

▼ GREENSTONE RIDGE TRAIL

GREAT SMOKY MOUNTAINS
NATIONAL PARK

THE SOUTH

The landscape of the South delivers mountains, gorges, and waterfalls galore—Shenandoah's Cedar Run-Whiteoak Circuit has seven trailside falls—along with a healthy dose of that famed hospitality.

From Diamond Point, West Virginia, the wild white water of the New River flows far below, and in the distance the namesake bridge spans the gorge in a single swoop. Endless Wall Trail led you here through thickets of mountain laurel and rhododendron, past rock climbers with their crash pads and chalk bags, and now you watch as fog fills the gorge from the bottom up, erasing the river as night falls. You'll have endless hiking options at Great Smoky Mountains, with its rolling mist-covered peaks, lush forests, and cascading waterfalls, but Big Creek Trail, broad and easy, promises the ultimate in backpacking refreshment: a swimming hole. Good thing you packed your bathing suit! Cypress trees blot out the sun, their knees poking up through mud and blackwater creeks beside Congaree's Boardwalk Trail. The wildlife has surprised you—wild pigs, an alligator, a cartoonish woodpecker—but more awaits around the next bend of the trail.

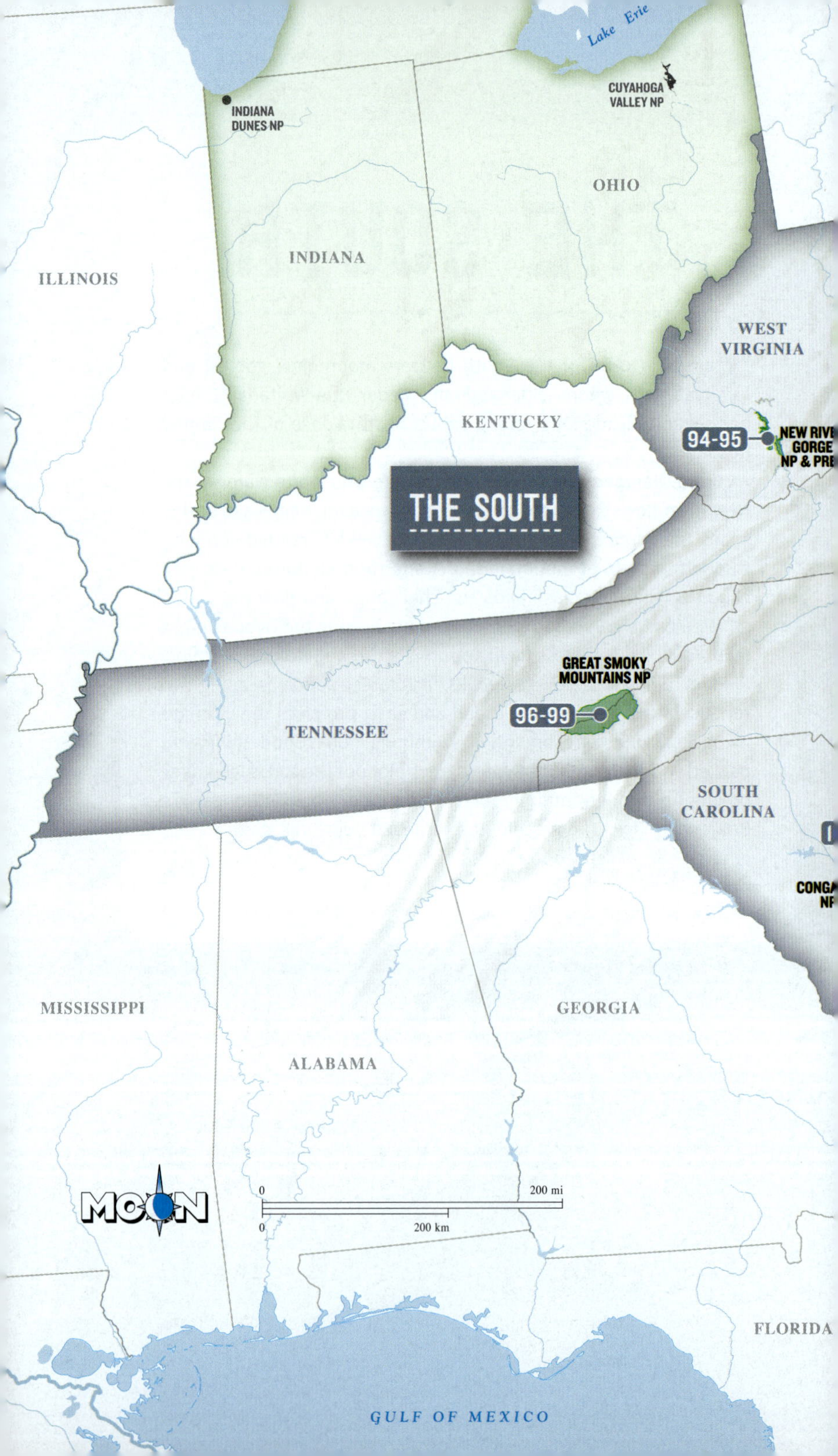

Lake Erie
INDIANA DUNES NP
CUYAHOGA VALLEY NP
OHIO
INDIANA
ILLINOIS
WEST VIRGINIA
KENTUCKY
94-95
NEW RIVE GORGE NP & PRE
THE SOUTH
GREAT SMOKY MOUNTAINS NP
96-99
TENNESSEE
SOUTH CAROLINA
CONGA NP
MISSISSIPPI
GEORGIA
ALABAMA
MOON
0
200 mi
0
200 km
FLORIDA
GULF OF MEXICO

YLVANIA
NEW
JERSEY
MARYLAND
DE
Washington DC
93
HENANDOAH
NP
VIRGINIA
NORTH
CAROLINA
ATLANTIC
OCEAN
© MOON.COM

90

HAWKSBILL LOOP TRAIL

SHENANDOAH NATIONAL PARK, VIRGINIA

The highest peak in the park, Hawksbill Mountain is named for the great number of hawks that can be seen circling on the thermals.

- **Distance:** 2.7 mi (4.3 km) round-trip
- **Duration:** 2-3 hours
- **Elevation Gain:** 758 ft (231 m)
- **Effort:** Moderate-strenuous
- **When:** Year-round
- **Trailhead:** Hawksbill Gap parking area

HIGHLIGHT: Taking in the 360-degree view from the summit

Hike to the top of Shenandoah's highest peak, watching for hawks and other raptors as you go. Not only will you have fabulous views of the Blue Ridge Mountains, you'll also join the Appalachian Trail for part of this hike.

Though this trail is short, sections of it are steep and rocky, so watch your footing as you hike. As with other Shenandoah National Park summit hikes, this one is rocky and requires a little bit of scrambling; no special rock-climbing gear or knowledge is required.

▲ BYRDS NEST SHELTER

▼ HAWKSBILL LOOP TRAIL

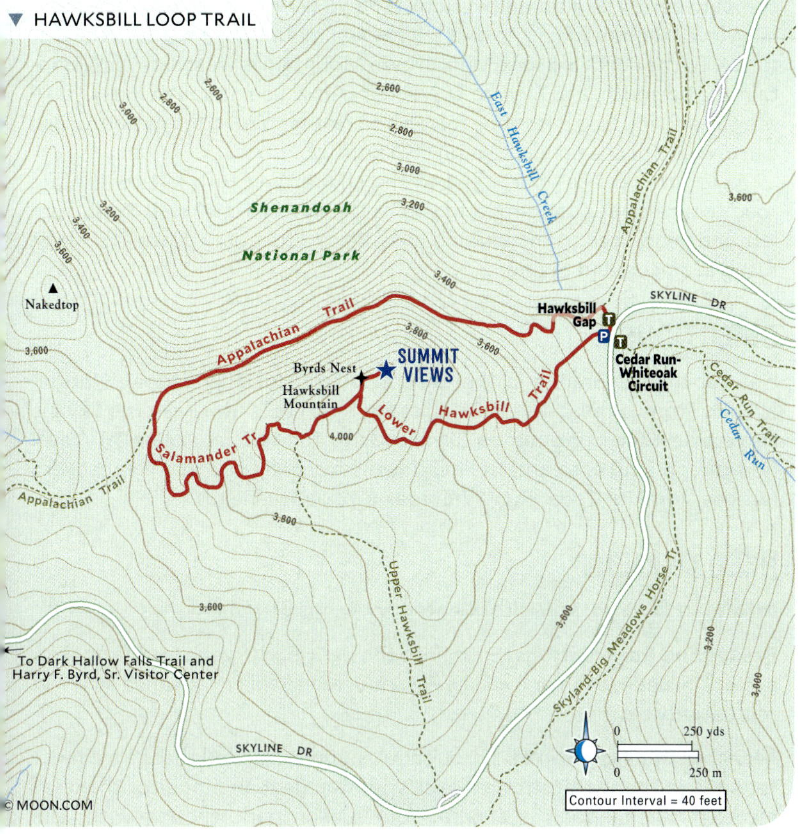

START THE HIKE

At the north end of the parking lot is the trailhead to the summit of Hawksbill Mountain (4,050 ft/1,234 m), the highest peak in the park. A spur trail about 100 yd (91 m) long leads to the **Appalachian Trail,** which you'll follow to your left and begin to climb. While you climb, keep your eyes open for raptors on the wing; they'll be most active during the raptor migration from mid-September through November, but arriving in late September-early October will give you both a sky full of hawks and mountainsides beginning to show autumn color.

The trail is rocky for the first 0.4 mi (0.6 km), then you reach a talus slope, then a short, clear section and a second talus slope. Along here you have great views of the surrounding valleys and mountains.

At 1 mi (1.6 km) in, you'll reach a cement signpost noting the Appalachian Trail mileage and arrows pointing to Hawksbill and to Fishers Gap. Make a hard left onto **Salamander Trail** and keep climbing. In 0.25 mi (0.4 km) you'll come to a very rocky point, so be careful of your steps. As you approach the top you'll join a fire road, making the rest of the route very easy. The summit is at 1.9 mi (3.1 km), so you're close.

On the **summit** you'll find the **Byrds Nest,** a shelter built for former US senator and Virginia governor Harry F. Byrd Sr. There's no water and no camping here. The summit overlook is 30 yd (27 m) or so away. The summit view is commanding. In every direction mountains fade into the distance. To the north is Stony Man, Brown Mountain is west, Graves Mountain to the south, and Skyline Drive just below you. If you're lucky you'll see the endangered peregrine falcon, the fastest bird in the nation, which can dive at speeds up to 120 mph (193 km/h).

To return, retrace your steps to the shelter and turn left on the fire road to a cement post directing you to the **Lower Hawksbill Trail.** Turn left and head back to the parking area. Be careful going down; it's rocky, steep in places, and taxing.

DIRECTIONS

Hawksbill Loop Trail is in the Central District of Shenandoah National Park. From Luray, take US 211 East for 9 mi (14.5 km). Take the Skyline Drive exit, then continue on Skyline Drive for 14.2 mi (22.9 km). You'll find the parking area and trailhead for Hawksbill Loop at Milepost 45.5 (across from the Cedar Run-Whiteoak Circuit Trailhead).

NEED TO KNOW

Info: Harry F. Byrd, Sr. Visitor Center, www.nps.gov/shen

Passes and Reservations: Entry into the park is $30/vehicle ($25/motorcycle, $15/pedestrian or cyclist). Passes are available in advance at www.recreation.gov.

Weather Considerations: Throughout summer and fall there's a chance for sudden thunderstorms, so pack your rain gear and monitor the day's forecast. Shenandoah is a great four-season park, though with winter weather comes the chance of snow and ice on the trail and the occasional closure of Skyline Drive. The best months for fall colors are

BEST NEARBY

Dark Hollow Falls Trail

▶ *Milepost 50.7 at the Dark Hollow Falls parking area*

Pair the short summit hike on Hawksbill with another short hike to a picturesque **waterfall** only a 10-minute drive away. **Dark Hollow Falls Trailhead** sits just 5 mi (8 km) south of the Hawksbill Gap parking area and offers a 1.4-mi (2.3-km) out-and-back hike to a 70-ft (21-m) waterfall. The trail is simple: Descend 440 ft (134 m) along the 0.75-mi (1.2-km) trail to the top of the falls, take your time checking them out, head to the base of the falls for a look, then hike back up the trail to the parking area. This hike is very popular thanks to the waterfall, the length, and the proximity to Big Meadows (and the lodge and visitor center here), but worth it. The trail is steep and rocky as you descend and will seem even more steep and rocky on the way back out, so take your time. Wildflowers and mountain laurel bloom alongside Hogcamp Branch (the stream feeding Dark Hollow Falls) throughout spring and summer. According to park naturalists, this waterfall was a favorite of Thomas Jefferson.

September-November. As with any time of year, check the weather forecast as you're planning your days on the trail.

Facilities: None at the trailhead.

▼ TRAIL TO HAWKSBILL SUMMIT

TOP EXPERIENCE

91

CEDAR RUN-WHITEOAK CIRCUIT

SHENANDOAH NATIONAL PARK, VIRGINIA

Eight waterfalls make this difficult hike worth the effort, especially when you take the time for a refreshing dip or wade in the plunge pools.

- **Distance:** 7.7 mi (12.4 km) round-trip
- **Duration:** 6-8 hours
- **Elevation Gain:** 2,274 ft (693 m)
- **Effort:** Strenuous
- **When:** Year-round, best June-Sept.
- **Trailhead:** Hawksbill Gap parking area

HIGHLIGHT: Swimming in waterfall pools along Whiteoak Canyon Trail

You can sum this loop hike up in three words: uphill, downhill, waterfalls.

START THE HIKE

From the **parking area,** follow the blue blazes onto **Cedar Run Trail,** which begins a gentle descent into the woods but soon grows steeper, with a few sections in the range of a -35 percent grade. Fortunately, the scenery—seven-story trees, trailside wildflowers and mushrooms, wildlife,

◄ HIKERS ON CEDAR RUN-WHITEOAK CIRCUIT

▼ MUSHROOMS ALONG CEDAR RUN TRAIL

▼ CEDAR RUN-WHITEOAK CIRCUIT

and a few scattered waterfalls—make this leg of the trip entertaining. At 1.3 mi (2.1 km) into the hike you'll reach a **pool and stream crossing,** and at 1.7 mi (2.7 km) you'll reach **Cedar Run Falls,** one of those "natural water slide" falls (when the water's high enough) and a deep plunge pool. A huge rock cliff—called **Halfmile Cliff**—stands on the northeast side of the creek and is one of many cliffs on this hike that offer freeclimbing and bouldering opportunities. At the 3-mi (4.8-km) mark you'll be at the bottom, ready to climb into waterfall country.

Once you've rested, it's time to ascend **Whiteoak Canyon Trail.** The trail can be steep and rocky, but you won't need to shimmy under or clamber over anything, just a few high steps and areas where you need to pay attention to your footing. On the climb up you'll pass at least **six sizable waterfalls** and many **smaller falls and cascades.** At some of these you'll find **plunge pools** deep enough for a refreshing dunk; at others you can wade or give your feet a break from the trail. Spur trails—often unmarked—lead a few dozen yards from the trail or from higher vantage points to the plunge pools and perfect picnic spots. Along the way you'll also spot several cliff faces and off-trail boulders frequented by rock climbers.

Follow Whiteoak Canyon Trail uphill for 2.7 mi (4.3 km) until you reach **Upper Whiteoak Falls** and the junction with Skyland-Big Meadows Horse Trail and Whiteoak Canyon Fire Road. Ignore the Horse Trail (it takes a sharp right turn) and Whiteoak Canyon Trail (which proceeds straight ahead), and follow **Whiteoak Canyon Fire Road** (to the left, marked with yellow blazes) for 2.2 mi (3.5 km) until you meet the junction with Cedar Run Trail, which leads 200 yd (183 m) or so to the parking area.

DIRECTIONS

Cedar Run-Whiteoak Circuit is in the Central District of Shenandoah National Park. From Luray, take US 211 East for 9 mi (14.5 km). Take the Skyline Drive exit, then continue on Skyline Drive for 14.2 mi (22.9 km). You'll find the parking area and trailhead for Cedar Run-Whiteoak Circuit at Milepost 45.5 (across from the Hawksbill Loop Trailhead).

NEED TO KNOW

Info: Harry F. Byrd, Sr. Visitor Center, www.nps.gov/shen

Passes and Reservations: Entry into the park is $30/vehicle ($25/motorcycle, $15/pedestrian or cyclist). Passes are available in advance at www.recreation.gov.

Weather Considerations: Throughout summer and fall there's a chance for sudden thunderstorms, so you should pack your rain gear and monitor the day's forecast. Shenandoah is a great four-season park, though with winter weather comes the chance of snow and ice on the trail and the occasional closure of Skyline Drive. As with any time of year, check the weather forecast as you're planning your days on the trail.

Facilities: None at the trailhead.

BEST NEARBY

Pale Fire Brewing Company

▶ *217 S. Liberty St., Harrisonburg; 540/217-5452; www.palefirebrewing.com; noon-10pm Sun.-Thurs., noon-11pm Fri.-Sat.; $8-35*

Pale Fire Brewing Company, a one-hour drive west of the Hawksbill Gap parking area in downtown Harrisonburg, serves up cold beers and hot Detroit-style pizzas. They're open late, which is perfect for evenings you come off the trail around sunset. The beer list focuses on IPAs but also includes sours, stouts, and seasonal offerings, and the pizzas are square, deep-dish pies with a perfect crown of crispy cheese on the edges. The folks here are friendly and fun, so don't hesitate to ask for a great breakfast recommendation while you're here.

Other: Before you set off, be sure to bring plenty of water and a lunch or substantial snack, as this is a true day-trip trail. Hiking poles will come in handy for the uphill and downhill sections, and if you plan on dipping into any swimming holes or wading in the creek, bring your bathing suit and a towel. Be aware that the water's cold here year-round, and that waterfalls and their plunge pools can be dangerous, so use caution. Part of this trail—Whiteoak Canyon Fire Road—is equestrian-friendly, so watch your feet for signs of horses and be a courteous hiker if you meet any riders on the trail.

▼ DOGS ON WHITEOAK CANYON TRAIL

92

BEARFENCE MOUNTAIN TRAIL

SHENANDOAH NATIONAL PARK, VIRGINIA

Hike to the top of Bearfence Mountain for a commanding, 360-degree view of Shenandoah National Park that dazzles throughout autumn and impresses with the daily sunrise and sunset.

- **Distance:** 1 mi (1.6 km) round-trip
- **Duration:** 1-1.5 hours
- **Elevation Gain:** 243 ft (74 m)
- **Effort:** Moderate-strenuous
- **When:** Year-round, best Sept.-Nov.
- **Trailhead:** Bearfence Mountain parking area

HIGHLIGHT: Catching a sunrise or sunset from the Bearfence Mountain summit

This short trail leads to a spot where you can take in a spectacular sunrise or sunset (or both), presenting a challenge and bit of bragging rights thanks to a rock scramble through a boulder field. No technical gear or real technical climbing experience is required—just common sense, a little upper-body strength, and the ability to determine when it's time to pack it in and turn back for the trailhead. Be advised that this hike is not for small children (especially those who need to be carried).

If you're a determined stargazer or astrophotographer, this can be a good place to set up, but there are easier places in the park where you can admire a dark patch of sky.

▲ AUTUMN VIEWS ALONG SKYLINE DRIVE

▼ BEARFENCE MOUNTAIN TRAIL

START THE HIKE

Cross Skyline Drive from the **parking area** and begin **Bearfence Mountain Trail.** It climbs uphill quickly, and at 0.1 mi (0.2 km) the blue-blazed trail crosses the **Appalachian Trail.** Continue straight on Bearfence Mountain Trail, which immediately gets rocky, and you'll begin to make your way through huge boulders.

The **boulder field** is only a couple of hundred yards long, though it feels longer and it's daunting despite its size. Rangers in Shenandoah do not recommend this hike for small children, especially if they need to be carried. Though it's not necessary to have rock-climbing expertise or equipment, the scramble here will test you: At times you'll scoot along on your rump; at other times you'll be on narrow ledges with fall exposure. Pick your way through the boulders, following the blue blazes, and at 0.4 mi (0.6 km) you'll reach the summit (3,640 ft/1,109 m), as evidenced by the view: You can see everything from here.

With the panoramic views from the top, this hike offers exceptional scenery throughout fall. These same panoramic views make **sunrise** and **sunset** especially gorgeous as the peaks and valleys in and around Shenandoah National Park glow with golden-hour hues. If you're climbing to the top for sunrise or sunset, be sure of your trail abilities and pack your headlamp; it's also advisable to make your way out of the boulder field before dark sets in.

There are two ways back, one a little shorter. You can return to the parking lot the way you arrived, an out-and-back route of only 0.8 mi (1.3 km), or you can turn right from the summit for a slightly longer loop. Continue on the trail for 0.5 mi (0.8 km) to reach a second junction with the Appalachian Trail. This time, turn right and follow the AT north to the first junction with Bearfence Mountain Trail, then turn left for the parking area.

DIRECTIONS

Bearfence Mountain Trail is in the Central District of Shenandoah National Park. From Luray, take US 211 East for 9 mi (14.5 km). Take the Skyline Drive exit, then continue on Skyline Drive for 25.1 mi (40.4 km). You'll find the parking area and trailhead for Bearfence Mountain at Milepost 56.4.

NEED TO KNOW

Info: Harry F. Byrd, Sr. Visitor Center, www.nps.gov/shen

Passes and Reservations: Entry into the park is $30/vehicle ($25/motorcycle, $15/pedestrian or cyclist). Passes are available in advance at www.recreation.gov.

Weather Considerations: In summer, rattlesnakes sometimes visit the rocks, so be cautious with your hand and foot placement during warmer months. Sudden thunderstorms can pop up during spring and summer, and in winter, snow and ice may cause difficult patches on the trail or force the occasional closure of Skyline Drive. As always, double-check weather and road conditions before you head out for the trail. Fall foliage season is the best time to do this hike. Peak leaf color generally happens in mid-late October.

Facilities: None at the trailhead.

BEST NEARBY

Big Meadows Lodge

▶ *Milepost 51 Skyline Drive; 877/847-1919; www.goshenandoah.com; mid-Apr.-mid-Nov.; $166-350*

Campgrounds and cabins abound in Shenandoah National Park, but if you're going to spend the night here, try for a reservation at Big Meadows Lodge. Located in the heart of the park just behind the Byrd Visitor Center, Big Meadows Lodge offers lodge rooms, small cabins, pet-friendly rooms, suites, and more. Many rooms have fireplaces, and sunset views from the lodge are dazzling. While you're here, you can stay fed at the **Spottswood Dining Room** (7:30am-10am, noon-2:30pm, and 5pm-9pm daily; $4-28) and **New Market Taproom** (2:30pm-10pm Sun.-Thurs., 2pm-10pm Fri.-Sat.; $7-18).

▲ VIEW OF THE BLUE RIDGE MOUNTAINS FROM BEARFENCE MOUNTAIN

93

OLD RAG MOUNTAIN TRAIL

SHENANDOAH NATIONAL PARK, VIRGINIA

Hiking Old Rag Mountain is a rite of passage for many visitors to Shenandoah National Park and offers stunning views.

- **Distance:** 5.8-9.3 mi (9.3-15 km) round-trip
- **Duration:** 7-8 hours
- **Elevation Gain:** 2,605 ft (794 m)
- **Effort:** Strenuous
- **When:** June-Oct.
- **Trailhead:** Old Rag parking area

HIGHLIGHT: Climbing over granite boulders to views of the Blue Ridge Mountains

Be sure of your fitness and skills before setting out on this hike because you'll be required to shimmy through narrow chimneys and between boulders, climb over rocks and boulders in the path, and jump from boulder to boulder in places. For this reason, I don't recommend this hike for younger kids and other hikers who aren't independent on the trail.

While this challenging hike is not one to take lightly, tough hikes like this pay out with truly astounding views and sections of trail that you'll talk about for years. With absolutely jaw-dropping panoramic views of the Blue Ridge and surrounding valleys, this hike is one for the books.

◀ ENJOYING THE VIEWS FROM OLD RAG'S SUMMIT

▼ BLUE BLAZES ALONG OLD RAG MOUNTAIN TRAIL

START THE HIKE

Park in the Upper, Lower, or Overflow lots and make your way to the **ranger check-in station.** After checking in, cross the footbridge and begin the blue-blazed trail as it climbs steadily, growing much steeper as you ascend the ridge. In 1.25 mi (2 km) you'll reach the top of the ridge and emerge onto the rocks. This is where the scramble begins. As you climb over granite boulders, you'll have some wide Piedmont views or closer **views of Weakley Hollow and the Blue Ridge Mountains.** Take a moment here to pull your gaze from the trail and admire your surroundings. In spring and summer the mountains are an undulating blanket of a hundred shades of green, but come autumn you'll have a treat in every direction: fall color blazing on the slopes of the Blue Ridge Mountains and lending shape and texture to distant fields and rolling hills.

At 2.8 mi (4.5 km) in, you'll be convinced you've reached the summit. A rocky outcropping here reveals views you could spend a day admiring, but despite the crowds sitting here taking a breather and a few pics, this is the first false summit; the trail continues through the trees for another 0.1 mi (0.2 km) and soon you'll see the second false summit. You can turn around here, retracing your steps for a 5.8-mi (9.3-km) round-trip hike to a beautiful viewpoint and a taste of the challenging trail. Or you can press on to the highest peak. If you press on, the boulder scramble gets tough, leading through narrow channels, a miniature cave, and up extremely steep and rocky slopes (at times you may wish for sticky climbing shoes). In another 0.7 mi (1.1 km) you'll reach the summit area, marked by a brown trail marker indicating the route down. The **true summit** is marked with a concrete post down a short (200-yd/183-m) side trail.

Some hikers turn back here, climbing down through that gnarly boulder field, but the **Saddle Trail,** which descends the back side of the mountain, is the preferred route. From the summit you'll descend along Saddle Trail 0.4 mi (0.6 km) to the **Byrds Nest Shelter No. 1** (day-use only; the only facilities are a picnic table), then follow the trail 1.1 mi (1.8 km) to the **Old Rag Shelter** (picnic tables, primitive privy), where you'll meet up with Old Rag Fire Road. Take this road 0.4 mi (0.6 km) and turn right onto **Weakley Hollow Fire Road** for 2.6 mi (4.2 km) to reach a parking area and a short set of stairs leading up to the **Ridge Access Trail.** Ascend Ridge Access Trail for 0.4 mi (0.6 km) to the T junction, turn left, and return to the parking area in 0.7 mi (1.1 km).

DIRECTIONS

Though Old Rag peak lies inside Shenandoah National Park, the trailhead is outside the park, near the community of Nethers. Before you head out to this trail, be sure to load driving directions on your navigation system or GPS as service gets spotty near the trailhead. From Luray, take US 211 East for 15.6 mi (25.1 km) to US 522 South in Sperryville. Follow the signs to Highway 231/F. T. Valley Road south and stay on this road for 7.8 mi (12.6 km). Turn right onto Highway 601/Peola Mills Road and continue until Highway 601 turns into Highway 707/Nethers Road. Just over 1 mi (1.6 km) from Nethers, you'll reach the parking area and trailhead to Old Rag Mountain.

NEED TO KNOW

Info: Harry F. Byrd, Sr. Visitor Center, www.nps.gov/shen

Passes and Reservations: Entry into the park is $30/vehicle ($25/motorcycle, $15/pedestrian or cyclist). Each hiker will also need to obtain an Old

BEST NEARBY

Spacious Skies Shenandoah Views

▶ *3402 Kimball Rd., Luray; 540/743-7222; https://spaciousskiescampgrounds.com/shenandoah-views; year-round; $22-120*

This campground sits just 2 mi (3.2 km) north of Luray, Virginia, a town with a number of hiker-friendly restaurants and the famed **Luray Caverns** (www.luraycaverns.com), and only 45 minutes (29 mi/47 km) from the trailhead; Skyline Drive sits 12 mi (19.3 km) east. At Spacious Skies you'll find plenty of RV and tent sites (from primitive to full hookups), and cabins and yurts fit for a couple or a small group. There's also a dog park, a seasonal swimming pool and playground, and a camp store on-site. It's easy to get to and makes a convenient base camp for exploring Shenandoah National Park.

▲ OLD RAG'S FALSE SUMMIT

Rag day-use ticket. Passes are available in advance at www.recreation.gov. For more information, see page 506.

Weather Considerations: Exposure near the summit is total, so if there's the chance of bad weather (especially lightning), keep an eye on the sky. Though Shenandoah is a great four-season park, before you take on this trail during the depths of winter, check the forecast as well as current road and trail conditions—winter snow and ice can create dangerous conditions on this hike and will occasionally force the closure of Skyline Drive and nearby roads.

Facilities: Primitive restrooms are available in the parking area, but bring your own water.

Other: Prepare for a full, strenuous day by bringing a map, good shoes, at least 2 quarts or liters of water per person, an emergency kit, food, and your trekking poles. Before you go, visit www.nps.gov/shen and watch the video about safety on Old Rag Mountain.

▲ OLD RAG SUNRISE

94

ENDLESS WALL TRAIL

NEW RIVER GORGE NATIONAL PARK & PRESERVE, WEST VIRGINIA

This easy hike to Diamond Point Overlook offers big cliffside views of the New River Gorge and provides access for rock climbers looking for challenging routes.

- **Distance:** 2.2 mi (3.5 km) round-trip
- **Duration:** 1 hour
- **Elevation Gain:** 184 ft (56 m)
- **Effort:** Easy-moderate
- **When:** Year-round
- **Trailhead:** Fern Creek Trailhead

HIGHLIGHT: Watching the sunset from Diamond Point Overlook

Endless Wall Trail can be hiked as a loop or an out-and-back. If you're hiking it as a true loop, be aware that the final 0.5 mi (0.8 km) will be along the shoulder of a rural county road with a narrow shoulder. For that reason, I recommend taking on Endless Wall as an out-and-back hike.

START THE HIKE

From the **Fern Creek Trailhead** you're only 1.2 mi (1.9 km) from the Diamond Point Overlook and the best views of the hike. Follow the trail and in 0.5 mi (0.8 km) you'll cross **Fern Creek** and, depending on the time of

◀ MOUNTAIN LAUREL ALONG ENDLESS WALL

▼ NEW RIVER GORGE BRIDGE

▼ ENDLESS WALL TRAIL

year, have a limited view of the **New River Gorge Bridge** (to the west). Continue on, and in 0.3 mi (0.5 km) you'll see a spur trail leading off to the right; this provides rock climbers access to the base of the cliffs, though there is another **viewpoint** less than 0.1 mi (0.2 km) down the spur. Pass the next climbers' access point on the right, and at 1.1 mi (1.8 km) into the hike you'll reach the spur trail to **Diamond Point Overlook;** follow this to the rocky clifftop and take in the view. Sunset is simply amazing here, and sunrise has the potential to be a star (though sometimes thick morning fog keeps visibility to a few dozen yards). When you're ready to turn back, make a left on **Endless Wall Trail** and you'll be back in the parking area shortly.

DIRECTIONS

Endless Wall Trail is in the northern area of New River Gorge National Park & Preserve. From Fayetteville, take US 19 North for 2.3 mi (3.7 km). Turn right on Lansing-Edmond Road/County Route 5/82 and drive for 1.3 mi (2.1 km). The parking area is on the right side of the road.

NEED TO KNOW

Info: Canyon Rim Visitor Center, www.nps.gov/neri

Passes and Reservations: No entrance fee or parking pass required.

Weather Considerations: Through summer and fall, there's a chance for sudden thunderstorms in this part of West Virginia, so pack your raincoat and keep a watch on both the sky and the forecast; summer can be surprisingly humid, so bring extra water. Winter and spring can see sudden, intense snow, but most often it's cold and snowfall is scant. You'll encounter heavy fog here throughout the year, most often during morning and evening hours; when you do get fog, wait a little while and it generally dissipates. For best fall colors, visit between mid-October and early November.

Facilities: Restrooms are available at the Fern Creek Trailhead.

Other: Endless Wall is a dog-friendly (on-leash, please) trail that also serves thousands of rock climbers every year. The rock climbers come to access the hundreds of rock routes on the long, running cliff here, and it's likely you'll see or hear some while you're out. For this reason, be very cautious near the cliff edges. No special equipment or skills are necessary to take on the trail and sightseeing portion, but I do recommend bringing a blanket or something comfy to sit on if you plan on hanging out for a bit and admiring the long view of the New River Gorge and the bridge in the near distance. A headlamp or flashlight is advisable if you'll be here around sunrise or sunset, and a decent set of binoculars can add to your sightseeing pleasure.

BEST NEARBY

Adventures on the Gorge

▶ *219 County Rt. 60/5, Lansing; 855/379-8738; https://adventuresonthegorge.com; year-round; $39-699*

This resort sits on the rim of the New River Gorge and offers up jaw-dropping views of the New River Gorge Bridge in addition to a full spectrum of amenities. The swimming pool overlooks the gorge and bridge; the collections of cabins (from rustic to deluxe), tent and RV sites, and glamping options sit nestled in the trees for maximum privacy; and a pentad of dining venues dish up everything from coffee and breakfast to late-night drinks and bites.

And this place is full of adventure, including zip-line and canopy tours (from $94 adults, $60 kids); guided hikes, rock climbing, and mountain biking (from $99 adults, $64 kids); white-water rafting on the New River (from $129) and nearby Gauley River (from $139); and more. The white water here is big—both the New and the Gauley boast multiple Class V rapids, but there are beginner- and family-friendly rafting trips available too. This might be me getting sentimental (I grew up only two hours away and my first white-water trip was with my Boy Scout troop on the New River), but while you're in the park, you owe it to yourself to experience it as a hiker and a rafter.

▲ DAWN LIGHT ON ENDLESS WALL TRAIL

95

NUTTALLBURG TRAILS

NEW RIVER GORGE NATIONAL PARK & PRESERVE, WEST VIRGINIA

This strenuous hike leads through decades of coal mining history to the ruins of a once-bustling coal town and gives you the experience of hiking in West Virginia's steep, rugged mountains.

- **Distance:** 4.6 mi (7.4 km) round-trip
- **Duration:** 4-5 hours
- **Elevation Gain:** 1,076 ft (328 m)
- **Effort:** Strenuous
- **When:** Apr.-Nov.
- **Trailhead:** Nuttallburg Headhouse Trailhead

HIGHLIGHT: Exploring the Nuttallburg ruins

The Nuttallburg Trails are a series of seven interconnected trails that tell part of West Virginia's history: coal mining. You'll first visit an old mine and headhouse (where coal was loaded onto conveyor belts for delivery to waiting train cars) where a long, covered beltline stretches to the river below. At the river you'll find the ruins of Nuttallburg, where the foundations of homes, businesses, and churches stand on mostly level patches of ground. The tipple (where coal was cleaned and loaded into train cars) and old coke ovens (used to turn coal into coke, used for smelting iron ore) are interesting. Nearby stand the remains of a church and school that served Black coal miners.

◄ VIEWS FROM THE CATWALK UNDER THE NEW RIVER GORGE BRIDGE

▼ MINE ENTRANCE

▼ NUTTALLBURG TRAILS

START THE HIKE

This difficult trail begins its unrelenting descent right off the bat, heading downhill on a wide, steep, gravel road. Follow this 0.7 mi (1.1 km) and detour off to the left to visit the **Headhouse,** coal mine, and other outbuildings. Cold air will blow out of the mine entrance and you should take advantage before you check out the beltline heading downhill. Return to the trail and begin the steepest part: switchbacks descending 0.8 mi (1.3 km) until they meet up with a onetime railroad line for a blessedly level trail that passes beneath the beltline (for a great photo opportunity). Stay to the right and follow this mostly-level trail until you reach the junction with **Town Loop Connector** in 0.3 mi (0.5 km). From here you can break off onto **Town Loop Trail** for a look at the ruins and to meet up with Tipple Trail in one of two places: right by the tipple or nearer the coke ovens.

When you've reached **Tipple Trail,** explore to the west to see what remains of the coke ovens and to reach the former Company Store and **ruins** at Seldom Seen, or explore to the east to the Black church and school. Many Black miners, often recruited from the South, migrated to Nuttallburg seeking employment and better economic opportunities. They worked alongside European immigrants, facing grueling conditions, racial discrimination, and segregation both in the mines and in the surrounding communities.

Wander here as you will, just don't detour onto the working railroad tracks, which cut off direct river access. Once you've rested a bit, and had a little water and a snack, it's time to climb. The first bit—that 0.5 mi (0.8 km) from the tipple to the base of the switchbacks—isn't too bad, but once you start up the steep slope (at times it's a 40 percent grade) the going gets tough. Stay on this trail until you get back to the trailhead, resting as often as you need along the way.

DIRECTIONS

The Nuttallburg Trails are in the northern area of New River Gorge Park and Preserve. From Fayetteville, take US 19 North for 2.3 mi (3.7 km). Turn right onto Lansing-Edmond Road/County Route 5/82 and follow this road for 2.5 mi (4 km). Turn right onto Beauty Mountain Road/County Route 5/83 and at 0.1 mi (0.2 km), turn right onto Nuttall Cemetery Road into the Headhouse parking area.

NEED TO KNOW

Info: Canyon Rim Visitor Center, www.nps.gov/neri

Passes and Reservations: No entrance fee or parking pass required.

Weather Considerations: Through summer and fall, there's a chance for sudden thunderstorms in this part of West Virginia, so pack your raincoat and keep a watch on both the sky and the forecast; summer can be surprisingly humid, so bring extra water. Winter and spring can see sudden, intense snow, but most often it's cold and snowfall is scant. You'll encounter heavy fog here throughout the year, most often during morning and evening hours; when you do get fog, wait a little while and it generally dissipates.

BEST NEARBY

Bridge Walk Tour

▶ *57 Fayette Mine Rd., Lansing; 304/574-1300; https://bridgewalk.com; 9am-4pm daily; from $60*

The New River Gorge Bridge is impressive: It's the largest single-arch bridge in the western hemisphere, the third-highest bridge in the United States, and the 13th-highest bridge on the planet. From the river to the base of the arch it's 876 ft (267 m)—that's one Statue of Liberty standing atop the Seattle Space Needle with a little room to spare. Once someone bungee-jumped a truck from it (seriously, it was filmed for a commercial). And you can slip into some safety gear and stroll across the 24-in-wide (61-cm) catwalk hanging under the bridge for views of the park and bridge unlike any other. This three-hour tour gives you a taste of history along with the thrill of the catwalk stroll, plus the photos you'll share of your feet dangling nearly 900 ft (274 m) above the river will be the envy of your friends.

Facilities: None at the trailhead. There are restroom facilities near the tipple.

Other: This hike is extremely steep and strenuous in places, so come prepared with plenty of water and a hearty trail snack.

▼ NUTTALLBURG BELTLINE

96

DEEP CREEK LOOP TRAIL

GREAT SMOKY MOUNTAINS NATIONAL PARK, NORTH CAROLINA

Best for beginners, the trail is easy and in good shape—plus you'll hike past two stunning waterfalls.

- **Distance:** 1.7-4.4 mi (2.7-7.1 km) round-trip
- **Duration:** 1-3 hours
- **Elevation Gain:** 607 ft (185 m)
- **Effort:** Easy
- **When:** June-Nov.
- **Trailhead:** Deep Creek Trailhead

HIGHLIGHT: Seeing Tom Branch Falls in autumn

A pair of waterfalls in the first 0.7 mi (1.1 km) makes this trail a dream for families with young hikers or hikers with mobility issues. The wide, flat trail—part of which is the remnant of a would-be scenic drive in this corner of the park—has a few puddles and damp areas, but nothing significant enough to stop a stroller or many mobility aids.

▲ TUBING DOWN DEEP CREEK

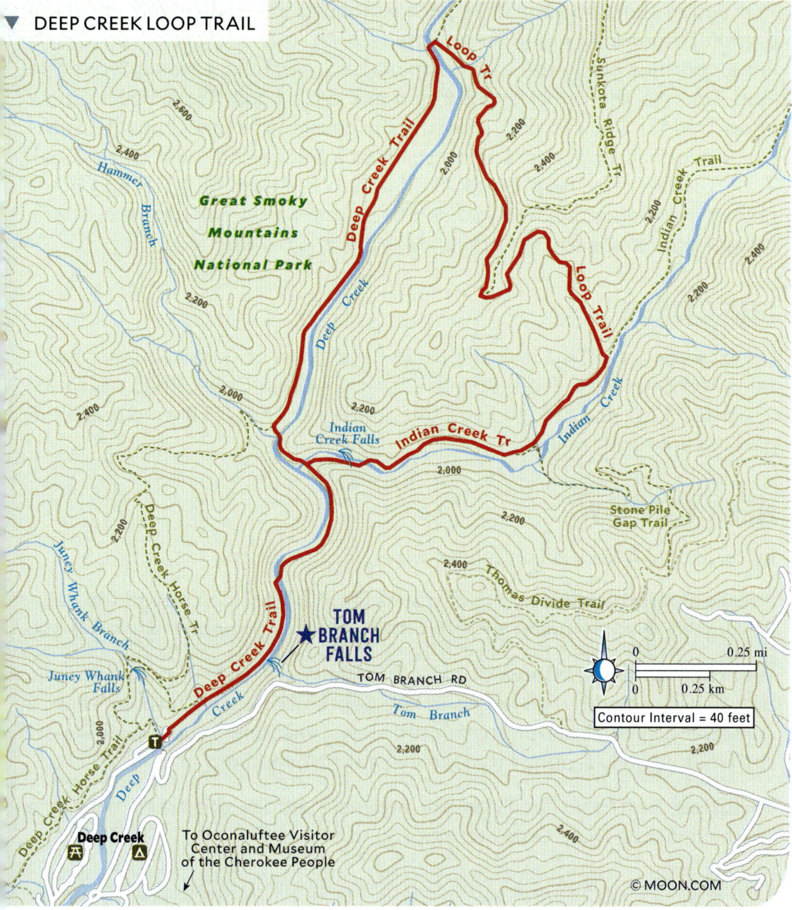

START THE HIKE

You'll find the trailhead for **Deep Creek Trail** 0.5 mi (0.8 km) up West Deep Creek Road, past the access to Deep Creek Campground. Just 140 yd (128 m) into the hike you'll pass the junction with **Juney Whank Falls,** a 0.75-mi (1.2-km) loop that leads to another small waterfall and terminates in the parking lot (adding this on at the end gives you a third waterfall without much additional effort). Continue straight and you'll encounter **Tom Branch Falls**—a 75-ft (23-m) plunge and spill into Deep Creek—in a spot where benches offer a place to admire the view and broad stone steps offer access to the creek for waders and folks headed downstream on their inner tubes.

Soon the path crosses Deep Creek via an automobile bridge and delivers you to a trail junction; keep to the right on the road-like Indian Creek Trail. As soon as you make the turn, you'll find a spur trail leading to **Indian Creek Falls**—a long, steep cascade surrounded by mountain laurel—though the falls are visible from the trail.

If you're short on time or require a mobility aid to hike, this would be a great turnaround point for a 1.7 mi (2.7 km) out-and-back hike. Otherwise, continue along the trail from Indian Creek Falls, passing Stone Pile Gap Trail (to the right) and turning left onto **Loop Trail.** You'll follow Loop Trail for 1 mi (1.6 km), climbing up, passing the junction with Sunkota Ridge Trail, then descending to cross a bridge and meet Deep Creek Trail. Turn left on **Deep Creek Trail** and in the next mile (1.6 km) you'll cross two bridges and find yourself back at Indian Creek Falls. From here, retrace your steps to Tom Branch Falls and the parking area.

DIRECTIONS

Deep Creek Loop Trail is in the Deep Creek area of Great Smoky Mountains National Park. From Bryson City, take Deep Creek Road north for 2.3 mi (3.7 km), and proceed straight another 0.5 mi (0.8 km) to reach the parking area and trailhead.

NEED TO KNOW

Info: Oconaluftee Visitor Center, www.nps.gov/grsm

Passes and Reservations: No entrance fee, but a parking permit ($5 daily, $15 weekly, $40 annually) is required. For more information, see page 512.

Weather Considerations: Both sets of falls are visible in any season, but when framed by fall leaves in late September-early October, they're something special. For unobstructed views, visit while the leaves are off the trees, usually around late October-mid-November.

Facilities: Restroom facilities are available across the creek from the trailhead at the Deep Creek Campground.

BEST NEARBY

Museum of the Cherokee People

▶ *589 Tsali Blvd., Cherokee; 828/497-3481; https://motcp.org; 9am-5pm daily; $12 adults, $7 ages 6-12, free ages 5 and under*

The Museum of the Cherokee People (formerly Museum of the Cherokee Indian) presents a vivid telling of the Cherokee's 11,000-year history in the region. From the retelling of traditional creation stories to the artifacts and objects that shine a light on the Trail of Tears and how a group of Cherokee resisted displacement to audio/visual and art elements telling more recent histories, you'll leave this museum knowing more about the Cherokee than any one history book could teach you.

Pair this with a visit to the **Qualla Arts and Crafts Mutual** (645 Tsali Blvd.; 828/497-3103; https://quallaartsandcrafts.org; 8am-5pm Mon.-Sat., 9am-4:30pm Sun. Mar.-Dec., 8am-4:30pm Mon.-Sat. Jan.-Feb.; free), a collection of traditional arts and crafts (basketry, wood and stone carving, weaving, beadwork, jewelry, and more) made by contemporary Cherokee artists. Even if you don't take a piece home with you, it's fascinating to see how contemporary artists use age-old methods and materials to express their—and the Cherokee people's—creative spirit.

▲ TOM BRANCH FALLS

97

ANDREWS BALD TRAIL

GREAT SMOKY MOUNTAINS NATIONAL PARK, NORTH CAROLINA

The highest grassy bald in Great Smoky Mountains National Park, Andrews Bald is a beautiful sight at the end of a nearly 2-mi (3.2-km) hike from Kuwohi.

- **Distance:** 3.6 mi (5.8 km) round-trip
- **Duration:** 3 hours
- **Elevation Gain:** 875 ft (267 m)
- **Effort:** Moderate
- **When:** July-Oct.
- **Trailhead:** Kuwohi (formerly Clingmans Dome) parking area

HIGHLIGHT: Appreciating summer wildflowers on Andrews Bald

Andrews Bald sits nearly 2 mi (3.2 km) down Forney Ridge Trail and is something of a rarity in the Smoky Mountains. Balds—like Andrews Bald and Gregory Bald (sitting high above Cades Cove)—are high-altitude meadows, and this one's the highest, at 5,860 ft (1,786 m). In summer, Andrews Bald is loaded with flame azalea and Catawba rhododendron, which color the meadow with orange-gold and rich rosy-purple blooms around mid-late June. In autumn the trail and bald give you the chance to hike among the changing leaves and take in the sweeping view of the North Carolina and Tennessee mountains while they're blazing with fall color.

◀ ANDREWS BALD

▼ TRAIL TO ANDREWS BALD

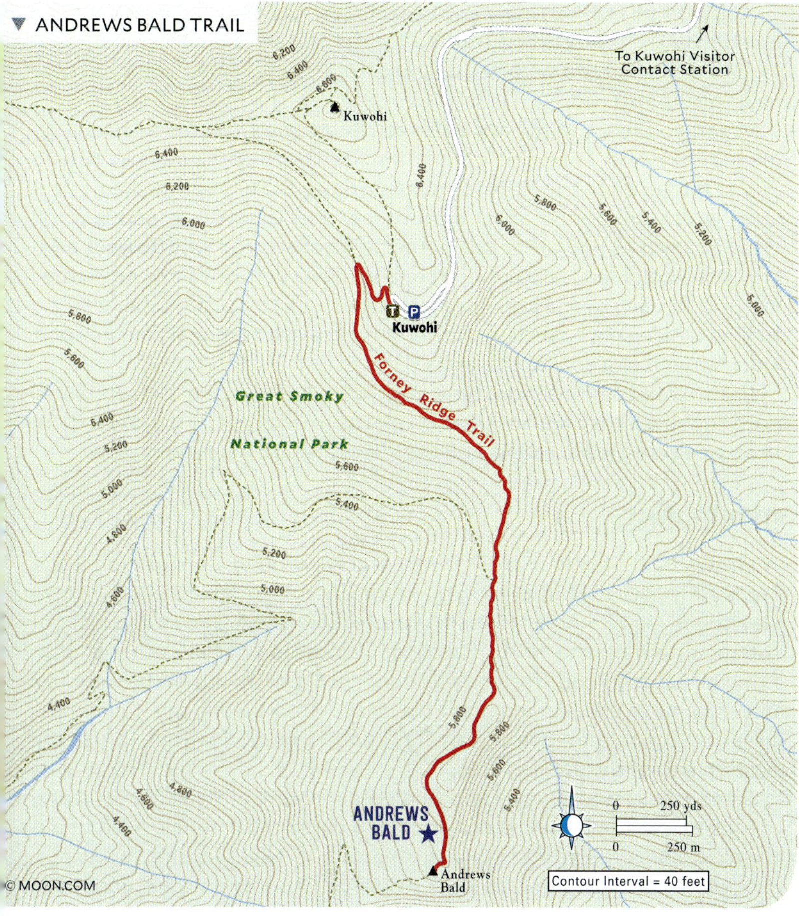

This hike begins at the Kuwohi parking area. Kuwohi—formerly known as Clingsmans Dome—is a sacred place for the Cherokee people and is the highest point within the traditional Cherokee homeland. The name change was approved in September 2024, following a formal request by the Eastern Band of Cherokee Indians (EBCI).

START THE HIKE

Head to the end of the **parking area** where the paved path leads to the summit of Kuwohi (formerly Clingmans Dome). Here **Forney Ridge Trail** splits off to the left, descending into the trees and leading to Andrews Bald. At 0.2 mi (0.3 km) you'll take a very sharp left turn to stay on Forney Ridge Trail. The first mile (1.6 km) of the hike is rocky, even with recent and ongoing trail maintenance, making for a tough bit of trail. Through this first section you may notice the forest looks a little ragged. That's thanks to the balsam woolly adelgid, a pest that devours Fraser fir trees, leaving snags—standing dead trees—in their wake.

At the 1.1-mi (1.8-km) mark you'll reach the low point of the trail and the junction with Forney Creek Trail (to the right). Take a breather and, staying on Forney Ridge Trail, press on uphill to Andrews Bald—you'll be there in 0.7 mi (1.1 km).

When you reach **Andrews Bald,** you'll find the trail disperses and almost disappears. That's ok; it's just a sign that other hikers have spread out a bit to explore the Bald, so you should too. In summer the flame azaleas (which only grow at high altitudes) and Catawba rhododendron draw butterflies and other pollinators, with scattered **wildflowers** adding more color and attracting more wildlife. Before following Forney Ridge Trail back to the parking area, I like to spend a little time here, refueling with a snack, reading a little, or maybe even grabbing a quick nap, and I recommend you do the same.

If you want to extend your time on Kuwohi, take the short, steep, paved path to the summit. An observation platform rises out of the trees there like some sort of spacecraft, and the views are 360 degrees of wow.

DIRECTIONS

Andrews Bald Trail is in the Kuwohi and Newfound Gap area of Great Smoky Mountains National Park. From Cherokee, take US 441 North/Newfound Gap Road for 19 mi (31 km) to Newfound Gap at the crest of the mountain on the North Carolina/Tennessee border. Turn left onto Kuwohi Access Road (formerly Clingmans Dome Road) and follow it 7 mi (11.3 km) to the parking area. Trailheads—to Kuwohi, the Kuwohi Bypass (leading to the Appalachian Trail), and Forney Ridge Trail—are at the eastern end of the parking area.

Since this is a busy area and finding parking is difficult, NPS recommends taking a shuttle instead of driving during peak times. A list of authorized shuttle providers is available on the NPS website (www.nps.gov/grsm); most shuttle services run March-October and cost about $25 per person daily.

NEED TO KNOW

Info: Kuwohi Visitor Contact Station, www.nps.gov/grsm

BEST NEARBY

Kuwohi Parking Area

▶ *Kuwohi Access Rd.; parking tags $5 daily, $15 weekly, $40 annual*

The parking area for Kuwohi, where this hike begins, sits at 6,300 ft (1,920 m) in elevation and offers 270-degree views of the mountains, making it a hotspot for sunrise and sunset photography. In peak times—autumn and during summer's crush of vacationers—the parking area can grow incredibly crowded. The crowds are thinner at sunrise, so get there early and admire the dawn before you head out on the trail.

Passes and Reservations: No entrance fee, but a parking permit ($5 daily, $15 weekly, $40 annually) is required. For more information, see page 512.

Weather Considerations: Mid-late June is best for viewing wildflowers, while late September-November offers the best fall colors. Kuwohi Access Road is closed for winter, generally December-April, but exact dates are dependent on weather.

Facilities: There are pit toilets in the parking area and modern toilets adjacent to the seasonal visitor center and small gift shop a few dozen feet up the trail. Potable water is not available.

▼ FORNEY RIDGE TRAIL

▲ ANDREWS BALD

98

ABRAMS FALLS TRAIL

GREAT SMOKY MOUNTAINS NATIONAL PARK, TENNESSEE

Hike through a lush forest to the picturesque Abrams Falls, known for its powerful flow and scenic beauty.

- **Distance:** 5 mi (8 km) round-trip
- **Duration:** 3 hours
- **Elevation Gain:** 617 ft (188 m)
- **Effort:** Moderate
- **When:** April-Nov.
- **Trailhead:** Abrams Falls Trailhead

HIGHLIGHT: Dipping your feet in the pool of Abrams Falls

At 5 mi (8 km), this hike makes for a great "long" trail challenge for novice and young hikers, and satisfies trail veterans thanks to Abrams Falls and the plunge pool. Along the trail you'll spot seasonal wildflowers, walk among autumn color, and find plenty of places to rest. After your hike, spend a few hours in Cades Cove looking for wildlife—the fields here are positively loaded with deer, turkeys, and even black bears.

▲ FALL FOLIAGE ALONG ABRAMS FALLS TRAIL

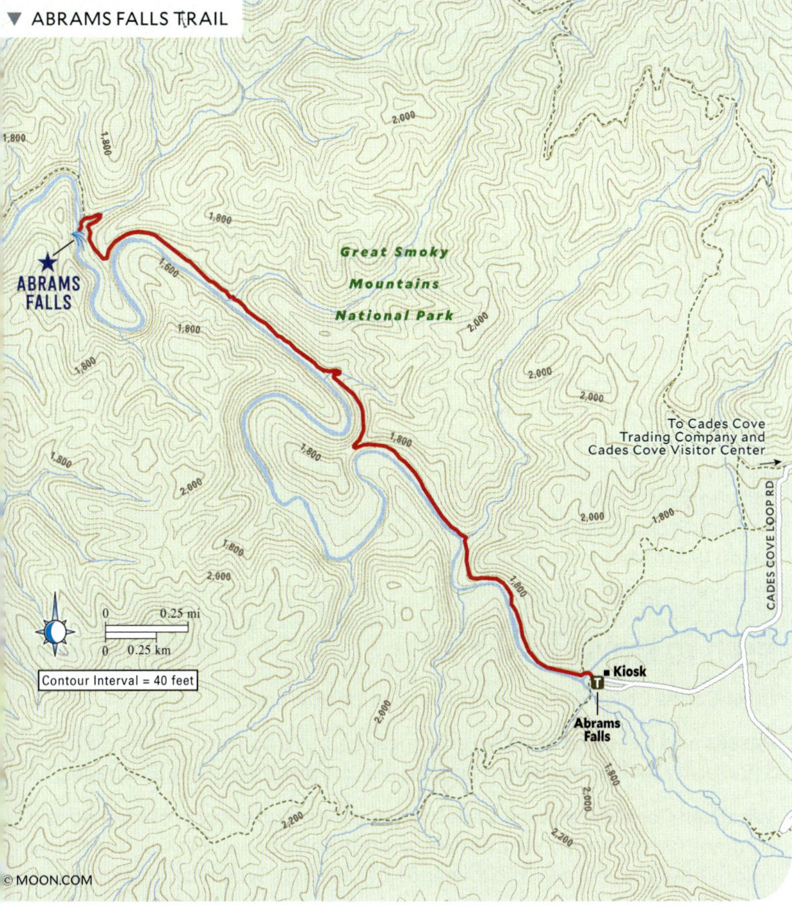

START THE HIKE

Several trails lead off into the woods from this parking area, but it's obvious which route to take—the most well-worn trail you see. If you're in doubt, follow the group in front of you, as Abrams Falls is the destination for most hikers who set off from this lot. Only a few steps from the trailhead is a **kiosk** that will set you on the right path.

The trail is pretty straightforward—it follows Abrams Creek all the way to the waterfall. The only real elevation gains come when you thrice leave the creek to climb up and around a ridge, crossing a feeder stream in the process. The first stream is Arbutus Branch, then Stony Branch, then Wilson Branch, which is very close to the falls.

After you cross Wilson Branch on a log bridge (these unusual bridges are icons of Smoky Mountains hikes), you'll follow the trail downstream, cross Wilson Branch once again, and arrive at the falls.

Abrams Falls is pretty, and in wet weather can be downright thunderous. Slick, mossy rocks make up the wall where the 20-ft (6-m) waterfall, which has the largest volume of water of any waterfall in the park, tumbles into the pool below. Tempted as you may be to take a dip after a sweaty hike, don't do it; the currents are strong, and a few folks have drowned here. That said, sitting at the edge of the pool with your bare feet in the water is a great way to refresh before you return to the trailhead.

DIRECTIONS

Abrams Falls Trail is in the Cades Cove area of Great Smoky Mountains National Park. From Townsend, take Laurel Creek Road 7.4 mi (11.9 km) to the Cades Cove entrance. Past the entrance, Laurel Creek Road becomes Cades Cove Loop Road. Continue driving on Cades Cove Loop Road for 5.1 mi (8.2 km), then turn right onto Abrams Falls Road and follow it to the parking area. (Note: The visitor center is approximately 0.5 mi/0.8 km past the turn onto the access road to Abrams Falls Trail; as Cades Cove Loop Road is one-way, don't detour to the visitor center before you hike, or you'll be in for a 5-mi/8-km drive from Cades Cove Loop Road to Hayatt Lane back to Cades Cove Loop and the trailhead at Abrams Falls Road.)

When you leave, turn right onto Cades Cove Loop Road and proceed 5.6 mi (9 km) around the loop until you reach the junction where the one-way road begins.

NEED TO KNOW

Info: Cades Cove Visitor Center, www.nps.gov/grsm

Passes and Reservations: No entrance fee, but a parking permit ($5 daily, $15 weekly, $40 annually) is required. For more information, see page 512.

Weather Considerations: Cades Cove grows incredibly crowded during summer (when family vacationers are out and about) and fall (when the color show draws tens of thousands of visitors), which can make Cades Cove Loop Road a virtual parking lot. Arrive early to avoid the traffic and

BEST NEARBY

Cades Cove Trading Company

▶ *10035 Campground Dr., Townsend, TN, at the Cades Cove Campground; 865/448-9034, bike rentals 865/448-2318; https://cadescovetrading.com; 9am-5pm daily Mar.-late Nov.*

For many folks, this is the first stop in Cades Cove. In addition to a great souvenir selection (my favorite Smokies tee came from here) and restrooms, there are snacks, grab-and-go bites, and a to-order deli serving burgers, sandwiches, and wraps ($4-9). This spot also serves as the campground store (campground check-in is just across the parking lot) and rents bicycles ($15/hour adults, $10/hour kids, $60/24-hour rental, group rental discounts available); if you arrive early enough on a Cades Cove's car-free Wednesday, you can rent a couple of bikes and pedal around the scenic loop.

to ensure you get a parking spot at the trailhead (parking is adequate, but not abundant).

Facilities: Primitive restrooms are available at the trailhead, but there is no potable water.

Other: Cades Cove is vehicle-free all day on Wednesdays May-September. This provides cyclists and pedestrians the time and safe roadways to explore Cades Cove a little more slowly, but if you're planning on a midweek hike, you might want to bring your bike to get you to the trailhead.

▼ ABRAMS FALLS

99

BIG CREEK TRAIL

GREAT SMOKY MOUNTAINS NATIONAL PARK, NORTH CAROLINA

This hike delivers both a waterfall—Mouse Creek Falls—and a swimming hole—Midnight Hole—on a streamside hike.

- **Distance:** 10.6 mi (17.1 km) round-trip
- **Duration:** 5-6 hours
- **Elevation Gain:** 1,316 ft (401 m)
- **Effort:** Easy
- **When:** July-Sept.
- **Trailhead:** Big Creek Campground and Picnic Area

HIGHLIGHT: Swimming in Midnight Hole

Big Creek is the site of a beautiful and seldom-visited frontcountry campground and has one of the best hikes for beginner day hikers and backpackers. Big Creek Trail, which follows an old motor road built by the Civilian Conservation Corps (CCC) in the 1930s, is smooth and wide with a very gentle grade for its entire length. It's more of an easy creekside walk than a hike, but it's long enough to make you feel accomplished when you're done.

◄ HIKERS ON BIG CREEK TRAIL

▼ BIG CREEK TRAIL

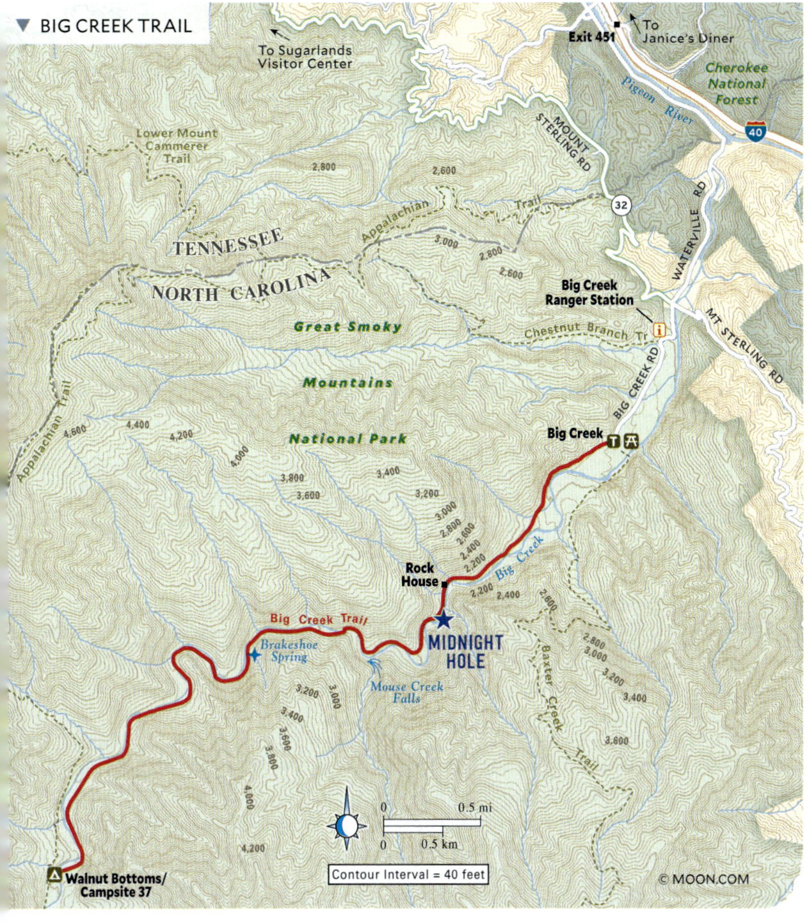

START THE HIKE

Roughly 1 mi (1.6 km) in from the trailhead you'll see **Rock House,** an impressive rock cliff that has sheltered more than a few loggers, Civilian Conservation Corps workers, hunters, and hikers from a rainstorm. Just beyond Rock House is **Midnight Hole,** where Big Creek flows through a narrow chute in the rock, then drops 6-7 ft (2 m) into a deep, dark pool before flowing on. Midnight Hole's broad, deep pool is one of the more popular swimming holes in the national park, but as few visitors make it to this isolated corner of the park, popular doesn't mean crowded. If you plan to swim, be aware the water is cold, even in summer, so a quick dip in spring or late fall isn't advisable. Bring a towel and your bathing suit, or if you're feeling bold—and there's no one around—just bring the towel and go for a dip au natural. Rocks and small boulders ring the swimming hole, so you'll find a place to dry off or just admire the view.

At 2 mi (3.2 km) in, you'll see **Mouse Creek Falls,** a 35-ft (11-m) cascade that drops right into Big Creek. It's a fantastic spot to sit, relax, take some pictures, and enjoy the woods. It's also a great spot to turn around if you don't feel up to the whole 10.6-mi (17.1-km) trip.

Push on past Mouse Creek Falls and you'll come to **Brakeshoe Spring.** In another 2.5 mi (4 km) you'll reach **Walnut Bottom** and Campsite 37. This is one of the best campsites in the park if you're going to make this hike an overnighter (which would require a permit). From here, it's time to retrace your steps back to the trailhead.

DIRECTIONS

To reach the trailhead, take I-40 exit 451 (Waterville) and join Waterville Road. You'll cross the Pigeon River and in 1 mi (1.6 km) (during which you'll cross the state line into North Carolina), you'll reach a four-way intersection at Mount Sterling Gap. Continue straight on Big Creek Entrance Road toward the Big Creek Ranger Station and the horse and group campsites, and reach the hiker parking area.

NEED TO KNOW

Info: Sugarlands Visitor Center, www.nps.gov/grsm

Passes and Reservations: No entrance fee, but a parking permit ($5 daily, $15 weekly, $40 annually) is required. There are no reservations or permits required for day use of this trail. For overnight trips and extended backpacking trips, permits are available at https://smokiespermits.nps.gov. For more information, see page 507.

Weather Considerations: Sections of the trail are rocky, so proper hiking shoes are recommended, particularly those with extra grip since the path can get muddy and slippery in wet conditions. June, July, and August have the highest amount of precipitation throughout the year.

Facilities: Flush toilets and potable water stations are available during the season at Big Creek Campground; cell phone service is nearly nonexistent, but an emergency phone is available at the **Big Creek Ranger Station** (236 Big Creek Park Rd.; 828/486-5910; Apr.-Oct.). Walnut Bottom is a primitive campsite with no facilities.

Other: The difficult part of this trail is the distance, so be sure to bring plenty of water and something to eat. **Note:** This trail was closed at the time of writing due to damage from Hurricane Helene. Check for updates before visiting.

BEST NEARBY

Janice's Diner

▶ *2765 Cosby Hwy., Cosby, TN; 423/613-5515; 7am-8pm daily; $2-12*

This cash-only spot in Cosby, Tennessee (16 mi/26 km, and 24 minutes, west of Big Creek), keeps it simple with a menu of home-cooking-meets-diner favorites. Biscuits, French toast, and loaded hashbrowns make breakfast a treat; for lunch or dinner go for the cheeseburger, fried bologna sandwich, or patty melt.

▲ MOUSE CREEK FALLS

100

BOARDWALK LOOP

CONGAREE NATIONAL PARK, SOUTH CAROLINA

This easy, accessible trail shows the highlights of the park, from huge, old-growth trees to the land and waterscape of an upland swamp.

- **Distance:** 2.3 mi (3.7 km) round-trip
- **Duration:** 1 hour or less
- **Elevation Gain:** 13 ft (4 m)
- **Effort:** Easy
- **When:** Year-round
- **Trailhead:** Harry Hampton Visitor Center

HIGHLIGHT: Walking among loblolly pines, water tupelo, and bald cypress trees

The Boardwalk Loop is an accessible trail, consisting of elevated and low boardwalks. A tiered ramp descends from the trailhead to the confluence of low and elevated boardwalks, a second ramp descends to the low boardwalk, and a third—at Weston Lake and a little trailhead there—brings the two boardwalks together again. This trail is marked with 20 information points (with explanations in a great little pamphlet) and offers dozens of views of truly impressive old-growth trees.

◀ ALLIGATOR AT WESTON LAKE

▼ WILD PIGS ALONG THE BOARDWALK LOOP

START THE HIKE

As you descend the ramp from the **Harry Hampton Visitor Center,** you're immediately surrounded by some impressively tall deciduous trees. Look among the near branches for the huge webs of golden orb weaver spiders, but also keep your eyes out for other wildlife: Squirrels are common on the drier sections of the trail, and you may see deer as well as the small wild hogs that live here (all the torn-up ground near the trail is from the hogs; their prints look similar to a deer, and you can easily see their tracks in the mud).

At 0.2 mi (0.3 km), take the low boardwalk and you're immediately in the swamp. The ground here is thick and muddy, and just a few inches of elevation change make a difference in the plant life here. Along the first stretch of the low boardwalk, you'll see impressive bald cypress trees with their "knees" rising from the mud and water around them. Cypress knees are an odd and beautiful sight, and you'll see thousands of them by the end of the hike.

When you reach the 0.7-mi (1.1-km) mark, the trail takes a hard turn left and you begin to find some **truly enormous loblolly pines (the tallest trees in the state), water tupelo, and more bald cypress.** Many of these trees are right beside the trail, but look deeper into the forest and you'll see trees 100 ft tall (30 m) and higher poking above the canopy. Along this stretch you stand a good chance of seeing a pileated woodpecker.

In another 0.5 mi (0.8 km), you'll reach the third ramp and ascend to the elevated trail. Take a minute here to observe **Weston Lake,** an oxbow lake where you might spot one of the few alligators that live in the park. Continuing along the elevated boardwalk gives you a different perspective on the landscape and the trees. Here you'll spot the South Carolina state tree—the cabbage palmetto—growing like mad. You'll also spot deer and possibly wild hogs, and if you're on the trail near sunset you'll hear the calls of barred owls echoing through the forest.

DIRECTIONS

The Boardwalk Loop is in the main area of Congaree National Park. From Columbia, take Highway 48 southeast for 18 mi (29 km); use "100 National Park Road, Hopkins," in your GPS rather than relying on general directions to the park. It's also easy to reach the park from downtown Columbia via public transportation. Route 61 (runs approx. every 8 minutes daily) and a transfer to Route 47 (runs every 2 hours Mon.-Sat., nonoperational on Sun.) on The COMET (https://catchthecometsc.gov; from $2), the regional bus system, will deliver most visitors from a central downtown location to the visitor center; an online route-planning map can provide specifics from your exact location.

NEED TO KNOW

Info: Harry Hampton Visitor Center, www.nps.gov/cong

Passes and Reservations: No entrance fee or parking pass required.

Weather Considerations: Summer brings high temperatures and humidity to this park and region, while heavy rainfall in winter and early spring can bring flooding. The low boardwalk usually floods—it's only a couple

BEST NEARBY

Palmetto Outdoor

▶ *803/404-8254; www.palmettooutdoor.com; shuttles run daily between Memorial Day and Labor Day, noon-3pm Sun.-Fri., 10am-3pm Sat.*

After experiencing Congaree from the Boardwalk Loop, join Palmetto Outdoor on a guided canoe trip ($100) through the national park. Knowledgeable and friendly guides will point out wildlife and flora of note while describing the natural and human history of the river and park. On these half-day excursions, you'll often have the opportunity to explore on land, so bring shoes and clothes that can get a little muddy.

Palmetto Outdoor doesn't have a retail shop; instead there's a seasonal outpost on the West Columbia Riverwalk where they rent river tubes and operate a shuttle for tubing enthusiasts; canoe and kayak trippers will meet their guides at the designated river access points.

of feet above ground level—but the elevated boardwalk seldom does. The entire park sits on a floodplain and experiences a dozen high-water events annually, prompting periodic trail and campground closures; information on closures, trail conditions, and weather is available at www.nps.gov/cong. Waterproof shoes are recommended.

Facilities: At the visitor center you'll find ample parking, gender-specific and family restrooms, as well as stations to refill your water bottles.

Other: You'll want plenty of bug spray on Boardwalk Loop or any other locations in Congaree National Park, but as the environment is sensitive here, please apply your bug spray in the parking lot. There's no special gear necessary for the Boardwalk Loop aside from plenty of water, but you'll want boots or something sturdy and waterproof if you're doing any other hiking.

▼ BOARDWALK LOOP

COWLES BOG TRAIL, INDIANA DUNES NATIONAL PARK

ESSENTIALS

PASSES AND FEES

ENTRANCE PASSES AND FEES

Entrance passes and fees range from free to $35 or more per vehicle; fees for motorcycles, bicyclists, and individuals on foot are slightly reduced. Once paid, most entrance passes are good for seven days. Many national park passes are available for purchase online. Some fees must be paid in person at the individual park entrances; some entrances, whether staffed or unstaffed, may be credit/debit card-only.

Specific Parks Notes

Indiana Dunes

Indiana Dunes National Park is next-door neighbors with Indiana Dunes State Park, and the two parks require separate entrance fees. It can get confusing, but you'll need to pay your $25/vehicle ($20/motorcycle, $15/pedestrian or cyclist) entry fee to the national park and a $7 fee for in-state license plates or $12 for out-of-state license plates for the state park. You can purchase the national park entry pass in advance at www.recreation.gov and buy your state park pass at the entry gate or online at www.in.gov/dnr.

Redwood

Redwood National and State Parks sits on the coast of California, entwined with three other state parks; trails lead from one park to the other and it can get confusing to first-time visitors and California residents alike. Redwood National Park doesn't charge an entrance fee or require a timed entry reservation, but at Prairie Creek, Del Norte Coast, and Jedediah Smith Redwoods State Parks, there is an $8 day-use fee payable at developed campgrounds and parking areas.

FEE-FREE DAYS

Admission is free on fee-free days:

- Martin Luther King Jr. Day (Jan.)
- the first day of National Park Week (Apr.)
- Juneteenth (June 19)
- Anniversary of the Great American Outdoors Act (Aug.)
- National Public Lands Day (Sept.)
- Veterans Day (Nov. 11)

TIMED ENTRY PASSES AND VEHICLE RESERVATIONS

National parks are wildly popular, which is a good thing and a bad thing. It's great to see more people engaging with the parks, enjoying the trails and scenery, and getting a much-needed dose of nature. But more people means more traffic, more congestion, and solutions that not everyone likes. Designed to mitigate congestion (and irresponsible actions like parking on roadsides, increased litter, and the like), timed entry passes help control the flow of traffic and visitors into the park, along certain corridors and scenic drives, and into specific areas of a park. Timed entry pass fees are usually in addition to entry fees.

Many uber-crowded parks are now requiring reservations (www.recreation.gov; fees vary) to drive certain **roads.** The reservation costs are usually in addition to entry fees. While each park's reservations open at different times, most offer two windows: 60-120 days in advance and 1-7 days in advance. The entry pass, timed ticket, and vehicle reservation regulations and fees can vary from year to year, so check with your park for current rules and fees before you go. Announcements about new policies are typically made November-December the year prior to implementation.

Many of us, this author included, have had difficulty securing our desired reservations, and unfortunately, there's little you can do other than try again with new dates and times. You can also try for walk-up reservations—many hike permits, backcountry camping or hiking permits, and frontcountry campsites set aside a portion of their reservations for day-of or week-of guests. So there are some second chances.

Note that this book doesn't cover all 63 US national parks or other elements of the National Park System (like scenic byways, recreation areas, or historic sites and battlefields), so if your parks trip includes a visit to a place not covered in this guide, check their website for current entry fees and timed entry regulations.

Specific Parks Notes

Acadia

In addition to your park entry fee, reservations ($6/vehicle) are required for driving Cadillac Summit Road late May-late October. Reservations are available only at www.recreation.gov. The hikes covered in this book do not require driving on Cadillac Summit Road.

Arches

In recent high seasons (Apr. 1-Oct. 31), all visitors have been required to purchase a timed entry ticket. Reservations (877/444-6777; www.recreation.gov; $2 pp on top of the park entry fee, paid on arrival) open three months in advance on the first of the month requiring the pass. Check before your trip to see if a timed entry reservations system is in place (www.nps.gov/arch).

Glacier

In addition to park entry fees, you'll need a vehicle ticket reservation (available only through www.recreation.gov; reservations $2/vehicle) for **Going-to-the-Sun Road** (when entering from the west) and the **North Fork** 6am-3pm daily late May-early September, and for **Many Glacier** 6am-3pm daily July-early September.

Haleakalā

If you plan on seeing sunrise in the **Summit District** or if you're hitting **Halemau'u Trail** before 7am, you'll need to secure a **Sunrise Reservation.**

It's only $1 and is available through www.recreation.gov, and it helps keep the overlooks and trailhead crowds manageable.

Mount Rainier

Timed entry passes are required for the **Paradise Corridor** 7am-3pm late May-early September; for the **Sunrise Corridor,** timed entry is required 7am-3pm early July-early September. Check www.nps.gov/mora for exact dates, rates, and availability closer to your trip.

Rocky Mountain

Timed entry passes (www.recreation.gov; $2) are required when visiting in summer. Advance purchase is required for timed tickets, although a portion of them are released one day prior, so if you're visiting last minute (or you forgot to buy your passes), find an area with internet access and try your luck. The Bear Lake Corridor is one of the most popular parts of Rocky Mountain National Park. In addition to park entry fees, you'll need a timed entry permit (www.recreation.gov; $2) for **Bear Lake Road** 5am-6pm daily late May-early October. Permit options include timed entry or timed entry + Bear Lake Road.

Yosemite

"Peak Hour Plus" reservations (www.recreation.gov; $2) to drive into or through Yosemite are required for travel 5am-4pm daily July 1-August 16, and 5am-4pm weekends and holidays April 13-June 30 and August 17-October 27. If you have in-park camping or lodging reservations, or a Half Dome or wilderness camping permit, show your permit or reservation and Yosemite personnel will waive the driving reservation requirement.

ANNUAL AND LIFETIME PASSES

Annual Passes

The **America the Beautiful Annual Pass** (www.recreation.gov; $80) admits entrance to all national parks and federal fee areas for up to one year. Most national parks also offer their own **Annual Pass** ($50-70) granting access to that one park for up to one year. All US fourth graders (https://everykidoutdoors.gov) are eligible to receive a free annual pass.

Regional Pass

If you're visiting multiple parks in southeast Utah, consider the **Southeast Utah Parks Annual Pass** ($55), which provides access to Canyonlands and Arches National Parks and Natural Bridges and Hovenweep National Monuments.

Senior Pass

US citizens or permanent residents age 62 and older have two pass options: an **Annual Senior Pass** ($20, $10 processing fee), good for one year, or a **Lifetime Senior Pass** ($80, $10 processing fee), which is valid for life. To purchase either pass, apply online (https://store.usgs.gov/recreational-passes) or bring proof of age (state driver's license, birth certificate, or passport) in person to any national park entrance station (processing fee waived at park entrances). In a private vehicle, the card admits four adults, plus all children under age 16. Four annual senior passes can be traded in for the lifetime senior pass.

Both senior passes grant the passholder discounts on fees for federally run tours and campgrounds; however, discounts do not apply to park concessionaire services like hotels, boat tours, and bus tours.

Access Pass

Blind or permanently disabled US citizens or permanent residents can request a lifetime **National Parks and Federal Recreational Lands Access Pass** (https://store.usgs.gov/recreational-passes; free, $10 processing fee) for access to all national parks and other federal sites. The pass admits the passholder plus three other adults in the same vehicle; children under age 16 are free. Passholders also receive a 50 percent discount on federally run tours and campgrounds. Proof of medical disability or eligibility is required for receiving federal benefits.

Military Pass

US military personnel and their dependents can acquire an **Annual Military Pass** (https://store.usgs.gov/recreational-passes; free), and veterans and Gold Star Families can get a lifetime **National Parks and Federal Recreational Lands Access Pass** (https://store.usgs.gov/recreational-passes; free) for access to all national parks and other federal sites. The pass admits the passholder plus three other adults in the same vehicle; children under age 16 are free. Passholders also get a 50 percent discount on federally run tours and campgrounds. Passes must be acquired in person at entrance stations; proof of service is required.

Volunteer Pass

Those volunteering in national parks or other federal lands can get an annual pass to all national parks by reaching 250 service hours. Service hours may be accrued in one year or across several years.

PERMITS AND RESERVATIONS

HIKING

To keep the trail experience high for all visitors, some parks have instituted trail-specific permits or reservations. In addition to easing parking problems, this helps with parking lot and trailside litter and the ongoing trail maintenance that comes with overuse. Some of the hikes covered in this guide require such a permit or reservation, but other trails you may discover while in a specific national park may require them, too, so check with your park's website before you leave and make the appropriate arrangements. Don't be disappointed if you can't get your desired reservation (it took me two attempts to secure an Old Rag day-use ticket in Shenandoah), just come with an alternate plan in mind or get a recommendation from a ranger once you arrive.

Specific Parks Notes

Redwoods

The Park Service limits the number of folks allowed on the trail to **Tall Trees Grove** each day (65 reservations available daily), so you definitely need to make a Tall Trees reservation if you want to visit. Reservations are free and available online (www.redwoodparksconservancy.org); when you confirm your reservation you'll be emailed a code (within 23 hours of your arrival) for the locked gate. You can apply for reservations up to 180 days in advance. During summer, holiday weekends, and other busy times, be sure to apply for your reservations well in advance. A handful of reservations are available the day before.

Shenandoah

The **Old Rag Mountain Trail** is immensely popular, and to control traffic on the trail, the Park Service instituted an Old Rag day-use ticket system in the summer of 2022. March-November, they issue 800 tickets per day through the online portal at www.recreation.gov (877/444-6777; $2), with 400 tickets made available 30 days in advance and an additional 400 released 5 days in advance. You'll need one ticket per member of your hiking party, and you'll need to pay the park admission (there's a park admission kiosk in the parking area; rangers check for both your parking pass and Old Rag ticket at the trailhead) if you want to climb.

Yosemite

During the summer, about 300 people a day make the trek to **Half Dome**'s summit, a number that is strictly regulated by a permit system. The permits are designed to limit the amount of hiker traffic on Half Dome's famous cables. Most hikers make the trek as a day hike, but whether you do it in one day or opt for an overnight backpacking trip, you need to have a permit. Permits are acquired via two lottery processes. The preseason lottery takes place throughout the month of March, with results announced in mid-April (apply online at www.recreation.gov or by calling 877/444-6777). If you don't succeed in scoring a permit in March, you can try for the daily lottery, which takes place every day the cables are in place. Only 50 permits per day are given out in the daily lottery, and you must apply for a hiking permit two days in advance of your hike.

Zion

A permit is required to hike any part of the West Rim Trail to Angels Landing. There's a seasonal lottery system ($3 pp; apply 1-3 months in advance; specific seasonal lottery windows listed at www.nps.gov/zion). You can also try your luck at getting a next-day permit ($6 pp); apply by 3pm the day before you want the permit. Both permit types are available at www.recreation.gov. And if you're bold enough to hike The Narrows from the top down, you'll need a permit (www.recreation.gov) for this full-route hike.

LODGES AND CAMPGROUNDS

During the busy summer months, accommodations can be hard to come by. It's common for national park lodgings to be fully booked up to 13 months in advance. Cancellations sometimes provide last-minute limited options. Most campground reservations are handled by www.recreation.gov, available six months in advance and often booked within minutes.

If you're planning a backcountry excursion, follow all rules and guidelines for obtaining wilderness permits for specific parks (www.nps.gov). Rules vary among parks, especially regarding fees, reservations, and procedures for picking up permits. Park-specific backcountry offices will have information on any health, trail, bear, or other alerts in the area. Check online for individual park Backcountry/Wilderness Trip Planners for assistance. For your safety, let someone outside your party know your route and expected date of return.

Specific Parks Notes

Capitol Reef

Camping is available for $25 per night and is reservable up to six months in advance. Backcountry camping, canyoneering, and rock-climbing permits are free and available at the visitor center.

Glacier

You can overnight at the rustic **Granite Park Chalet** (Belton Chalets; 888/345-2649; www.graniteparkchalet.com; July-early Sept.; $140 first guest, $95 pp after, bedding service $40 pp); reservations are required and online bookings for the upcoming summer go fast, starting in early January. Granite Park Chalet does not have running water, but it does have bottled water and snacks for purchase.

Grand Canyon

To stay overnight at any campsite below the rim, you must obtain a permit from the **Backcountry Information Center** (928/638-7875; $10 plus $14 pp per night). A lottery system governs **Phantom Ranch reservations** (www.grandcanyonlodges.com/lodging/phantom-ranch/lottery).

Grand Teton

In the popular backpacking areas of the Tetons, some campsites are assigned while others are designated to a backcountry camping zone. All backpackers are required to carry food in an approved **bear canister** (permit offices have loaners) and have a **wilderness camping permit.** Apply online (www.recreation.gov; apply early Jan.-mid-May; $20 plus $7/night/camper) to guarantee your permit in advance. First-come, first-served permits ($20 plus $7/night/camper) are available in person 24 hours before departure. Competition for walk-in permits is high in July and August; a line usually forms at the Jenny Lake Ranger Station or Craig Thomas Discovery & Visitor Center well before their opening. For more details, read the Backcountry Trip Planner on the park's website.

Great Smoky Mountains

Backcountry campers and Appalachian Trail thru-hikers will find information on permits through the **Backcountry Information Office** (865/436-1297; https://smokiespermits.nps.gov; 8am-5pm daily; backcountry permits

$8/night/camper, $40 maximum; Appalachian Trail thru-hiker permits $40). Reservations for the **Big Creek Campground** (reservations required; open May-Oct.; $30) are available through www.recreation.gov.

Isle Royale

The park's 36 campgrounds are free after you pay the entrance fee to the park. Campsites are first-come, first-served, and permits are required for all campers; if you're arriving by ferry onboard *Ranger III,* a park ranger riding along will issue your permit; otherwise, rangers will issue permits when you arrive on the island. Permits are free for small groups (fewer than six people) of campers and boaters; larger groups incur a fee (from $25), though they do have reserved campsites.

Mount Rainier

Hiking **Wonderland Trail** requires several nights camping in the wilderness, and that means you'll need a wilderness permit (www.recreation.gov; $6 nonrefundable lottery application or $6 reservation fee during the general on-sale; $20 recreation fee charged for all permits acquired through recreation.gov). See the Wonderland Trail listing on page 90 for a list of campsites and additional trip planning resources for Wonderland Trail.

Yosemite

Campsites are found close to the pair of **Cathedral Lakes,** but you will need to secure your wilderness permit far in advance in order to spend the night. Wilderness permits are available at www.recreation.gov 24 weeks in advance via a lottery system. It costs $10 for processing applications; if you receive a permit, you'll be charged an additional $5. You can have up to six permits at one time (meaning you can reserve for several trips all at once).

TRANSPORTATION

TYPES OF VEHICLES

Most of the trails in this book are accessible by normal passenger vehicles—cars, trucks, SUVs, minivans, and accessibility-modified vehicles—no 4WD required. A few of the more remote parks and trailheads do require a vehicle with high clearance, 4WD or AWD capabilities, or experience driving off-road. We've noted the parks and trails that require something more robust than the standard passenger vehicle.

Many visitors will fly to a destination, rent a car, and head to their chosen national park. If you're renting with the intention of driving off-road, be warned: Most car rental companies prohibit off-road driving and have limitations on towing/roadside service in off-road situations or increased penalties for damages to the vehicle (and don't think your credit card rental coverage or personal auto coverage will kick in here, because it won't cover breaking the rental contract). With the easy ability for GPS tracking, some car rental agencies may know if you try to hide the truth of your off-roading ways. When booking something 4WD, AWD, or off-roadable, call the car rental agency to check on availability and regulations for driving off-road (sometimes called off-pavement); they don't often keep these vehicles listed in online inventory, so a call will be more effective. If you're met with a "no" from the traditional car rental agencies, try contacting an overland shop where they outfit vehicles for off-road adventure; they may have connections, recommendations, or insights that will help you land the right off-road vehicle.

If you travel by RV, you won't have to worry about camping or lodging options, and many facilities, particularly farther north, accommodate RVs. However, RVs are difficult to maneuver and park, limiting your access to some trailheads and sights in national parks. Be aware that some national park roads ban RVs or restrict length. They are also expensive, both in terms of gas and the rental rates.

GAS AND CHARGING

The availability of gas for your car is limited inside the boundaries of our national parks. Many parks—Joshua Tree, Great Smoky Mountains, Congaree, and more—have no gas or fuel available, meaning you need to fill the tank (and your snack supply) at gas stations outside the park. For parks that do have gas stations, expect to pay prices well above the regional average.

Electric vehicle charging stations are starting to make a few inroads into the parks. Research availability before your trip; stations aren't as common as they are in cities. The NPS's **Electric Vehicle Charging Map** (www.nps.gov/subjects/sustainability/electric-vehicle-charging-map.htm) is a great resource.

ROAD CONDITIONS

Road closures are not uncommon, especially in winter in mountain parks. Traffic jams, accidents, mudslides, fires, and snow can affect interstate and local highways at any time. Before heading out on your adventure, check road conditions online with the applicable state highway department and the national park. Most national parks now maintain a hotline or presence on social media dedicated to updating road conditions; check with your national park for their specific method of letting you know about the roads.

In an emergency, dial 911 from any phone. The American Automobile Association, better known as **AAA** (800/222-4357; www.aaa.com), offers roadside assistance free to members; others pay a fee.

Be aware of your car's maintenance needs while on the road. The most frequent issues result from summer heat.

- Engine: If the car gets hot or overheats, stop for a while to cool it off. Never open the radiator cap if the engine is steaming. After the engine cools, squeeze the top radiator hose to see if there's any pressure in it; if there isn't, it's safe to open. Never pour water into a hot radiator because it could crack the engine block.

FOREST BATHING

There was a time I'd find myself distracted on the trail, too focused on the destination to enjoy the moment. When I read about shinrin yoku, known widely as "forest bathing," that changed, and I found that my connections to the natural world grew deeper, stronger, and more interesting. It transformed the way I approach some hikes.

Forest bathing originated in Japan as a way to help urbanites discover the healing, restive, restorative power of nature, all backed up by scientific studies that show how immersing ourselves in nature can reduce stress, lower blood pressure, and provide psychological benefits. And it works anywhere and everywhere.

It just so happens that it's easy to do—and our national parks are ideal places to practice a little forest bathing.

Try your hand at a bit of forest therapy next time you're on the trail; here are few suggestions on how to do it.

FIVE TIPS FOR FOREST BATHING

- **Pick the right location.** Find a trail, park, forest, or patch of nature that offers quiet and tranquility.
- **Unplug.** Disconnect from your electronic devices and digital distractions (I just flip my phone to airplane mode for a while and retrieve it from my pack later) so you can focus on nature. Remember to unplug from conversation too, so you and your hiking companions can focus on your inner worlds and the world around you, distraction free.
- **Engage your senses.** Observe the natural world with all your senses. Breathe deep, smell the flowers, note the fresh air of the forest. Touch leaves and stones, bark and petals, and note the textures. Get quiet and listen as the sounds of nature fill the void you left. Look at everything large and small, near and far: treetops, beads of dew on a leaf, the many greens of the foliage and the hues of wildflower blooms, the sky and clouds. Savor the place; breathe in and taste it on your tongue. Finally, tap into your memory—I think it's a sort of sixth sense—and find connections to this place and moment.
- **Slow down.** There's no destination in forest bathing, and no rush, so you can slow your pace to observe a place as you move through it, or you can stop, sit, and become part of the landscape for a time. Try to spend at least 10 minutes forest bathing, and if you hit the 10-minute mark, try for 20; the longer you do it, the more beneficial it can be.
- **Be present.** Focus on your breathing and set any intrusive thoughts aside for a moment. As your breath, heartrate, and thoughts slow, you create a space nature can fill, allowing you to immerse yourself in nature and the moment.

FIVE TRAILS FOR FOREST BATHING

You can practice forest bathing on nearly any trail in nearly any national park, but also in parks, wild spaces, and greenspaces near you; all you need is nature and a little solitude. Here are a few suggestions for hikes in each region that are ideal for forest bathing, but feel free to visit other trails and areas of your park to find the perfect spot for your practice.

- **Tall Trees Grove, Redwood:** Beneath the canopy of these titanic trees you'll find mosses, ferns, and a forest full of moments to discover. This trail's isolation adds to the quietude, deepening your experience (page 160).
- **Widforss Trail, Grand Canyon:** Find a spot between the edge of the woods and the canyon rim where you can observe both environments in quiet contemplation (page 206).
- **Teton Crest Trail, Grand Teton:** Long trails like this offer countless opportunities to practice forest bathing, from quiet moments in camp to solitary spur trails and overlooks (page 366).
- **Ledges Loop Trail, Cuyahoga Valley:** You'll find promontories to perch on, quiet nooks in the rocks, and trailside benches where you can sit and observe the natural world (page 424).
- **Big Creek Trail, Great Smoky Mountains:** Countless spur trails lead to boulders on the edge of Big Creek, or venture into the forest where you can observe the world in solitude for a while (page 492).

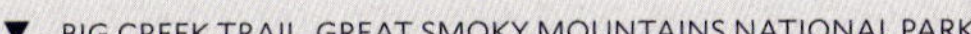

▼ BIG CREEK TRAIL, GREAT SMOKY MOUNTAINS NATIONAL PARK

- Tires: If you start to smell rubber, your tires are overheating, and that's a good way to have a blowout. Stop and let them cool off.

When descending steep mountain roads, use lower gears for the engine to force a slowdown rather than riding your brakes and wearing them down. During winter, a can of silicone lubricant such as WD-40 will unfreeze door locks, dry off humid wiring, and keep your hinges in shape. Mountain parks may require chains or traction devices for winter access.

PARKING

Parking can be an issue at well-visited parks, beloved trailheads and visitor centers, and during peak seasons and for special events. Some parks use timed entry for designated trails to reduce trailhead parking lot congestion and have taken measures—like fence and barrier installation and increased ranger patrols—to reduce roadside parking. If you want to minimize your own parking-induced stress and be a good steward of the parks, there are a few things you can do. First, show up at your trailhead early or at off-peak times to avoid the crowds. Second, park only in designated areas, not in a wide spot on the shoulder of the road; parking on the shoulder causes erosion and environmental damage and encourages other visitors to do the same, compounding the problem. Third, have a Plan B hike in mind.

I can't believe I need to address this, but here is it: Don't litter. Most parking areas in most parks have a place to properly dispose of trash and recycling, yet in park after park and on trail after trail I find trash. Cans, wrappers, bottles, even cigarette butts. Try using a bag from your grocery shopping as your in-car trash bag, and when it's convenient, drop the bag in the proper trash or recycling bin.

Specific Parks Notes

Great Smoky Mountains

Great Smoky Mountains National Park does not charge an entrance fee; instead, they use a parking pass system. The Park It Forward program (www.nps.gov/grsm/planyourvisit/fees.htm) launched in spring 2023 and instituted a required parking tag for anyone stopping for more than 15 minutes within the park. This means visitors cruising along the scenic **Newfound Gap Road** can stop to snap a pic and take in a little mountain air for a few minutes, but hikers like us will need that parking tag. Parking tags come in three varieties—daily ($5), weekly ($10), and annual ($40)—and are good only for the car they're in. Tags are available online, in person at visitor centers, and from kiosks around the park (including the Deep Creek Campground kiosk).

MAPS AND GPS NAVIGATION

Always travel with a printed map or guide; do *not* rely solely on GPS navigation, which is notoriously unreliable inside the national parks. Some park travelers relying on GPS get led to the wrong location, into dead ends, or onto closed roads, snowbound passes, or defunct roads. Carry up-to-date printed road maps and learn how to read them. Check seasonal access and weather conditions for all driving routes prior to travel.

Upon entering any national park and paying the park entrance fee, you'll be offered a free park map. These maps are good for paved road navigation and locating services, but they are not detailed enough for backcountry trails or rough 4WD roads. For topographical maps, download maps from **National Geographic** (www.natgeomaps.com) or order them from the **USGS** (http://store.usgs.gov).

INTERNATIONAL DRIVER'S LICENSES

If you are visiting the United States from another country and planning to drive, you need to secure an International Driving Permit from your home country before your arrival. (You won't be able to get one once you're here.) You must also bring your government-issued driving permit.

Visitors from outside the United States should check the driving rules of the states they will visit at www.usa.gov. Among the most important rules is that traffic runs on the right side of the road in the United States. Note that many states have bans on using handheld cell phones while driving. If caught, expect to pay a hefty fine.

GETTING TO THE PARKS

Having a car is typically the most convenient way to reach and explore most US national parks. Many parks are located in remote areas with limited public transportation options, and even within the parks, points of interest are often spread out over large distances. Parks closer to urban centers, such as Indiana Dunes and Congaree, may be accessible via public transport or rideshares. Still, a car generally offers the most flexibility for travel to and within the national parks.

NATIONAL PARK	NEAREST AIRPORTS	DRIVING TIME
	WEST COAST	
Denali	Ted Stevens Anchorage International Airport (ANC)	5 hours via AK 3 N
Wrangell-St. Elias	Ted Stevens Anchorage International Airport (ANC)	3.5 hours via AK 1
Olympic	Seattle-Tacoma International Airport (SEA)	2.5 hours via WA 16 W
North Cascades	Seattle-Tacoma International Airport (SEA)	2.5 hours via I-5 N and WA 530 NE
Mount Rainier	Seattle-Tacoma International Airport (SEA)	1.5 hours via WA 167 S
Crater Lake	Rogue Valley International-Medford Airport (MFR)	1.5 hours via OR 62
Yosemite	San Francisco International Airport (SFO)	3.5-4 hours via CA 120 E
Sequoia & Kings Canyon	Fresno Yosemite International (FAT)	1.5 hours via CA 180 E
Death Valley	McCarran International Airport (LAS)	From LAS: 2 hours via NV 160 W and CA 190 W
	Los Angeles International Airport (LAX)	From LAX: 5 hours via CA 14 N

(continued)

NATIONAL PARK	NEAREST AIRPORTS	DRIVING TIME
Joshua Tree	Palm Springs Airport (PSP) Los Angeles International Airport (LAX)	From PSP: 1 hour via I-10 E From LAX: 3 hours via I-10 E
Lassen Volcanic	Sacramento International Airport (SMF)	2.5-3 hours via I-5 N and CA 36 E
Redwood	Del Norte County Airport/Jack McNamara (CEC) San Francisco International Airport (SFO)	From CEC: 10 minutes via W Washington Blvd and US 101 N From SFO: 6 hours via US 101 N
Pinnacles	Mineta San Jose International Airport (SJC) San Francisco International Airport (SFO)	From SJC: 2 hours via US 101 S From SFO: 3 hours via US 101 S
Haleakalā	Kahului Airport (OGG)	1 hour via HI 37 and Hwy 378
Hawai'i Volcanoes	Ellison Onizuka Kona International Airport (KOA) Hilo International Airport (ITO)	From KOA: 2 hours via HI 11 From ITO: 50 minutes via HI 11
SOUTHWEST		
Grand Canyon	Flagstaff Pulliam Airport (FLG) Phoenix Sky Harbor International Airport (PHX)	From FLG: 1.5 hours via I-40 W and AZ 64 N From PHX: 3.5 hours via I-17 N
Saguaro	Tucson International Airport (TUS)	25 minutes to Saguaro East via E Valencia Rd 30 minutes to Saguaro West via I-10 W
Zion	McCarran International Airport (LAS) Salt Lake City International Airport (SLC)	From LAS: 2.5 hours via I-15 N From SLC: 4 hours via UT 36 and I-15 S
Bryce Canyon	McCarran International Airport (LAS) Salt Lake City International Airport (SLC)	From LAS: 4 hours via I-15 N From SLC: 4 hours via I-15 S
Capitol Reef	Salt Lake City International Airport (SLC)	3.5 hours via I-15 S and UT 24
Arches	Salt Lake City International Airport (SLC)	4 hours via US 6 E
Canyonlands	Salt Lake City International Airport (SLC)	4 hours via US 6 E
Mesa Verde	Durango-La Plata County Airport (DRO) Denver International Airport (DEN)	From DRO: 1.5 hours via US 160 W From DEN: 8 hours via US 285 S and US 160 W
Great Sand Dunes	Colorado Springs Airport (COS) Denver International Airport (DEN)	From COS: 2.5 hours via I-25 S and US 160 W From DEN: 4.5 hours via I-25 S

NATIONAL PARK	NEAREST AIRPORTS	DRIVING TIME
Big Bend	Midland International Air & Space Port (MAF) El Paso International Airport (ELP)	From MAF: 4 hours via US 385 S From ELP: 5.5 hours via US 90 E
ROCKY MOUNTAINS		
Rocky Mountain	Denver International Airport (DEN)	1.5 hours via US 36
Black Canyon of the Gunnison	Denver International Airport (DEN)	5 hours via I-70 W
Yellowstone	Bozeman Yellowstone International Airport (BZN) Jackson Hole Airport (JAC)	From BZN: 1.5 hours via I-90 E and US 89 S From JAC: 1 hours via US 20 E
Grand Teton	Jackson Hole Airport (JAC)	15 minutes via US 191 S
Glacier	Glacier Park International Airport (FCA)	30 minutes via US 2 E
Theodore Roosevelt	Bismarck Municipal Airport (BIS)	2 hours via I-94 W
Badlands	Rapid City Regional Airport (RAP)	1 hour via SD 44 E
GREAT LAKES AND NORTHEAST		
Acadia	Bangor International Airport (BGR) Boston Logan International Airport (BOS)	From BGR: 1 hour via US 1A E From BOS: 5 hours via I-95 N
Cuyahoga Valley	Cleveland Hopkins International Airport (CLE)	25 minutes via I-480 E and I-77 S
Indiana Dunes	Chicago Midway International Airport (MDW) South Bend International Airport (SBN)	From MDW: 1 hour via I-90 E From SBN: 1 hour via IN 2 W and US 20 W
Isle Royale	Thunder Bay International Airport (YQT) Duluth International Airport (DLH)	From YQT: 1 hour via MN 61 S From DLH: 3 hours via MN 61 N
THE SOUTH		
Shenandoah	Dulles International Airport (IAD)	1 hour via I-66 W
New River Gorge	Yeager Airport (CRW) Raleigh County Memorial Airport (BKW)	From CRW: 1 hour via US 60 E From BKW: 20 minutes via WV 41 N
Great Smoky Mountains	Asheville Regional Airport (AVL) McGhee Tyson Airport (TYS)	From AVL: 1.5 hours via I-40 and US 19 S From TYS: 30 minutes via E Lamar Alexander Pkwy
Congaree	Charlotte Douglas International Airport (CLT) Charleston International Airport (CHS)	From CLT: 2 hours via I-77 S From CHS: 2 hours via I-26 W

GETTING AROUND THE PARKS

As a way to ease congestion, improve the visitor experience, and be more environmentally sensitive, several parks have their own—sometimes novel—modes of transportation. This ranges from ferries and shuttle boats to complimentary bus and trolley routes within a park. As of this writing, a number of parks are considering expanding or opening new public transpiration routes, so check your park for updates before you leave the house.

Specific Parks Notes

Acadia

The **Island Explorer** (www.exploreacadia.com; free) buses offer 10 routes to and through Acadia National Park. Select buses are accessible, others offer bike racks, and all of them make regular stops throughout the park and will pick up hikers who flag them down. Island Explorer buses operate mid-June-early October. Schedules and live tracking are available via the **myStop** mobile app (available for both Apple and Android platforms).

Bryce Canyon

The summer shuttle (every 15-20 minutes 8am-8pm daily mid-Apr.-mid-Oct., shorter hours early and late in season; free) stops at Sunrise Point, Sunset Point, Inspiration Point, and Bryce Point. Sections of Bryce's main scenic drive may be closed in winter.

Crater Lake

A ticket for a boat tour or shuttle boat is required to access Wizard Island. The **Wizard Island boat tour** ($55 adults, $37 children 3-12) includes an interpretive talk by a park ranger, lake cruising, and a three-hour stop at Wizard Island. Tours depart at 9am daily in season. Including the stop on Wizard Island, the tour lasts approximately five hours total. The **shuttle boat** ($28 adults, $18 children 3-12) offers pick-up and drop-off and includes a three-hour stop on Wizard Island without the educational talk. Shuttles depart at 9am and 11:30am daily in season. The shuttle takes about half an hour to get to Wizard Island.

Boats typically run June-September. Approximately half the tickets for every tour or shuttle are available in advance, online (www.explorecraterlake.com), or by phone, and the other half are available 24 hours before each tour or shuttle at self-serve kiosks in the park's Crater Lake Lodge and Annie Creek Gift Shop. Any remaining tickets are sold at a booth in the parking area at the top of the Cleetwood Cove Trail.

Note: At the time of writing, the park announced boat tours would be suspended due to construction on Cleetwood Cove Trail. Check for updates before visiting.

Denali

Private vehicles are restricted within the park. In summer, private vehicles can't go beyond the Savage River Crossing at Milepost 15 along the park road. For this reason, you'll often be riding a bus. Buses come in two flavors: un-narrated transit buses ($33.25 ages 16 and up, free ages 15 and under) and narrated tour buses (reserve online at www.reservedenali.

com; from $116.25 ages 16 and up, $50.75 ages 15 and under). Transit buses are tan and tour buses are green; hikers should take the transit buses as they're intended to make frequent stops at trailheads and campgrounds, whereas the tour buses are essentially locked into a 4-5-hour tour and talk. Due to weather and road conditions, it's possible that both the transit and tour buses run shorter routes; refer to www.nps.gov/dena and to notices posted at visitor centers for current information. Note that camper buses—with fewer passengers but more room for gear—are made available for frontcountry and backcountry campers who have confirmed campsite reservations or valid backcountry permits. Bus services are available May 20-mid-September.

Glacier

The boat shuttle to shorten the **Grinnell Glacier** hike is run by **Glacier Park Boat Company** (406/257-2426; https://glacierparkboats.com; June-Sept.; adult one-way tickets $19.70, round-trip $39.45, ages 4-12 $9.85 one-way, $19.70 round-trip, free under age 4). Reserve in advance online.

Grand Teton

Jenny Lake Boating (307/734-9227; www.jennylakeboating.com; 7am-7pm daily early June-early Sept., 10am-4pm daily mid-May-early June and mid-late Sept.; round-trip $20 adults, $17 seniors, $12 kids, one-way $12 adults, $10 kids, no senior one-way tickets) runs the boat shuttle across Jenny Lake. Shuttles run every 10-15 minutes throughout the day. The last boat leaves the dock at the posted closing time. Reservations are not required.

North Cascades

The **Stehekin Shuttle Bus** (509/859-6070; www.stehekinvalleyadventures.com; $10 adults, $5 ages 2-11) carries hikers to spots along the Stehekin Valley Road, departing from Stehekin Landing and stopping at Stehekin Pastry Company (www.stehekinpastry.com), Harlequin Bridge, Stehekin Valley Ranch, and High Bridge (adjacent to **Agnes Gorge Trailhead**). It's 11 mi (17.7 km) to High Bridge. Shuttle services begin in early April and run through mid-October. During the slower shoulder seasons—early April-early June and late September-mid-October—shuttle services are by request, so make arrangements accordingly. At the peak of summer—early June-late September—shuttles leave Stehekin Landing at 8am, 11:30am, 2pm, and 5:30pm and leave High Bridge for the return trip at 9am, 12:30pm, 3pm, and 6:15pm.

Yosemite

The free **Yosemite Valley Shuttle** operates daily year-round, running a pair of loops to serve hikers, campers, and visitors. The Valleywide Shuttle makes 19 stops that include campgrounds and lodges, restaurants, and trailheads; shuttles arrive every 12-22 minutes and the service runs 7am-10pm. The **East Valley Shuttle** is limited to trailheads and campgrounds in eastern Yosemite Valley including Yosemite and Curry Villages; these shuttles arrive every 8-12 minutes 7am-10pm.

Yosemite Valley Lodge (www.travelyosemite.com) offers Yosemite guided bus tours to a number of locations in the park, including Glacier Point, the trailhead for the Panorama Trail (page 106). You can book a

one-way ticket (888/413-8869; www.travelyosemite.com; Glacier Point Tour available June 15-Oct. 13; $28.50) from the lodge to Glacier Point.

Zion

The **Zion Canyon Line** has nine stops between the Zion Canyon Visitor Center and the Temple of Sinawava in a trip of about 45 minutes. The **Springdale Line** runs between Zion Canyon Village and Majestic View Lodge. Both shuttles run daily March-November and briefly during December's holiday season (exact dates and times vary, check www.nps.gov/zion for schedules and details). During the Zion Canyon Line's operating season, the shuttles are the only vehicles allowed on the Zion Canyon Scenic Drive.

SAFETY

HIKING PREP

Choose an appropriate-length hike based on your abilities while also considering the elevation and steepness of the trail. Please know that most of the hikes listed in this book can be shortened (or lengthened); feel free to adjust accordingly. Once you have a plan, leave the hike information (name, location, trailhead, direction of travel) with a close contact, plus an outside time of when to act if they don't hear from you. Though satellite messenger devices and phones with GPS and SOS alert capabilities are increasingly common, these are battery-powered electronic tools that can fail. Be prepared with solid plans that you share with friends, plus knowledge about the backcountry and the following gear.

Experienced hikers and runners will tell you that proper footwear is everything. For the vast majority of hikes in this guide, "proper footwear" means a sturdy pair of hiking boots, though you can get by with trail runners or even sneakers on a few. With your hiking boots you may want to consider a cushioning or arch-supporting insole, and a pair of liner socks and heavier (wool or similar) hiking socks.

What to Pack for Day Hiking: The 10 Essentials

Even when hiking solo, I tend to pack more than necessary for a day hike; I usually carry a larger (22-26L) pack to fit it all. This helps when I'm hiking with children and/or dogs and need to carry extra items and snacks. The other end of the packing approach spectrum is ultralight—that is, carrying as little weight as possible, but still covering these 10 essentials. That's one of the benefits of using the 10 essentials as your packing guide—you can scale them to your hiking style. Of course, you'll also want a day pack that fits well and can comfortably fit your version of the following:

1. **Hydration:** Water bottle or bladder, minimum 1-2 quarts or liters of water; most hikers also carry a filtration system or purification

tablets. Your hydration needs will vary with temperature and environment, so always follow your park's guidelines (and bring an extra bit of water just in case).

2. **Nutrition:** Bring a few more snacks than you think you'll need, and not just the crappy bars that you'll never eat; bring something you like. Using a spare water bottle to mix up some hydration salts or "endurance fuel" powders to add essential electrolytes to your mix.
3. **Navigation:** Map and compass, GPS or satellite messenger device, and training/knowledge of how to use both.
4. **First-aid kit:** Adjusted for the length of your hike and the size of your group. I like to divide my hiking/backpacking kit into four sections based on the following scenarios: (1) cuts, scrapes, splinters, blisters; (2) burns; (3) meds for illnesses; and (4) trauma items like splints, sheers, tape, wraps. If you buy a premade kit, spend some time before your hike going through the contents and creating "what-if" scenarios to prepare yourself for the real thing.
5. **Light and power source:** Small, lightweight headlamp or handheld flashlight, even if you don't expect to enter any caves or be out after dark. Some lanterns can also charge your phone and other devices, or bring a separate power bank.
6. **Sun protection:** Sunblock, hat with a brim, sunglasses, SPF lip balm, lightweight sun hoodie.
7. **Insulation/layers:** Rain shell top/bottom and a midweight top, preferably lightweight wool or synthetics that keep you warm even when damp. In cold temperatures and seasons, wear a base layer of silk, synthetic, or merino wool long underwear. Add a wool or fleece mid-layer, and a packable puffy jacket for the summit. When starting a hike in the morning, I like to follow the adage "Be bold, start cold; start hot, sweat a lot" (Rob Steffens of Deuter Backpacks taught me that one while hiking Lost Man Pass).
8. **Fire:** A lighter, torch, and/or waterproof matches, perhaps a wad of Vaseline-soaked cotton or other small firestarter hack.
9. **Multitool or pocketknife:** For equipment repair or other unexpected needs.
10. **Emergency survival gear:** This can include an emergency blanket, tent/tarp for shelter, down quilt, or sleeping bag; a whistle; and SOS/satellite capability via phone or GPS device. Realistically, many short hikes and urban walking paths wouldn't require these items, but for more remote, longer hikes into wilderness areas, these things can save your life.

FIRST-AID TRAINING

Just as important as placing first-aid supplies in your pack is pre-trip training on how to use them. For first responders, "wilderness" is defined as being 1 hour or more away from a hospital, which describes many of the trails listed in this book. If you have the time, take a Wilderness First

Aid (WFA) course, often given over a weekend. If you can spare eight days, Wilderness First Responder (WFR) is an intensive, scenario-based course, usually taught in 60 hours over one week. Find courses via the Wilderness Medicine Institute and National Outdoor Leadership School (NOLS; www.nols.edu/wmi), American Red Cross, Colorado Outward Bound School, and Wilderness Medicine Training Center (www.wildmed-center.com).

HOSPITALS AND EMERGENCIES

Most national parks are tucked into remote locations where emergency services take longer to respond. Hospitals, emergency rooms, and urgent care facilities are often located outside the national parks in nearby towns several hours away. The larger parks with huge visitation numbers may have an urgent care clinic.

If you are injured in a park, dial 911 or the park phone number for emergencies. If cell service is not available, flag down a ranger or passing motorist to get help instead. Due to the remote locations of many national parks, do not rely on having cell phone service to call for help.

WILDERNESS SAFETY

For hikers, backpackers, climbers, and river travelers, be prepared to handle emergencies on your own. Be competent in administering first aid, self-rescuing, and providing your own evacuation. Only rely on calling for help in life-threatening situations or where severe injuries prevent you from being able to get out on your own.

Heat Exhaustion and Heatstroke

Being out in the elements can present its own set of challenges. Heat exhaustion and heatstroke can affect anyone during the hot summer months, particularly during a long, strenuous hike in the sun. Common symptoms include nausea, light-headedness, headache, and muscle cramps.

Dehydration

Many first-time hikers to high-mountain or arid parks are surprised to find they drink more water than at home. Wind, sun, altitude, and lower humidity can add up to a fast case of dehydration. It manifests first as a headache. Before launching at a trailhead, consult with rangers about current reliable water sources.

While hiking, drink lots of water—even more than you normally would. With children, monitor their fluid intake. In desert parks, plan to carry and drink 1 gallon (3.8 liters) of water per person per day. It's also a good idea to take electrolytes with your fluids, to keep the body's water and sodium levels from getting out of whack.

Hypothermia

Exhausted and physically unprepared hikers are at risk for insidious hypothermia. The body's inner core loses heat, reducing mental and physical functions. Watch for uncontrolled shivering, incoherence, poor judgment, fumbling, mumbling, and slurred speech. Avoid becoming hypothermic by staying dry. Don rain gear and warm moisture-wicking layers rather than cottons that won't dry and fail to retain heat. Get hypothermic hikers into dry clothing and shelter. Give them warm nonalcoholic and noncaffeinated liquids. If the victim cannot regain body heat, get into a sleeping bag with the victim, both stripped for skin-to-skin contact.

Poison Oak, Ivy, and Sumac

Poison oak, ivy, and sumac (my personal enemies on any trail) are vines or shrubs that inhabit forests. Common in western states, poison oak has three scalloped leaves. Found across the United States except for tropical islands and Alaska, poison ivy has three spoon-shaped leaves and grows along rivers, lakes, and oceans. With 7-13 leaflets, poison sumac grows in wet, swampy zones in the North and Florida. Contact with these plants may cause a rash and itching, which can be transferred to your eyes or face via touch. Your best protection is to wear long sleeves and long pants when hiking, no matter how hot it is. Tecnu can cleanse your skin after exposure to poison oak and poison ivy. Calamine lotion can help ease the rash and itching. The oils from these plants can stay active (and itchy) for months after contact, making it important to sanitize your boots, clothing, gaiters, and gear if you encountered or think you encountered any of these awful vines on your hike.

Ticks

Ticks and bug bites are unfortunate realities for hikers, and since the results from a bite can range from the inconvenient itch of a mosquito bite to a life-changing illness like Rocky Mountain spotted fever or Lyme disease, you need to take precautions before you hit the trail. Most bug sprays use DEET as their repellent, and you can find effective DEET sprays, lotions, creams, moist towelettes, and even DEET-impregnated clothing at outdoor retailers and at many department stores; simply apply it to your skin and you're off, though you may need to reapply periodically. Clothing impregnated with permethrin is also effective in repelling ticks and other bugs.

You should wear long sleeves and keep as much skin as possible covered (a good plan for avoiding sunburn, too), keep your shirt tucked in (so they can't crawl under and find a good hiding spot), and check your and your hiking companions' clothes for unwanted hitchhikers. It's a great idea to do periodic tick checks of your body, paying close attention to your armpits; groin; body hair, hairline, and beard; beneath your breasts; in folds or creases on your body; and in places where your clothing or gear straps touch the skin. These are all good hiding spots for ticks.

If you do find a tick attached to you, don't panic. With a pair of pointy tweezers, grab the tick behind the head and pull out gently and steadily (but don't twist) until, hopefully, you pull the tick free. If you pull and its head stays embedded, don't freak out—the head alone can't spread disease; it's merely inconvenient (and kind of gross). Wash the wound site well with soap and water, and apply rubbing alcohol or antiseptic to the area. Once bitten, keep an eye on the site for the next two weeks: If you see an expanding red bullseye around the wound or experience flu-like symptoms, it's time to head to the doctor.

Giardia

Lakes and streams can carry parasites like *Giardia lamblia*. If ingested, it causes cramping, nausea, and severe diarrhea for up to six weeks. Avoid giardia by boiling water (for one minute, plus one minute for each 1,000 ft/305 m elevation above sea level) or using a one-micron filter. Bleach also works: Add two drops per quart or liter and wait 30 minutes. Tap water in campgrounds, hotels, and picnic areas has been treated; you'll taste the chlorine.

Altitude

Some visitors from sea-level locales feel the effects of altitude at high elevations in the mountain parks of the Rockies and the Sierra Nevada. Watch for light-headedness, headaches, or shortness of breath. To acclimate, slow down the pace of hiking and drink lots of fluids. If symptoms spike, descend in elevation as soon as possible. Altitude also increases UV radiation exposure: To prevent sunburn, use a strong sunscreen and wear sunglasses and a hat. When I climbed Mount Whitney, I learned both of these lessons the hard way, earning a splitting headache and blistered ears on the way up. Rest, water, and a slower pace helped with the altitude issues, and you'd better believe I was diligent with the sunblock after I felt that first painful blister rise up.

WILDLIFE SAFETY

Bears

Bears are a beautiful sight in our national parks, but only from a distance. To stay safe in parks and areas with bear activity, the easiest rule to follow is this: keep 150 ft (46 m) between you and any bear you spot.

If you do see a bear, remain watchful and aware of where it is and what it's doing. Don't approach it or allow it to approach you. Note the bear's behavior: If it changes behavior (stops feeding, decides to travel in another direction, is startled, starts watching you), you're too close and you need to give the bear some space. Back away slowly, watching the bear the whole time, and calmly increase the distance between you and the bear. In most instances, this is enough.

You could encounter a curious or aggressive bear, though. If you do, change direction slowly and calmly as above, but if the bear follows you, stand your ground, act aggressively (yelling, shouting, or talking loudly), make yourself larger (by raising your hiking poles or backpack above your head), and throw stones or sticks or other non-food objects at it. Deploy bear spray or bear bangers (think big firecrackers designed to scare the bear) when the bear approaches within 20 yards (18 m).

Moose, Elk, and Sheep

Keep at least 75 ft (23 m) between you and any elk or bighorn sheep, and keep 120 ft (36 m) between you and any moose you spot.

Mountain Lions

If you see a mountain lion, maintain eye contact and make yourself large (raise your arms, lift your pack overhead). If the mountain lion approaches, make noise and wave your arms to let the lion know you're not food. Report any mountain lion sighting or wildlife incident to rangers at the first opportunity.

TRAIL ETIQUETTE

Hiking is a great way to get out of the concrete jungle and into the woods and the wild to explore places of natural beauty. Unfortunately, this manner of thinking is shared by millions of people. Following some basic rules of etiquette will ensure that we all get along and keep the outdoors as a place we can enjoy together.

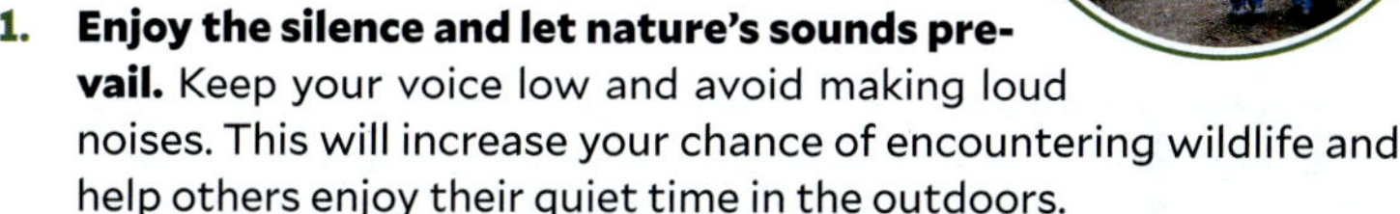

1. **Enjoy the silence and let nature's sounds prevail.** Keep your voice low and avoid making loud noises. This will increase your chance of encountering wildlife and help others enjoy their quiet time in the outdoors.
2. **Be aware of other trail users and yield appropriately.** If you hear someone coming up behind you who clearly is hiking faster than you, stand aside and let that hiker pass. On narrow trails, hikers going downhill should always yield to hikers going uphill. Get out of their way so uphill hikers can keep their momentum as they climb. Also, large groups of hikers should always yield to smaller groups or solo travelers.
3. **Be friendly and polite to other trail users.** A smile or a "hello" as you pass others on the trail is always a good idea. If someone steps aside to allow you to pass, say "thank you."
4. **Obey all posted signs and trail closures.** Only hike where it's legal. Do not invent shortcuts or hike across private property without the express permission of the owner.
5. **Hike only on established trails.** As soon as you walk off a trail, you trample vegetation. Never cut switchbacks; hillside trails are built with switchbacks to keep the slope from eroding. Just a few people cutting switchbacks can destroy a hillside.
6. **Yield to equestrians.** Horses can be badly spooked by just about anything, so always give them plenty of room. If horses are approaching, stop alongside the trail until they pass. If horses are traveling in your direction and you need to pass them, call out politely to the riders and ask permission. If horses and riders move off the trail and the riders tell you it's okay, then pass.

LEAVE NO TRACE

Keeping our national parks—or your local park, playground, or greenspace—clean, pristine, and ready for the next visitor to enjoy takes a tiny bit of effort on our part. The Leave No Trace principles are simple guidelines that help us minimize our negative impacts on the environment while allowing us to enjoy the fullness of the outdoors.

If you're not familiar with Leave No Trace, the name just about says it all, but the official guidelines are below; try to integrate them into all of your outdoors activities.

If you're familiar, skim the next part to brush up, and remember to encourage your hiking, hunting, fishing, and outdoors partners to practice them as well.

- **Plan ahead and prepare.** Hiking in the wilderness is inherently risky. Three mi (4.8 km) of hiking at the high elevations in Wyoming may be much harder than the same distance through your neighborhood park back home. Choose appropriate routes for mileage and elevation gain with this in mind, and carry hiking essentials.
- **Respect wildlife.** Bring along binoculars, spotting scopes, and telephoto lenses to aid in watching wildlife. Keep your distance. Do not feed any wildlife, even ground squirrels. Once fed, they become more aggressive.
- **Travel and camp on durable surfaces.** In frontcountry and backcountry camp-grounds, camp in designated sites. Protect fragile plants by staying on trails even in mud, refusing to cut switchbacks, and walking single file. If you must walk off the trail, step on rocks, snow, or dry grasses rather than wet soil and delicate plants.
- **Minimize campfire impacts.** Make fires in designated fire pits only, not on beaches. Use small wrist-size dead and downed wood, not live branches. Be aware: Fires and collecting firewood are not permitted in some places in the parks.
- **Leave what you find.** Flowers, rocks, and fur tufts on shrubs are protected park resources, as are historical and cultural items. For lunch stops and camping, sit on rocks or logs where you find them rather than moving them to accommodate your comfort.

▲ SQUIRREL EATING AN APPLE LEFT BEHIND, GLACIER NATIONAL PARK

- **Properly dispose of waste.** Pack out whatever you bring, including all garbage. If toilets are not available, pack out toilet paper. Urinate on rocks, logs, gravel, or snow to protect soils and plants from salt-starved wildlife, and bury feces 6-8 in (15-20 cm) deep at least 200 ft (61 m) from water.
- **Be considerate of other visitors.** Particularly be aware of cell phones and how their use or noise cuts into the natural soundscapes of the parks.

For more Leave No Trace information, visit www.LNT.org.

TRAVEL TIPS

ACCESSIBILITY

While some national park structures have been fitted with ramps and wider doors, many historic or remote structures remain inaccessible. However, most campgrounds designate specific campsites that meet the Americans with Disabilities Act standards.

There are many resources to help travelers with disabilities plan their trip. Check on the specific park's website and the NPS app for services pertinent to that park. Many parks have facilities, programs, and trails designed for those with wheelchairs and physical or mobility challenges. Most park brochures are also available in large print or braille, and some in audio format. Park videos often have captioned versions. Trained service dogs are permitted in many parks, but check on requirements; some parks with prevalent grizzly bear populations discourage them in the backcountry.

FIREARMS

Federal law allows legally carried firearms into the national parks. However, they are prohibited in visitor centers, ranger stations, fee-collection buildings, and other facilities. Those places are marked with signs at all public entrances. Discharging firearms in the park is illegal except when presented with "imminent danger."

WI-FI AND CELL SERVICE

Cellular service and internet connectivity within the national parks tend to be limited. In general, plan to be out of reach while you travel in the parks, where service is unavailable on many roads, trails, campgrounds, picnic areas, and lodges. National park visitor centers, ranger stations, and campgrounds rarely have Wi-Fi. Some park lodges may offer limited Wi-Fi for overnight guests, but connectivity will often be very slow.

Mobile Apps

The National Park Service has a free NPS smartphone app covering each national park. Download the app before you begin your trip because cell service and internet are limited inside the parks. Some sections can be saved for offline use. The app has information on alerts, visitor centers, hikes, geyser predictions, road closures, ranger programs, self-guided tours, and interactive park maps. Even with the app, your first stop for accurate, up-to-date information should always be a national park visitor center and the national park website.

TRAVELERS OF COLOR

National parks draw visitors of all ethnicities and races. While the parks have not always been inclusive places, they are public lands, meant for everyone to enjoy, and a great place to start adventuring outdoors. Here are some resources to help you prepare for your trip.

Misha Euceph hosts **Hello, Nature** (www.rei.com/blog/podcasts/hello-nature), an eight-episode podcast that visits popular national parks, exploring who the parks are for. During the episodes, Euceph shares her experiences as a person of color.

Other resources provide how-to guides for launching into outdoors pursuits such as hiking, camping, and backpacking, which are the backbone of many national park adventures. **Diversify Outdoors** (www.diversifyoutdoors.com) is a coalition of bloggers and social media personalities who are passionate about the outdoors and strive for equity, inclusion, and access for all. **Melanin Base Camp** (www.melaninbasecamp.com) features outdoors athlete bloggers, trip reports, and gear reviews. **Latino Outdoors** (https://latinooutdoors.org) has bilingual educational resources in their "How-To Vamos Outdoors."

LGBTQ TRAVELERS

The national parks are generally LGBTQ-friendly, but in the small rural towns surrounding the parks, don't expect to find much in the way of overt gay culture or nightlife. For perspective on visiting the national parks from two gay travelers, tune in to the podcast **Gaze at the National Parks** (https://gazeatthenationalparks.com). Avid hikers Dustin Ballard and Michael Ryan share their on-the-trail adventures in many of the US national parks, adding new destinations each season.

TRAVELING WITH CHILDREN

The National Park Service has designed ways to pique the interest of kids through educational activities online (www.nps.gov, under "Learn About the Park"), in-park activities, and visitor center hands-on exhibits.

Hiking with kids can either be a nightmare or a hoot. To make it more fun, take water and snacks along to prevent hunger and thirst from sapping their energy. Take extra layers to keep kids warm if the weather turns. Help them connect with the environment while hiking by asking them about what they see and why things are the way they are. If you make hiking a fun experience for them, they'll want to do it again.

Junior Ranger Programs

Junior Ranger Programs (www.nps.gov/kids/jrRangers.cfm) mix educational activities with experiences for families to do in the park. Most activities target ages 6-12. Pick up Junior Ranger activity guides ($3-5 or free) at any visitor center. Kids complete the self-guided activities and receive a Junior Ranger badge after stopping at a visitor center to get sworn in.

TRAVELING WITH PETS

Pets are allowed inside national parks, but only in limited areas: campgrounds, parking lots, and roadsides. They are not allowed on most trails and beaches, in the backcountry, or at most park lodges or motor inns. When outside a vehicle or in a campground, pets must be on a leash or caged. Be kind enough to avoid leaving them unattended in a car anywhere. Be considerate of wildlife and other visitors by keeping your pet under control and disposing of waste in garbage cans. Some national parks (such as Grand Canyon) provide kennel services for a fee.

HIKING AND OUTDOORS ORGANIZATIONS

When it comes to nature and our national parks, I believe a few things. First, there's a park for everybody. Second, no matter who you are, where you're from, or how you were raised (I'm an outdoors kid, my wife is a self-described indoors kid, yet we hike together), you can have a fantastic experience in the great outdoors. Third, there are a lot of ways to enjoy nature, but if we don't act responsibly and protect the woods and wilds and wonders of nature, folks a couple of generations down the line won't have the same opportunities. Which brings me to these lists. Below you'll find organizations devoted to preserving our parks, environments, and wild lands; groups dedicated to helping novice hikers have exceptional experiences in the outdoors; and those fabulous "Friends of" groups that serve the needs of specific national parks. By no means is this a comprehensive list, but each of these groups shares my love and passion for our parks, for growing the hiking and outdoors community, and preserving our precious environment.

HIKING

- **American Hiking Society** (8403 Colesville Rd., Ste. 1100, Silver Spring, MD; 800/972-8608; https://americanhiking.org): Working under the mission of "empowering all to enjoy, share, and preserve the hiking experience," the AHS lobbies federal and state lawmakers for more parks funding, assists in trail building and maintenance efforts, and helps connect hikers with hiking and outdoors groups near them (check their Alliance of Hiking Organizations for more).
- **American Alpine Club** (710 10th St., Ste. 100, Golden, CO; 303/384-0110; https://americanalpineclub.org): This group keeps a focus on climbers, but they're a wealth of information for outdoors lovers and help broaden the base of outdoors and parks lovers.
- **Outdoor Afro** (https://outdoorafro.org): Outdoor Afro helps connect the Black community to the outdoors through work on a national and local level. Across the country, they lead hikes, walks, and outdoors adventures, and you can find a group near you under the "Places" tab on the website.

CRYPTIDS AND ODDITIES

Out in the wilds of our national parks, you can see and hear some weird, unexplainable things. Reports of UAPs (Unidentified Anomalous Phenomena, or UFOs if you're of *The X-Files* generation like me) and sightings of creatures like Bigfoot, Spearfinger, and even Mothman in our parks make headlines and give rangers something to talk about over coffee. If cryptids—those unexplained and mythological creatures—and UAPs get you excited to hike, you're in for a treat. Here are several trails where you might just spot something weird in the woods, but don't limit your search for the unexplained to these parks, as there's weirdness to be found wherever you go.

MOTHMAN

Mothman, a red-eyed, moth-winged monster from my home state of West Virginia has been reported in New River Gorge National Park & Preserve and in Shenandoah National Park in Virginia. But both places are far from his home on the Ohio River, so take these sightings with a grain of salt.

- **Hawksbill Loop Trail, Shenandoah:** If Mothman heads to Shenandoah for a getaway, the sweeping views of Virginia's wooded countryside make this hike a great place to start your search (page 452).
- **Endless Wall Trail, New River Gorge:** This trail leads you through heavy woods to views of the New River Gorge, where you may spot Mothman in and among the trees or flying over the river below (page 470).

BIGFOOT

Also known as Sasquatch, this hairy, manlike creature stands 7-10 ft tall (2.1-3 m), has enormous feet, and is known for knocking on trees, howling and yelling in the night, and making the occasional appearance in badly shot video clips. Bigfoot sightings are most common in deeply wooded areas like the Pacific Northwest where parks like Olympic, Mount Rainier, and Yosemite provide plenty of places to live and roam.

- **Hurricane Hill, Olympic:** Hike to the top of Hurricane Hill to survey the stunning scenery and scout for Sasquatch hideouts; one look at this countryside and you'll see there are hundreds of hiding places (page 60).
- **Silver Falls Loop, Mount Rainier:** You should be safe on this hike because Bigfoot's not known for showering in waterfalls, but look for double-sized footprints in the sand and mud near the stream and plunge pool to see if he's been prowling around (page 86).
- **Cathedral Lakes, Yosemite:** Spend a night or two in this pristine wilderness and listen close for the sounds of Bigfoot knocking on and knocking over trees; just don't knock back or Bigfoot may decide to investigate (page 112).

THUNDERBIRD

These giant, birdlike creatures come straight out of the mythologies of several Indigenous traditions across the American West. Said to have

▲ FOG ROLLING INTO PARADISE, MOUNT RAINIER NATIONAL PARK

a wingspan some 20 ft (6 m), they sometimes control the weather—particularly thunderstorms—and other times appear as a portent of coming storms. Keep your eyes to the skies when you visit these trails and you may spot one.

- **Savage Alpine Trail, Denali:** You can see for miles and miles on Savage Alpine Trail, so if there's a Thunderbird soaring over this Alaskan parkland, you'll find it with ease (page 52).
- **Soda Canyon Overlook, Mesa Verde:** When clear skies turn stormy over this section of Colorado's Mesa Verde National Park, it just might be a Thunderbird soaring overhead (page 286).
- **South Rim Trail to Point Sublime, Yellowstone:** If there's a hike with a high chance of a Thunderbird sighting, this is it. The jaw-dropping scenery attracts all sorts of lookers, from hikers like us to mythological creatures like the Thunderbird (page 348).

WENDIGO

One of the two most frightening creatures on this list, the Wendigo, a cannibalistic beast associated with cold, famine, and madness, comes to us from a number of Indigenous stories in the western part of the country. All these tales agree that Wendigo is tall, terrifying, with glowing eyes, long claws, and the head of an elk or deer. Sightings are heaviest near parks like Glacier and Yosemite, as well as parks in Canada.

- **Half Dome, Yosemite:** Make the Half Dome trek an overnight affair and spend the dark hours looking for Wendigo's glowing eyes. If you don't spot this beast then, look for signs from the top of Half Dome (page 102).
- **Trail of the Cedars and Avalanche Lake, Glacier:** It's best to stick to a popular trail if you're looking for a creature like this—safety in numbers—but your best chance for an encounter will come after you spend a few nights in the woods, so book a remote campsite after you scout out the park on this hike (page 370).

(continued)

SKINWALKERS

Skinwalkers are powerful, shapeshifting witches who transform themselves into wolves or coyotes and terrorize humans. The Navajo people tell many tales about the Skinwalker, so your best bet is to look for this creature at parks in the Southwest like Grand Canyon and Canyonlands.

- **Bright Angel Trail, Grand Canyon:** Your view of the canyons and rugged landscape of the Grand Canyon might let you see a Skinwalker before they see you, keeping you safe to hike another day (page 202).
- **Chesler Park and The Joint, Canyonlands:** If I were a Skinwalker (who's to say I'm not?), I'd hide out in the maze of canyons at Chesler Park and The Joint, ready to pounce on slow hikers and groups who decide to investigate too deeply (page 276).

SPEARFINGER

This monster-witch hybrid comes to us from the Cherokee and their homeland in the Smoky Mountains where she's known as U'tlun'ta'. According to the Cherokee, Spearfinger lives in the Smokies and uses her long index finger—tipped with a sharp nail—to cut open her victims so she can feast on their livers.

- **Abrams Falls Trail, Great Smoky Mountains:** Cades Cove, the trailhead for this hike, is bound by high peaks and served as a Cherokee hunting land and later a community of European settlers, and it makes for a great place to look for Spearfinger. She's often out after dark, so once you finish your hike, stick around for a sky full of stars and fields full of wildlife, but hopefully no Spearfinger (page 488).

UAPS, UFOS, AND ALIENS

From strange lights in the sky to the supposed landing of alien spacecraft, parks from coast to coast have reported UAPs for decades. Parks with wide views of the stars offer the best odds for a sighting, so head west and keep your eyes peeled.

- **Skyline Trail Loop, Mount Rainier:** The "flying saucer" phrase and craze were born here back in 1947 after a pilot reported objects in the sky over Mount Rainier. Will you see the same? I hope so. And I hope you manage to snap a clear photo while you're at it (page 82).
- **Telescope Peak, Death Valley:** Like Joshua Tree, Death Valley is near Area 51, a US Navy weapons testing range, and several other military facilities, so when you're up on Telescope Peak, watch for dogfighting fighter jets and strange aircraft with possible extraterrestrial origins (page 134).
- **Lost Palms Oasis Trail, Joshua Tree:** Located near secretive military bases (like the legendary Area 51) and research facilities, Joshua Tree has a lot of reported UAP sightings, so pay a visit to this desert park around dawn or dusk to look for weird lights overhead (page 148).
- **High Dune Trail, Great Sand Dunes:** The night sky is incredible here, but a few blinking lights, odd orbs, or unexplained aircraft will have you believing in life beyond our little planet (page 290).

- **California Gay Adventures** (www.californiagayadventures.com): California Gay Adventures is an inclusive outdoors and hiking group based in Southern California that serves to introduce members of their community and community allies to fantastic outdoors experiences—no matter their level of comfort with the outdoors—by offering everything from day hikes to camping trips. Their sister organization, Pride Adventure Travels, spreads the outdoors love beyond US borders with epic trips.
- **Big City Mountaineers** (5394 Marshall St. #200, Arvada, CO; 303/271-9200; www.bigcitymountaineers.org): This group introduces youth from disinvested communities to the outdoors through monumental hiking and camping trips. They fund these trips through group hikes and trips under their Summit for Someone and Adventure for Someone programs.
- **AllTrails** (www.alltrails.com): Their mission is simple—to help the world find its way outside—and with a website and mobile app full of trails, maps, trail reviews, and more, they connect novice and veteran hikers to trails, treks, and experiences around the world. Do a deep dive into any national park and you'll find hundreds of user-generated maps and trail notes guaranteed to inspire a sense of adventure.
- **Hiking Project** (www.hikingproject.com): Thousands of trails and paths on their website and mobile app help hikers find a trail to explore. Maps and tips are user-generated, and they're full of useful, relatable information about a given park.
- **Hiker Babes** (www.hikerbabescommunity.com): Hiker Babes is a large, growing, diverse community of women with a passion for the outdoors. Their local chapters lead hikes and campouts and help novice outdoorswomen get comfortable on the trail.

ENVIRONMENT

- **The Sierra Club** (2101 Webster St., Ste. 1300, Oakland, CA; 415/977-5500; www.sierraclub.org): This well-known group has long been an advocate for the outdoors, conservation and environmental causes, and our national parks.
- **Leave No Trace Center for Outdoor Ethics** (100 North St., Boulder, CO; 800/332-4100; https://lnt.org): Leave No Trace serves the great outdoors by reminding us how easy it is to be responsible outdoorspeople. From simple "pack it in, pack it out" reminders to partnerships with tourism, corporate, and community groups that share their vision and values, Leave No Trace helps keep the great outdoors great.
- **National Parks Conservation Association** (777 6th St. NW, Ste. 700, Washington DC; 800/682-7275; www.npca.org): These national parks advocates lobby lawmakers to help preserve and expand parkland, and help increase park use and engagement through local and regional programming.

- **Appalachian Trail Conservancy** (799 Washington St., Harpers Ferry, WV; 304/535-6331; https://appalachiantrail.org): Dedicated to protecting, managing, and advocating for the Appalachian National Scenic Trail, this group has an outsize impact as their efforts consistently involve local and regional hiking and conservation organizations, trail crews, and volunteers with a passion for this legendary trail.
- **Pacific Crest Trail Association** (2150 River Plaza Dr., Ste. 155, Sacramento, CA; 916/285-1846; www.pcta.org): As protectors, advocates, and champions of the Pacific Crest Trail, this group seeks to keep this trail in great shape for all who use and love it.
- **Continental Trail Divide Coalition** (710 10th St., Ste. 200, Golden, CO; 303/996-2759; https://cdtcoalition.org): This group is devoted to maintaining and completing the Continental Divide National Scenic Trail, and their efforts include trail building and maintenance, lobbying and advocacy, and environmental work on behalf of the trail.

FRIENDS OF THE PARKS

- **National Parks Foundation** (1500 K St. NW, Ste. 700, Washington DC; 202/796-2500; www.nationalparks.org): The official nonprofit partner of the National Park Service, the foundation raises money to protect and enhance the parks, preserve the environment and wildlife in the parks, and encourage more use and exploration across the National Park System.
- **National Park Friends Alliance** (www.friendsalliance.org): The Friends Alliance doesn't serve a particular park, rather they serve the various "Friends of" groups dedicated to each of our parks across the system. By providing leadership, fundraising, and logistical support to the Friends of chapters, they expand the reach of each group and help create a more meaningful impact for each park.
- **Friends of Great Smoky Mountains National Park** (84 Coxe Ave., Unit 200, Asheville, NC; 828/452-0720; https://friendsofthesmokies.org): Friends of the Smokies provides fundraising and support for Great Smoky Mountains National Park, assists with trail maintenance, leads hikes and walks, and keeps locals and visitors engaging with the park in a positive manner.

Other "Friends" organizations serve parks across the National Park System and, frankly, there are too many to list here, so go to your park, navigate to the "Get Involved" tab, and follow the links to volunteer with the park or join their particular Friends of group.

INDEX

LIST OF MAPS

Great Lakes and Northeast

The South

PHOTO CREDITS

Title page: Bearfence Mountain Trail, Shenandoah National Park © NPS/M. O'Neill

Page 4: © NPS/D. Archuleta; pg. 5: © NPS/Marc Neidig; pgs. 6-7: © NPS; pgs. 8-9: © Idreamphotos | Dreamstime.com pg 9: © Wirestock | Dreamstime.com pg. 10 © Dana Schagunn | Dreamstime.com pg. 11: © NPS/Patrick Myers pgs. 12-13 © Paul Brady | Dreamstime.com pg. 14: © NPS; pg 15: © (top) Sean Pavone | Dreamstime.com, (bottom) NPS/Jacob W. Frank; page 16: © NPS/David Pinigis; pg. 17: © Eric Cote | Dreamstime.com; pg 18: © NPS/Michael Quinn; pg. 19: © NPS/Ivie Metzen; pg. 20: © Pichaitun | Dreamstime.com; pg. 21: © (top) Ztiger | Dreamstime.com, (bottom) NPS/Katy Cain; pg. 23: © Marek Poplawski | Dreamstime.com; pg. 24: © (top) Sdbower | Dreamstime.com, (bottom) Jon Bilous | Dreamstime.com; pg. 25: © Bryandericco| Dreamstime.com; pg. 27: © NPS/Lian Law; pg. 28: © (top) Always Wanderlust | Dreamstime.com, (bottom) Francisco Blanco | Dreamstime.com; pg. 30: © NPS/Hannah Schwalbe; pg. 31: © (top) Miroslav Liska | Dreamstime.com, (bottom) Zhukovsky | Dreamstime.com; pg. 32: © NPS/Neal Herbert; pg. 33: © NPS/Chalice Keith; pg. 34: © NPS/J. Manuszak; pg. 35: © © Daniel Sullivan | Dreamstime.com; pg. 43: © NPS/T. Chavis; pgs. 44-45: © NPS/Emily Brouwer; pg. 48: (top) David Gonzalez Rebollo | Dreamstime.com, (left) David Gonzalez Rebollo | Dreamstime.com, (right) Rinus Baak | Dreamstime.com; pg. 51: © Eileen Tan | Dreamstime.com; pg 52: © (top) Ivan Kokoulin | Dreamstime.com, (bottom) Ivan Kokoulin | Dreamstime.com; pg. 55: © NPS/Emily Mesner; pg. 56: © (top) NPS/Jacob W. Frank, (bottom) Ghm Meuffels | Dreamstime.com; pg. 59: © Bilderschorsch | Dreamstime.com; pg 60: © (top) Colin Young | Dreamstime.com, (bottom) Andrey Tarantin | Dreamstime.com; pg. 63: © Jaahnlieb | Dreamstime.com; pg. 64: © (top) Lisa Wood | Dreamstime.com, (left) Pierre Leclerc | Dreamstime.com, (right) Victoria Ditkovsky | Dreamstime.com; pg. 67: © Sean Pavone | Dreamstime.com; pg. 68: © (top) Sean Pavone | Dreamstime.com, (bottom) NPS/R. McKenna; pg. 71: © Sean Pavone | Dreamstime.com; pgs. 72-73: © Jenifoto406 | Dreamstime.com; pg. 74: © (top) Marek Rybar | Dreamstime.com, (left) Brian Logan | Dreamstime.com, (right) Brian Logan | Dreamstime.com; pg. 77: © Gregg Brekke | Dreamstime.com; pg. 78: © (top) NPS, (bottom & pg. 81) Courtesy of North Cascades National Park Service Complex; pg. 82: © (top) NPS/Emily Brouwer, (bottom) NPS/L.Shenk; pg. 85: © Chris Boswell | Dreamstime.com; pg. 86: (top) Martina Birnbaum | Dreamstime.com, (bottom) Kwan Tse | Dreamstime.com; pg. 89: © Svitlana Imnadze | Dreamstime.com; pg. 90: © (top) Wirestock | Dreamstime.com, (left) David Crane | Dreamstime.com, (right) Kelly Vandellen | Dreamstime.com; pg. 93: © Kelly Vandellen | Dreamstime.com; pg. 94: © (top) Tamifreed | Dreamstime.com, (bottom) Yggdrasill33 | Dreamstime.com; pg. 97: © Alex Grichenko | Dreamstime.com; pg. 98: © (top) Topseller | shutterstock, (bottom) SimonDannhauer | Dreamstime.com; pg. 101: © Kitleong | Dreamstime.com; pg. 102: © (top) Stephen Moehle | Dreamstime.com, (bottom) Marek Poplawski | Dreamstime.com; pg. 105: © Stephen Moehle | Dreamstime.com; pg 106: © (top) Thicoz | Dreamstime.com, (left) Hannoonnes | Dreamstime.com, (right) Steve Lagreca | Dreamstime.com; pg. 109: © Abigail Marie/AdobeStock; pgs. 110-111: © Johannes Onnes | Dreamstime; pg. 112: © (top) Always Wanderlust | Dreamstime.com, (bottom) Djschreiber | Dreamstime.com; pg. 115: © Always Wanderlust | Dreamstime.com, pg. 116: © (top) Oscity | Dreamstime.com, (left) Miroslav Liska | Dreamstime.com, (right) Luckyphotographer | Dreamstime.com; pg. 119: © Thomas Takacs | Dreamstime.com; pg. 120: © (top) Elis CorA! | Dreamstime.com, (bottom) Swathi Chirra | Dreamstime.com; pg. 123: © Swathi Chirra | Dreamstime.com; pg. 124: © (top) Stephen Moehle | Dreamstime.com, (bottom) Kwiktor | Dreamstime.com; pg. 127: © Debove Eric | Dreamstime.com; pgs. 128-129: © Debove Eric | Dreamstime.com; pg. 130: © (top) Alex Edmonds | Dreamstime.com, (left) Paul Lemke | Dreamstime.com, (right) Kevin Oke | Dreamstime.com; pg. 133: © Sarah Fields | Dreamstime.com; pg. 134: © (top) Sarah Fields | Dreamstime.com, (bottom) Roman Slavik | Dreamstime.com; pg. 137: © Kelly Vandellen | Dreamstime.com; pg. 138: © (top) Andreistanescu | Dreamstime.com, (left) Maria Luisa Lopez Estivill | Dreamstime.com, (right) Andreistanescu | Dreamstime.com; pg. 141: © Demerzel21 | Dreamstime.com; pg. 142 © (top) Nicholas Motto | Dreamstime.com, (bottom) Kelly Vandellen | Dreamstime.com; pg. 145: © Nicholas Motto | Dreamstime.com; pgs. 146-147: © NPS/Lian Law; pg. 148: © (top) Andreistanescu | Dreamstime.com, (bottom) Tracy Immordino | Dreamstime.com; pg. 151: © Andreistanescu | Dreamstime.com; pg. 152: © (top) Alessandra Rc | Dreamstime.com, (bottom) Snyfer | Dreamstime.com; pg. 155: © Patrick Barron | Dreamstime.com; pg. 156: © (top) Steven Prorak | Dreamstime.com, (left) Kojihirano | Dreamstime.com, (right) Andreistanescu | Dreamstime.com; pg. 159: © Stephen Moehle | Dreamstime.com; pg. 160: © NPS/Shaina Niehans; pg. 161: Maksershov | Dreamstime.com; pg. 163: © Taylor Cole | unsplash.com; pg. 164: © (top) NPS/John Chao, (bottom) Tristan Brynildsen | Dreamstime.com; pg. 167: © Stephen Moehle | Dreamstime.com; pg. 168: (top) Zrfphoto | Dreamstime.com, (left) NPS/Steve Olson, (right) NPS; pg. 171: © Galyna Andrushko | Dreamstime.com; pg. 172: © (top) Cheri Alguire | Dreamstime.com, (bottom) Kelly Vandellen | Dreamstime.com; pg. 175: © Kelly Vandellen | Dreamstime.com; pg. 176: © (top) Vlue | Dreamstime.com, (left) Vacclav | Dreamstime.com, (right) Mihaela Nica | Dreamstime.com; pg. 179: © Hawaii Tourism Authority (HTA) / Taku Miyazawa; pgs. 180-181: © Hawaii Tourism Authority (HTA) / Tor Johnson; pg. 183: © (top) Mike7777777 | Dreamstime.com, (bottom) Heeb Photos | eStock Photo; pg. 185: © Mike7777777 | Dreamstime.com; pg. 186: © (top) MNStudio | Dreamstime.com, (left) Maria Luisa Lopez Estivill | Dreamstime.com, (right) Elio Mattia | Dreamstime.com; pg. 189: © MNStudio | Dreamstime.com; pg. 190: © (top) George Burba | Dreamstime.com, (bottom) Mike7777777 | Dreamstime.com; pg. 193: © David Hayes | Dreamstime.com; pgs. 194-195: © NPS/Michael Quinn; pg. 198: © (top) Josemaria Toscano | Dreamstime.com, (bottom) Kristie Gianopulos | Dreamstime.com; pg. 201: © Lunamarina | Dreamstime.com; pg 202: © (top) Joshua Huang | Dreamstime.com, (left) Robin Runck | Dreamstime.com, (right) Santiago Rodriguez Fontoba | Dreamstime.com; pg. 205: © Thomas Takacs | Dreamstime.com; pg. 206: © (top) NPS/Allyson Mathis, (bottom) Arlene Waller | Dreamstime.com; pg. 209: © Kelly Vandellen | Dreamstime.com; pg. 210: (top) Nicholas Motto | Dreamstime.com, (bottom) Lhb Companies | Dreamstime.com; pg. 212: © (left & right) Billy Mc Donald | Dreamstime.com; pg. 213: © Lhb Companies | Dreamstime.com; pg. 215: © Arlene Waller | Dreamstime.com; pg. 216: © (top & bottom) Lirina Kozhemyakina | Dreamstime.com; pg. 219: © Luckyphotographer | Dreamstime.com; pg. 220: © (top) William Wise | Dreamstime.com, (left & right) NPS; pg. 223: © Patrick Jennings | Dreamstime.com; pgs. 224-225: Yggdrasill33 | Dreamstime.com; pg. 226: © (top) Kobus Peche | Dreamstime.com, (bottom) Galyna Andrushko | Dreamstime.com; pg. 229: © Straystone | Dreamstime.com; pg. 230: © (top) Rinus Baak | Dreamstime.com, (left) Steve Lagreca | Dreamstime.com, (right) Maryswift | Dreamstime.com; pg. 233: © Larry Gevert | Dreamstime.com; pg. 234: © (top) Frank Bach | Dreamstime.com, (left) Robert Bohrer | Dreamstime.com, (right) Oren Gelbendorf | Dreamstime.com; pg. 237: © Robert Bohrer | Dreamstime.com; pg. 238: © (top & bottom) Stephen Moehle | Dreamstime.com; pg. 241: © Brocreative/AdobeStock; pg. 242: © (top) William Perry | Dreamstime.com, (bottom) Pierrette Guertin | Dreamstime.com; pg. 245: © Deepfrog17 | Dreamstime.com; pg. 246: © (top) Sergio Boccardo | Dreamstime.com, (bottom) Hpbfotos | Dreamstime.com; pg. 249: © Legacy1995 | Dreamstime.com; pgs. 250-251: © Paul Brady | Dreamstime.com; pg. 252: © (top) Katerina Devlin | Dreamstime.com, (bottom) Robin Runck | Dreamstime.com; pg. 255: © Peter Mautsch / Maranso Gmbh | Dreamstime.com; pg. 256: © (top) Pierre Leclerc | Dreamstime.com, (left) Tristan Brynildsen | Dreamstime.com, (right) Bjoern Alberts | Dreamstime.com; pg. 259: © Chon Kit Leong | Dreamstime.com; pg. 260: © (top) Lunamarina | Dreamstime.com, (left) Ralf Broskvar | Dreamstime.com, (right) William Perry | Dreamstime.com; pg. 263: © Colin Young | Dreamstime.com; pg. 264: © (top) Nuvista | Dreamstime.com, (bottom) Stephen Moehle | Dreamstime.com; pg. 267: © Lhb Companies | Dreamstime.com; pg. 268: © (top) Asboard90 | Dreamstime.com, (bottom) Paul Smith | Dreamstime.com; pg. 271: © Asboard90 | Dreamstime.com; pg. 272: © (top & bottom) Cynthia Mccrary | Dreamstime.com; pg. 275: © Cynthia Mccrary | Dreamstime.com; pg. 276: © (top) Kelly Vandellen | Dreamstime.com, (bottom) Madeleine Deaton | Dreamstime.com; pg. 279: © Colin Young | Dreamstime.com; pgs. 280-281: © NPS/Emily Ogden; pg. 282: © (top) Dominic Gentilcore | Dreamstime.com, (left) Kenny Tong | Dreamstime.com, (right) Maurie Hill | Dreamstime.com; pg. 285: © Njarvis5 | Dreamstime.com; pg. 286: © (top) Jeffrey Ross | Dreamstime.com, (bottom) Swdesertlover | Dreamstime.com; pg. 289: © Laurens Hoddenbagh | Dreamstime.com; pg. 290: © (top) Michael Ver Sprill | Dreamstime.com, (left) NPS, (right) Zi Magine | Dreamstime.com; pg. 293: © Wayne Mckown | Dreamstime.com; pg. 294: © (top) Ztiger | Dreamstime.com, (bottom) Sdbower | Dreamstime.com; pg. 297: © Ztiger | Dreamstime.com; pg. 298:

© (top) ImagoDens | Dreamstime.com, (bottom) Kelly Vandellen | Dreamstime.com; pg. 301: © ImagoDens | Dreamstime.com; pgs. 302-303: © Martin Kramer | Dreamstime.com; pg. 304: © (top) Pbclub | Dreamstime.com, (bottom) Kanokwalee2 | Dreamstime.com; pg. 307: © Bill Kennedy | Dreamstime.com; pgs. 308-309: © NPS/Tobiason; pg. 312: © (top) NPS/Jacob W. Frank, (bottom) Mark Collins | Dreamstime.com; pg. 315: © Colin Young | Dreamstime.com; pg. 316: © (top) NPS/Jim Westfall, (left) Mitgirl | Dreamstime.com, (right) Brenda Denmark | Dreamstime.com; pg. 319: © Brenda Denmark | Dreamstime.com; pg. 320: © (top) Brian Wolski | Dreamstime.com, (left) David Spates | Dreamstime.com, (right) Bobby J Norris | Dreamstime.com; pg. 323: © Ronda Kimbrow | Dreamstime.com; pg. 324: © (top) Brian Wolski | Dreamstime.com, (bottom) Pancaketom | Dreamstime.com; pg. 325: © Pancaketom | Dreamstime.com; pg. 329: © Noamfein | Dreamstime.com; pg. 330: © (top) Stephen Moehle | Dreamstime.com, (bottom) Zrfphoto | Dreamstime.com; pg. 333: © SI Photography | Dreamstime.com; pg. 334: © (top) Lorcel | Dreamstime.com, (left) F11photo | Dreamstime.com, (right) Ken Desloover | Dreamstime.com; pg. 337: © Chon Kit Leong | Dreamstime.com; pgs. 338-339: © NPS/Neal Herbert; pg. 340: © (top) Jeffrey Ross | Dreamstime.com, (bottom) Hellmann1 | Dreamstime.com; pg. 341: © Donyanedomam | Dreamstime.com; pg. 343: © Yggdrasill33 | Dreamstime.com; pg. 345: © (top) NPS/A. Falgoust, (left) Linda Bair | Dreamstime.com, (right) Kelly Vandellen | Dreamstime.com; pg. 347: © Kelly Vandellen | Dreamstime.com; pg. 348: © (top & bottom) NPS/Jacob W. Frank; pg. 349: © NPS/Jacob W. Frank; pg. 351: © Widyada Chongtrakul | Dreamstime.com; pg. 352: © (top) Chengusf | Dreamstime.com, (left) Chengusf | Dreamstime.com, (right) Giovanni Gagliardi | Dreamstime.com; pg. 355: © Wirestock | Dreamstime.com; pg. 356: © (top) Kelly Vandellen | Dreamstime.com, (bottom) Kwiktor | Dreamstime.com; pg. 259: © Kwiktor | Dreamstime.com; pg. 360-361: NPS/T. Chavis; pg.362: © (all) Mkopka | Dreamstime.com; pg. 365: © Linda Mohammad; pg. 366: © (top) Chris Hartman | Dreamstime.com, (bottom) Brian Flaigmore | Dreamstime.com; pg. 369: © Kelly Vandellen | Dreamstime.com; pg. 370: © (top) F11photo | Dreamstime.com, (bottom) Bernard Dunne | Dreamstime.com; pg. 371: © Chris Labasco | Dreamstime.com; pg. 373: © Claire White | Dreamstime.com; pg. 374: © (top) Wirestock | Dreamstime.com, (left) Kelly Vandellen | Dreamstime.com, (right) Linda Mohammad; pg. 377: © Jeremy Christensen | Dreamstime.com; pg. 378: © (top) Alexy Kamenskiy | Dreamstime.com, (bottom) Dan Breckwoldt | Dreamstime.com; pg. 381: © Alexy Kamenskiy | Dreamstime.com; pg. 382: © (top) NPS, (left) Granitepeaker | Dreamstime.com, (right) Henryturner | Dreamstime.com; pg. 385: © Mkopka | Dreamstime.com; pg. 386: © (top) Jamie Frattarelli | Dreamstime.com, (bottom) Dwight Hegel | Dreamstime.com; pg. 389: © Dejavu Designs | Dreamstime.com; pg. 390: © (top) Richard Wood | Dreamstime.com, (left) Patrick Barron | Dreamstime.com, (right) Richard Wood | Dreamstime.com; pg. 393: © Davidshenbo | Dreamstime.com; pgs. 394-395: © Paul Brady | Dreamstime.com; pgs. 396-397: © Cheri Alguire | Dreamstime.com; pg. 400: © (top) Jerry Whaley | Dreamstime.com, (left) Zhukovsky | Dreamstime.com, (right) Jim Ekstrand | Dreamstime.com; pg. 403: © Michael Ver Sprill | Dreamstime.com; pg. 404: © (top) Ivan Kokoulin | Dreamstime.com, (bottom) Cheri Alguire | Dreamstime.com; pg. 407: © Cheri Alguire | Dreamstime.com; pg. 408: © (top) Paget Kidd | Dreamstime.com, (left) Meinzahn | Dreamstime.com, (right) Colin Young | Dreamstime.com; pg. 411: © Jon Bilous | Dreamstime.com; pg. 412: © (top) Robert Grabowski | Dreamstime.com, (bottom) Mary Katherine Wynn | Dreamstime.com; pg. 415: © Cheri Alguire | Dreamstime.com; pg. 416: © (top) Tang Man | Dreamstime.com, (bottom) Kenneth Sponsler | Dreamstime.com; pg. 417: © Bradley Monahan | Dreamstime.com; pg. 419: © Kelly Vandellen | Dreamstime.com; pg. 420: © (top) Leonid Andronov | Dreamstime.com, (bottom) Brian Welker | Dreamstime.com; pg. 423: Kenneth Keifer | Dreamstime.com; pg. 424: © (top) Theresa Lyon | Dreamstime.com, (bottom) Ken Desloover | Dreamstime.com; pg. 427: © Kenneth Keifer | Dreamstime.com; pgs. 428-429: NPS/Jackie Boesinger Meredyk; pg. 430: © (top & bottom) NPS; pg. 433 © NPS; pg. 434: © (top & bottom) NPS; pg. 437: © Jon Lauriat | Dreamstimecom; pg. 438: © (top) Jon Lauriat | Dreamstimecom, (bottom) Gerald D. Tang | Dreamstime.com; pg. 441: © Kelly Vandellen | Dreamstime.com; pg. 442: (top) NPS/Kelly Morrissey, (bottom) NPS; pg. 443: © Qube002 | Dreamstime.com; pg. 447: © Derrick Jaeger; pgs. 448-449: © NPS/Chalice Keith; pg. 452: © (top & bottom) Jon Bilous | Dreamstime.com; pg. 455: © Jon Bilous | Dreamstime.com; pg. 456: © (top) Ivan Kokoulin | Dreamstime.com, (left & right) Jason Frye; pg. 459: © Jason Frye; pg. 460: © (top) Jon Bilous | Dreamstime.com, (bottom) Dreamstime.com | Vadim Startsev; pg. 463: © Jon Bilous | Dreamstime.com; pg. 464: © (top) NPS/B. Kuhns, (left) NPS/L. O., (right) Jason Frye; pg. 467: © Jason Frye; pgs. 468-469: © NPS/N. Lewis; pg. 470: © (top) Sean

Pavone | Dreamstime.com, (left & right) Jason Frye; pg. 473: © Jason Frye; pg. 474: © (top) Edward Lange | Dreamstime.com, (left & right) Jason Frye; pg. 477 © Edward Lange | Dreamstime.com; pg. 478: © (top & bottom) Jason Frye; pg. 481: © Jason Frye; pg. 482 © (top) Dreamstime.com | Kelly Vandellen, (left) Jerry Whaley | Dreamstime.com, (right) Dreamstime.com | Melinda Fawver; pg. 485: © Billy Mc Donald | Dreamstime.com; pgs. 486-487: © NPS/Andrea Walton; pg. 488: © (top) Dreamstime.com | Mark Scott, (bottom) Carmen Sisson | Dreamstime.com; pg. 491: © Jason Frye; pg. 492: © (all) Jason Frye; pg. 495: © Dean Pennala | Dreamstime.com; pg. 496: © (all) Jason Frye; pg. 499: © Jonathan Mauer | Dreamstime.com; pgs. 500-501: © NPS/K. George; pg. 502: © NPS/Alex Vanderstuyf; pg. 505: © NPS/M. Quinn; pg. 508: © Travnikovstudio | Dreamstime.com; pg. 511 © Kelly Vandellen | Dreamstime.com; pg. 518: © NPS/Patrick Myers; pg. 523: © NPS/J. Chao; pg. 524: © NPS; Pg. 525: © NPS/Neal Herbert; pg. 527: © NPS/Ivie Metzen.

ACKNOWLEDGMENTS

This book would not be possible without the help, input, and support of a small army.

First, thank you, Lauren Frye. You keep it together at home when I'm on the trail, and your advice and wisdom are always welcome. It's been fun watching you fall in love with the outdoors and I can't wait for our next adventure.

Thank you, Taylor Brown, your work ethic is a constant inspiration, especially on days I'd rather not be at the keyboard.

Thank you to the tremendous team at Moon. Vy, Hannah, Ann, Lucie, Kat, and everyone else, you bring my words to the world and I'm forever grateful.

Thanks to Aryn and Zach. Your maps, photos, trip reports, unabashed enthusiasm for our national parks, and undying love for a road trips rocks; let's get on the trail soon.

Thanks to my fellow Moon authors for helping your readers find moments of beauty in the national parks and great outdoors.

Thanks to our national parks workers. Without you rangers, volunteers, trail crews, and maintenance folks, we couldn't experience the wonders of nature in the same way.

Finally, thanks to you, readers and fellow hikers. The miles you burn on the trail, the nights you sleep under the stars, and the hours you spend planning your next trip make every minute of writing, research, and hiking worth it. Hope to meet you on the trail one day.

Travel with Moon through California & the PNW

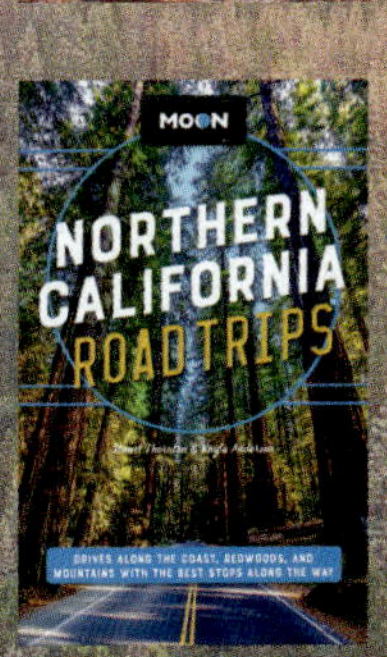

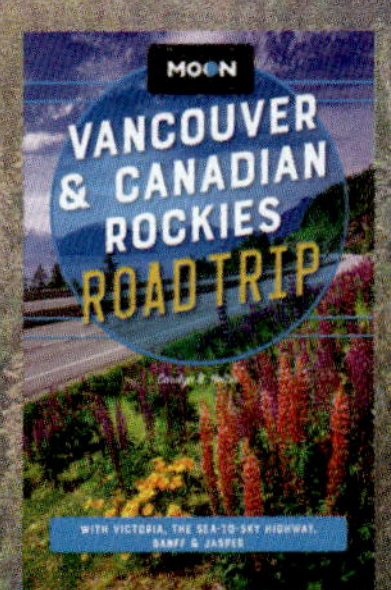

National Parks Travel Guides from Moon

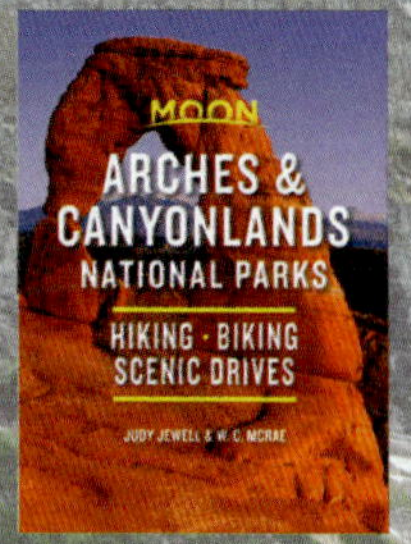

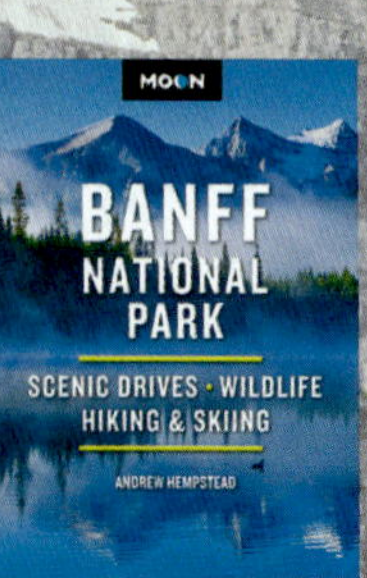

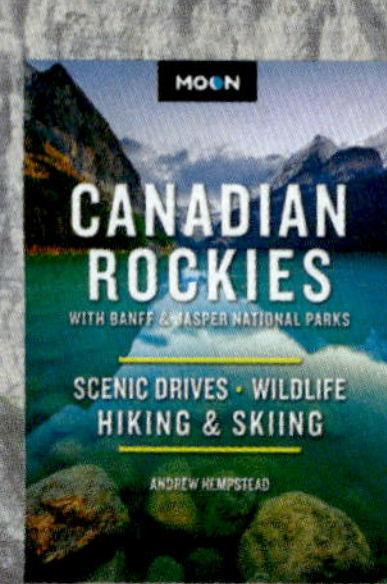

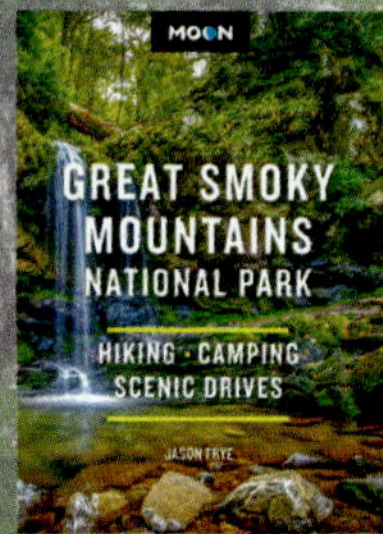

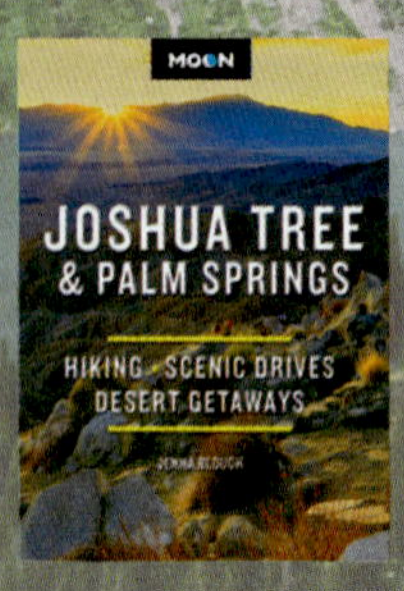

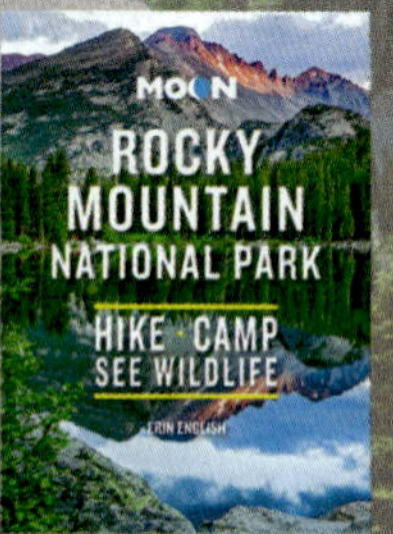

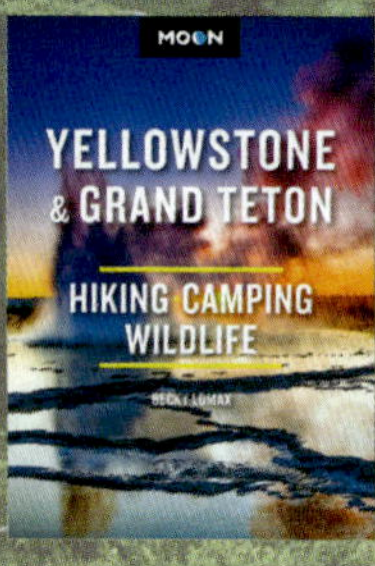

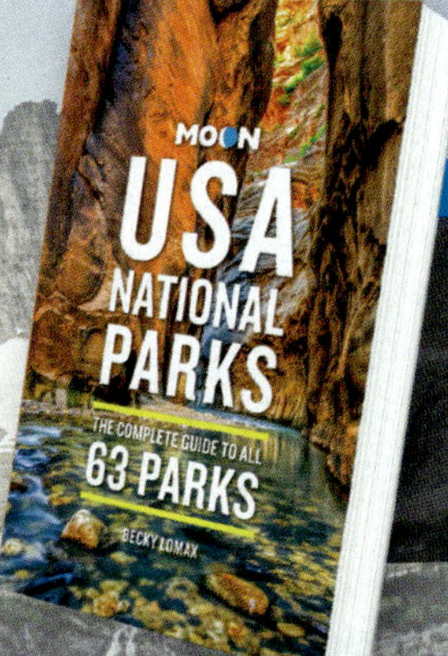

Get the bestselling all-parks guide, or check out Moon's new Best Of Parks series to make the most of a 1-3 day visit to top parks.

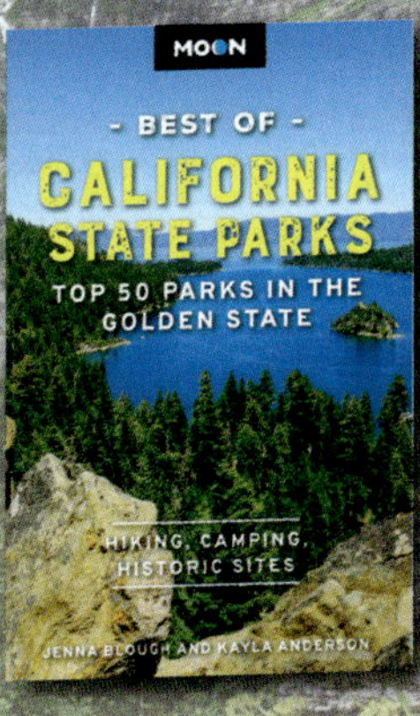

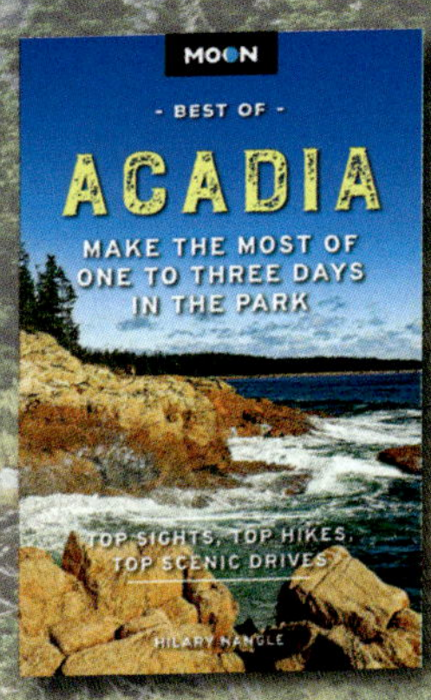

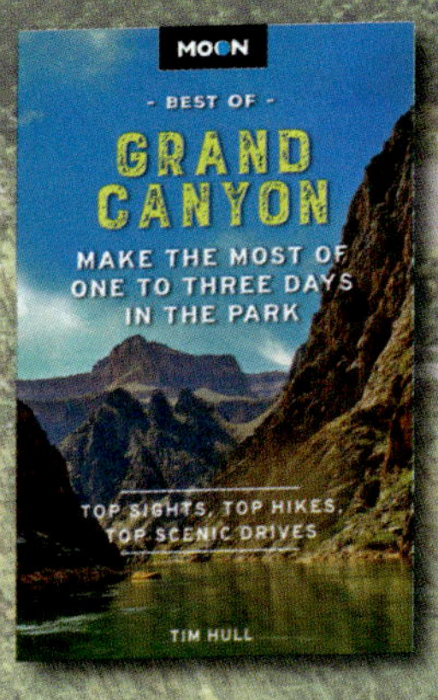

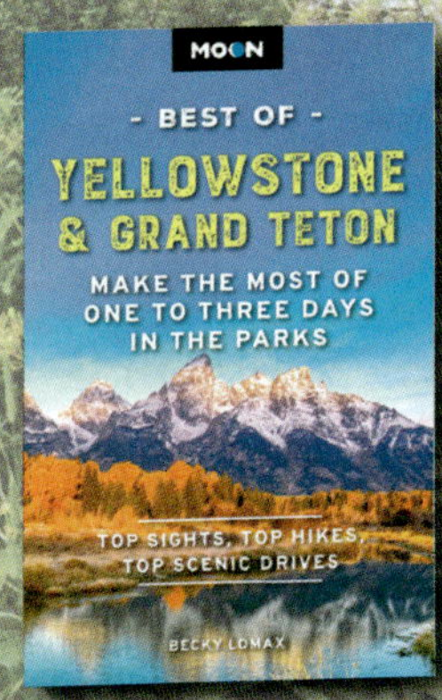

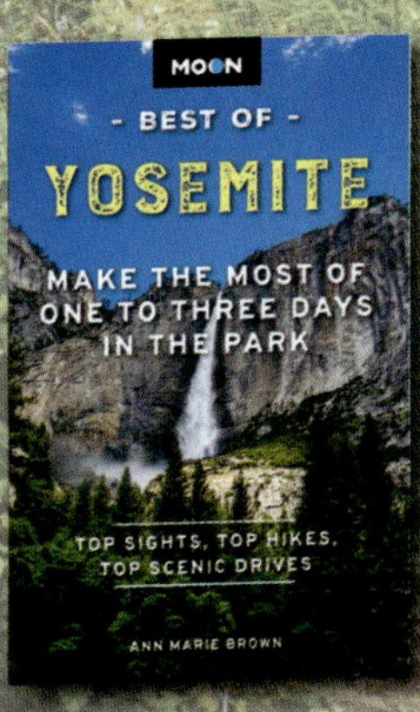

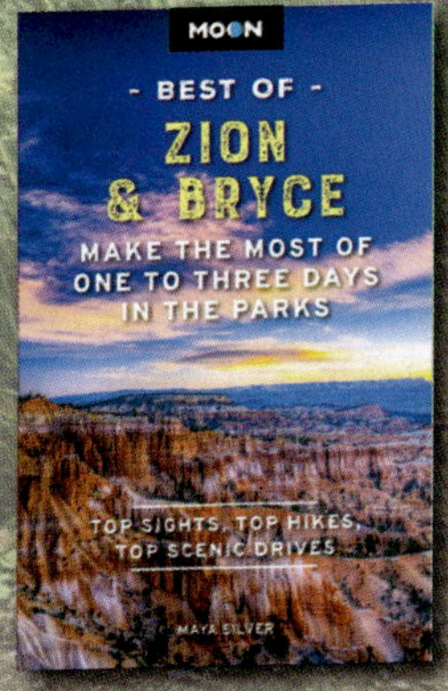

ROAD TRIP GUIDES FROM MOON

MOON
SOUTHERN CALIFORNIA ROAD TRIPS
DRIVES ALONG THE BEACHES, MOUNTAINS, AND DESERTS WITH THE BEST STOPS ALONG THE WAY

MOON
ROUTE 66 ROAD TRIP
Jessica Dunham
DRIVE THE CLASSIC ROUTE FROM CHICAGO TO LOS ANGELES

MOON
SOUTHWEST ROAD TRIP
Tim Hull
DRIVE THE LOOP FROM LAS VEGAS TO SANTA FE, VISITING 8 NATIONAL PARKS ALONG THE WAY

MOON
NEW ENGLAND ROAD TRIP
SEASIDE SPOTS, MAJESTIC MOUNTAINS, FALL FOLIAGE, COZY GETAWAYS

MOON
VANCOUVER & CANADIAN ROCKIES ROAD TRIP
WITH VICTORIA, THE SEA-TO-SKY HIGHWAY, BANFF & JASPER

MOON
YELLOWSTONE GRAND TETON & GLACIER ROAD TRIP
Carter G. Walker
CONNECT MONTANA & WYOMING'S NATIONAL PARKS

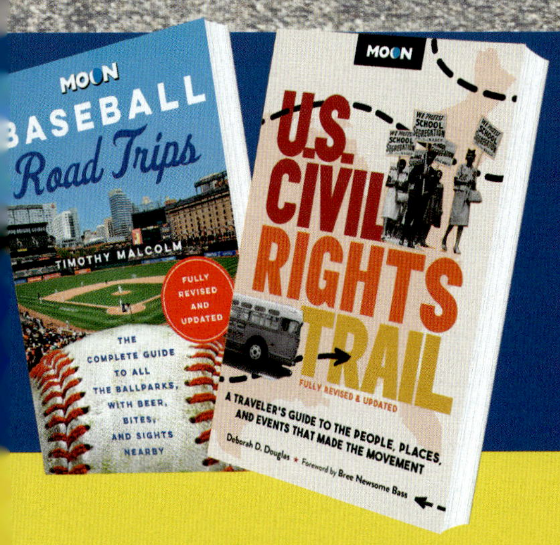

Explore the U.S. with expert authors like baseball writer Timothy Malcolm and journalist Deborah D. Douglas!

MAP SYMBOLS

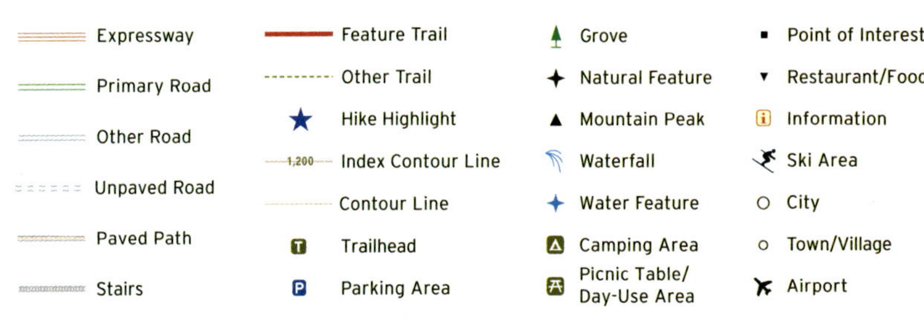

CONVERSION TABLES

°C = (°F - 32) / 1.8
°F = (°C x 1.8) + 32
1 inch = 2.54 centimeters (cm)
1 foot = 0.304 meters (m)
1 yard = 0.914 meters
1 mile = 1.6093 kilometers (km)
1 km = 0.6214 miles
1 fathom = 1.8288 m
1 chain = 20.1168 m
1 furlong = 201.168 m
1 acre = 0.4047 hectares
1 sq km = 100 hectares
1 sq mile = 2.59 square km
1 ounce = 28.35 grams
1 pound = 0.4536 kilograms
1 short ton = 0.90718 metric ton
1 short ton = 2,000 pounds
1 long ton = 1.016 metric tons
1 long ton = 2,240 pounds
1 metric ton = 1,000 kilograms
1 quart = 0.94635 liters
1 US gallon = 3.7854 liters
1 Imperial gallon = 4.5459 liters
1 nautical mile = 1.852 km

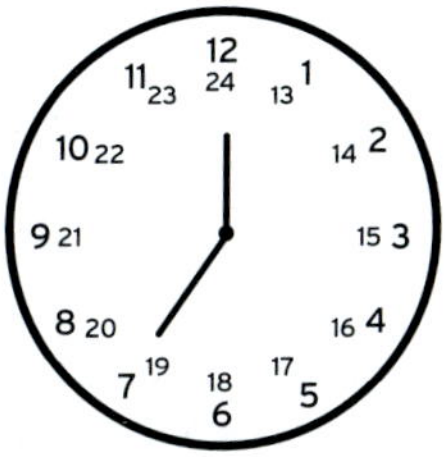

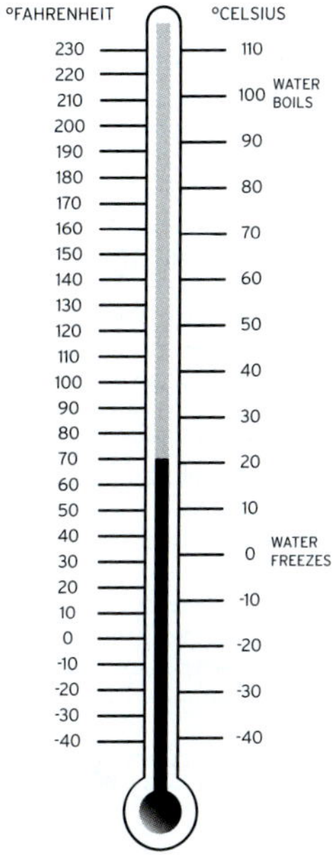

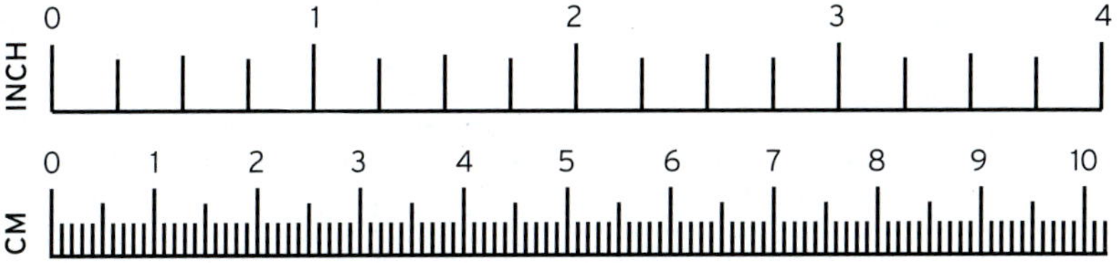

°FAHRENHEIT °CELSIUS

WATER BOILS (100 °C / 212 °F)

WATER FREEZES (0 °C / 32 °F)

INCH 0 1 2 3 4

CM 0 1 2 3 4 5 6 7 8 9 10

MOON USA NATIONAL PARKS HIKING

Avalon Travel
Hachette Book Group, Inc.
555 12th Street, Suite 1850
Oakland, CA 94607, USA
www.moon.com

Editor: Vy Tran
Managing Editor: Hannah Brezack
Copy Editor: Ann Seifert
Graphics and Production Coordinator: Lucie Ericksen
Cover Design: Toni Tajima
Interior Design: Lucie Ericksen
Map Editor: Kat Bennett
Cartographers: John Culp, Kat Bennett, Mark Stroud (Moon Street Cartography)
Proofreader: Callie Stoker-Graham
Indexer: Greg Jewett

ISBN-13: 979-8-88647-082-6

Printing History
1st Edition — October 2025
5 4 3 2 1

Front cover photo: hiker on Queens Garden Trail, Bryce Canyon National Park © DuncanImages / Alamy Stock Photo
Back cover photos (top to bottom): hiker on Mist Trail, Yosemite National Park © Martinmark | Dreamstime.com; trail to Angels Landing, Zion National Park © Zeljkokcanmore | Dreamstime.com; Glacier National Park, Montana © Wirestock | Dreamstime.com

Printed in China by R.R. Donnelley Dongguan

All recommendations, including those for sights, activities, hotels, restaurants, and shops, are based on each author's individual judgment. We do not accept payment for inclusion in our travel guides, and our authors do not accept free goods or services in exchange for positive coverage.